# Seeing Things

# Seeing Things

*Deepening Relations with Visual Artefacts*

Stephen Pattison

scm press

© Stephen Pattison 2007

The Author has asserted his right under the Copyright,
Designs and Patents Act, 1988,
to be identified as the Author of this Work

British Library Cataloguing in Publication data

A catalogue record for this book is available
from the British Library

978 0 334 04149 8

First published in 2007 by SCM Press
13–17 Long Lane
London EC1A 9PN

www.scm-canterburypress.co.uk

SCM Press is a division of
SCM-Canterbury Press Ltd

Typeset by Regent Typesetting, London
Printed and bound in Great Britain by
William Clowes Ltd, Beccles, Suffolk

# Contents

For Charmian

# Preface

This book was the basis for the Gifford lectures, delivered in the University of Aberdeen in 2007.[1] I interpreted the lecturer's task as being to: think big; explore a topic that is significant for many people; take the world and different ways of exploring it seriously; communicate clearly, using language and concepts that ordinary people can grasp; and help people think about what sort of practical and ethical response might be made to greater understanding.

The topic that seems to have chosen me is exploring the nature of relationships that people in the West have with visual artefacts, together with human responses to, and responsibilities for, them. I try to bring images and artefacts out of the realm of undifferentiated 'stuff' or 'things' into the arena of human community and communication to suggest a more intimate way of perceiving and relating to them through 'haptic' or touching sight. I hope readers will agree that this is a large and important topic, potentially of interest to everyone on a planet that is increasingly populated with visual objects and artefacts, as well as people.

I owe substantial debts to many people in the pursuit of a protean topic only slightly less demanding than 'life, the universe, and everything'. Formally, I must thank the electors to the Gifford lectureship for inviting me to give the lectures. It was, indeed, a great and unexpected honour. I am particularly grateful to Iain Torrance, convenor of the electors at the time when I was invited, who continued to show a lively, helpful interest in my halting progress towards them. His successor, Trevor Salmon, and members of the Gifford Committee, made me very welcome in Aberdeen.

Thanks are due to the Principal and Fellows of Jesus College, Oxford, who provided me with congenial facilities to pursue the basic research for this book in the academic year 2004–5 while I was a visiting senior research fellow there. Martin Kemp and his colleagues at the Centre for Visual Studies in Oxford made me very welcome as a research associate. The British Academy supported me with a small personal research award, and the Vice-chancellor of Cardiff University very generously paid my salary for a semester. At the sharp end of things, Peter Blood, John King and John Watt acted as heads of the Cardiff School of Religious and Theological Studies, Peter Sedgwick picked up some of my teaching responsibilities, and other colleagues took on parts of my duties. Duncan Forrester, Don Browning, Frances Young, John Hedley Brooke and Chris Rowland wrote many references for me in trying to obtain funding and opportunities of various kinds. My thanks to each and all of them.

Exploring perception and the significance of artefacts cannot be the province of any one discipline. I am grateful to the following for sharing their time, wisdom and knowledge with me. Psychologists: Hadyn Ellis, Peter Halligan, Mark Williams, Chris Frith, Gordon Claridge, Laurence Weiskrantz, Mansur Lalljee, Silke Göbel, Michael Jackson. Historians of art and visual culture theorists: Martin Kemp, Geraldine Johnson, Marius Kwint, Gavin Parkinson, Jas Elsner, Kelley Wilder, David Morgan, Cathy Oakes. Philosophers of Art: Andrew Edgar, Katerina Reed-Tsocha, John Hyman. Intellectual historians: Rhodri Lewis, John Hedley Brooke, Ruth Harris, Sophie Ratcliffe, David Cram, Allan Chapman. Sociologists of Science: Steve Woolgar, Catelijne Coopmans. Theologians: Chris Rowland, Paul Joyce, George Pattison, Gordon Lynch, Susanne Sklar, Patricia Gibbons, Mary Charles Murray, Francesca Stavrakopoulou, James Woodward, Josef Lossl, Dan King, James Hegarty, Jolyon Mitchell, Sallie McFague, Barbara Hayes, Nick Bradbury. Anthropologists: Chris Gosden, Elizabeth Edwards, Gabriel Hanganu, Chris Pinney, Polly Nooter Roberts, Allan Roberts, Geoffrey Samuel. I am also grateful to John De'Ath and Stuart Hodson, for sharing important visual experiences with me, and to colleagues who in 2003 attended an interdisciplinary symposium in Cardiff, 'The Visionary Mode', supported by the British Academy. The ideas that emerged on that occasion have remained a constant stimulus.

Chris Rowland has been a staunch friend and supporter throughout this project and I was fortunate to spend a lot of time with him in Oxford during my visit there. David Morgan, one of the most generous and interesting academic encouragers I have ever met, turned into the fairy godparent of this work after a memorable conversation I had with him at the Victoria and Albert Museum in London. Gordon Lynch has helped me to formulate ideas and provided new sources of stimulus and information at every turn. Indeed, it was Gordon who facilitated the meeting with David at the V and A. I have been greatly blessed by the interest of these three friends who, happily, seem to believe in this project more than I do myself. I am extraordinarily indebted to them for listening to inarticulate rants, for reading scrappy, speculative drafts, and for keeping faith in times of authorial doubt. I hope they will neither be disappointed in the final result, nor feel in any way responsible for its faults and defects.

A special word of thanks to Janet Bellamy who edited down the first draft, making suggestions for substantial modification which have done much to clarify the direction and shape of the book's argument. I am more grateful than I can say for this difficult, supererogatory work. Thanks, also, to Reed Malcolm for helping fundamentally to shape and improve the book. Many thanks to Barbara Laing at SCM Press who believed in the project enough to publish it. My primary debt is to Charmian Beer, who lived with the book and the lectures for six years, as I did.

This book started life as a work about religious vision and seeing, provisionally entitled, *Seeing God*. Since there is relatively little about religion or God here, I guess I will now have to write a second volume. So watch this space.

## Notes

1  For more on the Gifford lectures see www.giffordlectures.org and Witham (2005). For a synopsis and texts of the lectures themselves see www.abdn.ac.uk/gifford/.

# List of illustrations and plates

Figure 1. Lacan's notion of interlocking gaze, p. 28.

Figure 2. The differences between the human and non-human world, p. 152.

## Plate section

1. Athanasius Kircher, *Ars Magna Lucis et Umbrae*, 1646.
2. Albrecht Durer, *Draftsman drawing a nude*, c. 1525.
3. Anthony Gormley, *The Angel of the North*.
4. Laurence Broderick, *The Bronze Bull*.
5. Herbert Bayer, *The Lonely Metropolitan*, 1932.
6. Mary of Burgundy, *Book of Hours*, late 1470s.
7. Toby jug.
8. Giotto, *St Francis having a vision before the Crucifix in San Damiano*.
9. Jake Cress, *Oops* and *Self-portrait*.

# Introduction

The true mystery of the world is the visible, not the invisible.

Oscar Wilde

With an admirable economy we see only so much as is needful for our purposes; but this is . . . just enough to recognize and identify each object or person; that done, they . . . are no more really seen. In actual life the normal person really only reads the labels as it were on the objects around him and troubles no further. Almost all the things which are useful . . . put on . . . this cap of invisibility.

Roger Fry, *Vision and Design*

This book questions the way people in the West look upon the world and things, so that we might have the possibility of seeing more critically, broadly, and widely. Sight is one of the main ways in which humans perceive and relate to the world. However, it is mostly assumed rather than actively reflected upon. Objects designated as 'art', and the realm of aesthetics, attract some active attention and reflection. However, most of the visible world is ignored, and effectively invisible, in the context of our 'ordinary blindness'. The range of things that we choose to see and value is arbitrarily limited. The ways in which we see and relate to them are mostly crude and unnuanced. We have so much, but see so little.

The book should be of value to anyone interested in broadening their understanding of what it means to see and to relate to material artefacts of all kinds. It considers how humans engage with the visual dimension of material existence, with images, and with visually perceptible artefacts of all kinds. It argues that humans need to enter into more personlike relationships with the created visible artefacts that share the human world, for the sake of the artefacts themselves as well as for that of the humans who created them. While artefacts like oil paintings and films attract a great deal of attention already, many humble, everyday objects, made by humans, deserve far more consideration than they normally receive.

I

Most of us pay inadequate critical attention to the visual aspects of existence and to the conscious and unconscious relationships that we might, or do, have with visible objects. This deprives us of more interesting, self-conscious relationships with the material world. It also has substantial ethical risks. If we do not take the visible world seriously, and appreciate adequately the things that are in it, we are likely to exploit and destroy it. This may well deliver us into a world that actually has no future. So we need to become much more aware and concerned about the world of visual objects in general, what it does to us, and we do to it. This 'turn to the visual' requires expansion and explanation.[1]

The visual dimension is fundamentally important in structuring human thinking and experience.[2] All sentient beings live in a world structured round sight. Despite living in an age of what might be characterized as 'visual overload' or hyper-visuality, many people do not actively reflect upon their ordinary visual experience or their relationships with visual objects, whether in the realm of 'high art', or in everyday experience.

Not having a critical awareness of relationships with visible artefacts does not mean that these relationships do not exist. Being unaware of their nature and effects, we may not be able to appreciate them fully, or to change them. The ability to appreciate and modify visual relationships is important because relationships with objects are part of what makes humans what they are.

Modern people in the West draw an invisible, but absolute, dividing line through reality, strongly distinguishing animate from inanimate beings. Beings on one side of the line, those who breathe and die, especially if they possess the mysterious qualities of consciousness, intentionality and language, have been accorded high status in world religions and philosophies.[3] Those regarded as inanimate have been relegated to a radically inferior position; they are regarded as objects that can be used and disposed of at human whim. Essentially, the inanimate and material world, including the world of visible objects of all kinds, is treated as being a separate adjunct to the community of persons.

The cost of this devaluation of the material realm can be high. It distorts the reality of human being and existence. Humans are not just shaped and formed by their relations with other humans, but also by their relations with material reality and the objects within it. Objects help to make us what we are at every level of our existence. Chairs, for example, not only contribute symbolically to social perceptions of status and style, they also shape human bodies by curving the spines of their occupants and giving them varicose veins.[4]

To be responsible participants in the animate/inanimate world, we need to become more aware of the kinds of relationships we do and could have with objects. Looking at some of the features and relationships we have with visible objects and the realm of the visual is one way of beginning to open up the debate about values and relationships that needs to occur if we are not rapidly to reduce the world to crud. Considering the visible world and visual images and artefacts within it is a good way of selectively beginning to address some of the emerging practical and intellectual issues concerning human relations with the material world in general.

It is arbitrary to divide off the visual dimension of human perception from other parts of sensory and perceptive experience. It is not just the visual world that is important, but also the world known through hearing, touch, and the other senses.[5] Sensual perception is not the province of separate, clearly demarcated individual senses; it is the sum of those senses interacting with the whole of the external world. Perception is a whole-body phenomenon. However, traditionally in Western literate culture and thought, hearing and sight (the 'distant' senses) have been privileged as the most important senses; of these two, sight and apprehension of the visual world has often been accorded the role of most important sense.

In the last two centuries, the primacy of sight has become even more significant, and visual culture has developed and proliferated. With the extension of sight by microscopic, telescopic, electronic, digital and other means symbolized by instruments such as electron microscopes, scanners, cameras and photographs, we are all too aware of living in a world structured round sight and the visual. Images rain upon us in all spheres of life, proliferating, diversifying and becoming more complex and sophisticated by the day. So the sphere of sight and the visual, which is well researched and reflected upon by many historical and contemporary disciplines (for example, anthropology, psychology, art history, history of science, sociology, literature), even if it is only partially understood, is a good place to begin to consider the nature and significance of human relations with the material world.

## Living in a visual world

The contemporary Western world is brighter, more colourful and more saturated with humanly created images and artefacts than that of our ancestors. The visual crowds in on us all day long; there is so much to delight or dull the palate of sight.[6]

With the advent of street and other kinds of lighting, night has been turned to day.[7] Shops and leisure venues are full of brightly coloured and carefully packaged goods designed to seduce the prospective buyer. Advertisements, once long verbal tracts treating of the virtues of products, have been refined to clever images, sometimes without words at all. The centrality of the static, book-bound written word has given way to the dominance of the moving images of film and TV in the lives of many, both for information and for entertainment.[8]

Meanwhile, there may well be more full-time professional artists and designers making a living from their craft today than have ever lived on earth.[9] Which is not to mention the thousands of photographers, amateur and professional, who snap and manipulate millions of images of all kinds every day. Image-making is also important in science; using computers and digital technology, we can see, or at least think we 'see' things that are invisible to the naked eye by virtue of size, nature or distance.[10] I can lie in bed with my laptop and look at the surface of Titan, one of the moons of Saturn, at the press of a key. If I get bored with this, I can insert a DVD into the same machine to amuse myself.

Technologies of illumination, image production and visual manipulation have advanced exponentially over the last two centuries. The invention of electric light has been supplemented by the advent of the photograph in the mid-nineteenth century, the invention of cinephotography in the early twentieth century, and latterly by the development of computers. Digital technology has enabled a move from analogue reproduction of images which not only makes images more immediately manipulable, but also more transmissible and able to represent aspects of existence that would otherwise be invisible and unknowable. Hence the unborn child, previously hidden till the moment of birth, can now be represented on a screen by its mother's bed as ultrasound audio waves are converted into images while, by virtue of magnetic scanning, tumours lying deep within the dark and unseeable brain can become three-dimensional images suspended in pixels that can be examined in detail.[11] Likewise, the virtual digital manipulation of images can allow film-makers to animate and create special effects in films that would have been unimaginable only 30 years ago. I could make quite a sophisticated film on the laptop with which I am writing this book. With a screen of 9 x 5.5 inches, it is twice as powerful as the one I bought only five years ago.

We have moved from a situation in which earthly life and activity was regulated almost completely by the rising and setting of the sun, in which the majority of created visual artefacts were often crude, or produced by expensive and elusive professionals, and where all colours were produced from often rare natural products, into a sophisticated, complex world of light and sight. Images and sights bombard us from the moment we wake till we close our eyes in sleep. And the world behind our eyelids is not image-free, filled as it is with thoughts, dreams and visions. Even blind people cannot escape from a world heavily structured by sight, image and vision.

The turn to the visual, the rise of visual culture, or however one wants to characterize the kind of visually saturated society we think we now inhabit, has been accompanied by the very recent rise of visual studies.[12] Traditionally, the critical humanistic study of visually significant phenomena was the province of art history. Following Vasari, the focus of the discipline was on the appreciation and analysis of fine and classic art, that is paintings, sculpture and architecture.

Only in the late twentieth century did it become apparent that there is more to the visual than understanding the work of an elite group of clearly designated 'artists'. At this point, some critics from a variety of disciplines began to analyse aspects of popular culture such as films and television programmes. Partly inspired by the sociological, philosophical and anthropological approaches that emphasized popular, non-elite activities and animated the rise of cultural studies in the late 1960s, there has been a growing desire on the part of some scholars from a variety of disciplines to consider critically all aspects of visual culture, whether it be 'high' or 'low' (Levine 1988). Thus alongside studying the paintings of Rembrandt and Dürer, visual-culture analysts turn their attentions to the theatre as spectacle, to the waxworks as popular art form, to everyday forms of pottery and decoration, to images used in science, to popular images in religion, to television programmes and films, to advertisements and graphic design, to the construction and use of images and the visual in the production and representation of science.

A vibrant, if small, interdisciplinary community of those who want to think about the visual as a category containing aspects of sight, image production and consumption, and representation, is now becoming established. This loose coalition of critical analysts of the contemporary visual world would regard formal art images and ways of looking at these as only one part of a wider quest to understand the significance of images and what enters the purview of the visual in all its plurality. Unfortunately, even analysts of non-elitist visual culture have largely failed to give much attention to the visible but humble artefacts that constitute the everyday world. It is within the exciting quest for an interdisciplinary, pluralist approach to all things visual that the present study is situated. While my concern is basically with everyday visible artefacts of a static kind, this move would not have been possible without the advent of visual studies.

However, one of the emergent implications of visual studies is that there is an inverse relationship between the number and commonality of visual artefacts and the amount of conscious scholarly attention paid to them. So, 'high art' objects like statues and oil paintings, which constitute a tiny part of the visually available artefactual world, have received huge amounts of detailed scrutiny and analysis, while common, everyday objects like toasters and shelves have tended to be ignored. There is what seems to be a hierarchy of attention which follows elite concerns and runs something like this:

• Paintings, drawings and sculptures and other representational works of art
• Architecture
• Films and TV programmes
• Photographs
• Designed objects of aesthetic or stylistic importance
• Decorations
• Hand-crafted everyday objects
• Mass-produced objects.

This hierarchical order of attention means that ordinary objects owned and used by people in everyday life are accorded little significance. This is important here because my concern lies with relations with all kinds of visibly available objects. However, there is little theory that can be drawn upon to discuss or understand these objects. Thus, I will have to use insights, theories and methods derived mainly from the study of highly significant visible artefacts like pictures and sculptures to begin to articulate relationships between humans and humble objects that may often be ignored even though they significantly shape the everyday lives of people.

# Introduction

## The seer sited

I could say that I bring to the study of sight, vision and images nothing but a pair of eyes and a set of important unarticulated theoretical and practical assumptions that have been modified in exploring the protean realm of the visual and its contents. This has been a process of 'auto-iconoclasm'; I have had to shatter and change my ideas about seeing, sight, images and artefacts quite drastically – with profit and pleasure, as well as some real discomfort and distress. Some of my assumptions have turned out to be quite shameful prejudices.

But this is not quite accurate. I also bring two critically important positive things. First, I am curious about the whole realm of the visual. I want to know more about what I see, why I see it or don't see it, the nature and conditions for seeing and how I interpret what I see so that it has meaning and value for humans. How did I, and countless others, come to be living in a world dominated by the visual, by images, representations and artefacts, and have so little critical understanding of, or grip upon, it? What are the images and artefacts that I see doing to me and what effect, if any, do I as beholder or observer have on them? Is the realm of the visual just a kind of background tableau against which I live my life, ignoring it most of the time? Or am I involved in important and dynamic relationships with visible artefacts and objects that are fundamental to the kind of person I am and the kind of world I live in? I started on this project of exploring the visual by thinking that this was basically a kind of self-education in art criticism and interpretation. However, I have come to think that the whole sphere is broader, more important, and more challenging than this.

The other thing that I bring to the sphere of sight, vision and the visual is my professional training in theology and religious studies. While I am an interdisciplinary scholar with some training in art history and visual studies, my disciplinary home lies in a particular branch of theology, practical theology.[13] Practical theologians are generally interested in the relationship between belief and practice from the standpoint of themselves having a critical faith commitment. They are 'critical inhabitants of action-guiding world-views'. So they are interested in seeing how beliefs and practices that people live by in the everyday world coalesce or live in tension with each other.

Life, whether conceived as 'sacred' or 'secular', is full of action-guiding world-views, beliefs and faith assumptions that are mostly ignored and simply taken for granted as 'reality'. Furthermore, lying behind all practices and beliefs there are assumptions about the ultimate

7

nature of reality, deep metaphors and understandings of what the world and human beings are really like.[14] Sometimes these understandings owe much to religious or quasi-religious faith systems, sometimes not. But at all times, one can ask questions about what people believe (consciously and articulately, or unconsciously and inarticulately) and how this manifests or fails to manifest itself in their lives and practices. So I am particularly interested in the action-guiding assumptions that underlie contemporary perspectives and practices in the realm of the visual.

Practical theology is deeply concerned with the nature of human beings and their relations with the other human beings and the world around them. The material environment and the artefacts in it help to shape and condition human beings. Similarly, humans shape the material world in reciprocal relationship. So it is appropriate to ask questions about the nature of relations with the neglected artefactual world to promote the well-being of both humans and the visually available objects with which they interact.

Clearly, the notion of promoting well-being for humans and material things implies a commitment to exploring ethics and values; this is another element of the practical theological approach. Rather than adopting an uncommitted, analytical stance, I am concerned both to understand more about the nature of visual relationships between humans and artefacts as they presently exist, but also to try and identify more appropriate norms for governing these relationships. As I have already suggested, unless humans become more ethically aware, responsive and responsible in their relations to visually available artefacts, there are possibly very negative implications for the future of the human race and the world in general. I will commend the need to enter into deeper, more personlike relationships with artefacts if we are to deal with them more appropriately.

Practical theology is so called because it is concerned with action and practice. The guiding question in this discipline is, ultimately, 'So what?' What difference does this way of understanding things have on the lives of contemporary people? How might they change their way of acting and thinking so that they have better, more life-enhancing relationships in all parts of their existence? So one thing that I try to do is to suggest some ways in which it might be desirable to change our ways of perceiving and interacting with visible artefacts in practical terms.

A final contribution that a theologian might bring to the present subject is knowledge of religious traditions and practices. Seeing, sight and vision are important elements of most religions. In the West, the

Christian tradition has influenced the science and practice of sight and vision in a multitude of ways. For example, much early optical theory was evolved in the context of a theological search for truth. I hope that it will prove useful to allude to the experience and thought of religious communities in attempting to assay the significance of relationships with visible images and artefacts. This book makes no assumptions about religious belief or commitment. However, it would seem unnecessarily coy if I were not to draw upon my specific subject knowledge from time to time in order to illuminate topics under discussion.[15]

## An interdisciplinary approach

Sight, vision, perception, and relations with the visible material world, are huge topics. They impinge upon fundamental understandings of humans and the universe they inhabit. On a planet governed largely by the daily rhythm of light and darkness, where most people are sighted, and life is conditioned fundamentally by sight and vision, this area is, in principle, relevant to everyone on earth.

No single discipline or focus of enquiry can grasp the whole of this sphere. One is stuck with partial insights and approaches drawn from a great variety of different academic and non-academic spheres of activity and enquiry, from the hard sciences to the performing arts.

Physicists, for example, are interested in the nature of light and the ways it behaves.[16] Working along the scientific matrix, optometrists are more concerned with how the stimuli created by light are processed to produce binocular vision. Behind the eyes lies the brain where images are processed and interpreted. This processing and interpretation of images is of increasing interest to neuro-psychologists who often use complex scanning devices to understand the neural pathways and mechanisms that enable people to see.[17] Beyond the laboratories of the neuro-psychologists lies the work of psychiatrists and clinical psychologists who have to deal with and interpret the normal and abnormal visual experiences of service users.[18] Many people have unusual visual experiences which sometimes take the form of delusions or visual hallucinations.[19] These form part of a continuum of human visual experience.

Many humanities disciplines, both theoretical and applied, also have much to offer in contextualizing and expanding the study of visual perception and relationships.

Art history has been the traditional locus for the study of artefacts

and things visual. Quite recently, art history has begun to expand its
purview to consider the place and function of all visual artefacts, beginning, for example, to look at the place of visuality and representation
in advertising and science, or the place of the visual in the design and
function of everyday objects such as cutlery or street furniture. Thus
it begins to move beyond the appreciation of the formally beautiful
into the area of cultural understanding and criticism. Here it intersects
with social sciences such as anthropology and sociology which locate
vision, seeing and images in the context of social structures, practices
and meanings.

Anthropology has a particularly important part to play in the study
of vision, sight and images beyond the aesthetic. There is an increasing
number of studies in so-called 'visual anthropology' which comment on
the significance of objects and vision for the creation and maintenance
of meanings and persons in human societies.[20] The anthropological perspective looks beyond image and likeness as artistic object and begins
to relate all manner of visual objects to a much wider agenda about the
significance of representations in human social life as a whole. Sociology, too, through its critiques of the rise, use and consumption of art
and through its commentaries both on the visually related institutions
such as museums and tourist sites and the use and meaning of visual
objects, offers its own voice to this complex area.[21]

Philosophy has developed a whole area of discourse on the interpretation and appreciation of the human artistic endeavour, usually
designated aesthetics. Beyond aesthetics, philosophers are involved in
debates about the nature of perception, the nature of images, and how
images and the visual should be interpreted.[22] History, both of ideas
and practices, also has much to offer. The experience of vision, images
and artefacts is inevitably involved in space and time as much as it is
involved in social realities. Historical perspectives increase awareness
of the particular constraints under which visual categories and experiences develop, contextualizing the production of all kinds of images
and artefacts.

These are just a few of the scientific and humanist disciplines that
can fruitfully contribute to understanding of sight, vision, images and
relations with artefacts. Practitioners working in the fields of design,
craft, image creation, and curating museums also have their own
distinctive insights to offer.[23] Frequently, these are ignored within the
humanist academy.

The whole field of the visual cannot be the province of any one disciplinary perspective. Like personality, the visual is experienced as a

whole, but analysed in parts. Scholars, however, often tend to stay closely within their own narrow furrow of expertise. Frequently, they fail to have the enriching conversations that might lead to broad understandings of universal phenomena that would make academic life more interesting and creative and produce insights that would be of value to the human race generally.

Having said this, however, many disciplines, if they reflect upon themselves, would recognize that they are in fact already interdisciplines, drawing ideas from common wells of concepts and methods. So, for example, anthropologists and historians of art often acquire many of their most illuminating ideas and methods from philosophers like Heidegger and Gadamer, or psychoanalytic writers like Lacan.

Trying to work in an interdisciplinary way always runs the risk of misunderstanding, ignorance and partiality – so there is a need for awareness of the limits of what one is doing.[24] However, without such endeavour it is impossible even to suggest synthetic understandings and ideas which might be to the benefit of a number of disciplines and human beings in general rather than just for a particular specialism.

## The purpose of this book

What might you gain if you continue to read this volume?

My first aim is to provide *a more critical and complex view of the nature of visual artefacts and relationships with them.* I have to admit to having had naive and unexamined attitudes in relation to this field. I have been astonished by what I did not know and have taken for granted in my assumptions about sight, visuality and the significance of images and visual objects for life, action and thought. In particular, I have had to open my eyes to the significance and function of visual objects that do not function as overt 'art'. Art and its products are not the only, or even the most important, components of the visual realm. Images and artefacts come in many other forms than classic, rectangular easel-painting shapes. We have experiences and relationships with all manner of created visually perceptible objects that attract and repel our gaze.

I hope here to share some of my discoveries and questions in the hope that you will find your visual and intellectual life enriched by problematizing and expanding your view of this area. There are few fields that are so complex as that of sight and vision. I hope you will enjoy undertaking the kind of revision of assumptions and prejudices about vision, images and visual artefacts that I have undertaken in re-sighting/-siting myself in relation to the visual.

My second main aim is *to encourage exploration of some of the implications for ethics and action of understanding vision, images and artefacts in a more complex way.* Traditionally in Western society, we have distinguished very clearly between that which is alive and that which is devoid of life and dead, and we have felt free to use the latter for the sake of the former without any qualms. Indeed, it has often been regarded as admirable to despise the world of objects and things for the sake of 'higher' ends like human relationships, or service of the divine. The world of objects is, then, mostly treated as providing means for the benefit of the animate rather than as having value in its own right.

This absolute, somewhat arbitrary, distinction is questioned here. One of my reluctant learnings in the sphere of sight and the visual has been that people clearly attribute some personlike qualities and have some human-like relationships with inanimate objects in the world (for example, people give their motorcycles and violins names, speak to their computers to encourage them, immortalize themselves in buildings designed by, or named by, them). The traditional clear division between the animate/human and inanimate/thing worlds can be unhelpful. Humans are who and what they are as much because of their relationships with objects and things as because of their relations with gods or other people. We shape our environment and the things in it. But they also shape us. If this kind of relationship can be recognized, so that the psychological self is extended to become an embodied social self in a material world, there is a case for asking what kind of relationships of responsibility we might, or should, have to these objects. If we create visible objects that invite rejection, thoughtless use, or invisible subordination, then we do not show them much respect. We can then throw them away or abuse them as we see fit, much as people treated slaves or infants in the past. This might be pragmatically justifiable if the population of the world were stable or contracting, while material resources expanded infinitely. However, late capitalist consumption is producing a situation in which we buy more and more, but natural resources are diminishing.

I will argue that we need to come to love and respect the material world better, cherishing the objects within it and revaluing them so we know and appreciate those that we live with. Indeed, I suggest that we need to create relations of appreciative friendship and companionship with at least some artefacts, so we treasure and appreciate them more. We might then move into a properly materialistic culture that values and respects the material rather than seeing artefacts as symbols of some other, inarticulate, human need. As it is, materialism is a frightening spiritual heresy that is presently in danger of helping to destroy the world, animate and inanimate together, because it does not help us to deal with our deep inner needs or halt the inexorable trends towards ephemerality and disposability that characterize consumption.

The casualty of this is the downgrading and contemptuous way in which objects are often treated. We probably need to learn to treat them much more like persons deserving respect and love, rather than like stuff that has no meaning. If we moved towards consciously endowing the material with some personlike aspects we would perhaps need less of it. Just as we can only really love a few people, maybe we need to move to a stage where we properly love a few objects so that we don't need to have or exploit hundreds of ignored and disparaged ones. An important part of loving someone or something might be to learn how to gaze upon it and with it attentively rather than looking through or past it to find that elusive something else that will not ultimately satisfy either the eye or the heart. It is within my lifetime that we have begun to believe that pre-natal foetuses and animals have some grounds for being accorded personlike rights and qualities. Perhaps the time has come to look more closely at the world of inanimate objects in this kind of light.

I have a number of contributory subordinate aims. The first of these is *to outline and, where necessary, problematize theories and practices of seeing and vision*. Most individuals on a day-to-day basis find opening their eyes and negotiating their way round a visible world easy and instinctive. However, there are many theories and ways of seeing that can complicate the taken-for-granted. In almost every dimension of sight and vision there are competing, and possibly incommensurate, understandings of the nature and importance of what is going on. It is probably not helpful that so many different understandings and activities are comprehended by the deceptively short words, 'seeing', 'sight' and 'vision'. I will not provide a unified understanding of sight and vision in this book. However, I will attempt to make readers critically aware of a range of the many ways in which vision and visually related phenomena are analysed, understood and represented.

Beyond the many different theories and understandings of sight and vision that intertwine in everyday life, it is also *worth exploring the ambivalent, sometimes contradictory roles and valuations in thought and practice in which seeing, sight and vision become embroiled*. In part, this can be accounted for by very different activities and concepts being placed together and being in tension with one another. However, while vision is often taken to be our most powerful, useful sense, there is considerable debate and uncertainty about its usefulness and veracity. Is the visual the realm of ultimate truth and accurate witness? Or is it the place where we are all vulnerable to illusion and deception? The politics of vision and the visual pervade both secular and religious worlds. They continue to arouse strong emotions as people feel both the power and pull of what is seen, while also wanting to cast doubt on its reality and legitimacy.

While the realm of sight, the visual, and images is vast, a few pockets of interest and attention have tended to monopolize the attention of thinkers. There is much writing and theorizing about objects regarded as art created by a clear tribe of named artists. However, there is much less about objects that are simply designed or crafted by anonymous labourers. Similarly, in the religious sphere, there is still much analysis of arguments about the validity of representing the sacred in icons or the rights and wrongs of destroying religious imagery, but a great deal less about the everyday relations that people have with devotional objects. And no real concern at all about what might be the ethical implications of visual interpretations and relations of phenomena that are not necessarily strictly religious at all. Within this book, then, one main intention is *to broaden thought and awareness about the visual, images, artefacts and representations beyond limited consideration of idols, icons, the aesthetic, and high art, into everyday and other areas of perception and life.*

The sense of sight has often been regarded as the most important and sophisticated of the senses. It is closely linked with reason, thought and mentation – hence the proliferation of sight- and light-related words to describe aspects of the intellectual. The word 'theory' itself is linked to the Greek word for sight. This network of associations points to an important limitation in understanding sight in the modern world; it is often isolated from the other senses, and particularly from the proximate senses of touch, taste and smell that are held to interact more immediately with the material world. Just as thinking and reason have been regarded as disembodied, separate parts of the person, separated from embodied aspects of perception like emotion, so sight and vision have shared a separation from the material world, often being regarded as somewhat ethereal and idealized. One of the most important purposes of this book, then, will be *to reconnect seeing with all the other senses and the material world, rescuing it from artificial isolation from physical reality.*

It has become a commonplace of perceptual theory that no one sense is any more important than any other in helping humans to relate to the world. We are whole-body perceivers who need all our senses if we are to really gain a full grasp of what is before us. So although we may divide the senses into, say, five discrete and separate functions, for the sake of analysis or convenience, this distorts our real perceptual process. Thus, for example, when people want to gain a real sense of what they are seeing, they will often automatically reach out to touch the object they are looking at. Sight is often closely related to the sense of touch and used alongside it or with one sense substituting for the other. This has led some theorists to coin and explore the notion of the 'haptic' in vision. The haptic denotes the sense of vision that touches, caresses and interacts more mutually with objects, rather than just surveying them from afar.

In this book, then, one of my intentions is *to try partially to review the senses in which vision might be reconceived as a haptic, materially connected sense working in tandem with, rather than isolation from, the other senses in a single sensorium.* This with a view to ensuring that vision is redeemed from being conceived only as a distant, objective, detached evaluatory faculty that is ultimately uninterested in the intimate feel of the material world. If seeing and theorizing are reconceived in a more haptic way, there is more possibility of having a thicker, more appreciative theory and practice of seeing and also a fuller, more responsive, and more responsible, relationship with objects in the material realm. This is important for developing the ethical implications for seeing and relating to objects within the sphere of the visual. Thus I argue here for a turn to the haptic in visuality.

Just as vision has perhaps become artificially dissociated from the other senses, and has been shaped into a system of metaphors for abstract, detached thought, there has been a long, astonishingly bitter antagonism between word and image both within religion and in the wider world. For many intellectuals and theologians, the word and the oral represent the most authoritative and reliable discourse. Mostly, the visual image is to be mistrusted as misleading, illusory and untrustworthy in its illusions and ambivalences. These 'logocentrics' are often strongly committed to substituting words for images, reducing figure to language, and generally subordinating the visual to the verbal.

A similar antagonism to words can be found in parts of the artistic and other visually focused communities. Here, the word may be understood as a hindrance to visual expression and understanding by people whose main form of expression and understanding is not primarily verbal. Isadora Duncan is reputed to have said something like, 'If I could have said it, I would not need to dance it!'

Sometimes the 'logocentrics' and 'ocularcentrics' have clashed overtly, as in the instances where religious or intellectual iconoclasts have demanded the destruction of images and idols. More often, there has been stand-off, indifference and mistrust between the two broad groups with each pursuing its own path. Very occasionally, there have emerged performers like William Blake, gifted in both verbal and visual fields.

I will not revisit all aspects of the conflict between word and image or fully evaluate the issues at stake between them. But I do want *strongly to suggest that word and image mostly belong together and can be separated only artificially*. Both add to understandings and perceptions of reality and are equally indispensable. The Greek verb *graphein* denotes both writing and image-creating. Words on pages are in fact images themselves, constructed often from characters and letters to which much artistic design attention has been given. Frequently, too, words and images work best when they are put alongside each other, providing complementarity and critique. Text with pictures is often more illuminating than text without, while paintings in galleries often benefit from words, within or around them, which help explain and expand their meanings.

Because I am a logocentric academic, whose business is the written word, I will try to redress the bias towards images and the visual by considering what the strengths and limitations of the image are, and how images and the visual can contribute to wider understandings of the world. I will also try to unpack some of the reasons for the historic antagonism towards images from the intellectual community with a view to considering the various possible uses and values of images when they are denuded of the unnecessary fear and ignorance that have often accompanied consideration of them from Plato onwards.

One reason why images may be despised, rejected or suspected by logocentric intellectuals and others is that they are deemed to have power and influence that is not easy to define, understand or control. For generations, people have reverenced images in religion and used them as a means of mediation with the divine. The prominence of images continues largely unabated in many contemporary religious traditions – even in some forms of Protestantism. Some people continue to think of this active relationship with images as being idolatrous. But it is not just in the realm of religion that images come under suspicion. Many intellectuals lament the prominence of the visual and images in all parts of contemporary life, seeing this as deflection from really understanding and dealing with the world. Some of these same intellectuals, on the other hand, are also to be found spending time and money on visiting galleries to stand in front of famous images, or indeed to acquire images of their own with which to decorate their homes. So any progressive assumption that the power and influence of images is diminishing as Western culture becomes more 'sophisticated' and self-critical is probably unsustainable.

This being the case, it behoves me *to explore what power and influence images have, whence this comes, and how this is, and has been, interpreted.* What is it that makes some images of huge influence and significance for many individuals? How do images acquire this and what is the nature of the context and content that allows a relationship of significance to occur? If we fail to understand the historic and continuing power and influence of images and visual artefacts, we are in no position to evaluate the significance of that power and influence or to take responsibility for our relationships with them. To be a sophisticated and responsible seer is to understand a little of what might make images potent and important beyond merely adoring, fearing, or being indifferent towards them.

Finally, to God. This is not a work of theology. However, I am a theologian; so it would be strange if I were not to show some interest in the religious dimension of images, artefacts, sight and seeing, particularly as they might relate to the ways in which we see the world and might relate to it morally and in other ways. Furthermore, the God of the Western monotheistic scriptural religions – Judaism, Christianity and Islam – which have done much to shape common culture in the West, has a very interesting, not to say problematic relationship to visuality and the realm of the material visibility. Religion has also influenced ways of seeing and conceptualizing visibility and material reality. Among other things, Christianity has contributed to the split between animate and inanimate realms. So my final intention in this book is *to consider the role that religion, particularly Christianity, has played in shaping understandings of, and relationships with, the realm of visual artefacts.*

A few more words now on what this book does not do. First, I am concerned with the whole realm of the visual and images, not primarily with religious images, or with objects such as films that seem to have a fairly easily interpretable religious significance. Second, this is not a book primarily about art. It is not a guide to art, art history, art appreciation or art criticism, though it draws on all these areas, and others, to develop broad critical perspectives on the whole topic of visuality, imaging, and relationships with artefacts. It focuses on relations within the visual realm and all the kinds of visible artefacts that might be encountered there because it is not just original 'masterpieces' with which ordinary people have significant relationships.

Third, I want to disavow the narrow pursuit of the philosophy and aesthetics of the visual. Since the late eighteenth century, much effort has been devoted to considering what makes art art, what the qualities are that make the beautiful universally considered to be beautiful, etc.[25] Another set of philosophical concerns has revolved around the nature of perception and how we know what we are seeing, how we are deceived or deluded, etc. However, my concern is to begin to understand and analyse some general aspects of the experience of people in general rather than to address a very narrow and well-trammelled agenda which is only of real interest to a few.

Finally, although I am personally interested in all aspects of visual experience, interpretation and meaning, and want here to extend thinking about the significance about the visual and relationships beyond the realm of fine art, I will confine my thinking almost entirely to humanly manufactured artefacts and creations. I will largely exclude the natural world, untouched by humanity, from consideration. My focus on dimensions and objects within the visual created by humans is not motivated by lack of interest in the wider ecological order. It is simply a way of limiting the subject matter of the book to a reasonable size. However, if I am right in my overall assertion that we think too little about the nature of our seeing, and the ethical implications and responsibilities that emerge from this, some of the ideas advanced here might be applied to the appreciation of non-humanly created visual objects and phenomena such as landscapes, fields, planets, oceans, etc. Our gaze on the natural order is not innocent or naked.

## The shape of this book

The purpose of this book is to problematize and expand understandings of vision and visual relationships so that we might perhaps see differently and more critically. Thus, each chapter of the book takes an issue or theme related to seeing and vision with a view to broadening and complexifying taken-for-granted assumptions and expanding understanding and concerns.

The book starts by considering the nature of sight and vision. In Chapter 1, I outline some of the main theories and insights about the nature of vision currently available in the Western world in a variety of disciplines, scientific and other. I discuss the complexities of the nature of sight generally as function, practice and metaphor. I suggest that vision and sight have become reified and separated off from the other senses in the majority Western scopic regime of ocularcentric perspectivalism. This regime indicates an approach to visual phenomena and objects that is basically distant, detached, disembodied and disengaged. The scopic regime of the 'arrogant eye' and its limitations are pointed up and discussed.[26]

If the scopic regime of the 'arrogant eye' is to be rejected in favour of fostering more intimate fellowship with visual artefacts, then an alternative approach is required that allows the emergence of a more intimate, loving gaze. Chapter 2 introduces and explains the elements comprising the scopic regime of haptic, or 'touching', vision. Haptic vision reconnects vision with the body and other senses, as well as allowing sight to draw nearer to perceptible objects. It allows people to get close to and become involved in more intimate relations with the world. The recovery of a haptic or more tactile, whole-body, notion of sight as perception might change some of the unhelpful biases and gaps that have determined many notions of sight in the contemporary world. In particular, a haptic concept of sight emphasizes the holistic, embodied and relational aspects of vision. The notion of haptic vision as a scopic regime is highly metaphorical, fragmented, and in some ways incoherent. However, elements of it are often present in the way that contemporary Western people interact with visual objects. It thus fits better with some aspects of contemporary Western viewers' experience than with ocularcentric perspectivalism. The metaphor and practices of haptic sight inform the quest in the rest of the book to develop friendship and fellowship with visible objects of all kinds.

Having given some preliminary attention to ways of seeing and the nature and assumptions of seers, Chapter 3 turns towards the other pole of visual relationships, that is objects of perception and sight. In so doing, it is necessary to learn from visual theory in art and elsewhere, so this chapter considers the nature of visual images. I look at the complex idea of the image. Images are both material and immaterial, sometimes taking an embodied or visible form, sometimes not, and often flitting between mind, text and material visual representation. Images, then, are more complex and diverse in both form and substance than we perhaps commonsensically think.

While images and visual artefacts are to be found throughout society, there is often resistance to taking them seriously. It is common to hear logocentric intellectuals of all kinds, particularly theologians, deploring the proliferation of images and visual media, apparently to the detriment of the word. Chapter 4 considers the relationships between word and image. I suggest that while in both theory and practice word and image are inseparable, in the contemporary Western intellectual world, images remain subordinated to words. This often prevents viewers from taking images and visual objects seriously. Thus, logocentric culture needs to overcome its scopophobia if it is to appreciate the importance of visual objects and artefacts. There can be no nuanced relationship or fellowship with visual things if viewers are prejudiced against them from the start. I begin to consider why many images and visible artefacts are either feared or ignored in Western capitalist society, and to ponder the power that they seem to have over viewers, a theme that is developed in the next two chapters.

Whether logocentric intellectuals like it or not, people do, in fact, engage in important relationships with visual objects of all kinds. What, then, gives visual artefacts like pictures power to move or grasp us so we find ourselves engaged in relationships with them? Here I start to explore the notion that people have quasi-personlike relationships with visual objects and images and to enquire into the factors that might influence and predetermine those relationships. Taking up the notion of sight or vision as relational, embodied, 'haptic' activity, in Chapters 5 and 6 I look in detail at how the relations between humans and visual material objects might be formed, construed and influenced.

I identify three sets of factors which might impinge upon relationships with visible artefacts. Antecedent factors predispose people to have relations with objects. They include personal psychology, social narratives, expectations, myths and other things that prepare people before they encounter an image or artefact. Contextual factors include setting, lighting, position, and the other phenomena that impinge on perceptual relations with particular visual objects. Finally, inherent factors are those features of individual artefacts that might enable them to become 'sticky' so that they enter into relationships with their viewers. Just as relations with people are complex and multi-dimensional, there are many factors that might work individually and separately to produce possibilities of relationship and connection between people and artefacts.

Images and visual artefacts are not just communicative symbols or representational images. They have material bodies. These inhabit the same spatial world as that occupied by humans. They enter into bodily, non-symbolic relations with humans, helping fundamentally to shape us in symbolic and non-symbolic ways. This might partly explain why

Western moderns, especially disembodied, rationalistic intellectuals, are uncomfortable with them, and want to subvert their importance.

In the modern Western world, artefacts of all kinds are regarded as inanimate, dead, and so incapable of entering into personlike relationships. It was not ever thus. The material world has not always been perceived as completely other to the human world, and artefacts are, of course, the product of human activity and so have that of humanity about them. In Chapter 7, I look back over the history of human relations with artefacts to consider how they came to be regarded as wholly different, unpersonlike, dead, and alien from the human sphere.

Chapter 8, then, goes on to consider the ways in which images and artefacts might be seen as containing personlike attributes in the contemporary world. Having already established that people continue to have complex relationships with material objects, this chapter considers various theories of how personlike attributes and residues might be found in artefacts so that, for example, some people feel that they are addressed, or engaged, by them. Is the notion that objects speak on their own account just a metaphor, or is it possible that real communication does occur between animate and inanimate agent-like beings? Artefacts are not in all ways personlike – they do not suffer or have independent intentionality, for example. However, they do share some of the characteristics of their creators. While trying to avoid theories that anthropomorphize, re-animate or re-enchant the world, this chapter argues that there is a real basis for personlike relations with visible artefacts. Most Western moderns, not just children with dolls, find themselves involved at some level in some kinds of relationship with artefacts. So it behoves us to become more aware, critical and articulate concerning the significance of these. The discussion about relations between humans and artefacts is earthed in a discussion of the symbolic and non-symbolic relations with photographs.

Until this point, the book is mainly descriptive and phenomenological, building up the case that people can, and do, enter into personlike relationships with artefacts. The work now takes a more normative, prescriptive direction. It explores the ethical implications and practicalities of trying to enter more fully into relations with visible objects of all kinds. This is under the guiding perceptual paradigm of haptic vision, the kind of multisensorial vision that allows a more intimate, subject–subject relationship with things in the world.

In Chapter 9, objections to engaging in personlike relations with artefacts, such as the dangers of animism and idolatry, are engaged with. I try to create a case for the importance of closer relationships with artefacts, not least because they have such an important role in shaping the human world. Objectification and domination of objects under the detached gaze of the 'arrogant eye', have served neither humans nor artefacts well. I develop the case that humans need to love and care much more for the artefacts they have created, trying to enter more actively into relations of fellowship and friendship with them. We need to appreciate visual objects of all kinds to a much greater extent than we have done hitherto. This implies attending to them, respecting their ends and intentions, trying to see them for what they are, and not just for what they might do for us, attempting to understand them, and generally displaying many of the other attitudes and behaviours found in human personal relationships. We need to love them better and to see them with an appreciative and sensitive loving gaze. Instead of seeing through objects, humans need to become more engaged with their embodied materiality. More than that, we need to wonder with and at them, as we do at some of our fellow human beings.

This requires the development of a loving, haptic gaze that allows more involvement with things. In Chapter 10, some suggestions are then made as to what practices and attitudes might begin to constitute an appropriate, loving attitude to visual artefacts. How might humans use their eyes differently, and better, so that relations with objects might be richer and deeper for the sake of the artefacts themselves, their human viewers, and the whole of the material world?

The final chapter addresses the role that religion, specifically Christianity, might play in developing more personlike relations with objects in the visible world. Christianity, especially Protestant Christianity, has played a substantial part in creating contemporary Western attitudes to the material world. There are a number of factors that might make Christians anxious about developing a more haptic, appreciative and respectful attitude to artefacts. These are considered before a case is made for a more positive theology and practice of relating to objects. I argue that creating friendship and fellowship with objects is not incompatible with the Christian theological tradition. Indeed, there are many elements in that tradition that might support a very constructive approach to creating personlike relations with artefacts, not least the central doctrines of creation and redemption through material incarnation. Like St Francis, contemporary Western Christians need to develop an attitude to the artefactual realm that does not see through, or past, objects, but sees them as having their own valued place within creation.

# Introduction

## Seeing the things in this book

Due to the expense of reproduction and licensing, there are only a very few illustrations in this volume. However, many visual objects are alluded to and discussed. This might seem both paradoxical and frustrating in a book about visuality. I apologize for any inconvenience and frustration caused. However, a Google search, especially in Google Images, will produce images of most of the things I mention in the text in a matter of seconds – and in colour, too. So if you wish to access the missing images in the book, or, indeed, to see more representations of some of the images included, then please start surfing.

## Notes

1 If the last century has been characterized by a 'linguistic turn', the next development that might be expected is a turn to the material, emotional and perceptual. This realm lies beneath and beyond the verbal and symbolic.

2 Parker (2003).

3 Ingold (2000, p. 46).

4 Cranz (2000).

5 For example, Howes (2003, 2005).

6 Pallasmaa (2005, p. 21) notes, 'The only sense that is fast enough to keep pace with the astounding increase of speed in the technological world is sight. But the world of the eye is causing us to live increasingly in a perpetual present, flattened by speed and simultaneity.' He also notes, 'The hegemony of vision has been reinforced in our time by a multitude of technological inventions and the endless multiplication and production of images – "an unending rainfall of images . . . ".'

7 Schivelbusch (1995).

8 Stephens (1998).

9 Harvey (1989, p. 290), Julier (2000, pp. 10–11).

10 Weibel (2002, p. 670) argues that while representational images are becoming less important in art, they are becoming central to science.

11 Duden (1993), Kemp (2000b).

12 For example, Elkins (2003), Mirzoeff (1999, 2002) and Sturken and Cartwright (2001).

13 Woodward and Pattison (2000).

14 See further Pattison (1997).

15 Sadly, within theology, there is a strange absence of interest in the materiality of visual objects, especially objects whose origins lie outside the influence of Christianity and the Church, and a neglect of approaches to them other than the aesthetic, semiotic or sacramental. Miles (1985, p. 2) points out the Western tradition is one of 'eyesight becoming insight', so that seeing becomes a kind of 'feeling-toned insight' and the material is seen through. Mostly, theologians seem to be interested in the symbolic meaning and interpretation of objects designated to be widely culturally significant by virtue of their being deliberately created as art or architecture (Tillich 1989), especially if those objects can be harnessed to theological and ecclesial purposes

such as engendering devotion (Drury 1999). Thus Brown (2004) is interested in the sacramental potential of a limited number of 'important' artefacts and buildings, but largely fails to deal with the unremarkable things that chiefly mediate human meaning, identity and community in the everyday world. Theology is generally interested in high, rather than popular culture, and in nurturing religious imagination, 'good taste' and aesthetic discrimination (Burch Brown 2000; De Gruchy 2001; Dyrness 2001; Begbie 2002; Monti 2003). It largely ignores the 'kitsch' with which many people surround themselves in their ordinary lives (holiday souvenirs, mass-produced ornaments, photographs, statues of saints, etc.), especially if this appears to have no apparent 'deeper' symbolic religious value, and it is little interested in the materially based religion and implicit theology of popular religious cultural artefacts. Most theologians, for example, take no account of contemporary designers and the designed objects that form the ubiquitous context for daily living. However, some theological attention has been paid to architecture and the built environment (Gorringe 2002). There is now some movement, mainly within US art-historical scholarship, towards considering the importance of the material in the religious lives of ordinary people (McDannell 1995, Morgan 1998, Morgan and Promey 2001), but this has yet to percolate the world of theological and philosophical reflection. Elkins (2004) argues that most contemporary theology is unable or unwilling to engage with cutting-edge movements in art, which are often hostile to or critical of traditional religion, but this judgement is contested (Pattison 1998, Dyrness 2001, Begbie 2002). Theologians have shown quite a lot of interest in analysing films (e.g., Miles 1996); these are the most literary of visual artefacts and come well within the comfort zone of word-based theology.

16 Zajonc (1993).

17 Snowden, Thompson and Troscianko (2006).

18 Ramachandran and Blakeslee (1999), Ramachandran (2003), Sacks (1985, 1991, 1995).

19 Nettle (2001), Frith and Johnstone (2003), Claridge and Davis (2003).

20 Banks and Morphy (1997), Pinney and Thomas (2001).

21 Chaplin (1994), Tanner (2003).

22 Collingwood (1958), Carroll (1999), Lopes (2005).

23 Elkins (2000b), Nooter Roberts and Roberts (1997).

24 Moran (2002).

25 Davies (1991), Carroll (1999), Freeland (2001).

26 McFague (1997).

# I

# Catching Sight:
# Vision, Sight and Visuality

The gradually growing hegemony of the eye seems to be parallel with the development of western ego-consciousness and the gradually increasing separation of the world; vision separates us from the world whereas the other senses unite us with it.

Juhani Pallasmaa, *The Eyes of the Skin*

## Introduction

It is not easy to get a grip, conceptual or practical, on sight, vision and visuality. The intellectual and scientific history and self-understanding of humanity is bound up with understanding vision, seeing and light, from Plato's 'heliocentric' philosophy onwards.[1] To undertake a detailed survey of this area would require many volumes, each taking very different areas and approaches.

Here I want to touch briefly and selectively upon some of the main concepts, debates, insights and confusions that illuminate and confound students of sight and vision today. Vision and seeing are not straightforward matters, nor are the ideas and analytic theories that surround them. It is particularly important to give some account of specular vision, the kind of theory of sight and visuality sometimes known as distant sight, ocularcentrism, or Cartesian perspectivalism. This has perhaps been the dominant model underlying Western society and everyday human visual practices and assumptions over the last few centuries.

## Conceptual preliminaries

There are three main ways of understanding sight.[2] First, it can be understood as a *perceptual experience*. This is sight understood as basically a physical, physiological and psychological phenomenon, closely related to the operations of eye and brain within the ecology of light perception and optics. It is this understanding of sight that engages the interests of psychologists, optometrists and neurophysiologists.

Second, sight can be regarded as a *social practice*. One prominent emphasis in recent visual theory expounded by art theorists, historians and philosophers has been the influence of social and historical factors upon both ways of understanding sight, for example different scientific theories of light and vision – and ways in which people see and represent the visual. Why do people think it is important to look at particular things in particular ways at particular moments in time? Why did perspectival vision appear in Western paintings in the fifteenth century and then dominate representation until the twentieth century? Why did the Japanese have different non-perspectival conventions in their art?[3] Why do contemporary scientists colour digitally derived scans of the interior of the brain and what conventions do they use for such colouration?

Social and cultural conventions and codes also impinge upon the ways humans see. We are taught to see and how to interpret the significance of what we see, by others. Thus, if they gain vision, people who are blind from birth at first experience a kind of chaos. The conventions and codes also impinge fundamentally upon ways of representing what is seen.[4] If you look at a sixteenth-century drawing of a rhinoceros, it will not correspond to a modern photograph of the same species.[5] Both the medium and the conventions of representation are different.

One way of characterizing this social dimension of sight from the more physical is to distinguish vision and visuality. Vision is 'what the human eye is physiologically capable of seeing', while visuality can be thought of as 'the way in which vision is constructed in various ways' (Rose 2001, p. 6). However, physical and social dimensions cannot be entirely separated: 'Although vision suggests sight as a physical operation, and visuality sight as a social fact, the two are not opposed as nature to culture: vision is social and historical too, and visuality involves the body and psyche' (Foster 1988, p. ix).

Within any particular era or culture there will be a certain 'scopic regime'. A scopic regime is 'an integrated complex of visual theories and practices' (Jay 1988, p. 4).[6] Foster argues that, 'With its own rhetoric and representations, each scopic regime seeks to close out these differences: to make of its own many social visualities one essential vision, or to order them in a natural hierarchy of sight.'[7]

The third aspect of sight to be distinguished is that of *discursive construct*. This refers to the way that sight and vision give rise to metaphors, images and constructs that shape thought and thinking. The

Western intellectual tradition, building upon Greek preoccupations with light, reason and sight, has been structured by visually related ideas.[8] Thus, knowledge is seen as light, ignorance as darkness, incomprehension as blindness, thought as speculation, and so on. Western ways of thinking about knowing and reasoning are essentially related to ideas of light and sight – a phenomenon sometimes known as ocularcentrism. Even in everyday life and conversation, visually related language and concepts are prominent.[9]

To summarize, there are three different fundamental ways of conceptualizing sight and vision. They continuously interact with, and dynamically affect and interpret, each other in a hermeneutic circle. Furthermore, 'there is no privileged vantage point outside the hermeneutic circle of sight as perceptual experience, social practice, and discursive construct' (Jay 1994, p. 587). Thus it is very difficult to understand any particular dimension of sight on its own or to understand it clearly. It is possible to get completely confused about the nature of the realities that are being alluded to in any particular sight-related discourse.


## Practical realities

It is now possible to go on to think about the perceived realities of sight in the contemporary world. Here confusion and ambivalence deepens.

Art historian James Elkins (1997, p. 11) writes this about commonsensical sight within the Western scopic regime:

> At first, it appears that nothing could be easier than seeing. We just point our eyes where we want them to go, and gather in whatever there is to see . . . Seeing does not interfere with the world or take anything from it, and it does not hurt or damage anything. Seeing is detached and efficient and rational. Unlike the stomach or the heart, eyes are our own to command: they obey every desire and thought.

However, learning from psychoanalytically related ideas about sight, Elkins recognizes that far from being passive or objective, looking is driven by passion and desire. Sight is very active. It can be invasive, both bringing and causing pleasure and pain. It affects both the things that are seen and the person who sees. Nor does it take things in passively. Looking is fundamentally influenced by desires and longings, and can function as a kind of appetite.[10]

While humans may conceive of themselves as being isolated monadic viewers, according to the French psychoanalyst Jacques Lacan, we exist in a complex reciprocal, modificatory web of mutually seeing and being seen (see Figure 1):

> as I look at someone or something it looks back, and our gazes cross each other . . . I see and I can see that I am seen, so each time I see I also see myself being seen. Vision becomes a kind of cat's cradle of crossing lines of sight . . . (Elkins 1997, p. 70)

Sight is incomplete and partial. Human seers have the subjective impression that their visual world is unified, comprehensive and stable. However, visual scientists and others have demonstrated that this is an illusion. There is no direct perception of the world in the eye, just an interpretive representation in the brain. Vision is created as much or more within the brain as within or before the eye.[11] Each of our eyes receives slightly different sense data from the world. This must be made sense of to provide a unified representation. Within the eye, only the central part, the fovea, is capable of sight of the kind needed to distinguish details. It is surrounded by an area of peripheral vision which is sensitive mainly to movement, not to detail. And there is a blind spot on the retina which is filled in by the brain. This means that there are always things of which we cannot be directly physically aware, though we are not conscious of this.

The visual system (the eye and brain combined) accommodates the fact that the eyes are constantly moving, scanning and receiving incremental sense data which are generated by constant, tiny saccadic eye movements. If we keep our eyes absolutely still, as we might think we are doing when we gaze on a loved one or a picture, we cannot see anything at all.[12] Just as sharks cannot breathe if they stop swimming, we cannot see if our eyes stop moving. The sense of immediacy of stable vision we think we enjoy actually takes time to assemble. This means

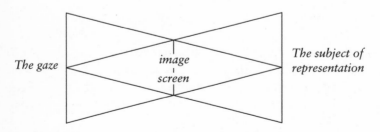

*The gaze* — *image / screen* — *The subject of representation*

*Figure 1: Lacan's notion of interlocking gaze (see Lacan 1981, p. 106).*

that our incremental creation of representations is historical. Furthermore, human vision is more drawn to edges and movements than to the details of objects.[13]

Perhaps the best way to conceptualize sight and vision is as a series of informed, selective predictive hypotheses about reality based on past knowledge and experience, as well as on present sensory data. There are many gaps in it.[14] This does not stop vision providing humans with the information they need for action, perception and effective living. However, sight is not as comprehensive and trustworthy as it superficially and intuitively seems to be. Most of the things we think we see are only rough approximations:

> [W]hen you are looking more or less straight ahead, everything at the edges is radically undependable . . . It's hard to realize that you have not been seeing familiar objects like distant trees but drawing conclusions based on tiny samples and guesses. (Elkins 1997, p. 100)

When the unconscious wishes and fears that may determine attention, gaze and sight are added in, we may see even less. Some images are so offensive that we must look away from or ignore them. For centuries, viewers failed to notice or discuss the naked penis of the infant Jesus in Renaissance paintings, evidence of 'deflected seeing' and visual repression perhaps.[15] In the modern world, we are familiar with the phenomenon of people being unable to look at or remember sights which are too traumatic or overwhelming.

Sighted people, then, can be characterized as partially blind. Indeed, sight can be regarded as a kind of enclave within blindness in which blindness and sight are traded off one another.[16] 'The paradox of seeing is that the more forcefully I try to see, the more blind I become' (Elkins 1997, p. 210).

There are many ways in which vision occurs and fails to occur within the contemporary Western scopic regime.[17] Elkins describes the limits, issues and problems that occur for seeing from the perspective of individualized, atomistic, sovereign psychological selves living in a context of capitalist modernity. In this kind of world, seeing is confined to the material and the psychological, to what is taken to be the realm of material appearance.

However, there are other scopic regimes, ways of seeing, and ways of understanding seeing, for example, religious seeing. In the past, for prepsychological selves, the worlds of visionary seeing and ordinary seeing overlapped and were not firmly separated from one another.[18]

Since the rise of science and triumph of rationalism in the Enlighten-ment, the notion of material sight has tended to displace the value of religious and spiritual seeing. Those in Western society who think they have visions, see apparitions, or have prophetic dreams are regarded as deviants, or as mentally deranged, by psychologically minded moderns. However, this dismissal of 'extraordinary' experience may simply be another kind of blindness which confines Westerners' vision to a thin, limited view of 'reality'. It is not uncommon for people in some com-munities and contexts in modern Western society to have experience of dreams, visions and apparitions.[19] Contemporary travel writer William Dalrymple reports this experience just a few miles from Jerusalem in the late 1990s:

> There is nowhere in the East where it is quite as easy to summon up Khidr [St George] as in his birthplace at Beit Jala [near Bethlehem].
>
> 'Ask anyone,' said Fr. Methodius . . . 'Stop anyone in the street outside and ask them if they have seen St George . . . '
>
> The first person we came across was an elderly Muslim gentleman . . . I asked him whether he had ever seen St George.
>
> 'Of course', he said. '. . . I see him frequently – he is always coming and going on his horse.'
>
> 'You see this in dreams?'
>
> 'No, when I am awake, in daylight . . . Whenever we have problems he comes and helps us.' (Dalrymple 1998, p. 343)

Dalrymple's interlocutor refuses to modify his account of being an inhabitant of a particular scopic regime to fit in with the interloper's assumptions about the world and perception.

What we might be tempted to call delusion, or fantasy, forms an important part of many contemporaries' normal visual experience, not just in so-called primitive societies.[20] Many individuals have unusual visual experiences, but this does not make them ill or mad. Western arbitrary exclusion of this as madness, or loss of touch with reality, may be another example of ideological filling in of intellectual scoto-mas (blind spots).[21] Within the positivistic Western scopic regime we accept from scientists the notion that invisible energy waves are real but cannot be seen because of physical ocular limitations. Simultaneously, we reject the idea that there might be other kinds of seeing and visibili-ties than objectifying observational perception of external appearances, despite the fact that these same scientists point up the arbitrary and partial nature even of our physical seeing.

The arbitrary censorship of apparently non-material 'seeing' might be another instance of our unwillingness to deal with vision in its pluriformity. It makes sense to atomized, autonomous psychological selves, who have a well-defined, boundaried sense of self and other, inner and outer. However, the psychological individual is a socially and historically contextualized entity of quite recent origin in the development of Western society.[22] There is no reason to think that it is superior to other kinds of selves that may have more fluid boundaries and be open to rather different perceptions and experiences.

Vision and sight are, indeed, 'not what we think' (Pylyshyn 2003). Different socially inflected scopic regimes, with their distinctive theories, types, and experiences of vision, can exist alongside one another, despite the illusion that perhaps all seers have, that what they and their like see is 'reality'. There are more holes than continuities in human vision. Perhaps we should admire people who can see more and differently rather than less and the same. We should at least accord them respect and some interest in their experience if we are to avoid scopic imperialism.

## The way we see now – sight, vision and their discontents

> The sight is so much the noblest of the senses, as that it is all the senses. As the reasonable soul of man . . . becomes all the soul of man, and he hath no longer a vegetative and sensitive soul, but all is that one reasonable soul, so, says St Augustine . . . all the senses are called seeing . . . Employ then this noblest sense upon the noblest object, see God, see God in everything . . . (Donne 1990, p. 139)

Even within our contemporary world, conscious of embodied sensual pluralism, for most sighted people sight remains the sense most valued.[23]

The exaltation of sight draws on a tradition emanating from the origins of Western thought. Aristotle writes in the *Metaphysics*:

> All men by nature desire to know. An indication of this is the delight we take in our senses; for even apart from their usefulness they are loved for themselves; and above all others the sense of sight. For . . . even when we are not going to do anything, we prefer seeing (one might say) to anything else. (Magee and Milligan 1998, p. 35) [24]

Situated at the top of the erect human body, this powerful sense seems close to the brain and consciousness within some kind of hierarchy of perceptive capacities.[25] As Donne, following Augustine, suggests, it can seem to be the most sophisticated of the senses, acting as a kind of master-model for perception and also as a measure and judge of the others.

While we might now hesitate to describe sight as the 'noblest' of the senses, we still set enormous store by the sense of vision. It apparently allows immediate and co-ordinated access to the present world. It provides distance on objects, allowing us to judge their significance and get them into perspective without our having to interfere with, or touch, them. It allows us to judge distances, to gather large amounts of data rapidly, literally to have foresight so we can work out quickly where to go and how to act.[26] Beyond its functional and informational potential, it also allows us aesthetic pleasure, human communication and illusory play.[27]

Most sighted people would be devastated by the threat of blindness, with the loss of the visual world and the freedom to move around freely in it.[28] So it is unsurprising that sight has been the most researched sense as well as being perhaps our best-developed and best-understood sense.

In many ways, however, we mistake and misunderstand the nature and significance of sight. We overestimate its significance and importance for gaining knowledge of the world. Whole schools of philosophy have been founded on the assumption that to think and have the images in the mind that would allow us to reason and imagine, we need to be able to internalize images through the eyes from the outside world.[29] However, blind people can think well and have perfectly adequate imaging and imaginary capacities without the benefit of sight.[30] They rightly argue that the sighted consistently over-value vision. Much of the data that comes from any one sense is superfluous and most things can be known, appreciated and understood perfectly well by people who are deficient in any particular sense. Non-sighted people can gain adequate access to and understand most of the phenomena in the visual world without the benefit of eyesight.[31] Dreams, images and visions are not the exclusive preserve of the sighted.

Related to these misunderstandings, we are perhaps inclined to believe that sight is a sense on its own, a uniquely powerful and useful sense that can function autonomously and independently of all the others. This assumption is unfounded. Sight is in many ways affected by, dependent upon, and integrated with, other senses such as hearing, touch and bodily position.[32] Touch, in particular, is very important for confirming the nature of what we see. Furthermore, if sight is possibly our most powerful sense it is also the sense that is most easily deluded, subject as it often is to illusion and deception. It only takes a little mist or a sleight of the hand to fool the eye completely. Doubting Thomas was doing what most would when he protested that he would not believe that Jesus was risen until he could touch him (John 20.26–9).[33]

So why do we continue to endow sight and vision with nobility, fascination and priority, to the exclusion of the other senses? It is difficult to account fully for the aura that continues to give sight the status of quasi-autonomous 'super-sense'. One powerful predisposing factor is probably the close association of sight with rationality and thought itself. The Western intellectual tradition has tended to identify rationality as the most distinctive feature that humans have, compared with other living beings. Reason and understanding are often couched in terms of illumination.[34] Indeed, Platonic metaphysics was an ocular-centric, heliocentric philosophy of the emanation of creative light that formed the visible order. While light floods the eyes with sight, reason floods the mind engaged in *theoria* with knowledge of the physically invisible reality of ideas.[35]

The metaphorical usage of sight and vision to construct and understand the sacralized human intellect then acts to dignify physical seeing with an aura of divinity.[36] As rationality is to the divine, so physical sight is to reason. Here we are firmly in the hermeneutic circle where sight as perceptual experience, social practice and discursive construct constantly mutually construct and modify one another.[37] We overestimate physical sight and seeing, perhaps because we overestimate the power of disembodied pure reason and the mind. If reason is supposed to be cool and detached, as it is often held to be, then in a complex mutual reintrojection of metaphors and practices, sight will share these characteristics.

The so-called specular view of the mind, whereby it is conceived as a kind of inner mirror or even as a kind of theatre where some kind of inner spectator or homunculus (a human-like figure in the mind) muses upon ideas and images abstracted from the sensual world, was consolidated in the seventeenth century at the dawn of the modern, scientific world by philosophers such as Locke and Descartes. At this point, many of the properties accorded to the eye and vision were transferred to the mind.[38] These thinkers were much influenced by the paradigm of the camera obscura. This device was a dark chamber into which images of the outside world were projected through a small hole, providing independent image without substance (see Plate 1).[39]

The camera obscura became a philosophical metaphor, as well as being a model for optics.[40] The implications of adopting this as a model for the mind were far-reaching. First, it created a clear division between the inner and outer worlds. The mind was regarded as separate from the physical world. It was the mind, not the eye, that really saw. It acted as a camera obscura into which images which could then be used for thought came. The mind acts as a kind of inner observer with its own 'inner eye', the 'mind's eye'.

Second, it reinforced the idea of an independent, incorporeal observer cut off from the material world, helping to create the notion of a free, sovereign individual subject inhabiting a private space clearly separated from the public domain, an 'interiorized, disembodied, subject' (Crary 1990, p. 40). Mind becomes objective, God-like spectator.[41]

Third, and related, it creates the notion of mind as an inner space that can be observed. Fourth, it fosters the idea that there is a single viewpoint from which things can be perceived. Most importantly, it provided a model both for reflective introspection and self-observation while simultaneously creating a way of observing material phenomena in the external world.[42] Descartes gave 'encouragement to both speculative and empirical concepts of vision' (Jay 1994, p. 80).[43]

Within this distinction between mind and matter, the introspective and the empirical methods,

> philosophy's projects became dedicated to the 'rigorous' and 'scientific' divination of the accurate and most appropriate transportation of the 'outside' into the 'inside'. The conventional highway for this transport has been . . . primarily sight. Such empirical . . . theories . . . have marked out the epoch of modernity: a period we might describe as the 'opening of vision'. (Jenks 1995, p. 3)

Although this scopic regime of detached, disembodied Cartesian perspectivalism (as Jay (1988) denotes it) has been modified, and a variety of scopic regimes have flourished within and around it, it has powerfully shaped the contemporary Western world.

An important development in thinking about the theory and practice of vision over recent years has been the assertion of relativism, pluralism and multi-perspectivalism. It is, therefore, possible to identify a number of scopic regimes which co-exist simultaneously in the contemporary world. So some people think we live in a scopic regime of socially controlling gaze and surveillance. Others think the dominant scopic regime can best be characterized as that of mechanical vision in which most 'seeing' is done 'virtually' by machines, digitally, and without the benefit of human eyes. Simultaneously, there are people who continue to see 'religiously' and 'spiritually'. And many Americans apparently have an extramission theory of sight whereby they believe that they see by means of rays going out from the eyes.[44] Perhaps many of us move through different scopic regimes and notions as we do through our other values, practices and assumptions.

Despite this pluralism, a basically Cartesian idea of sight continues to underlie many of the assumptions Western people make about sight. While I 'know' that the images in my mind are not impresses of external sensations but rather complex representations that in no way appear on a screen, it is difficult not to feel that my mind is a proscenium for inner visual experience.[45] This is what introspection is like. Thinking feels like working with images in the theatre of the mind. The reality of the idea that thinking is probably beyond words and images is almost impossible to grasp if I take my intuitive experience seriously.

Meanwhile, my inner world is supposedly situated within an external reality where science is still held by many to be synonymous with authoritative, objective and detached observation that has nothing to do with the biases of subjectivity and introspection.[46] Some aspects of Cartesian ocularcentric perspectivalism and the implications of the specular mind seem, then, far from dead, perhaps especially in the lives of ordinary users of the eyes and the mind.

A scopic regime is 'an integrated complex of visual theories and practices' (Jay 1988, p. 4). In Western individualized psychological culture, we are still heirs to the 'Cartesian theatre' view of the mind and sight.[47] However, this ocularcentric way of seeing has come under increasing criticism.

This way of understanding the world with and through vision separates the subject from the world; it objectifies everything outside the self. It provides the illusion that everything outside the self is lifeless and can be objectively observed.[48] Things in the external world become reified and deprived of significance other than that bestowed by the observer. Thus they can be instrumentally used without qualm while the intellectual observer has the sense of being in a separate realm of rationality (so-called intellectual logocentrism).[49] Vision becomes an 'immaculate perception' in which the external appearances of things are taken to be the sum total of reality (see Nietzsche 1969, p. 144). The seer can ignore issues of social construction, conflict and politics because what there is to see is all that is of significance. Thus empirical observation becomes 'mindless' and 'valueless', focused on the quantitative and non-reflexive (Jenks 1995, p. 5).

A unitary gaze from a single viewpoint suppresses the possibility of plural viewpoints and is then taken to be indisputably valid. The observer, looking at nature, can ignore matters of interpretation or notions that the gaze may be representational and interpretative. Indeed, many scientists have aspired to this kind of unambiguity of positive vision which produces a world of unequivocal 'facts'. The 'artfulness of sight' based on its being interpretative is suppressed by the veracity of universally valid observation (Jenks 1995, p. 10). The observer is not an embodied, erotic being with a particular point of view and vision affected by desire. He or she is a generalized, dispassionate godlike being with a single, accurate linear perspective who literally 'sees through' things, ignoring their materiality.[50] Even divinity becomes an object in the view of the Cartesian observer rather than humans being the objects of God's vision.[51] The disciplined, linear vision of the Cartesian viewer is regimented and total, aspiring to unambiguous clarity and providing a basis for technological control (see Plate 2).

Ocularcentric scopic regimes, Cartesian and other, have come under extensive criticism over the last two hundred years, particularly in France. Philosophers have attacked this way of seeing because of its apparent neglect of body, time, action and context and its espousal of an illusory, eternally valid, disembodied, contemplative perspective. Feminists have attacked this kind of 'rational gaze' for its intrusive patriarchal will to power over women and nature and its disrespect for the proper veiling of reality – so-called 'phallogocularcentrism'.[52] Postmodernists have attacked its 'blindness' to so many of the things that matter, such as the bodily, affective and intersubjective aspects of life.[53] Social analysts have tried to situate sight and vision within the contextualized construction of power and control.[54] Psychoanalytic writers have attempted to write back aspects of embodied desire and communication into the 'optical unconscious'.[55] Artists and writers such as Dadaists and Surrealists have tried to subvert the visually obvious in order to open up the wonder and instability of the visual.[56] A phalanx of twentieth-century French thinkers has decried and denigrated the dominance and nature of vision and sight in thought and life.

It would be wrong to give the impression that ocularistic perspectivalism has been unchanging, monolithic, universal or unified. For example, eighteenth-century Baroque art embodies a playful, fanciful, non-linear approach to sight and vision which is quite at odds with the cold rationalism that is portrayed as underlying the Cartesian scopic era.[57] However, attending to the nature and limits of this kind of paradigm helps to draw out some possible continuing working assumptions about sight and vision in contemporary Western thought and practice in a scopic regime which still works on many of the inhabited beliefs of ocularcentric perspectivalism, for example, the notion of pictorial realism, the objectivity of scientific observation.[58]

## Conclusion

Having outlined something of the criticisms of ocularcentric sight and visuality in their Cartesian and post-Cartesian forms, I next propose a view of vision and sight that counters and questions many of the assumptions that may have influenced the ways that we conceptualize and value vision and sight. I will introduce the notion of 'haptic vision' which has been suppressed beneath and within Cartesian and other modern scopic regimes such as spectacle, social control, mechanical seeing, with their emphasis on objectivity, detachment and distance in visual perception.

## Notes

1 See Jay (1994, p. 270) for heliocentrism.

2 See Jay (1994, p. 587) for this typology.

3 For more on these questions see Gombrich (1977), cf. Alpers (1983), Bryson (1983), Holly (1996).

4 Cf. Zeki (1999, pp. 91ff.) and Bryson (1983). Zeman (2004, p. 200) notes, 'The sight that greets . . . newly seeing eyes is a "chaos of continually shifting, unstable evanescent appearances".' He quotes the nineteenth-century scientist, William Herschel: 'Seeing is an art that must be learned: we cannot see at sight' (Zeman 2004, p. 199). Mitchell (1986, p. 118) notes that the 'innocent eye is blind'.

5 Kemp (1990).

6 I have some reservations about the word 'integrated' in Jay's definition. I would rather remove this word in the interests of being more accurate, but have left it in for completeness. I think a scopic regime can actually be a rather loose mélange of factors that have consonances and dissonances even while, as constituents of a kind of 'ideal type', they hang together.

7 Foster (1988, p. ix). Heywood and Sandwell (1999, p. x) offer a more detailed topography of levels of analysis of visual phenomena: visual practices in everyday life, the sociology and politics of the visual order, the historical formation of theoretical sciences and their construction, and critical discourses about visually organized paradigms and practices.

8 Rorty (1980), Jay (1994).

9 'In western society . . . visual ability has become conflated with cognition, and in a series of very complicated ways' (Jenks 1995, p. 1). Blindness then becomes a metaphor for stupidity, lack of understanding etc. (Barasch 2001).

10 For more on the nature of, and problems with, sight see, for example, Arnheim (1969, pp. 13ff., 37ff.) and Snowden *et al.* (2006).

11 Pylyshyn (2003, p. xiii), Zeki (1999, pp. 13ff.).

12 Snowden *et al.* (2006, ch. 2).

13 For more on all these matters see Gregory (1998, 2004), Snowden *et al.* (2006).

14 Gregory (1998, p. 5). Pylyshyn (2003, p. 446): 'Vision routinely goes beyond the information given; a percept is invariably a generalization of the individual properties of a unique stimulus.'

15 Elkins (1997, p. 118), cf. Steinberg (1996).

16 Cf. Derrida (1993) for the integral place of blindness in seeing and representing. Mitchell (2002, p. 90) argues: 'Visual culture entails a meditation on blindness, the invisible, the unseen, the unseeable, and the overlooked . . .' For the phenomenon of 'blindsight' whereby blind people can see some things without conscious awareness of it, see, for example, Ramachandran and Blakeslee (1999, pp. 75–6), Snowden *et al.* (2006, pp. 319–21).

17 For more on how different societies and cultures shape the sensorium and ways of perceiving see, for example, Howes (2003), Marks (2000), Seremetakis (1994) and Stoller (1997).

18 Freud (1991), Carruthers (1998), Flannery-Dailey (2004). Translating the visionary into the realm of material visuality, some contemporaries take photographs of the divine (Berryman 2006).

19 For example, Wiebe (1997), Christian (1992), Zaleski (1987), Connell (1997) and Maxwell and Tschudin (1990). Cf. Harris (1999) and Taves (1999).

20 Nettle (2001, ch. 1).

21 'According to Helmholz [a nineteenth-century physiologist and visual scientist], there is not a single blind spot, there are many, scattered throughout the field of vision. Each person has defective spots in his retinas (negative scotomas) and defective neurons in his visual cortex, so that we are more or less blind in spots without ever knowing it: an exact analogy to our intermittent awareness in the visual field. There are objects in every scene that we don't see . . . ' (Elkins 1997, p. 219).

22 For more on the rise of the individual, psychological, atomized, autonomous self see, for example, Carrithers, Collins and Lukes (1985), Strathern (1998), Taylor (1989), Danziger (1997) and Ingold (2000).

23 For more on sensual pluralism see, for example, Marks (2000), Howes (2003, 2005) and Stoller (1997). On the contemporary supremacy of the visual, Jay (1994, p. 543) writes: 'Vision . . . is normally understood as the master sense of the modern era, variously described as the heyday of Cartesian perspectivalism, the age of the world picture, and the society of the spectacle or surveillance.'

24 Plato (1977, p. 65): 'I reckon the supreme benefit for which sight is responsible is that not a word of all we have said about the universe could have been said if we had not seen stars and sun and heaven.'

25 Freud speculates that human civilization is founded on 'the triumph of the eye over the nose' as humans raise themselves from the ground into the erect position and thus distance themselves from the genitalia and smelly parts of the nether regions (Jay 1994, p. 333).

26 See Jonas (1966, pp. 135ff.) for these points.

27 Pylyshyn (2003, p. 133). Lowe (1982, p. 7) notes: 'Seeing in contrast to hearing, touching, smelling, and tasting is pre-eminently a distancing, judgmental act. The data of the other four senses come to us, so that perceptually we connect our selves to what is proximate. But sight is extension in space, presupposing a distance . . . We can hear, touch, smell, and taste in any position we like . . . But seeing is most certain when

we assume an upright posture . . . Within this frontal, upright, horizonal extension, seeing is judgmental. The other four senses can be very refined and discriminating; but only sight can analyze and measure. Seeing is a comparative perception of things before our selves, the beginning of objectivity. That is why sight has been closely related to the intellect.'

28 According to the Royal National Institute for the Blind (*Today* programme, BBC Radio 4, 6 September 2006), nine out of ten Britons say that sight is the sense that they would least like to lose. For powerful insights on the nature and meaning of sight, see Hull (1991, 2001). Hull lost his sight in adulthood. He once told me that he was 'glad' that he lost his sight rather than his hearing as hearing is the more sociable sense, so deafness cuts the deaf person off from other people. Hearing is a more reactive and less directed sense than sight. 'Sound and silence come upon one from beyond. Sound is, however, experienced internally. Things seen are experienced objectively' (Hull 1991, p. 126).

29 Aristotle (1986, p. 210): 'It is necessary that, whenever one is contemplating, it is some image that one is contemplating; for the images are like sense-data but without matter . . . What, then, distinguishes the primary thoughts from being images? Is it not better to say that neither they nor the others are images, but that they cannot occur without images.'

30 Pylyshyn (2003, p. 400), Magee and Milligan (1998, pp. 190ff.), Hull (1991), Sacks (2005).

31 See further Magee and Milligan (1998, pp. 179ff.), Kleege (1999), Ree (1999).

32 Ingold (2000, pp. 243ff.) makes a powerful case for the integration of senses in a single flow in which perception is unified. For more on the individual senses see, for example, Ackerman (1990), Ree (1999) and Watson (1999). Gorringe (2002) provides a theological perspective.

33 Interestingly, while Jesus invites Thomas to 'place your finger here and see my hands', Thomas does not actually touch him and haptic confirmation is deferred.

34 'Since the days of Greek philosophy sight has been hailed as the most excellent of the senses. The noblest activity of the mind, *theoria*, is described in metaphors mostly taken from the visual sphere' (Jonas 1966, p. 135). See also Blumenberg (1993), Nightingale (2005).

35 Cf. Crary (1990, p. 43) and Rorty (1980). Jonas (1966, pp. 145–52), among others, suggests that it was certain properties of physical sight that gave rise to fundamental modes of conceptualizing thought. Thus, the apparent constancy of present visual experience might give rise to the idealized notion of unchangingness as compared to the fleeting succession of non-visual sensations. The apparent non-interference of vision with the world it perceives might allow the formation of the notion of objectivity and thought that exists independently of that which it perceives, so form and idea can be separated from matter. The experience of being able to see things at considerable distance might give rise to ideas of foreknowledge and mental distance.

36 This divinization of reason was supported by theological metaphysics and optics which closely related knowledge of light to knowledge of God. Cf., for example, Jay (1994, chs 1 and 2), Crombie (1953), Nicholas of Cusa (1997), Hills (1987). Perhaps until the time of Newton and even beyond, the exploration of light and sight was part of the contemplative quest to find God, the light of lights, the source of light, and the all-seeing eye (Jay 1994, p. 89). See also Funkenstein (1986).

37 Jay (1994, p. 236) notes, 'The tenacious hold of ocularism was abetted by the oscillation among models of speculation, observation, and revelation. When one or

another faltered, a third could be invoked as the foundation of a still visually privileged order of knowledge.'

38  See further Nelson (2000a, p. 7).

39  For more on the workings of the camera obscura see Steadman (2001, pp. 4–24).

40  Crary (1990, pp. 25ff.) and Jay (1994, p. 76).

41  'Vision assumes some of the central predicates of the Judaic-Christian God – it is troped as an ocularcentric "view from Nowhere", a secular variant of a God's-Eye View of Things' (Sandwell 1999, p. 40).

42  Crary (1990, p. 40). The camera obscura is bound up with the development of interiority and figures a nominally free autonomous individual, an isolated subject enclosed separated from the exterior world. See Crary (1988).

43  See Judovitz (1993) for more on Descartes' view and theory of vision.

44  For these attitudes see respectively, for example, Foucault (1979), Virilio (1994) and Nelson (2000a, p. x).

45  Dennett (1993), Pylyshyn (2003).

46  See further Midgley (1989, 2001).

47  For the Cartesian theatre of the mind see Dennett (1993).

48  'You kill things to look at them', Damien Hirst has said in a caption to one of his still-life works, *Forms without life* (1991), Tate Modern Collection, London.

49  For these points see Levin (1988, pp. 3ff.).

50  See further Holly (1996, p. 15), Bryson (1983).

51  Levin (1988, p. 115), cf. Berger (1972, p. 16).

52  Jay (1994, pp. 197ff., 493ff.).

53  Gardiner (1995).

54  For example, Foucault (1979), Debord (1995).

55  For example, Krauss (1994).

56  See Bataille (1982), Hopkins (2004).

57  Jay (1988). 'Decades have passed since Panofsky pointed to the conventionality of perspective and Heidegger to its complicity with a subject willed to mastery; years since Merleau-Ponty stressed the bodiliness of sight, Lacan the psychic cost of the gaze, and Fanon its colonialist import' (Foster 1988, p. xiv).

58  Ingold (2000, pp. 286f.) rightly points out that sight as a sense is not inherently distancing or objectifying, any more than any other sense. He follows Houlgate (1993) in arguing that 'it is unreasonable to blame vision for the ills of modernity', and he arraigns the critics of Cartesian visuality for not so much giving an account of actual visual practice but instead providing 'a critique of modernity dressed up as a critique of the hegemony of vision'. I generally agree with Ingold, but I think he (a) underestimates the usefulness of Jay's (1988) concept of a scopic regime, which would embrace both thought and practice, and (b) fails to address the reality that many contemporary Westerners do think of vision as distancing and behave as if this is the case. So Cartesian visuality is a phenomenological reality in everyday life, albeit that it functions also as a metaphor for modernity as a whole.

# 2

# Touching Sight:
# Rediscovering Haptic Vision

The eye is the organ of distance and separation, whereas touch is the sense of nearness, intimacy and affection. The eye surveys, controls and investigates, whereas touch approaches and caresses.

Juhani Pallasmaa, *The Eyes of the Skin*

## Introduction

In the contemporary Western world, and especially in the shadow of a dominant ocularcentric Cartesian scopic regime, sight and vision have often been treated as separate from the other senses. With their connotations of the distant, the observational, the detached, the inward, the thoughtful, and the rational, they have tended to be synonyms for abstracted, non-involved relating to the world, with connotations of transcendence and that which lies beyond. The spectator stands by rather than being involved. Detached viewers have distance and perspective on the world. The visionary sees into another, unreal world behind this one. The seer prophesies and foretells the intangible future. However, this kind of understanding of sight is, in fact, relatively new, contextual and limited.

Until the Renaissance, and even beyond, sight was firmly located alongside the other senses in a more integrated sensorium. It was even thought of as a kind of touch.[1, 2] More importantly, the whole action of seeing was thought to be a direct and active substantial engagement and encounter with material reality. In this chapter, I suggest that the concept of 'haptic vision', if not all its mechanisms and former understandings, can usefully be deployed to understand more adequately the experiential phenomenology of seeing. Seeing can be an intimate, visceral experience that touches and moves.[3] Concepts and insights that rescue it from captivity to the notion of the unseen, untouched distant observer are required. This will allow visual experience to be richer and more nuanced, and deeper relationships with visual artefacts might then be developed.

41

## Haptic vision: history and background

The Greek verb, *haptein*, means to seize, to grasp, or to touch. The origins of 'haptic vision' lie in early Greek optical theory in which sight was a materially based experience. Some kind of material change needed to occur to link seen objects to the eye. The Atomists, first philosophical theorists of the mechanism of sight, argued that visible objects give off some kind of image, effluence, or skin, formed of consolidated air, called an *eidolon* or simulacrum which makes its way into the eye. This is so-called intromission theory, whereby some material aspect of the seen object penetrates the eye.[4]

Plato developed a similar kind of materially based theory of vision. He put forward an extramission theory whereby a gentle fire in the human body flows out of the eyes and coalesces with its like, daylight, 'forming a single uniform body in the line of sight, along which the stream from within strikes the external object'. The stream then somehow comes back into the seeing body and produces in the soul 'the sensation which we call sight'. The object seen also produces a kind of 'flame that streams off bodies of various kinds and is composed of particles so proportioned to our sight as to yield sensation' (Plato 1977, pp. 62, 94).

Plato, like the Atomists, regarded seer and seen as being linked in some sort of physical way through the medium of light and particles. Sight was not abstract, passive and distant, it was physically relational, a kind of active touching, penetrating and being penetrated. This idea of mutual erotic penetration between seer and seen was highly influential in the development of early philosophy.[5]

Interactive, material, haptic theories of sight survived for many centuries. The rhetoric of post-Cartesian vision and science more generally 'favours the passive voice'. By contrast,

> ancient and medieval writing about vision is more active, for seeing itself was performative . . . hence the fear that someone could bewitch by a glance and the transformative effects upon a pilgrim of viewing a holy site or person and a believer of praying to an icon by voice and sight. (Nelson 2000a, p. 4)

Thus, pilgrims to the Holy Land did not distinguish between visual and tactile piety, as Western moderns might.[6] In Byzantine culture, too, seeing was about active connection between seer and image; it was haptic as well as optic:

> Vision . . . connected one with the object seen, and, according to extramission, that action was initiated by the viewer . . . Photius can speak of the mind

grasping the figures in that distant apse mosaic, and John of Damascus can write of embracing the icon with the eyes as well as the lips. (Nelson 2000b, p. 153)

Hearing was associated with passivity, discontinuity, difference and temporality while 'seeing implied continuity, connection, presence, immediacy, and an active subject' (Nelson 2000b, p. 155). Looking was acting and engaging, not simply experiencing.[7]

St Augustine had a basically haptic view of sight which structured his thought about the inner longing for God.[8] He joins Gregory of Nyssa in ascribing tactile qualities to the eyes in gaining the vision of God – the eyes, inner and outer, physical and spiritual, touch the divine. While sight was deemed to be the most important sense, and touch was thought to be inferior to it (though necessary for survival), paradoxically, it was thought to share the characteristics of touch – contact, participation, active initiative: 'Writers used tactile language to convey vision's superiority' (Frank 2000, pp. 106, 108).[9]

Both intromission and extramission implied a more active, material, directly connective kind of seeing than is familiar in the modern West. Intromission, particularly, implies the inner absorption of images from species, with both words and images making a direct impression on the mind.[10]

The haptic or material nature of sight may help to explain why for medieval Christians, just witnessing the consecration, or seeing the elevation of the host at Mass, rather than consuming it, was thought to be efficacious. It also partly accounts for the power conceded to the evil eye and the sight of other objects that might penetrate and affect the mind.[11]

Geraldine Johnson advances an interesting hypothesis about haptic vision and sculpture in early modern Italy. She argues that 'in the case of sculpture in particular, models of reception should be developed that are not based on optical interpretations alone, but that instead consider the tactile reception of three-dimensional art objects as well' (Johnson 2002, p. 61). Touch, she argues, has been ignored in favour of pure optical seeing in the creation, appreciation and ownership of sculptural figures. Tactility was part of the artist's creation of an object, the owner's possessive grasp, and of the devotional or talismanic touch of religious devotees. Even if people did not actually touch sculptures, for example, in churches, they could imagine an 'in-principle' or imaginary implicit tactile relationship with them that would powerfully enrich their sense of active relationship and sight:

[F]or religious devotees, touch would have a talismanic or devotional quality, as when pilgrims strained to touch carved reliquaries and saints' tombs, or when wooden statues of Christ were removed from supporting Crucifixes for processions and ceremonies associated with Holy Week. Documents also describe nuns ritually handling life-size statues of the Christ Child, with these objects occasionally giving the illusion of magically coming to life in the women's arms. (Johnson 2002, p. 66)

Even Alberti, in constructing his theory and practice of perspective, relied upon some notion of visual rays that actively connect the seer and the seen object.[12] And haptic, connective notions of vision can be found in John Donne's poem, 'The Exstasie', too:

Our hands were firmly cimented
With a fast balme, which thence did spring,
Our eye-beames twisted, and did thred
Our eyes, upon one double string. (Donne 1949, p. 38)

Cartesian ocularcentric notions of sight did not entirely displace or subordinate the haptic dimension, or completely sunder the intimate relationship between sight and touch.[13] In eighteenth-century thought, 'haptic and optic are not autonomous terms but together constitute and indivisible mode of knowledge' (Crary 1990, p. 64). There was great interest in how these two senses complemented each other, particularly in relation to the blind. It was perhaps only in the nineteenth century, with the pre-eminence given to sight within a scientific world-view, that the tactile and other senses were completely subordinated within the optical and a final, decisive separation was achieved between tangibility and visuality.[14] This separation of the senses cleared the way for the domination of sight understood as pure, abstract vision in the society of spectacle which elevates sight above touch.[15]

We perhaps conceive ourselves to inhabit an ocularcentric scopic regime of non-haptic, abstract vision, independent and autonomous of the other senses. This regime of gaze, spectacle, surveillance and visual virtual reality is cut off from the smelly, tactile, auditory distractions of the other senses in our appreciation of reality. However, this world has only come lately into existence in the West in its most abstract form.[16] It is probably not universal. So, for example, in contemporary Indian religion it remains normal for people to engage in embodied 'corpothetic', as opposed to aesthetic, distant, relationships with images of gods in ritual contexts. 'Corpothetics' can be understood as 'the sensory embrace of images, the bodily engagement that most people (except Kantians and modernists) have with artworks' (Pinney 2001,

p. 158). Similar corpothetic relations can be found in Western religion and everyday life.[17] Furthermore, ocularcentric abstraction has been fundamentally challenged by the 'friends' of touch and integrated sense knowledge.

While the idea of tactile or haptic dimensions to vision may formally have been ignored, hidden and repressed, the reality of haptic sight has never actually gone away.

## Friends of haptic vision

The apotheosis of specular, disembodied, ocularcentric Cartesian-type vision occurred in the eighteenth and nineteenth centuries. Its dominance was challenged in the last century by critics who attempted to reintegrate vision with the other senses and relocate it firmly within the body.[18] These critics may be characterized as 'denigrators of vision' (Jay 1994). While they may not often use the term 'haptic vision', their attempts to present a thicker, more corporeal notion of sight support the recovery of the haptic dimension of sight. Thus the early twentieth-century Impressionist painters challenged realist perspectivalism in an attempt to regain a sense of the actual experience of sight and light.[19] Painters like Cezanne made '*visible* how the world *touches* us' (Merleau-Ponty 2004, p. 283. Emphasis original).

At around the same time, the philosopher Bergson attacked ocularcentrism and asserted the equality of all the senses in whole body perception of the recorporealized, contextualized cognitive subject. The transcendent, contemplative eye was re-sited within the acting temporal body, while the model of subjectivity constituted primarily from vision was deemed fallacious. The Surrealist thinker Bataille dethroned the eye and questioned the whole basis of heliocentric thought, pointing up the capacity of the sun and light to blind and destroy. The mutilated eye often appears in Surrealist images as a symbol of the rejection of disembodied sight as the best model of knowledge and human action.[20]

The German philosopher Martin Heidegger and the French phenomenologist Maurice Merleau-Ponty are key figures in decentring the perceiving subject and situating it within the visual field of objects rather than outside it. De-objectifying and de-reifying sight, they emphasize the spontaneous participation of the whole body and all the senses in perception.[21] They challenge the individualist psychological understanding of sight as a one-way bridge whereby disembodied images of the outside world are internally represented in the mind.[22] Sight is not

an objective, independent, individually directed psychological capacity. The eye is not a camera or a flashlight that objectively scans things
without engagement. Rather it is involved in a complex set of interpen-
etrative, subjective, reciprocal relationships that constantly change.

Merleau-Ponty grounds perception in total embodied experience of
reciprocal encounter. Indeed, he argues that perception is constituted
by a reciprocal relationship of partners that actually constitutes the
partners as perceivers and things that are perceived. Perception, then,
always involves an open-ended, unfinished interplay between the spontaneous, perceiving body and that which it perceives.[23] The fleshly body
is part of the material, enveloping world, seen and touched by, as well
as seeing and touching, the flesh of the world.[24] In any visual encounter,
perceiver and perceived affect each other profoundly. The embodied
eye is seen and touched by, as well as seeing and touching, the visible
world. Perceived things are 'encountered by the body as animate, living
powers that actively draw us into relation' – there is no strong division
between animate and inanimate things in this preconceptual experience
(Abram 1997, p. 90).

Merleau-Ponty often alludes to the importance of touch and the haptic nature of vision. This happens within the 'chiasm', or confluence,
of the body and the senses.[25] Here subjective experience and objective
existence are seamlessly, synaesthetically fused, so the sensuous body
is integrally connected to the sensual world. The dance of perceptual
reciprocity engenders and supports linguistic reciprocity, so that even
language is rooted in non-verbal fleshly exchange.[26] Merleau-Ponty
writes movingly of the haptic, connective nature of sight:

> What there is then are not things identical with themselves . . . nor is there a
> seer who is first empty and who, afterward, would open himself to them – but
> something to which we could not be closer than by *palpating* it with our look,
> things we could not dream of seeing 'all naked' because the gaze itself *envelops*
> them, *clothes* them with its own flesh. (Merleau-Ponty 2004, p. 249. Emphasis
> added.)

An important figure in the rediscovery of embodied, haptic vision
was the psychoanalyst, Jacques Lacan. Against the abstracted, subjective eye he argues,

> What determines me . . . in the visible, is the gaze that is outside. It is through
> the gaze that I enter light, it is from gaze that I receive its effects. Hence . . . the
> gaze is the instrument through which light is embodied, and through which
> . . . I am photo-graphed. (Lacan 1981, p. 106. Emphasis omitted.)

Gaze is something that pre-exists the subject. It is a field, almost a substance, which infants arrive in, constituting them personally as tangibly as nourishment or experience.[27] The notion of gaze as a constructive social field has been further developed by thinkers such as Foucault.

Roland Barthes also makes a significant contribution in recognizing that

> Science interprets the gaze in three (combinable) ways: in terms of information (the gaze informs), in terms of relation (gazes are exchanged), in terms of possession (by gaze I touch, I attain, I seize, I am seized): three functions: optical, linguistic, and haptic. (Jay 1994, p. 441)

Most famously, perhaps, Barthes contributes the haptic notion of the *punctum* to ideas about looking at photographs. In some images there is an element 'that rises from the scene, shoots out of it like an arrow, and pierces me . . . A photograph's punctum is that accident which pricks me (but also bruises me, is poignant to me)' (Barthes 2000, pp. 26–7).

More recently, feminist critics such as Luce Irigiray have criticized the distancing of sight from the embodied experience:

> More than any other sense, the eye objectifies and it masters. It sets at a distance, and maintains a distance. In our culture the predominance of the look over smell, taste, touch and hearing has brought about an impoverishment of bodily relations.[28] (Jay 1994, p. 493)

Plate 2 contains a suggestive illustration of the sort of tendencies that Irigiray is criticizing here.

Actually, there is nothing inherently objectifying about physical sight. What Irigiray and others are criticizing is a mind set, a scopic regime, a set of theories, metaphors, attitudes and practices that might characterize culture as a whole. Physical sight, then, is used as a symbolic surrogate for criticizing the attitudes and practices of a whole social order.[29]

There are many, more recent theoretical critics whose writing has impinged extensively on the revaluation of sight as embodied and haptic rather than distant and abstract. However, I now turn specifically to understandings of perception as a discrete topic.

## Thickening perception

One of the greatest potential contributions to the revaluing of the haptic dimension of sight recently has come from experimental psychology exploring the function and relationships of the senses. Psychologists now believe that perception is a very active process involving the brain with its previous experience and knowledge in creating perceptual hypotheses about the world.[30] It is not the eye that sees, though sight would be impossible without it. It is the eye-brain working together in an integrated system that creates visual perceptions. These complex perceptual representations constitute our knowledge and experience of reality. Sometimes, they turn out to be wrong; thus we experience illusions, and perception has to be modified.

In a sense, then, the notion of extramission or active gaze returns, because what we believe we see or perceive is actually a hypothetical projection onto the 'real' world. The eye is not like the hole of a pinhole camera, or camera obscura, into which images enter to be shown on a hypothetical passive screen in the mind. Nor is the mind a wax tablet upon which images impress themselves, like a seal upon wax.

Recent psychological work has also demonstrated that perceptions are integrated interpretative constructs which draw upon signals from all the senses, as well as upon perceptual and conceptual knowledge built up from past experience. Different parts of the perceptual system, audial, visual and haptic, interact with and affect each other physiologically. Hence the phenomenon of synaesthesia whereby people see sounds or hear colours.[31] There is a reasonable consensus that all the senses work together to produce a more or less unified percept of the world.[32] Thus visual activity, such as looking at the person we are speaking to, and reading their lips, helps us to hear better. Similarly, locating the direction of sounds through the ears informs us where we might direct our eyes and visual attention better.[33]

Psychological work has demonstrated that the apparently unitary integrities of individual senses are made up of different functions and systems. So, for example, there appear to be separate functions for registering movement, colour and shape in the brain's visual processing systems.[34] Furthermore, probably a few more senses should be added to the classic five listed by Aristotle. Thus proprioception (the monitoring of inner bodily sensations), gravity (balance), and heat sensitivity can be added to supplement vision, hearing, touch, taste and smell.[35] And touch itself can be split into senses of actively touching and passively being touched.[36] It is impossible for people to tickle themselves because one sense of touch cancels out the other.

This inclusion and specific analysis of different types and elements of senses has modified the assumption that sight is isolated on its own as the pre-eminent element in perception. There is, however, some evidence that people are more likely to believe and be led by their eyes than by the other senses. Thus in the so-called 'McGurk effect' it can be observed that people's auditory perception of the pronunciation of a syllable like 'pa' will be changed if they see someone mouthing a different, but similar, symbol like 'ka' (Gregory 2004, p. 333).

Clinical experimental psychology has also demonstrated the importance of touch for sight. From the seventeenth century it was wondered whether, if a blind person gained the use of their eyes, they would be able to recognize and interpret visible objects that they previously had knowledge of through touch.[37] In the twentieth century, Richard Gregory worked with a man, S. B. At the age of 52, S. B. had a corneal transplant that allowed him to see for the first time. To Gregory's surprise, S. B. was able to identify and interpret many objects and phenomena previously experienced by touch. Confronted by objects of which he had no previous knowledge, his instinct was to close his eyes and touch them, rather than look at them, to gain understanding. He famously exclaimed, 'Now that I've felt it I can see' (Gregory 1998, p. 157).

S. B.'s experience, replicated in others, shows that people can effectively learn to see before they have sight. There is a transfer of knowledge from one sensual system to another. This relativizes the exclusive importance of sight, because blind people have access to most of the knowledge sighted people possess. Most importantly, it highlights the power of touch to supplement and modify sight:

> Touching is the most realistic and reassuring of the five senses. What we see or hear, we always want to verify by the tactile sense of touch. Touching is tangible and substantive. It is the ultimate perceptual connection between a subject and an other . . .[38] (Lowe 1982, p. 6)

Another extension of thinking about integrated sight and touch occurs when perception is understood as a relationship, not just as internal individual experience. If you are used to thinking of perception psychologically, as a faculty of the mind or brain located within the individual person, you probably think of it as the means or process whereby the outer world represents itself internally in the mind. It seems like a kind of bridge to the external world.

This very individualistic understanding is challenged by philosophers who argue that perception should be regarded as a relationship between a perceiving subject and an object. Levin (1999, p. 186), for example, suggests that 'vision is, above all, a capacity for responsiveness.' This implies that it is a relational potential, not an internal faculty contained and wilfully controlled by the seer. Perception is not a separate, internal event in the mind which is distinct from the object perceived. Rather, the human perceiver and that which is perceived are bound together like partners in a marriage. Without one of the partners, there is no marriage, no perception. Perception exists within and between perceiver and perceived, not in isolation as a capacity or faculty of persons:

> The act of perceiving unites the subject with the perceived. And the content of the perceived . . . affects the subject's bearing in the world. Perception is therefore a reflexive, integral whole, involving the perceiver, the act of perceiving, and the content of the perceived. (Lowe 1982, p. 1)[39]

This view of perception as relationship does not explicitly mention a haptic element. However, it implicitly favours a view of perception as dynamic relationship in all its aspects, involving the whole perceiving body. The intimacy and union of perception posits a touching, smelling, tasting body, not just a disembodied pair of eyes that are inwardly referential. Again, this provides the basis for an important corrective to ocularcentric, Cartesian understandings that sharply separate mind and matter, inner and outer, sight and touch. We are touched and moved (note the haptic language) by objects as we enter into perceptual relations with them.[40] This multidimensional, intersensorial, relational view of sight as only part of perception opens up a different way of relating to the world of objects and things. It permits the re-entry of the haptic dimension of vision that has often been ignored.

While many understandings of sight may have ignored the dimension of touch, contemporary everyday experience and practice have never put aside this element in seeing.

## The continuing reality of haptic vision

Scopic regimes – integrated complexes of visual theories, representations and practices – often run parallel and contemporaneously in different sub-cultures. It may be that dominant contemporary Western visual understandings and practices tend to emphasize the distance of the seer from the seen. However, it would be wrong to assume that haptic vision has no part in the contemporary West.

All sighted people begin life as babies. Observation of infants reveals that they not only look at objects that have attracted their attention, they reach out to touch and taste them.[41] Infants may learn by touch before they can make much sense of visual data, so there is a 'haptic-visual' transfer of information (Stern 1985, pp. 47ff.). For the infant, its carers and the wider material ecology are not just sights to be seen, but tactile objects to be grasped and known with all the senses to the greatest possible extent.[42] Perhaps this is why so often one hears around small children, 'Now don't touch'. This instruction indicates the way in which we gradually teach ourselves to separate out the senses from their initial integration. When well-disciplined Westerners reach adulthood, they have learned that the non-invasive, non-haptic senses such as sight, hearing and smell can be used more or less freely, while they must keep their hands to themselves, except in certain clearly understood relationships and contexts.

The price of this socialization is the fragmentation of sensual experience and the repression of the haptic in vision. Furthermore, we do not become non-haptic seers just because we have grown up. The repressed returns; if it is not acknowledged and befriended, it can uncomfortably haunt our lives while we fail to recognize its significance.[43]

That the discipline and repression does not entirely work is demonstrated by the return of the haptic, sometimes in places where people hope it has been eliminated. If you go to a museum or art gallery, you will usually find there security devices such as surveillance cameras and guards, partly to prevent artefacts being touched. There is anxiety that viewers will 'go too far' and handle the exhibits. Sometimes you can see them getting closer to the exhibit and almost feel their longing to touch it. The feeling of repression is almost palpable in this kind of situation, particularly if people are looking at interestingly textured objects, or objects that were possibly intended to be touched by their owners. Standing in front of a textured Van Gogh painting like *Sunflowers*, or a Michelangelo sculpture, while keeping one's hands to oneself, may be an act of supreme self-discipline.[44]

Viewers often long to touch. The self-denial involved in not touching is 'a ritualized practice of restraint and attention' (Stewart 1998, p. 30). It is almost unbearable, and can only partly be mitigated by purchasing the tangible replicas and images of objects in the gallery shop that can be taken home for close personal inspection and manipulation. This practice of taking home material objects or *eidola*, skins of the objects seen that in some way replicate and have a relationship with the tangible original, has been an important part of visits since pilgrimages began at the dawn of historical time.[45] This reflects the apparently basic human need to have haptic-visual relations with things. Perhaps, then, it is not surprising that many educated people in the US claim to believe that vision depends upon extramission of rays from the eyes.[46] Nor is it strange that when the Scottish tourist authorities did some market research overseas with people who might visit Scotland, they discovered that prospective visitors wanted to touch tombstones, buildings and other parts of the environment, not just to see them.[47]

The fact that barriers exist to prevent touching is probably evidence in itself that often people do illicitly touch visible objects.[48] Probably a lot of touching goes on in museums and art galleries, but it is not alluded to by either the keepers or the touchers. For example, some curators at a well-known London museum were changing the display of a Mithraic statue and so moving it. Underneath it, they found fifty or sixty bits of paper and other small objects stuck to the statue with chewing gum and other means.[49] Clearly, people did not feel able to confine their relationship to the image to looking without touching. In Los Angeles, a 2003 exhibition at the University Fowler Museum of Cultural History associated with the Senegalese Sufi saint, Amadou Bamba (1853–1927), witnessed visitors touching the portraits and examples of the writing of the saint, then touching their foreheads. The curator of the exhibition explains, 'The images transmit *baraka*, so to touch such an image is one of the most effective ways to obtain the blessing power' (Nooter Roberts 2006). Fortunately, the curator had warned the security guards that the normal rules about not touching should be suspended. Images of this particular saint, although not placed in a religious setting, evoked a directly tactile and corporeal experience.[50]

It is fascinating to see how people when unrestrained by internal inhibition or external prohibition will often touch objects that they find visually interesting. People reach out to touch the rusty surface of Anthony Gormley's *The Angel of the North*, though this is so large that you cannot get your eyes, never mind your hands, round it (see Plate 3). Other, less gargantuan public statues also get a good deal of handling, particularly if they are in any way sexually suggestive. *The Bronze Bull* by Laurence Broderick in the Bullring in Birmingham is constantly fondled and climbed on by passers-by (see Plate 4), while the generally dull bronze surface of the statue of Juliet in Verona has two breasts that gleam from continuous fondling by tourists. At Madame Tussaud's in London, hundreds of people do not so much look at effigies of the famous as grope them.

Not all haptic engagement with visual artefacts is kindly and appreciative. Much art on public display is handled aggressively, mutilated and destroyed. Taussig (1999, pp. 9ff.) documents the systematic mutilation of a public statue in Australia of the Queen and the Duke of Edinburgh. In Birmingham in 2003 a polyester statue in a main square was burned down. Three years later, *The Bronze Bull* was badly scratched (see Plate 4). Velasquez's *Rokeby Venus* in the British National Gallery was slashed by Mary Richardson in 1914 (Freedberg 1989, pp. 409ff.). Michaelangelo's *Pieta* in Rome was assaulted with a hammer, as Duchamp's *Fountain* has been many times. Much 'viewing' remains a very 'hands on' experience.

The practice of both touching and seeing objects of religious devotion has never died out in the West, particularly in Catholicism. The religious act of pilgrimage often culminates in a haptic encounter with the main object of devotion – touching the tomb, kissing the reliquary, icon, or crucifix. To see the divine and be seen by it, to enter into relationship with it, is often to touch as well as to gaze. In 2005, I watched a succession of women in a Catholic church in Madeira gazing at a rather ordinary-looking plaster statue of the Sacred Heart of Jesus as they prayed. Finishing their devotions, they got up and touched the feet of the statue then crossed themselves with the same hand used for the touch. One woman was teaching her little son to do the same. Touching the object of devotional gaze deepens and completes a visual relationship.[51]

In abstracted, thin, ocularcentric Western scopic regime and the intellectual culture it supports, the haptic dimension of vision is associated with childishness, primitivism and immaturity; we may aspire to deny and repress it. However, humans are multiply sensate, embodied beings whose sense of self and world is not constructed by the autonomous action of the eyes on their own. Like so many other habits and skills learned in infancy, it is difficult to abandon the haptic dimension of vision. And it must be questioned whether it is desirable to ignore such an important dimension of sensual experience. Perhaps we should cultivate touching, smelling and tasting in relation to artefacts, as well as seeing, to modify, deepen and extend perceptions and experiences of the visible world.

## Envisioning haptic vision

From the foregoing it may seem that I am advocating that people should physically touch visual artefacts more to deepen their relations with them instead of just looking at them in abstracted, aesthetic, Kantian mode. The recognition that physically touching things happens, and might usefully happen more, may be helpful. However, I am making a more subtle point. To commend haptic vision is not just to recognize and occasionally legitimate touching as well as looking, it is to acknowledge the value of an alternative scopic regime. A scopic regime is 'an integrated complex of visual theories and practices' (Jay 1988, p. 4). Scopic regimes are constituted by perceptual experiences, social practices and discursive constructs. Haptic vision is therefore a complex of attitudes, theories, metaphors and practices, a complex way of relating phenomenologically to the world, not just the application of hands to things.

Drawing attention to this kind of way of understanding and working with vision problematizes the hegemony of isolated, ocularcentric, abstract, decontextualized, disembodied vision that appears to separate people from the realm of artefacts and material images. It fits in with recent attempts to reintegrate the senses and relate them more widely to the perceived material world using, for example, a paradigm of 'intersensoriality': 'While the paradigm of "embodiment" implies an integration of mind and body, the emergent paradigm of emplacement suggests the sensuous relationship of body-mind-environment. This environment is both physical and social . . .' (Howes 2005, p. 7).

This echoes the concern of critics like Walter Benjamin who wanted 'to undo the alienation of the corporeal sensorium, to restore the institutional power of the human bodily senses for the sake of humanity's self preservation' (Buck-Morss 1992, p. 5). For Benjamin, the early twentieth-century contemplative, aesthetic gaze had unhelpfully parted from the original meaning of aesthetics as the sensory experience of perception.[52]

What, then, might an intersensorial, corporeal scopic regime based round haptic sight imply? Laura Marks, a film theorist, provides perhaps the most subtle indication of what a haptic approach to sight and visually available objects might mean. She explores the way in which films call on the embodied memory of the senses. Audio-visual images are multi-sensory. They intersect with and arouse the bodily senses, awakening pre-symbolic memories in the whole sensorium. This bodily interaction is haptic vision. Haptic visuality is understood in metaphorical terms: 'it is as though one were touching the film with one's eyes' (Marks 2000, p. xi). However, it is firmly embodied, drawing upon the corporeal senses and the body as a whole.

Marks distinguishes distant, symbolic optical vision from haptic vision:

optical visuality . . . sees things from enough distance to perceive them as distinct forms in deep space . . . Optical visuality depends on a separation between the viewing subject and the object. Haptic looking tends to move over the surface of its object rather than to plunge into illusionistic depth, not to distinguish form so much as to discern texture. It is more inclined to move than to focus, more inclined to graze than to gaze. (Marks 2000, p. 162)

Haptic images pull viewers in close, and force them to look at the images themselves rather than becoming involved in symbol or narrative.[53]

Engaging in haptic, close-up, intersensory visual relationships engenders a dynamic intersubjectivity in which boundaries are muddied, and viewer and object viewed come to constitute each other. While haptic visuality may not involve actual touch (it is not usually possible for the film viewer to touch the image on the screen, for example), an intimate, erotic sensual relationship is evoked in which meaning is visceral, not symbolic.[54] Attentive recognition involving a 'participatory notion of spectatorship' occurs; in this, both perceiver and object perceived touch each other (Marks 2000, p. 147). The viewer relinquishes her sense of power and mastery over the image – she is overwhelmed and enters into a kind of mutuality based on yielding-knowing characterized by lingering and caressing gaze.[55] An appreciative tactile knowing based on compassionate involvement and productive embrace emerges, and the viewed object comes to matter personally and bodily to the viewer.

Marks' account of haptic visuality is made up of a mixture of theories, metaphors, attitudes, experiences and practices. It is difficult to disentangle these elements from each other. This is compounded because she is trying to engage with sensual phenomena that are pre-symbolic and pre-verbal.[56] Marks uses words to describe a multi-sensorial phenomenon which is basically non-verbal, though hopefully not unintelligible. However, her notion of haptic sight provides substance to what haptic visuality might be in theory and practice in approaching visually available objects. This understanding of visual relationships might open up new ways of engaging with artefacts generally.

## Conclusion

Denial does not usually produce integration. We need to question whether the withholding commandments that symbolize the ocularcentric specular regime of modern capitalism – Look but don't touch, and, Don't touch it if it is not yours – are appropriate for understanding and experiencing vision. Enforced disembodied ocularist spectacularism has probably impoverished our perception of the world. It continues to diminish our visual relations with the objects within it. It colludes with the downgrading of the material world so that our relationships with it easily become casual and exploitative. A rediscovery of the haptic dimensions of vision might do something to redress this and help form part of a more dynamic, 'just and loving [and creative] gaze' which may help us both to grow in looking and 'grow by looking' (Murdoch 1985, pp. 34, 31).[57]

'Haptic vision' as an alternative scopic regime is not a monolithic, integrated set of theories and practices, any more than ocularcentric spectacularism. It is multi-perspectival, full of holes, inconsistencies and incoherencies, arising as it does from several different theoretical and practical sources. (So, for example, even biologically, touch is not a unitary phenomenon; it consists of perceptions of pressure, pain, heat, vibration, texture, touching, and being touched or tickled.[58]) It might best be regarded as a loose, porous, poorly articulated, reactive scopic regime compared to that of Cartesian ocularcentrism which it lives alongside and permeates. That said, however, the notion of haptic vision highlights some important ways of amending notions and practices of perception that may allow significant insights about human relations with visual objects to emerge: 'Perhaps, freed of the implicit desire of the eye for control and power, it is precisely the unfocused vision of our time that is again capable of opening up new realms of vision and thought' (Pallasmaa 2005, p. 35).

This leads on to more questions about the nature of the material world and the fears that humans may have about the power of images and visual artefacts that inhabit it. I now turn from thinking about sight, seers and perception, to the objects of gaze. If sight is relational, it is important to consider the partners within the relationship. This means looking more closely at images and objects and the various ways in which they might be able to relate to human beings. I begin by looking at understandings of images.

## Notes

1 See Nelson (2000a), Nightingale (2005). Aristotle (1986, pp. 168–96), the first literary categorizer of the five senses, thought that taste and seeing were both forms of touch. In the classical world, those senses that were most involved in the world were the least prized, while the 'distant' senses of hearing and sight, associated with mentation, reason and culture, were hierarchically placed above them (Stewart 2005, pp. 61–2).

2 The material nature of visual relationships is also found in the relationship between objects and visual representations of them. The defender of the use of images in Christianity, John of Damascus, sees images as a physical extension of their prototypes, just as shadows are extensions of the person. The New Testament supports the idea that shadows can act as agents, cf. Acts 5.15. Barasch (1992, p. 212) writes: 'In popular beliefs the elusive connection between the prototype and the copy tends to become a physical unity of sorts . . . the link is only partial . . . but . . . one of substance . . . No wonder, then, that the god or saint portrayed can use the picture as a means of intervening in the affairs and fate of people.'

3 Tillich (1989, p. 235) writes of seeing Sandro Botticelli's *Madonna with Singing Angels* in Berlin, just after World War One, 'As I stood there, bathed in the beauty its painter had envisioned so long ago, something of the divine source of all things came through to me. I turned away *shaken*.' Emphasis added. De Bolla (2001, pp. 2–3) similarly talks of being struck mute by art works.

4 'Leucippus and Democritus "attributed sight to certain images, of the same shape as the object, which were continually streaming off from the objects of sight and impinging upon the eye". There is no question about the corpuscular nature of these images or *eidola*' (Lindberg 1976, p. 2). For general background on historical theories of light and vision, see, for example, Lindberg (1976), Park (1997) and Zajonc (1993).

5 Bartsch (2000, pp. 74ff.). Cf. Nightingale (2004).

6 Nelson (2000a, p. 11). Cf. Frank (2000).

7 Early medieval visual experience of the divine 'focused upon instantaneous and powerful effect, which struck or engraved the heart' (Hahn 2000, p. 169).

8 'The visual ray of the physical eye which unites the soul to the objects of its habitual attention provided Augustine with a powerful description of the vision of God, a coordination of physics and metaphysics which grounded his "vision" of the process and goal of human life' (Miles 1983, p. 142).

9 Frank (2000, p. 108) quotes Gregory of Nyssa thus: 'Who can help but love such a beauty provided that he has an eye capable of *reaching out* to its loveliness.' Emphasis added.

10 See further Camille (2000).

11 See Rubin (1991, pp. 63–4), Gravel (1995).

12 Nelson (2000a, p. 5). Alberti (1966, p. 46): 'For these same rays extended between the eye and the plane seen come together very quickly by their own force and by a certain marvellous subtlety, penetrating the air and thin and clear objects they strike against something dense and opaque, where they strike with a point and adhere to the mark they make.'

13 Descartes himself 'equates vision with touch, a sense which he considers to be more certain and less vulnerable to error than vision' (Judovitz 1993, p. 71). Crary (1990, p. 57) notes, 'From Descartes to Berkeley to Diderot, vision is conceived in terms of analogies to the sense of touch.'

14 See Crary (1990, pp. 62, 19). Cf. Classen, Howes and Synnott (1994, p. 88).

15 Debord (1995, p. 17) writes, 'the most abstract of the senses, and the most easily deceived, sight is naturally the most readily adaptable to present-day society's generalized abstraction'.

16 For background to the splitting up, and abstraction, of the modern Western sensorium see, for example, Howes (2005), Seremetakis (1994), Marks (2000), Classen, Howes and Synnott (1994).

17 De Bolla (2001, p. 49), for example, describes his affective, aesthetic experience of looking at some pictures thus: 'looking is not like a visual activity at all – it is more like a recognition of presence, or a feeling of and for presence.'

18 Looking at technological developments, Crary (1990, p. 150) highlights the way in which interest in sight focused on the physiology of sight and the visual mechanisms in the body. He notes of the decades 1810–40: 'Dominant discourses and practices of vision, within the space of a few decades, effectively broke with a classical regime of visuality and grounded the truth of vision in the materiality of the body. One of the consequences of this shift was that the functioning of vision became dependent on the complex and contingent physiological makeup of the observer, rendering vision faulty, unreliable, and . . . arbitrary' (Crary 1999, pp. 11–12). It is against this technological and scientific background that some of the theoretical developments discussed here should be seen.

19 Jay (1994, p. 159).

20 For these points, see Jay (1994, pp. 187, 207, 222ff.).

21 Krell (1993, pp. 139ff., 307ff.), Merleau-Ponty (1968, 2004).

22 See Merleau-Ponty (1968, 2004), Levin (1988, 1993, 1999).

23 See Abram (1997, ch. 2) for an excellent account of the phenomenologists, Husserl, Merleau-Ponty and Heidegger. Matthews (2006) provides a clear guide to Merleau-Ponty's main ideas about embodiment and relational perception.

24 Merleau-Ponty (1968, p. 127).

25 Merleau-Ponty (1968, pp. 130–55).

26 Abram (1997, p. 90). For more on preconceptual, non-verbal knowledge and experience in perception and relationship see, for example, Gendlin (2003)

27 See Figure 1 on p. 28 above for an illustration of Lacan's notion of gaze as a web of encounter.

28 This relatively early view of gaze in patriarchal society as always distancing, non-mutual, objectifying, dominating, etc. has been modified and challenged by more recent feminist scholars. Marks (2000, ch. 3) argues that we need distant, objectifying, optical sight as well as intimate, mutual haptic sight, for example, to drive cars. Scarry (2000) points out that sight is likely to change the perceiver, so vision is seldom just one-way mastery.

29 Ingold (2000, pp. 286f.) follows Houlgate (1993) in arguing that 'it is unreasonable to blame vision for the ills of modernity', and he arraigns the critics of Cartesian visuality for not so much giving an account of actual visual practice but instead providing 'a critique of modernity dressed up as a critique of the hegemony of vision'. I generally agree with Ingold, but I think he (a) underestimates the usefulness of Jay's (1988) concept of a scopic regime, which would embrace both thought and practice, and (b) fails to address the reality that many contemporary Westerners do think of vision as distancing and behave as if this is the case. So Cartesian visuality is a phenomenological reality in everyday life, albeit that it also functions also as a metaphor for modernity as a whole.

30 For example, Gregory (1998, 2004), Pylyshyn (2003), Zeki (1999, ch. 3).

31 See further, for example, Harrison (2001).

32 Jonas (1966, p. 154): 'The basic fact, of course, is that vision is the part-function of a whole body which experiences its dynamic involvement with the environment in the feeling of its position and changes of position.'

33 Gregory (2004, p. 333).

34 Gregory (1998, 2004).

35 Elkins (1997, pp. 136–7). Cf. Aristotle (1986).

36 Heller (2000, pp. 1–3) points out that there is some confusion about the use of words like 'haptic', 'tactual' and 'tactile'. Haptic can mean active touch whereby we touch or take hold of something. Tactile and tactual can be used to denote passive touch whereby stimulation is imposed on a passive recipient. None of these meanings are fixed and complete clarity is not needed in order to prosecute the case for more haptic visual relations, but it is important to understand possible differences of usage. To be touched is not the same thing as touching. Heller also identifies 'dynamic touch' whereby a person uses a tool to examine the world, for example a blind person using a cane to gain information about shape, distance, etc.

37 This is the so-called 'Moyneux question'. See further Locke (1997, pp. 143ff.). Cf. Ree (1999, pp. 334ff.) and Paulson (1987, pp. 21ff.).

38 An evolutionary biological argument can be made that sight is fundamentally based in touch because eyes are basically pieces of specialist skin that evolved to become sensitive to heat and eventually light (Gregory 1998, Parker 2003). Pallasmaa (2005, p. 10) argues that, 'All the senses, including vision, are extensions of the tactile sense; the senses are specializations of skin tissue, and all sensory experiences are modes of touching and thus related to tactility.' Macmurray (1991) similarly argues that touch is the fundamental, basic sense. I have not placed weight upon this evidence here because it risks a kind of biological essentialism which is unhelpful in exploring the nature of a haptic scopic regime which I see as being composed of a mixture of socio-historically influenced phenomena, metaphors, interpretations, theories and practices, not just biological 'facts', however helpful they may seem.

39 Merleau-Ponty (1968, p. 76) puts it elliptically, poetically and haptically thus: 'I am no longer the pure negative, to see is no longer simply to nihilate, the relation between what I see and I who see is not one of immediate or frontal contradiction; the things attract my look, my gaze *caresses* the things, it *espouses* their contours and their reliefs, between it and them we catch sight of a complicity.' (Emphasis added.) See Ingold (2000, pp. 243ff.) for a thoroughgoing, existential and holistic theory of perception. Ingold completely rejects the mind–matter, individual–environment, thought–reality dualisms that cause problems to most post-Cartesians to suggest that perception is a 'kind of scanning movement, accomplished by the whole body . . . which both seeks out, and responds to, modulations or inflections in the environment to which it is attuned. As such, perception is not an "inside-the-head" operation performed upon the raw material of sensation, but takes place in circuits that cross-cut the boundaries between brain, body and world' (Ingold 2000, p. 244).

40 Stewart (1999, p. 32): 'To be in contact with an object means to be moved by it . . . And this pressure perceived by touch involves an actual change: we are changed and so is the object.'

41 See Gregory (2004, pp. 637–9). For more on the visual development of infants see Atkinson (1995), Trevarthen (1995), Ayers (2003, ch. 2) and Stern (1985, pp. 47ff.).

42 Arguably, 'the early mutuality of the mother's nipple and the child's mouth is the paradigm for the reciprocity found in all tactile experiences' (Stewart 1998, p. 31). Perhaps the prevalence of preverbal experience in the apprehension of the visible is why de Bolla can talk of affect-driven mutism as a main response to works of art. He describes the phenomenological decomposition of the sense of sight into another sense, 'a compelling sensation of tactility in vision, *as if sight included the sense of touch*' (de Bolla 2001, p. 49). (Emphasis added.)

43 Freud (1985b, p. 323).

44 Berger (1972, pp. 88ff.) notes that 'what distinguishes oil painting . . . is its special ability to render the tangibility, the texture, the luster, the solidity of what it

depicts. It defines the real as that which you can put your hands on.' Commenting on Holbein's, *The Ambassadors*, he notes 'this painting, whilst remaining purely visual, appeals to, importunes, the sense of touch . . . What the eye perceives is already translated . . . into the language of tactile sensation.' Zwijnenberg (2003) argues that Leonardo deliberately plays with the power of painting to evoke the kind of tactile experience that viewers might have with sculpture.

45 See further, for example, Coleman and Elsner (1995) and Maniura (2003). Some pilgrims used to purchase mirrors which had held the image of the treasured object in them to take home.

46 Nelson (2000a, p. 9).

47 'In Nov 2003 VisitScotland commissioned DTZ Pieda to undertake a survey . . . of 6,100 ancestral tourists . . . All respondents had Scots ancestry . . . The research didn't ask . . . about propensity to "touch the past". It was through the open-ended prompts about what "you expected most from an ancestral trip to Scotland" that the theme of physically touching something came through strongly as a prime expectation: "Some things you just have to touch"/ "I stood for ages, my hands touching the walls of the croft my family lived in for generations" – these are typical of hundreds of similar comments' (Colville 2006).

48 Stewart (1999, p. 32) points out not only that sculptures were much touched in the past but also that 'Those works that we cannot touch are repositories of . . . the touch and care of their makers and conservators.'

49 I am grateful to Jas Elsner for this unpublished anecdotal evidence.

50 Museums and galleries are gradually becoming more intersensorially interactive, haptic places. See Edwards, Gosden and Phillips (2006). In the University Science Museum in Oxford I was brought up short by a stuffed lynx near the entrance, easily within reach of children, that had a forbidding looking notice on it saying, 'Please *do* touch'.

51 See Pinney (2001). Pinney denotes this kind of relationship as a 'corpothetic' one. In India mutual gaze between image and worshipper which allows communion between gods and their devotees is called Darshan and it is a vital part of religious practice. See further, for example, Davis (1997), Eck (1998).

52 'The original field of aesthetics is not art but reality – corporeal, material nature' (Buck-Morss 1992, p. 6).

53 Haptic and optic visuality are complementary, not mutually exclusive. Both are needed: 'it is hard to look closely at a lover's skin with optical vision: it is hard to drive a car with haptic vision' (Marks 2000, p. 163).

54 'Tactile epistemology involves thinking with your skin . . . ' (Marks 2000, p. 190).

55 Marks (2000, pp. 151, 169).

56 Smell, taste and touch are embodied senses which have a memory in the body. But their knowledge and memory, while real, is not articulate or verbal. See further, for example, Seremetakis (1994), Stoller (1997).

57 Bergson (2004, p. 124) discusses embodied 'attentive perception' as the key to approaching images.

58 Gregory (2004, p. 637).

# 3

# What is an Image?

The contemporary image establishes a presence that saturates daily life and imposes itself as a unique and obsessive reality . . . it broadcasts a visual and social order; it infuses modes of behavior and belief; it anticipates, in the visual field, evolutions that have not even yet given rise to conceptual or discursive explanation.

Serge Gruzinski, *Images at War*

## Introduction

In the previous two chapters, the focus was upon the viewer of objects and ways of seeing. I suggested that seeing might usefully be thought of as relational, even haptic, corporeally involving, and intersensorial.

Relational, tactile viewing can be provoked by the viewer or the object looked at – or by both (Marks 2000, p. 170). In the next few chapters, I turn away from human viewers to try to understand why some visual images and artefacts can evoke an active, visceral response in those who look at them. Images and objects that provoke such responses can be described as 'auratic'. Aura is 'the quality in an object that makes our relationship to it like a relationship with another human being' (Marks 2000, p. 81). Before seeking out what makes images and artefacts actually, or potentially, auratic, thus susceptible to humans entering into personlike relations with them, it will be helpful to understand more about what images are. Like sight and vision, they are not necessarily what they common-sensically seem to be.

At the centre of the visual world lies the physical, visible image. Many books on the visual take the nature and meaning of the image for granted. In the optical context, an image can be thought of simply as anything you see when you have your eyes open. So a natural landscape provides an image to the eye, as does a face, a table, or a painting. In the more specialized realm of the artistic and pictorial, an image can be regarded as the deliberately worked area of any visible artefact. Thus a painting or sculpture provides an image of a certain size and shape.

Mostly, I will stay close to these two basic understandings of what an image is. However, it is useful to provide some intellectual hinterland to understandings of the nature of images because actual images and notions of image and imagery are mobile; they wander through different kinds of discourse and terrain, and influence each other. Often, image and imagery do not denote any direct encounter with the visible world at all. This mobile and ambivalent aspect of images engenders 'the play of images'.[1]

## The play of images

You may have had the experience of seeing a person whose voice you have heard but whom you have never met face to face. Probably in the flesh they will not be quite what you expected. You have formed an inner, mental, non-material image of the person; it is then confronted with some kind of external appearance which is different. There is a difference, then, between inner and outer images, images in the mind and those that exist in the visible world. Similarly, when you see a film of a favourite novel, you can find yourself confronted with a concretization of the character completely unlike the image in your head. Different mental images can be differently perceived and materialized by others – script writers, directors and actors in this case.

This kind of example also shows how images can change as they move from one kind of representation or materialization to another. You acquired your image of Mr Darcy in *Pride and Prejudice* from reading a book in which Jane Austen embodied her own mental image of this character. But the image you perceive is probably different from Austen's mental image; it is also different from the embodiment of the image in film as portrayed by an actor. Thus, images are mobile across genres – they might be found in literature, in pictures, in films, plays, or simply in people's minds. The mobility and play of images as they transmute and transform themselves in different genres and interpretations can be delightful. Occasionally, it can also be frustrating.

This mobility and play of images is found in religion. The art historian, Cathy Oakes (1997), argues that in the medieval period images of the Virgin Mary were constructed in the light of narratives and writings about her when her cult came to prominence. Her image was first a literary one. However, as statues and other objects came into being, the image of the Virgin in devotional and other writings was influenced by the visual perception of her image, and new narratives and literary images of the Virgin were created. The Virgin's image travelled between the written and the visual, changing physically and theologically as it went.

A similar kind of mobility can be observed in other kinds of devotional practice. At the beginning of his religious life, St Francis of Assisi spent time gazing on an image of the crucified Christ (see Plate 8). Not only did he experience this image speaking to him, he also modelled his imagination and life on this Christ so that he actually became a living image of Christ to his followers. Towards the end of his life, he received the wounds of Christ, completing his identification with, and embodiment of, this image of the divine. Thus an image of the invisible God, manifested in the incarnate human Jesus, and represented materially in the Gospels and images such as the crucifix, once again moves into the life and mind of a living human being.[2]

## The complexity of images

The language of sight and the visual is often ambivalent. It is used as much to describe thought and the intellectual realm as the world of physical apprehension.[3] So, for example, reason is equated with light and knowledge or learning with illumination – when I say, 'I see', I often mean, 'I understand'.

Thus with images, we can start with the apparent and everyday. However, quickly the idea and reality of image slips its moorings with taken-for-granted visual reality and enters the intellect and imagination. Image quickly moves into the position of being heavily overlaid with secondary, metaphorical meanings such as idolatry (false or misleading images) and unreality or illusion (an image substitutes in an illusory way for the real).

It is, therefore, difficult to 'see' or conceptualize images clearly. They are entangled in an undergrowth of multiple use and interpretation, individually and as a conceptual class. Beyond the art gallery (where image denotes the artistically worked part of an object, or some loose idea that an image is what is represented on the retina), one enters the arena of thought, metaphor, multiple understanding, as in mental image. This conflation of the unseen, general and intellectual with the specific, material and local is typical of the visual realm; meanings are unstable as one walks through a kind of hall of mirrors. It is necessary, therefore, to become more sensitive to the range of meanings and uses that may impinge upon almost any discussion of images.

Images, in theory and practice, are slippery and difficult to comprehend. Visual images are unstable and dynamic, and differently perceived by different viewers. They can involve multisensory apprehension and interpretation.[4]

Introducing the concept of the 'family of images', Mitchell notes two important things about imagery:

> The first is simply the wide variety of things that go by this name. We speak of pictures, statues, optical illusions, maps, diagrams, dreams, hallucinations, spectacles, projections, poems, patterns, memories, and even ideas as images . . . The second . . . is that the calling of all these things by the name of 'image' does not necessarily mean that they all have something in common. It might be better to begin by thinking of images as a far-flung family which has migrated in time and space and undergone profound mutations in the process. (Mitchell 1986, p. 9)

It is possible to describe a 'genealogy' of different institutional discourses related to images. At the top is the idea of the image 'as such' with basic meanings of likeness, resemblance and similitude. The discursive 'children' of this 'parent' understanding are found in various specialized discourses. The *graphic* contains language about pictures, statues and designs. The *optical* deals with images in terms of mirrors and projections. In the discourse of *perception*, sense data and appearances are the manifestations of the image. In *mental* discourse, dreams, memories, ideas and fantasies are the ways in which images arise. Finally, in the discourse of the *verbal*, metaphors and descriptions can be dealt with as kinds of images.[5] This typology indicates the variety of different ways that image-related ideas and concepts pervade many parts of life and thought.

Having usefully muddied the conceptual waters around the apparently obvious idea and reality of 'the image', I will work through some main current understandings of images to show their differences and significance. I will start with the everyday and most apparently visual, and then move on to more abstract and, perhaps, surprising ideas.

## An image is what can be seen

Light rays meet an object and this then becomes visible to organs sensitive to certain wavelengths of radiation, that is eyes. When rays of light enter the eyes through the lens, an inverted image of what is seen is then projected on the retina at the back of the eye. This, then, is an optical image. An image is simply what is seen, not necessarily a work of art or humanly crafted artefact. A star, a landscape, a chair, or an animal produces an image in this optical sense.

However, the sense of immediate apprehension of what is seen is extensively influenced by complex neurological and interpretative processes beyond the retina, in the brain. So even within this basic understanding of the image the importance of mediation, interpretation, viewpoint, etc. must be remembered. Consider those conversations where someone says they think they can clearly see something while you cannot see what they are pointing at, never mind the significant features they so clearly behold.

## Images are created, visible human artefacts, especially art works

A more specialized understanding of image prevails in the art world. Here, an image is understood to be the deliberately worked, manipulated, or changed surface of objects that make them into works of art, for example, photographs, sculptures, paintings. So the measurements of a painted image – 20 x 37 inches, for instance – denote the part of the work that has been humanly worked to render a particular object visible.

More loosely, image denotes any visible artefact intended to be looked at by an audience. These are images in the strict sense, such as statues and pictures.

To this categorization, other artefacts can be added, for example, photographs, graffiti, designed objects like cars, advertisements, etc. and creations that include dynamic human imaging, such as ballet and human sculpture. All these phenomena are created to be looked at and to have an aesthetic effect upon viewers. This view of images would not exclude children's pictures – it does not imply any evaluation of the content or aesthetic value of any particular artefact.

## Images are copies or likenesses

'According to ancient etymology, the word *image* should be linked to the root *imitari*' (Barthes 1977, p. 32). One of the most important common understandings of images is that they are imitations, or copies. So a photograph or portrait, in representing a person, is often understood as a copy, or likeness, of that person. 'That's so like her,' people say when they see an accurate, recognizable representation. The same sense of image as copy or representation occurs when people notice that a child 'is the image of his mother'.

Part of the pleasure evoked by images is that they can play with our sense of reality and unreality. So people delight in *trompe l'oeil* or minutely accurate, naturalistic art such as that done by Pre-Raphaelites which can appear more real than the world it seems to copy.

Alongside this narrowly imitative representation, representations that could not be found in the normal visual world can be enjoyed. Picasso's fragmented, multi-perspectival Cubist portraits, for example, can still provide a sense of recognition and appreciation of the person portrayed. Perhaps a better example is that of political cartoons or caricatures. These often exaggerate features of the person depicted to an absurd extent, but still provide a basis for recognition of the original.

The whole area of copying and imitation in images will be addressed later. However, the mimetic (imitative or copying) aspect of images is one of their most important, powerful characteristics. The magic of mimesis appears to bring the dead back to life, to make the absent present, to visually subvert the nature of reality.[6] Leonardo da Vinci aspired to make copies of reality that would appear lifelike, thus demonstrating the godlike creative powers of the eye and the artist. Sometimes he succeeded – he created a shield painted with the head of a monster that frightened all who saw it because it looked so real.[7] Shakespeare has scenes in which 'statues' fool people by their veracity and then seem to come alive. A similar inverse playing with mimesis and reality occurs when humans in public spaces imitate artefacts like mummified pharaohs.

The mimetic dimension of the relation between copies and originals is one of the most dynamic aspects of image production and consumption. It has inspired both admiration and fear in many different cultures, including our own.[8] Plato (1955, pp. 370ff.), for example, condemned artists copying nature because he thought that it would deceive people about reality. Mimesis is closely related to the power and animation of images and is an important basis for human fascination with them.

## Images are representations

The term 'representation' is often used as a synonym for 'portrait' or 'likeness', rather similar to a copy. However, a representation does not have to be exactly like what it represents. A copy is always a representation, but a representation is not necessarily always a copy. Often visual images share many of the characteristics or features of the objects they purport to represent, for example, the same shape or colour. However, they need not necessarily do so. So, for example, the emblem of the crown can represent the sovereign, but it only images one tiny bit of the sovereign's appearance. Similarly, a rock or stone can represent divine presence without looking at all humanoid, let alone divine.[9]

This important distinction between likeness, copy or similarity, and representation, prompts the recognition that visual images, like words, should be regarded as signs or 'signifying practices' in a semiotic system (Hall 1997, p. 4). Like words, images do not necessarily have a direct correspondence with the things they represent. Images construct and transmit meanings in language-like codes which can be understood within cultures with particular world-views and life worlds.[10]

This suggests that humanly produced visual images like paintings should not just be seen as straightforward descriptions or denotations of the realities they purport to depict, for example, landscapes, persons. They are also sites for the production and consumption of meaning. Arguably, then, created visual images should not be regarded as direct imitations of the world, but as things that only represent reality.[11] They reflect and create meanings within a particular historical and cultural context with its own coded understandings and interpretations of the meaningful and 'real'.

Even realistic or naturalistic images are coded representations. It is not easy to discern the code in 'realistic' art because realism obscures the work of representation.[12] So when we look at photographs we may think that they just present us with a simple, direct view of reality. We do not realize that meanings have been encoded in the type of image that has been taken, its viewpoint, its editing, production, presentation and context and that further, socially intelligible, if not articulated, meanings will emanate from its interpretation by viewers.

Visual images are, in some ways, like verbal images; they are humanly created representations that are 'polysemic' and produce symbolic meanings (Barthes 1977, pp. 38–9). This makes it easier to 'read' them better, more systematically, and with critical suspicion. Instead of taking an image at face value, it can be contextualized and its obvious, and its more hidden, referential and symbolic meanings, can be deciphered. Understanding the context, grammar, rhetoric and symbolism of visual images reintegrates them with the representation and symbolization found in other activities such as literary production.[13]

Visual images become part of the realm of representation and analysis in history and culture, not unique, ineffable exceptions to normal communication and meaning creation. This corrects the naive belief that, in dealing with visual images, what you see is what you get. Insofar as any image is regarded as having significance, its significant representation is bound up with human meaning-making; our vision has been educated and biased in apprehending it.

## Images are metaphors or similes in language

It is a commonplace of literary criticism to talk of images contained in texts. Often this means that comparisons, metaphors and similes are used linguistically to evoke understandings, and to create mental images or 'pictures' in the mind. Thus the poet Burns compares his love to a 'red, red rose', while Gerard Manley Hopkins uses the metaphorical image of the kestrel to evoke Christ in 'The Windhover'. This use and understanding of the notion of image fits in with the observation that images are not simply or solely visual, but can also be contained within different representations and texts visual, literary, performative, and other.

## Images are pure ideas

The notion of images being closely related to words as well as visualizations is linked to the understanding of images as pure ideas. For Christian theologians, an important understanding of the way in which God shapes the world is through the divine word. Words and 'ideas', invisible purposes and forms, can shape and form the world without diminishing their originator. A person who speaks words impacts upon reality, expressing purposes and intentions, but they are not personally depleted or reduced because they have uttered breath. Thus Genesis and the Gospel of John begin with God's word going forth to shape and change the world. In John's Gospel, the word actually becomes incarnate as a visible image, Jesus Christ. This expresses how the essence of divinity can be retained in the Godhead while also actualizing itself in a separate human being. This creative, purposive aspect of verbal performance, the magic and power of words to do things to and for people, and to image the unseen in the material world, is an important aspect of thinking about the power of all kinds of images.

For some early thinkers about images, like Maimonides and Augustine, 'The true, literal image is the mental or spiritual one; the improper, derived, figurative image is the material shape perceived by our senses, particularly the eye.' Ancient philosophical understanding held that 'images were to be understood as something inward and invisible' (Mitchell 1986, pp. 32, 39).[14]

The notion that images are 'pure ideas' may seem strange in the context of thinking about concrete, visible, material images (Bryson 1983, p. 94). However, it should be remembered that much of the language of vision and the visible has had a fundamental shaping effect upon our understanding of and vocabulary about the mind and the intellect. Words like 'theory' owe their origin to the Greek word for seeing – to theorize is, in a sense, to see. For Plato, the kind of 'seeing' undertaken was the viewing of metaphysical forms by means of contemplation.[15]

Similarly, the word 'idea' is related to the word *eidolon* or image. Moderns might associate the word *eidolon* with the notion of idol, by which a false or misleading image is denoted. However, in the classical world this idea of image or form was closely related to seeing, thinking and knowing, without the negative cathexis of over-involvement in concrete objects that it now possesses.

## Images are the concrete manifestations of ideational forms

This understanding of images is distantly rooted in Platonic philosophy which held that behind the world of material reality was an immaterial world of ideas or forms. These ideas or forms manifest themselves in progressively more material, pluriform ways hierarchically, from pure thought or reason to inanimate objects, from the unified self-thinking one, to the diversity of animate and inanimate beings in the material world. The world of appearances is a pale imitation of the invisible world of ideas or forms which is accessed through the use of reason.[16] Insofar as anything exists, it reflects the reality of an underlying universal idea, or what Christianity (which took on a great deal of Platonism) might call a divine blueprint and plan.

This understanding of the visible and material bearing the impress of the rational and immaterial might seem improbable at first sight. However, this understanding still has some currency in thinking about the relation between inner and outer images. Most of us feel ourselves to make mental images within ourselves in the form of impressions of others, plans we might have, ideas for creating things.

So, for example, I can imagine an ideal armchair that would just suit my conditions for comfort. If I am skilled, I can then bring this armchair into existence by manipulating wood and other materials so that my mental image has concrete reality in the chair. Thus ideas or mental images can become (at least approximately) manifest in the contemporary world.

This example provides some phenomenological undergirding for the concept that images and ideas can precede and shape concrete reality.[17] Indeed, arguably, mental images are more important than concrete reality because without them it would not be possible to shape the world to human convenience. Thus it might be maintained that immaterial ideas and images are more significant than their outward manifestations in material reality. By using my powers of observation and deduction from looking at material forms like armchairs, I can extrapolate an overarching idea or image of what an armchair is and then modify this to create my ideal chair. So the power of mental images, ideas and reason should not be underestimated in thinking about the nature of images.

## Images can be both material and immaterial

Somewhat related to the last understanding of images, implicit in it to some extent, and less dualistic, is the notion that images can be both material and immaterial, inner and outer, either simultaneously or successively. Good examples of this ability of images to be real but either hidden within people or materially displayed can be found within religion. I have already mentioned St Francis' internalization from an outer image, then later manifestation, of the crucified Christ. Francis' practice of looking at an image to internalize it and then manifesting aspects of it in personal and communal practice, is common in religious meditation.[18] Christians pray to imitate Christ and that the divine image in which humanity is made may be restored in them and revealed in their life and works.

Turning to a more specific example, Martin Luther attacked iconoclasm and defended the use of crucifixes, recognizing that inward, internalized images cannot be eliminated by the destruction of their physical representations:

> [W]hen I hear the word of Christ, there delineates itself in my heart the picture of a man who hangs on the cross . . . If it is not a sin, but a good thing, that I

should have Christ's image in my heart, why then should it be sinful to have it before my eyes? (Koerner 2000, p. 205)

Beyond Christianity, anthropologists witness to the manifestation of images in persons inspired and taken over by gods in ritual dances and other religious practices.[19]

There is, then, a complementary relationship between inner, mental and outward, material images. Many attempts at iconoclasm actually fail to destroy images which often continue to manifest themselves in material forms when opportunity arises. When the Spaniards conquered Mexico in the sixteenth century, they flooded the land with material Christian images to supplant the 'idols' of the indigenous population. However, it was years before they actually extinguished the inner divine images of those they subordinated.[20] Internalized, immaterial images have great stamina and lasting power in individuals and cultures. Within contemporary Western culture, the image of the Nazi swastika continues to manifest itself on bodies and in groups from time to time.

## Images are invisible or only partially visible

It is possible to regard images as either wholly invisible, or only partly and intermittently visible. This kind of understanding is consistent with the kind of Platonic view that the world of appearances is a shadow or imitation of immortal invisible forms in the realm of ideas. But it can be justified in terms of visual pragmatics also. Because of the constant saccadic movement of our eyes whereby they are never still, and therefore only see part of any image at a time, we are partly blind and never see the totality of an image.[21] We can only gain a partial glimpse of any visual figure, glancing rather than gazing at it. Similarly, the perception that there are multiple perspectives on any aspect of reality so that no one can see the whole of an object in all its dimensions, nor from all perspectives, implies a kind of practical partial sight or limited seeing. And visual theorists working with the Lacanian notion that interlocking gaze forms a kind of screen through which seer and seen both see each other and cannot see also emphasize the partial nature of image perception.[22]

The notion of invisible or only partially visible images is important in Christian religion and theology. While some Jewish scholars maintained that in principle God was visible in the form of a man, they also believed that it was impossible to see God and live.[23] The basic invisibility of the image of God, and the impossibility of seeing God in God's totality, was maintained in Christianity. It was reinforced by Greek ideas of the invisibility of the One, the supreme rationality that governed the universe. However, Christianity also had to accommodate the incarnation of God in Jesus Christ, a human being who could be seen and even depicted in his human form. This enabled the Orthodox Church to embrace material icons which allowed people to glimpse heavenly realities, at least in part.[24] In the Western church, images of Christ and other sacred figures like Mary, and occasionally even of God the Father, also proliferated. However, Christianity in general maintains that, on earth, God cannot be seen in God's essence and totality.[25] As St Paul suggests, God can only be seen indistinctly and indirectly as through a mirror (1 Cor. 13.12). The images of God and sacred figures are to be treated as partial reflections of divine reality. There is a unending flow of visual and verbal images that complement each other and point beyond themselves that may lead people to 'see' or understand more of God in devotional life. However, these do not amount to a complete vision of God. God and God's image are essentially inaccessible and veiled. The divine is therefore effectively invisible, though its presence can be signified, and even to some extent mediated, through material and intellectual images.

Indeed, arguably, in Western images, the real image of God in its truth and beauty is actually hidden behind an aesthetic of ugliness represented by images of the suffering Christ. These images of divine ugliness make no attempt to represent God as God is and function negatively or apophatically to point to what God is not. Thus Christianity, while at one level embracing images to gain some mediated access to divinity, affirms the fundamental invisibility and incomprehensibility of God.[26]

## Images are mobile across genres and media

Images can be found 'inside' people's minds (in dreams, fantasies, visions), externally represented in words (spoken and written), in visible artefacts (for example, pictures, sculptures), in human performances (for example, divine possession, liturgy, theatre), and in the shape and behaviour of individuals and groups.[27]

As images move across media and genres, they can enter into a dialectic and dialogical relationship with each other over time, modifying each other as they go. Aspects of the image of Jesus Christ illustrate this.[28] Some of Jesus' early followers deposited a verbal image of this man in the books of the New Testament. Within the first few centuries of the church's existence, people had begun to create images of the man Jesus for devotional and other purposes.[29] There were also additional written and verbal teachings about Jesus which altered visual representations of him. So, for example, images of the crucified Christ were very rare in the early church, and in the first thousand years of the church Jesus was represented as alive on the cross, conquering death with his eyes open rather than as suffering and dead.

It was only in the thirteenth century, with Franciscan teaching on the suffering Christ, that images of a dead Christ became commonplace.[30] The fourteenth century saw the rise of the *devotio moderna* in which ordinary people were encouraged to meditate on images of the life of Christ so that they would become more like him in their lives.[31] Their mental images were aided by the many visual images and pictures that they saw in churches. This was not just so people would have pious mental pictures, but so that they would imitate Christ and tangibly recreate his image in the world by their practices.

Thus a complex dialectic relationship was set up between images of Christ in literary works like the New Testament and devotional books, oral teaching in sermons, visual imaging through pictures and ritual participation (in which the priest imaged Christ in celebrating the Mass), the ideas that people had of Christ in their heads, and the image of Christ that they manifested in the world by their individual and corporate lives and actions. This same kind of relationship between inner images and various kinds of external representation of the image of Christ is still alive today in churches throughout the world. It provides just one example of images travelling across media, genres and cultures.[32]

## Images are often types or generalizations rather than unique artefacts

When one is perceiving a particular image it can be forgotten that, mostly, images conform to certain recognizable types. Thus there are many fifteenth-century pictures of the Virgin Mary that share common features. Images gain much of their social and psychological power from conforming to certain expected conventions that make them more memorable in general terms and less memorable as particular images. The brain seems to function to find commonalities and patterns as a way of negotiating a way through life.

The process of generalizing images and creating types can also be observed in social life. Stereotypes allow us to order the mass of complex and inchoate data we receive from our sensual and social experience into generalities, patternings and typifications. This is a useful way of making sense of ourselves and reproducing society. Images, then, are cultural representations that follow codes and conventions of 'available cultural forms of presentation' (Dyer 2002, p. 2).[33]

Typing and generalization allows people to cope with and recognize the significance of different kinds of images. Unfortunately, they often do not think carefully and specifically about particular images. These are then generalized into one so their details and specificity are suppressed.

## *Images are happenings or events*

Images, however defined, can be regarded as dynamic, changing phenomena that manifest (or fail to manifest) themselves in many different ways. They are happenings or events, not just things or ideas. In this sense, they are, and remain, alive.[34]

Drawing on anthropological insights, art historian Hans Belting (2005, p. 302) writes: 'Images are neither on the wall (or on the screen) nor in the head alone. They do not exist by themselves, but they happen; they take place whether they are moving images or not. This happens through transmission and perception.' The better to understand this assertion, it will be helpful to give some account of Belting's theory of images. Mental images and physical images can be distinguished. However, there is an indissoluble, dynamic, continuous, dialectical link between them so that they function as two sides of the same coin in human experience of images. So, in a way, 'Dreams and icons . . . are dependent on each other' (Belting 2005, p. 304).

For analytic purposes, image, medium, and body can be further distinguished. Images start in the embodied person. To be externalized from the embodied mind, an image needs a medium, 'the agent by which an image is transmitted'. Thus it can acquire a substitute material body in which it can be manifest (for example, in a sculpture, a picture). Our bodies are the living medium for images that make us perceive, project, or remember them. Images, then, are negotiated between media and bodies. By the same token, images are nomadic, manifesting in different kinds of media, including human bodies:

Bodies receive images by perceiving them, while media transmit them to bodies. With the help of masks, tattooing, clothing, and performance, bodies also produce images of themselves or, in the case of actors, images representing others ... (Belting 2005, pp. 315–16, 311)

Images can also transcend media, living simply in mental space in dreams, visions and fantasies (Auge 1999). These mental images form one end of the inner/outer continuum. Concretions of images in pictures, sculptures and other material representations are at the other end of the continuum.

This concept of dialectical, dynamic, event or 'happening' images is a corrective to the notion that an image is static and fixed for ever, like the *Mona Lisa* in the Louvre. There are many more images than the *Mona Lisa* that deserve attention; these exist in a far more dynamic relationship with human bodies and activities than is often realized.[35]

## Images are multisensorial phenomena

Images exist in different media and genres. Furthermore, they are not monosensorial phenomena based exclusively around the sense of sight. Within ocularcentric regimes of thinking and knowing it can be forgotten that internal images and representations are the product of generalized experience from all our senses, not just visual or quasi-visual experience.[36] Bergson argues that images, like memories, are apprehended within the embodied sensual self in 'attentive recognition' whereby 'a perceiver oscillates between seeing the object, recalling virtual images that it brings to memory, and comparing the virtual object thus created with the object before us' (Marks 2000, p. 48). An image is a complex of all the sense impressions that a multisensory, embodied perceiver receives and as they engage with the carnal memory. Images and representations within human minds are thus multisensorially composed and affected, dwelling as much in bodily senses and memories as in the mind.[37]

Modern psychologists are unable, as yet, to say much about the nature of inner representations as these can only be consulted and analysed by subjective introspection. However, there is some agreement that these 'pictures' that we have in the mind are not just a straightforward, accurate transfer and recall of things that have impressed themselves on our retinas alone.[38] We have representations of experiences in the mind, but it is not clear in what they consist. Some psychologists graciously acknowledge that we are not much further on in understanding the nature of inner representation than seventeenth-century philosophers like Locke and Descartes.

There is further consensus that inner representations are not just composed of sights or visual data, particular or generalized. Rather, encounters with, and recollections of, external images are often influenced by data from senses other than sight, even if this is often unconscious. The beautiful picture we remember so vividly may remain in the mind because of the company we were with, the smell of the place we were in, or our internal state at the time (hunger, excitement). Often, when people want to excite recollection of, or participation in, an image, they will try to activate senses other than that of 'internal sight'. Ignatius of Loyola, for example, in trying to get people to realize and internalize an image of Christ asked them to participate in imagined scenes from the Scriptures using touch, smell, taste and hearing as well as sight. His aim was to develop a 'thick' multidimensional, haptic sense of the image of Christ, not just a 'picture' in the mind.[39]

## A specific example

To illustrate some of the rather theoretical understandings advanced above about the nature of images, I will briefly analyse a picture from the *Book of Hours* of Mary of Burgundy, probably painted in Ghent in the late 1470s (see Plate 6).

This almost unique picture is intriguing. It seems to depict the vision that a devout reader might expect to have when reading a devotional text (art has great difficulty in representing metaphysical or inward vision, for obvious reasons).[40] I will apply the categories developed above to this image.

In the first place this is clearly an image in the general optical sense that it is *visible to the eye*. In this particular case, it is also definitely an image in the sense of being *a created, visible, human artefact*, though it might be anachronistic to call it an art work, since it was probably created for devotional, not aesthetic, purposes.

It is not clear that this is an *imitation, likeness, or copy* of any particular people. Perhaps the lady reading the book at the front of the picture and the donors surrounding the enthroned Virgin may be people known to the artist; maybe they paid for the image to be created.[41] It may also be that this image copies aspects of other similar images (perhaps lost now) in its selection of subject matter, postures, etc.

This image is certainly a *representation*. It is not a realistic representation, accurately depicting a particular scene; its connotative and symbolic significances are much more important than any kind of direct, denotative reference to the visible world. Prima facie, this is a representation of devotional practice using a text which allows the reader to see invisible heavenly realities in the form of the Virgin Mary and her child. Semiotic theorists of images would argue that fully to understand the nature of this image, we might need to know a great deal more about the social and historically prevalent codes of meaning and symbolization that pertained when it was created. Without the benefit of such detailed knowledge, it seems that the symbolic meaning of this picture is to point the viewer towards contemplation of the heavenly vision of the Virgin as the reader/viewer contemplates the picture and the text it accompanies.

Fascinatingly, this image is centrally connected to the linguistic world of *metaphors and similes* because it is contained within a book of hours, a devotional text. The woman at the front is reading a similar book, full of verbal images, which has presumably fuelled her prayers and devotions so she can 'see' internally the heavenly scene beyond. The book has provided her with verbal, and possibly visual, images. These have precipitated into the space of her imagination so that she can actually envisage what a vision of the Virgin might be like.

Arguably, the image we are considering is one that concretizes *pure ideas*. God and the Virgin are transcendent, heavenly beings, not visible figures in the everyday world. The artist has drawn on his or her skills to make visible an unseen world to which devotees, using their minds and God-given capacity for reason and contemplation, should aspire. In this sense, this image is a *concrete manifestation of ideational forms*. Although the divine and heavenly realms are hidden from the physical gaze of human beings, they can be imaged and concretized in physical images like the Virgin. It is perhaps less controversial and difficult to represent the Virgin rather than God the Father; she is a human being and is thus more within the realm of material forms than the Godhead itself. At a more mundane level, this image can be taken as the manifestation of an ideational form in that it is the outworking of the image that an artist had in his mind. Like God, sometimes characterized as the artist of creation, the artist has externalized a part of his mind in creating this manifest form.

This particular picture illustrates the fact that images can be *both material and immaterial*. The image is clearly material, being made of paper or parchment and various artists' materials like pigment. There may be verbal images suggested by the text that the woman in the fore-front of the picture is reading; perhaps she is supposed to be meditating upon these. If so, perhaps the image of the Virgin in the background, a concrete image in this particular picture, is supposed to be a representation of what is in the former's thoughts and imagination. The representation of the Virgin is a materialization of ideas and images that both painter and viewers would have also had immaterially in their minds and thoughts, independently of this particular picture.

Probably no viewer of this image would mistake it for the whole of the Virgin Mary. The image is only one, partial representation of the reality of the Virgin who is also encountered immaterially and invisibly in believers' hearts and minds. Thus the full and total vision of the Virgin remains *invisible, or only partially visible.* It is part of the conceit of this picture's conceptualization that it tries to materialize a kind of spiritual vision which is in principle invisible through physical media that cannot depict the transcendent reality of devotional vision. Iconoclasts like Protestants have often criticized others like Catholics for mistaking visible material images for divine beings themselves. In fact, most people are perfectly able to distinguish between the image, however revered and respected, and the immaterial reality it represents, just as few people mistake a photograph for the full reality of the person imaged in it, however much they treasure the representation.

The image probably represents internal ideas of the Virgin, but also appears to show the Virgin being represented visually and possibly in text. Readers will probably be familiar with the different ways that the Virgin has been portrayed in literature like the Bible and plays, in pictures and sculptures, etc. Thus this particular image of the Virgin is *mobile across genres and media.*[42]

While this image may be unique in some aspects, this kind of representation of the Virgin holding the infant Jesus on her lap from a frontal viewpoint is quite common. It represents *a type or generalization, rather than being an entirely unique artefact.* This is a religious image intended to be instantly recognized and familiar so that devotees might have a mediated relationship with and through it. The same kind of generalization and typing can be found in lots of important, socially shared images. Originality and innovation were not necessarily prized in images that were intended to perform a devotional, reverential function rather than providing fresh visual stimulus.[43] The originality of this picture lies in its creator's attempt to depict a presumably invisible phenomenon, namely an individual's devotional vision, using visual media.

This picture is a *happening, an event,* because in perceiving it with our embodied gaze something of the image becomes internalized in our minds. It was clearly intended to communicate an image in a dynamic form that would interact with the senses and minds of those who saw it, possibly helping to transform their hearts and lives, and to make religious realities more vivid. After five centuries, it lives on in the pages of its host book of hours and in reproductions, continuing to produce effects and meanings. For some people, indeed, it might still serve its original purpose as a devotional aid, helping them to commune with the transcendent and invisible. And beyond this particular image, there are many other images of the Virgin that modify and intersect with this one in the minds of viewers to help form a composite, if not fully visible, image of Mary.[44] The ideal mental image of the Virgin survives well in the contemporary West, shaping minds, hearts and bodies.[45]

The image is *multi-sensorial.* Its complex, intricate design and deep, varied colours alone make it viscerally 'sticky' and attractive to viewers. Furthermore, the image of mother and child is a primal, iconic one which will evoke bodily memories and responses from anyone who has been nurtured as an infant. It is difficult to articulate this sensual, embodied response in detail because it is pre-verbal and largely non-symbolic. However, there can be little doubt that this image is precisely intended to elicit a holistic response from embodied devotees, drawing them in at a level beyond that of the intellect.

While images like this iconic one are certainly worthy of consideration and analysis, I hope soon to move away from this useful example to look at more mundane contemporary images and artefacts, many of which would not be conceived of as high art or have so much symbolic or lasting significance.

## Conclusion

The concept of 'image' has many, and shifting, meanings in both general and specific terms. Images can have both inward and outward aspects; the relationship between these aspects may be complex. Images can be conceived as dynamic, not necessarily visible things, sometimes having a kind of immortality in people's minds which only sometimes, and perhaps partially, manifests itself in material representations. In some ways, visual images, words, and other kinds of physical representation (for example, plays, ritual actions) are integrally related to one another and join in a kind of modifying play which allows images to

develop and change. Images are living things that can travel both physically and mentally through various media. Sometimes they manifest in
physical media or bodies, and they appeal to the whole sensorium and
embodied memories. While material, visible images of all kinds are to
be the focus of the rest of this work, there is an experiential and theoretical hinterland to the manufacture and interpretation of all kinds
of images which complexifies any view that we might take of a particular image encountered. 'All images are polysemic' (Barthes 1977,
pp. 38–9). They embody and engender varieties of very different meanings and interpretations. Images are generative and dynamic as they
enter into relationships with human users and interpreters over time
– they are also slippery and elusive. Images shimmer before and within
us: we cannot completely comprehend them. They are intriguing, but
also frustrate attempts to understand them. They may draw us on, and
in, but ultimately they withhold their essence and are hidden as well as
manifest. This hiddenness may, in fact, contribute to their power and
attraction.[46]

## Notes

1 Holly (1996, pp. 25–6) and Gadamer (1989, pp. 101ff.).
2 See Pinney (2001) for the importance of pictorial representations of gods acting
as preliminary legitimations for the much more important and active imaging of the
god in the bodies of inspired believers in India.
3 See Rorty (1980), Blumenberg (1993).
4 Mitchell (1986, p. 14).
5 Mitchell (1986, p. 10).
6 Taussig (1993). Cf. Belting (2005), Freedberg (1989).
7 See Kemp (2001b, pp. 26–34), Vasari (1991, pp. 288–9).
8 Consider the imaginative hold that the idea of humanoid robots who cannot
be distinguished from human beings has in films like *Blade Runner*. Cf. Gruzinski
(2001).
9 Freedberg (1989, pp. 33–6). Cf. Gell (1998).
10 Chaplin (1994, p. 1) argues that representation 'implies that images and texts
. . . do not reflect their sources but refashion them according to pictorial or textual
codes, so that they are quite separate from, and other than, those sources.' Images
and texts as coded representations articulate and contribute to social processes. The
notion that visual and textual representations form part of language-type codes
permits the use of terms such as 'rhetoric' in relation to images. All depictions and
visual representation can thus be seen as 'socially constructed arguments about the
natural world' rather than as straightforward realistic portrayals (Chaplin 1994,
p. 184). Accustomed to this way of 'arguing', we fail to see that visual representation
conceals artifice beneath familiarity and custom, so we just 'see' 'it'.
11 See, for example, Bryson (1983) and Mitchell (1994).
12 Bryson (1983, p. 134).

13 Kress and van Leeuwen (1996).

14 Bergson (2004, pp. 124ff.) argues somewhat differently that attentive perception to an image is a matter of bringing historical, inward representations of things into play with external objects. Perception image and memory image converge to produce the image to which the viewer attends.

15 Greek ideas about seeing, theory and thought actually had a very concrete origin in socio-cultural material practices associated with the civic institution of *theoria*. 'In the traditional practice of *theoria*, an individual (*theoron*) made a journey or pilgrimage abroad for the purpose of witnessing certain events or spectacles ... at its centre was the act of seeing, generally focused on a sacred object or spectacle ... This sacralised mode of spectating was a central element of traditional *theoria*, and offered a powerful model for the philosophical notion of "seeing" divine truths. ... by linking philosophical theorizing to an institution that was at once social, political, and religious, the fourth-century thinkers identified theoretical philosophy as a specific kind of cultural practice ... According to Plato, the philosopher is altered and transformed by the journey of *theoria* and the activity of contemplation. He thus "returns" as a sort of a stranger to his own kind, bringing a radical alterity to the city' (Nightingale 2005, pp. 3, 4, 5).

16 Mitchell (1986, pp. 10–11).

17 Ingold (2000) vehemently attacks the notion that material performances and objects are the application of mental plans on the one hand to material reality on the other. He argues that creations are emergent from a confluence of material, environmental and mental elements. This view is tangentially supported by Elkins' (2000b) perceptions on painting where images emerge at least as much from the nature of matter used as from the mind of the painter. See also Ball (2002) for the influence of matter on painting. The problem here is the absoluteness of the mind–matter split common in Western society and the over-valuation of reason over matter so that material creation ideally conforms matter to prevenient mind.

18 See Derbes (1996), Francis of Assisi (1963, p. 311). Cf. Teresa of Avila (1957), Belting (2005).

19 See, for example, Stoller (1997), Pinney (2001).

20 Gruzinski (2001).

21 Bryson (1983, p. 131).

22 See above (p. 28) for Lacan. Morgan (2005b, p. 2): 'Visual piety is a kind of sacred exchange, a way for both parties to see and to hide aspects of themselves from one another. The image is a screen on which visibility takes place as well as a screen that renders the seer partially unseen.' Taussig (1999) and Meyer (2006) argue that vision and visuality should be viewed as part and parcel of the dialectics of revelation and concealment. Making something visible presupposes an invisible, hidden, or secret realm. This theme of hiddenness in images is perhaps echoed in theorists who argue that images are fundamentally built around absence as much as presence: 'Images traditionally live from the body's absence ... This absence does not mean that images revoke absent bodies and make them return. Rather, they replace the body's absence with a different kind of presence. Iconic presence still maintains a body's absence and turns it into what must be called visible absence. Images live from the paradox that they perform the presence of an absence or vice versa ... When absent bodies become visible in images, they use a vicarious visibility' (Belting 2005, p. 312). See further Lacan (1981, pp. 105ff.), Holly (1996, 2003), Bull (1999) and Meyer and Pels (2003).

23 Wolfson (1994).

24 Ouspensky (1992), Barasch (1992).

25 Dillenberger (1953), Turner (1995).

26 Koerner (2000, 2004a). Cf. de Gruchy (2001) and Turner (1995). Meyer (2006) argues that visual and material mediation is an integral part of religion – religion and media are co-constitutive. So there is no useful distinction to be made between divinity and material reality. Divinity cannot be 'real' within religion without mediation. 'Once religion is understood as a practice of mediation, media . . . images, spirit mediums, written texts, sound, films – appear . . . as an inalienable condition on which any attempt to access and render present the divine and to communicate among religious practitioners ultimately depends.'

27 For bodily manifestations of image, cultural memory, and the divine, see, for example, Pinney (2001), Taussig (1993), and especially Stoller (1997, pp. 48ff.).

28 See, for example, Pelikan (1997), MacGregor (2000).

29 Finney (1994), Mathews (1999), Jensen (2000).

30 Derbes (1996). Cf. Pelikan (1997, pp. 103ff.), MacGregor (2000, pp. 122ff.).

31 Van Engen (1988).

32 Holly (1996, p. 1) notes that 'Images that can no longer be seen, only imagined, have been part of the history of art for a very long time.'

33 'The role of the stereotype is to make visible the invisible, so that there is no danger of it creeping up on us unawares; and to make fast, firm and separate what is in reality fluid and much closer to the norm than the dominant value system cares to admit' (Dyer 2002, p. 16).

34 Elkins (2001, pp. 76–7) notes that it is part of the role of images to alter, fade, and perhaps ultimately totally transmute or die in the mind. 'Memories are lovely things because they are unstable. Each time you recall something it changes a little, like a whispered secret that goes around a room and gradually changes into nonsense.' It can be asked whether the actual material image, and accuracy in its recall, is the most valuable aspect of relating to an image, or whether the transmutation of a 'living image' in the mind does not constitute just as important a part of the life of the image. Presence and accuracy may sometimes stop this transmutation, restricting and confining the image's life course. Perhaps the 'inaccurate' image in the mind is as significant as the material image or reproduction in the external world.

35 An interesting footnote to the idea of mobile, dynamic images is provided by Walker Bynum (2002) who enjoyed seeing Vermeer's *Woman with a pearl necklace* in an exhibition of the artist's work even though looking at the catalogue afterwards she learned the picture was not included, so could not have been there. This leads her to speculate in an open-ended way upon the power of images, internal and external, to 'move', even in the contemporary Western 'psychological' world.

36 Stern (1985, pp. 98ff.) and Bergson (2004).

37 Marks (2000, p. 73). Stoller (1997) shows that historic embodied image memories of whole groups can become concretized in rituals and dances in some cultures.

38 Pylyshyn (2003).

39 Ignatius of Loyola (1996).

40 Stoichita (1995).

41 It is likely that the figure is Mary of Burgundy herself. See Duffy (2006, p. 30).

42 Oakes (1997).

43 Bryson (1983, pp. 37ff.).

44 Brading (2001), Orsi (1985), Morgan (1998).

45 Another example of images lasting over time and in all manner of media from the

domain of religion is the vision of the divine chariot in Ezekiel 1. This image, possibly emanating from a direct prophetic encounter with the divine, was recorded in writing and has been refracted throughout the Bible (for example, in the Revelation of St John) and thereafter through Jewish and Christian mystic literature and practice to the present. Lieb (1991, 1998) shows how Ezekiel's image of the divine chariot supported by four living creatures has manifested itself in whole or in part in literature such as Dante's *Divine Comedy*, Milton's *Paradise Lost*, in paintings such as those by Chagall, and even in contemporary films and popular culture. A fictional re-manifestation of the image can be found in Patrick White's *Riders in the Chariot* (1996). Ezekiel's visionary image continues to haunt Western civilization more than two millennia after it was first seen and/or recorded. It remains elusive, being partly revealed at times but often hidden in the minds and imaginations of the inhabitants of Western culture. For more on chariot mysticism see Wolfson (1994), Scholem (1995).

46  See Bull (1999), Meyer and Pels (2003).

# 4

# Obstacles to Taking Images and Visual Artefacts Seriously

Images are winning – materialistic, entertainment-besotting, civic-life deplet-ing images; vain, phony, surface-loving, fantasy-promoting, reality-murdering images.

Mitchell Stephens, *The Rise of the Image and the Fall of the Word*

## Introduction

Living in a world saturated with visual images and artefacts, it might be hoped that we would have befriended them, and be knowledgeable about and comfortable with them. We tend, however, to be visually illiterate, and blind to many of the images around us. This is particular-ly so with common things in everyday life, such as book covers, kettles, furniture and buildings. Occasionally, we may be struck by a particu-larly powerful or memorable image, but interest may be momentary as we fail to analyse the nature and effects of the visible aspect of things.

There is considerable resistance to taking visual images and visuality seriously.[1] This chapter explores some of the factors that may contrib-ute to this. While it focuses specifically on a discussion about imag-es, the kinds of factors that make images dubious or invisible inflect understandings and suspicions of objects in the visual world generally.

'Image' in this context designates the visual aspect of all humanly created artefacts, whether they are intended to be 'art' or not.[2] Most images understood thus are not art, but they are deliberately crafted. Those that are artistically created include films, video games and adver-tisements. Beyond these art objects, there are scientific images, scans, designed objects, and so forth.[3]

First, I will consider the practical virtues and value of images. Next, I will set out some of the general intellectual arguments advanced against visual images as a whole. The suspicions of the intellectuals are ampli-fied within the Christian theological tradition. I will then outline some of the cultural and practical factors that may make it difficult for us to take images seriously. Finally, I will further explore the relationship between word/reason and image, arguing that the perceived rift and conflict between them has been unhelpfully exaggerated.


## The virtues of images

Visual images educate, inform, entertain, delight and worry people. They can seem magically powerful and entrancing, reaching the parts of people's minds and perceptions that words do not. They do not lack defenders and propagandists in the contemporary world. Unfortunately, the defence of visual images tends to focus upon intentionally representational art-like images such as those found in painting and science.[4] However, considering the value of this segment of specialized images, especially representational mimetic images, may help to raise awareness of the significance of visual images and artefacts generally.[5]

Visual images are *'marvelously accessible'* (Stephens 1998, p. 61). While some images may be enormously complex, elaborate and rich, the public accessibility of images is one of their great strengths. Anyone within sight of an image can look at it, often at the same time as many other people, without diminishing or changing the image or their own enjoyment. Images have helped illiterate people to participate in society and culture because they better embody narratives and myths than written words. Visual signs and images overcome some of the problems of not sharing a common language, even in the literate world.

In principle, visual images may be much more *publicly available and democratic* in consumption than words. They may have a better correspondence than words to human experience of space because they tend to be more spatially extensive rather than linear.[6] Images occupy real space, albeit temporarily (as in the case of a flickering film or computer image), while words in their oral flow are more abstract and less tangible; they reveal their meaning and significance gradually.

While some images are indeed rich and complex, many are quite simple and can be *very easily understood*, at least at a basic, inarticulate and uncritical level. Road signs, or family photographs, quickly and easily yield up information and, in the case of the latter, memories.

Furthermore, images are *fun to look at and sensually gratifying*. Even if the construction or symbolic meanings of images are not understood, it is still possible to enjoy looking at, for example, the colours and shapes in advertisements or Renaissance paintings. I am particularly fond of the way that Fra Angelico uses intense lapis lazuli blue in his pictures and I enjoyed his colour palette long before I knew anything about its symbolic significance. Even abstract art or black and white films can provide this kind of visceral enjoyment of shape, colour, and so forth.

Most cinema-goers, and many gallery-goers, would probably agree that images can have a powerful and immediate *emotional impact* on them that words and descriptions often do not. Consider the silence of cinema crowds at the end of a particularly absorbing film. Or the stunned public amazement, then real anger, on the publication of photographs of American soldiers humiliating prisoners in Abu Ghraib prison in Baghdad after the 2003 invasion of Iraq.

One of the main features of visual images in this respect is that they are *concise*. A lot can be communicated in a very limited space. A visual image can yield up a great deal of information almost instantaneously, unlike communication by the word, which necessarily takes longer as meanings and arguments unfold. Consider the power of a cartoon instantly to make a sharp point in a newspaper.

An advocate for the value and virtue of images, Barbara Stafford (1996, pp. 1–17), has noted that humanities scholars have treated images merely as an adjunct to texts and words. She argues that images have their own *unique contribution to make to understanding and knowledge*. They can quickly juxtapose data and make connections that words cannot. An example of this is the use of images in science or the use of diagrams.[7]

Beyond this, however, images have their own distinctive expressive power that can *connect with the pre-linguistic or a-linguistic parts of the human brain and understanding,* as well as with the emotions that enable the capacity to grasp the world. Images have their own irreducible contribution to make to knowledge and understanding. Indeed, unitive images can allow us to *grasp knowledge whole* in a way that language does not easily allow. Thus people should take images seriously on their own terms and to ask what the content and visuality of images autonomously adds to understanding and enjoyment. Within this 'high' doctrine of the independent reality and visual autonomy of images, we should think of images as actually *being the content of information and knowledge.* They are essential, not expendable, add-on aids to comprehension and experience that might be gained by other means.

Whatever their value and virtues, visual images still encounter much suspicion and opposition. Much of this is rooted in historical sources and arguments.

## Intellectual reservations about images

Western intellectuals, and educated people generally, are often enthusiastic proponents of the written and spoken word. Historically, they represent a privileged minority group in society, the majority having been illiterate and focused more on oral and visual communication.[8] Furthermore, intellectuals usually assert the value of words and ideas over images because this is their own area of currency and competence. We can have little idea of what non-literate people have thought about images down the ages – their thoughts were not written down.

Plato was the founder of ocularcentric philosophy and the importance of vision and the eye for philosophy (*theoria*). However, he was also the father of the suspicion of actual images, damning both the images themselves, and those who created them. The problem with images was that they were rather unintelligent mimetic representations of objects that were themselves imitations of the ultimately real divine Forms.

Not only do the representational images of poets and artists fail to reflect truth and reality, they are superficial. Worse, if they are good imitations, they deceive simple people about reality:

> The artist's representation is . . . a long way removed from truth, and he is able to produce everything because he never penetrates beneath the superficial appearance of anything. For example, a painter can paint a portrait of a shoe-maker or a carpenter or any other craftsman without knowing anything about their crafts at all; yet, if he is skilful enough, his portrait of a carpenter may, at a distance, deceive children or simple people into thinking he is a real carpenter. (Plato 1955, p. 374)

This short quotation embryonically contains the charges against which visual images are arraigned to this day. They are superficial, illusory, deceptive, misleading and trivial, fixing naive viewers on appearances so they ignore the depth and wisdom of reality and truth. They appeal (along with poetry and drama) to the lowest, that is non-rational, part of the mind, associated with pleasure and pain, representing a corrupting threat to social and political order.[9] Paradoxically, many of the things that were advanced by the modern advocates of visual images as valuable are, in Plato's view, reasons for rejecting and suspecting them.[10]

In more recent, postmodern scholarship, valuing the superficial, unstable play of images on the surface of reality has become popular. However, much traditional thought has emphasized the need to go behind surface appearances of things to discern deeper forms and meanings. Thus superficiality has been condemned.

Not only are images superficial, they *deceive* people about the nature of reality. This is most apparent in techniques such as *trompe l'oeil* and perspective where a flat surface is made to look as if it contains depth and corresponds to three dimensional reality. While ordinary people have delighted in this kind of pleasurable illusion, and artists like Leonardo have been proud of their ability to create it, intellectuals have been quick to point out that this is in fact a kind of deception.[11] If the aim of life is to get at the reality of things, then deception should be discouraged; it weakens accurate perception of the true nature of things. There is a persistent reality issue about art images:

> [They] look real but are fake. They pretend to be what they are not. They lie. The portrait is a mute, lifeless substitute for the person; the idol, a superficial knockoff of the god. But that idol is also attractive and easy to see. It can detract from the more amorphous glories of the god. (Stephens 1998, p. 60)

Furthermore, imitating real things in visual representations can *devalue* the things of which they are representations, so the representations seem more real than the things they represent (Stephens 1998, p. 60). So, for example, public views of the Royal Family, and perhaps their own public presentation, become governed by an image or portrayal.

Baudrillard has explored the idea of simulacra – images or representations that appear to be copies of a reality, but of a reality that has never existed and presents no original to copy from. Within virtual reality, it is perfectly possible for a representation to be nothing but a representation of itself. Thus, Disneyworld, for example, is a never-never land that presents 'a play of illusions and phantasms' (Baudrillard 1994, p. 12). For the consumers of the virtual simulacra that abound in the contemporary world, there may be a fundamental confusion about where reality actually lies. Images, then, can confuse people about where reality lies. Worse, they can actually hide reality beneath a glittering skin of reality-simulating illusions.

While pleasure is not always condemned by intellectuals, they have tended to discourage *distraction and triviality*.[12] Recognizing the allure of images, their eye-catching attraction and capacity to amaze and amuse, many philosophers down the ages have worried that they fix people's attention on the apparent so they ignore that which is less easily discernible. This is analogous to people remaining childish and failing to mature to use their powers of reason, language manipulation and analysis to understand the world; they remain imprisoned in a sub-rational infancy aided and abetted by glittering, shiny images. The creation of visible images was seen by philosophers like Hegel (1993) as a necessary but intermediate stage on the way from primitive sensuality to the highest forms of human endeavour in religion and philosophy. For Hegel, and for others before and since, words, particularly poetry, point the way towards the highest forms of art and human endeavor because they allow humans to explore their interiority.[13] Serious human life and flourishing relates to the inner life of the mind, not to the external sensuality of the visual image.

Lurking behind many of the criticisms of visual images above, apart from a privileging of intellectual activity, may be discerned a *fear of the magical power of images* inherent in their mimetic, life-imitating capacities:

> They steal likenesses. They do what only the gods should be able to do: they recreate the living and preserve the dead. It is hard not to see this as black magic . . . They are, in this way, inherently unnatural – further evidence of magic.[14] (Stephens 1998, p. 60)

In a rationalist world-view, magic of any kind is held to be deeply suspect, associated as it is with irrationality, populism and superstition.

One of the main, if not explicitly stated, intellectual reservations about images is that *they are not words*. While words can change their meanings and significance, they are more stable in their content than images. The representations an artist makes are not verbal communications or signs. Images may carry several meanings or significations, but these are not necessarily obvious or stable. They can therefore offer a 'resistance to meaning' (Barthes 1977, p. 32). An image can be richly polysemic. At the same time, images are concrete and do not unambiguously convey abstract ideas or meanings. There is an irreducibly visual content to the image which makes it different from the words and concepts found in propositions and sentences.[15] Despite the popularity of the concepts like 'reading pictures' which presuppose that images will turn into some kind of written text that can be verbally anatomized, images will not entirely conform to linguistic understanding and rational analysis.[16] This frustrates intellectuals and makes them wary of them, as they are of emotions.

Some of the fear and envy that appears to underlie suspicion about the power of images among logocentric academics may emanate from the fact that seeing precedes speaking; visual perception comes before linguistic expression. Neuropsychologist Semir Zeki (1999, p. 9) notes the priority and superiority of visual perception over words in pondering why it is difficult to express the beauty or value of a painting:

> The reason is perhaps to be found in the greater perfection of the visual system, which has evolved over many more millions of years than the linguistic system; it is able to detect a great deal in a fraction of a second . . . language is a relatively recent evolutionary acquisition, and it has yet to catch up with and match the visual system in its capacity to extract essentials so efficiently.

The ineffable quality of images frustrates linguistic imperialists devoted to the all-powerful word.[17] Thus, historically, many philosophers have minimized the importance of images, emphasized their dangers, or interpreted and analysed them in such a way that they are effectively turned into words.[18]

Not all philosophers have contributed suspicion and scepticism to the use and understanding of images. In the shadow of Kant and Hegel, a whole branch of philosophy has grown up over the last two centuries entirely concerned with aesthetics and the nature of art.[19] Mostly, aesthetic concern has been directed towards a limited range of art images deemed to be of cultural importance. It has also been much influenced by understanding good taste and the quest to identify what is laudable and beautiful in art, following in the tradition that the quest for beauty might be a way of gaining access to important truths about human nature and reality and developing good taste might be personally improving.[20] This agenda is now diversifying, but it has yet to pay much attention to non-art images.

Substantial doubts about the value and power of images have been powerfully expressed within the Western intellectual tradition down the centuries. These have contributed to a general sense that images are either to be ignored, despised or distrusted. Intellectual rational logocentrism has had very practical outworkings. Literature and other word-based disciplines like history have had a prominent place in the academy for centuries. However, the study of the visual, even of high art, has been a minority pursuit. Art history departments are often relatively new and small compared with their counterparts in linguistically based disciplines. Those who study images such as television and film that are not regarded as high art have to fight for a place within the academy. Paradoxically, 'media studies' academics have often tried to make themselves as logocentric as they can, to the detriment of real empathic understanding of the visual nature of their subject matter. The study of visual images that are not recognized as art or entertainment is in its infancy and almost non-existent. There is an inverse relationship between universal availability and salience of images and the amount of critical attention given to them. Led by intellectuals with a narrow range of assumptions and concerns, perhaps we have all been complicit in denying ourselves deeper appreciation of the visual dimension of our experience.

## Theological objections and reservations

The Western Christian theological tradition has contributed a good deal to the denigration, dismissal and suspicion of visual images. There has been much image-making and consumption within Christianity, especially within its Eastern Orthodox expression. This has been theorized and promoted in a strictly limited way, but there has been much ambivalence as to the place and importance of images in general, and religious images in particular.

This ambivalence starts within Judaism. Its roots are in the anti-iconic Deuteronomic tradition, particularly in the Decalogue. The second commandment suggests that any kind of image-making is completely and diametrically against the expressed will of God:

> You shall have no other gods to rival me.
> You shall not make yourself a carved image or any likeness of anything in heaven above or on earth beneath or in the waters under the earth.
> You shall not bow down to them or serve them. (Exod. 20.3–5a NJB)

Not only is God not to be represented, but no likeness is to be made of anything. This commandment has never been completely observed, even in Judaism.[21] Paradoxically, only a few chapters later (Exod. 25, 26), Yahweh commands the creation of an ark, great winged creatures and other visual artefacts to be placed in the sanctuary which he will inhabit, and there is some evidence of considerable artefactual manufacture and use in pre-exilic Judaism. A *comprehensive* ban on images of all kinds can thus be distinguished from a *restrictive* view of images prohibiting only the making of images of the divine or those images which might be treated as idols.[22] Whether or not the commandment was ever fully observed in Judaism, it formed the basis for the suspicion and condemnation of images of all kinds within Judaism and Christianity. It has been appealed to, and restored to prominence, at times when iconoclasm and condemnation of idols have been important, for example, during the Reformation. Even at these points, however, this commandment was usually interpreted restrictively, not comprehensively.[23]

It is never clear in the Bible why God forbids the making of mimetic representational images of natural things or of the deity. It might be inferred that this was because God was invisible and had no physical, visible form. However, it is clear in parts of the Old Testament that God was thought to have the form of a human being, and was perfectly capable of making that form visible in limited ways in dreams, theophanies (for example, to Jacob and Moses (Gen. 28.10–19, Exod. 33.18—34.35) and visions (for example, Ezek. 1). However, God did not allow people to see God's visible form because this was dangerous for them.[24]

This tradition of the physical visibility of the deity virtually disappeared in Christian theology influenced by Greek philosophy.[25] Here the divine was beyond the reach of physical sight, human understanding and circumscription. Thus in the first millennium of the Byzantine church there was debate about whether divinity could be represented visually and, if so, in what ways. It was broadly resolved that while God the Father was invisible and so could not be represented at all, his manifestation in the incarnate Son, Jesus the human being, could be portrayed. Indeed, iconodules (defenders of icons and divine images) argued that icons partake of divinity within the material world and allow people to be drawn up into the sphere of divinity itself.[26] The issue of images in general was not at stake in the iconoclastic controversy – only images of the divine.

The theological arguments in the West which have been advanced against images, particularly religious images, have followed clear and predictable lines.[27]

First, images that represent the divine *distort and misleadingly represent the form of God*. God is invisible, formless, immaterial, and beyond any kind of human imagination or imaging. So any material or visible representation is necessarily a misrepresentation of the being of God.

Second, following Augustine and others, it is argued that images can *fix people's eyes and minds on the earthly, material realm* and discourage them from going upwards and inwards to find the transcendent God who is to be found in the soul and mind.

Third, images, particularly if they are powerful images, can *seduce people by the gratification of the eye*. People therefore risk becoming fixed upon the image and the pleasure it gives, failing to encounter the living God beyond the image itself. Thus they do not mature in faith in the invisible and become fixed upon the material world. John's Gospel, for example, emphasizes that faith should be in the Christ who cannot be seen, and that physical seeing can even be seen as faithlessness (John 20.29).

Fourth, there is the constant danger of *idolatry*. Idolatry was vigorously condemned in the Old Testament (see, for example, Isa. 44.9–20). Ever since Moses destroyed the golden calf which the Israelites created in the desert (Exod. 32.1), it was recognized that followers of God could lapse into worshipping the dead, inanimate work of their own hands.[28] This argument is about images that might supplant God. However, some parts of Christianity have seen this incipient idolatrous tendency as such an immanent and tempting danger that it has been applied to all religious images. Critics like Calvin therefore held that there is no place for religious images of any kind within the context of church and worship.[29]

Images that gain power and status of their own can easily become *devourers of resources and property* that could be used for other, more godly purposes. This argument surfaced strongly in the Reformation. While religious images were being fêted with gifts and attention, the human beings who embodied the divine image were being neglected and God was not being appropriately recognized in them.[30] (In the contemporary world it is perhaps worth considering how much money is spent on charitable appeals for 'art treasures' – here, again, images could be portrayed as active consumers of resources that might be deployed elsewhere in the interests of honouring the image of God in humans.)

Sixth, it was argued by reformers that *images distract from the word of God*. The Protestant tradition emphasized that God's principle means of communicating with, and being present to, humans is through the divine Word. This was incarnated in Jesus, but is also witnessed to by the words of Scripture and set forth in preaching based upon the living words of Jesus and Scripture. It is this word of the gospel that saves and divinizes, and in which God can be 'seen', not in images.[31] Indeed, visible images of God or any other kind of being may distract people from hearing and obeying the living word of God. The task of the Church is then to preach, not to provide images for people that may confuse them, preventing them from attending to the word.

Other arguments have been advanced by Christians against images. Kierkegaard, in the context of nineteenth-century individualist romantic aestheticism, argued that visual images can lead people to base their lives upon human creativity. He condemned aesthetic images for denying the temporality of human existence. They freeze moments in time and are inappropriately used to console people who need, instead, to transcend images to realize their true temporal situation bounded by the reality of death.[32]

The Christian tradition has not always been wholly opposed to the use of images. Early on, Pope Gregory the Great argued that 'the image is for the illiterate what the text is for those who read' (Barasch 1992, p. 204).[33] The use of images for didactic purposes has always had some legitimacy, even in Calvinist circles; Bibles and other written religious works have often been copiously illustrated to allow better assimilation of the narrative and message and so to deepen the response of the faithful.[34] Calvin and many of his followers did not object to many non-religious images as such if they did not provide trivial distraction which might prevent Christians from seeing God in the 'theatre of the world' and in their fellow human beings (Dyrness 2004, p. 76). Following John of Damascus, Eastern Orthodox Christians continue to believe that a limited range of iconic images provide a mediating means for humans ascending from the material realm to the divine.[35]

Thus the Christian tradition as a whole formally allows limited legitimacy to some visual images within religion. It generally has no problem with non-religious visual representations outside the context of the church. Mostly, it has not adopted Tertullian's position, that images, art and artists are adversaries of God and allies of the devil.[36] However, the acceptance and appreciation of images is strictly conditional upon their not coming between humans made in the image of God and their divine prototype. Generally, then, the Christian tradition, like Judaism and Islam, hedges their creation and use around with qualifications and warnings. The overall balance of thought, particularly in the West, has not affirmed visible images except insofar as they are used to illustrate and spread the message and truths of the gospel and belief in the transcendent, invisible God.

Even the Catholic Church, which gives considerable importance and respect to visual images as a means to contemplating, worshipping and understanding the divine, has not developed a theology which links this to central tenets of Christian doctrine. The use of images is a matter of useful devotional practice, not an essential element of faith. This poses some problems when certain images, for example Our Lady of Guadalupe, become semi-independent loci of divine presence and grace.[37] Catholic theologians would agree with their Protestant counterparts that material images are, at best, a means to apprehending the divine. They are not direct expressions of divine presence.

Centuries of suspicion of religious images within North European

Protestant culture have shaped contemporary Christian attitudes and practices. So many literary and musical artefacts are used in worship, but the use of images has been limited. And while there has been no shortage of secular visual images created in Protestant culture, there has been resistance to according them anything other than aesthetic or decorative status. One practical outworking of this suspicion is that the relationship between art, artists and organized Christianity has tended to be a delicate, and often a non-existent, one. Some contemporary Christians believe that it is time to engage more fully with art and artists, particularly if they can be put to the service of mission and worship.[38] However, there is hostility on both sides which will not quickly be quelled.[39]

Theological wariness about visual images has not stopped Protestants from entering into important relationships with images, religious and other. For example, some evangelical Americans have significant encounters with a portrait of Christ.[40] There is, however, something of a taboo against taking these relationships seriously and articulating their nature.

As inhabitants of Western culture, our ordinary everyday attitudes to images have been heavily influenced by the intellectual and religious ideas considered above. However, there are also other, less theory-laden factors which contribute to our indifference to images.

## Practical, cultural and everyday limitations

Why do ordinary people pay so little attention to visual images of all kinds? I suspect that lying behind our indifference and lack of curiosity lies a set of fairly random factors that conspire together to blunt critical awareness and engagement.

The most obvious factor is that we are mostly surrounded by visible, humanly created images of all sizes, shapes and classes, from taps and patterned furnishings through product packaging to TV images and computer screens. Given the ubiquity and plurality of images, many designed to fit in and not to draw attention to themselves, their nature and effects can easily be ignored. Where would one start to distinguish and attend to created visual images if one wanted to? By contrast words, whether in books or other contexts, often arrest and draw our gaze, seeming pregnant with direct communication and meaning.

Similarly, the huge variety of ordinary images, merging into a common background, deprives them of claims to attention and significance. Not being special, they are ignored. Despite being full of design, meaning and purpose, ordinary objects are simply used for their most obvious purpose without note, comment or understanding. Their visual image is of little interest. And the longer an image is around, the more ubiquitous it becomes, the less interest and thought it may attract.

There is, however, a whole other restricted group of images – sculptures, paintings and the like – that are taken to be of supreme significance for culture. Privileging one group of images as 'important art' means that other images are further relegated to insignificance. We are encouraged to focus on classic, beautiful images like Monet's *Water lilies* or Canova's sculptures. But this means that more common, ordinary images, for example, the designs on packaging, the shape of artefacts, receive little attention.[41] Many people would be unable to mention the name of more than one of the contemporary designers who have probably fundamentally shaped their domestic world with familiar objects.[42]

Another consequence of making 'art' the category within which all significant visual images should be considered is that many feel that art has little to do with them. Art is the province of an esoteric elite of artists or art historians. Images are art, and art is for aesthetes. Perhaps abstract art is the most obvious locus for this kind of defeat by visual images of ordinary appreciation and understanding. Witness the annual popular puzzlement and dismay at the images and artefacts short-listed for the Turner prize. Art and the visual can only truly be appreciated by those who are extensively trained in performance and analysis. So we stop thinking about the visual altogether, except to look at the few bits of art that we actually feel we can enjoy, perhaps because they are familiar, or have colours and shapes that viscerally appeal to us.

This last point is perhaps related to the prevalence of general visual illiteracy in Western society. While people are taught in schools to use, and sometimes enjoy, words and numbers, visually related activities like art and dance are often regarded as optional extras for those who are naturally good at them. So many people leave education insensitive to, and inarticulate about, the realm of visual images. They may even feel humiliated and inadequate in relation to the visual.

Humiliation and inadequacy, born of ignorance, incompetence, rejection by an elite group of experts, contempt for esoteric culture, or whatever, are supplemented by a sense that attention to images is childish. As children, we look at picture books, draw and paint. This is left behind when we become literate; there may, then, be a tendency to associate visuality with our immature, pre-verbal selves. It may even be that it is only when pictures and images can be turned into an esoteric verbal vocabulary that we can find a way of appreciating a restricted range of images in adulthood.[43]

We might also have decided at some level of our being that visual images are not only childish but also superficial. While print and words may be associated with depth and understanding in the self, the obviousness of visual images may be associated with lack of profundity. What you see is what you get; it is all there in front of you, with nothing hidden. So the thoughtful must look elsewhere to find something more demanding. This prejudice originates with Plato. It is a kind of implicit elite aestheticism which suggests that visuality is inherently trivial and not complex enough for proper intellectuals. Only if the visual can be made into an intellectual puzzle, demanding years of ascetic training before the initiate eventually becomes part of an exclusive in-group that understands the mysteries of images, is it worth attending to visual images.[44]

Lurking beneath the feeling that images, if they are to be taken seriously, should be inaccessible, complex, and hard to understand, may be a Protestant ascetic and elitist attitude that only that which has to be striven for can be valued. Many of the critics of visual culture have appealed precisely to this kind of thinking.[45] There is no gain without pain. So, if images and visual artefacts are immediately and pleasurably available, then they must be worthless and undeserving of attention.

But images can, of course, provide unpleasant amounts of pain and discomfort. The advent of child pornography on the Internet, if nothing else, reminds us of the fact that images can be very disturbing and possibly destructive, both for those who are involved in their production and those who see them.[46] Many people throughout history have argued along the lines that we become what we see and gaze at because we internalize it.[47] The visual ingestion of images means that perhaps the reason that some of us are not willing to use our eyes, or only to use them to gaze on a very limited range of images, is because we fear the harm that might come from it.[48]

Visual images may also be taken to be deceptive and so to be actively distrusted.[49] In an age of computer-generated and modified images, people are aware that all visual representations can be altered. So, for example, election candidates can change the heads of the people in old photographs so that they are perceived to be in better, or less salubrious, company. An ordinary person using a computer program can turn mundane holiday snaps into works of art. The widespread capacity to morph the visual to show what the editor wants people to see, rather than providing a direct representation of reality, contributes to scepticism about the value of images. Visual scepticism may then contribute to an aversion to taking visual images of all kinds seriously.

The various points I have made about popular cultural obstacles constitute a miasma of factors that may negatively condition responses to visual images and artefacts. This contributes to a kind of fatalistic visual indifference or uncritical myopia in everyday life.

## Summarizing objections and reservations about visual images

Overall, a rather negative view of images emanates from the Western intellectual tradition, Western Christian theology, and contemporary Western literate culture. These sources all ignore images that are not deliberately created to attract attention; they focus on art images rather than on images that are created, for example, by designers and craftspeople. They tend to the view that words are safer, more reliable, and more important than images, despite the everyday prevalence of images of all kinds. All acknowledge that images have a strange kind of power and mystery – the power perhaps coming from a certain incomprehension. They each attribute considerable dangers and temptations to images. Insofar as they acknowledge the irrational, emotional, visceral, sensual attractions of images, they appear always to have in mind that these contain the potential for hurt and harm. Insofar as images remain stubbornly visual and refuse to be linguistically deciphered and/or to turn into words with clear meanings, they are regarded as insignificant, superfluous, or merely decorative. While logocentric rationality, theology, and common experience, all accord some value to images, this is conditional and limited. At best, they provide light relief, illustration and some pleasure at the edges of life rather than being central to human self-understanding and existence.

In light of all this, it is unsurprising that many people are visually illiterate and fail to appreciate the images and visible artefacts around them and the relationships that they have with them. I will finish this chapter with a brief excursus on the fraught relationship between words and images. This arises as an issue in thought, theology and cultural practice.

## Word and image – a difficult relationship

In contemporary Western culture there is a tendency for words and images to be placed in opposition to each other. Our culture and education is mainly verbal and literate. Philosophy, too, is verbally shaped and expressed, and theology, within the scriptural tradition of Christianity, is substantially biased towards the word and linguistic expression for doctrinal and practical reasons. Often, in everyday life and seeing, images seem to be drowned or silenced by the noisy words surrounding them. So, for example, in art galleries, spectators often spend more time reading the labels than looking at the actual pictures. Thus words become 'a substitute for seeing, replacing the material, visual presence of the picture with labels, anecdotes, and the reassurance of the famous-artist brand name' (Mitchell 1996, p. 209).

Image and the word are easily positioned as other, and alien, to one another. Visual images, in particular, are often presented as an alien threat that must be reduced to words to be taken seriously.[50] The relationship between words and images is an asymmetrical one, with images as the junior partner. Visual images are often subjected to analysis in words and texts. *Ekphrasis*, the verbal representation of visual representation, frequently occurs, and approaches to images are significantly modified by developments in language. This compliment is not usually repaid.[51] Texts are not usually read in the light of visual images, and developments in visual imaging rarely transform words and literature. Furthermore, there is a grave danger that, in turning visual images into language, they are not allowed to alter thought and theoretical practice as they might.[52] Even in the words used to talk about images, particularly in modern semiotic and cultural analysis, there is a danger that the actual physical visual dimension of the work is marginalized as the works are reduced to words and textual deciphering.[53] Similarly, there is a 'will to semiotics' in some recent feminist image criticism. This also threatens to reduce artworks to texts, to focus on the meanings of the spectator, and to exclude the multivalent and material visual dimensions of images.[54] Hebdige (1995, p. 109) warns that 'interpretation conveys "a contempt for appearances" and creates "a shadow world of meanings" that threatens to engulf the original forms in order to replace them . . . interpretation thus represents "the revenge of the intellect upon art".'

For some contemporary critics this 'revenge', the reduction and subordination of the image to the word and text, is entirely desirable. Stivers (2001), for example, laments the supplanting of words and concepts by images and numbers in contemporary academy and culture. This contributes to a 'dumbing down' of intellectual and critical capacity. Within the theological realm, Ellul (1985) rails against 'the humiliation of the word' by the invasion of images and the visual into all areas of life. He condemns visual images, particularly technologically created images, as *inter alia*, superficial and picturesque, servants of techno- logical manipulation, reductive substitutes for life and reality, killers of thinking, analysis and memory, excluders of reason, critical discourse, explanation and reflection.[55] Images have evacuated and eviscerated the verbal and truthful, creating an everyday idolatry. This is contrary to the biblical witness, primarily focused on the spoken word and 'opposed to everything visual' (Ellul 1985, p. 71).

With such absolutist thinking, it is not surprising that visual images have occupied such an inferior place in public and academic life and thought. I want now to try to bridge the schism between word and image. It is more helpful to dwell on their similarities and complementarity than to emphasize the gap between them.

Extreme protagonists of words seem to believe that words and texts are innocent of most of the dangers and harmful features inherent in visual images. However, Plato found all art forms, including literature, drama and poetry, untrustworthy. They could all mislead, emotion- ally arouse and confuse, and lead astray. While words might be less pernicious than visible images, they were only different in kind, not necessarily in their effects. Similarly, while words may have more sta- ble meanings and denotations than visible images, they can hide truth as well as revealing it. People lie and deceive as much with words as with photographs and visual images. Furthermore, words give a very limited, partial impression of objects in reality: they can '"cite" but never "sight" their objects' (Mitchell 1994, p. 152).

Words have the potential to distort the nature of God and become idolatrous. While a formless, invisible God cannot be captured or cir- cumscribed in a visual image, the same is true of words or concepts. To the extent that words or concepts are believed to contain the divine reality, they, too, are in danger of becoming idols. Arguably, verbal and conceptual idols and images are more pernicious than their visible counterparts because they cannot necessarily be seen and examined for what they are, inhabiting hearts and minds rather than material space.[56] It may be speculated as to whether a purely visual religious cult might be more welcoming, spacious and tolerant than those that are focused upon words and doctrines with their power to define and so exclude.

I will now explore some of the ways in which words and images dynamically interact and accompany each other to argue for their fundamental complementarity. Words and visual images cannot be usefully separated or placed in a hierarchy. They are involved in an endless spiral of mutual interaction. It may be that seeing comes before the use and creation of words, but words come before the creation and use of visual images and art.[57]

Written words and visual images both share the characteristic of visual representation. Both are meaningful patterns on surfaces, and both are necessary: 'Like art and non-art, word and image persist because they correspond to institutional habits and needs' (Elkins 1999, p. 84). In Greek, *graphein* meant to write, to draw, or to scratch on a surface. This kind of multiple meaning reunites writing and visual image-making, better reflecting a reality in which words, notations (for example, music) and images are often found together. Beholding words and images often happens simultaneously. In practice, they constantly modify perceptions and understandings of each other. Furthermore, written scripts are themselves a particular kind of visual image. You are looking at words dressed in the clothes of a particular, carefully designed font that may well influence your willingness to read them. Some written presentations of words, for example calligraphic scripts, are decorated and elaborated in redundant, but visually pleasing, ways that make them direct objects of aesthetic appreciation beyond the meaning of the words they embody. On any written or printed page the presentation of words provides the 'faint aroma of a picture' – you are reading a *portrait* page at the moment. Similarly, viewers get pleasure from pictures that 'toy with the traits or writing and the habits of reading' (Elkins 1999, pp. 101, 194). There are no image- or word-free zones in the world. Notations, words and images should be rescued from arbitrary isolation from each other and appreciated simultaneously and together.

A dialectical, unstable relationship exists between words and images in which they continuously modify and affect one another. There is an 'inextricable weaving together of representation and discourse, the imbrication of visual and verbal experience' (Mitchell 1994, p. 83). This is intellectual as well as practical, for both words and images are used in mentation.[58] Theory itself is a kind of seeing, not just the construction of sentences using words.[59] Furthermore, even linguistic meaning is not necessarily conveyed phonetically; sign language used by deaf people is predominantly a visual phenomenon. This kind of holistic perception cuts through the phony 'war' between images and words, suggesting that we should think about 'image/texts'.

It is necessary to suture the apparent wound perceived to exist between these two very similar representational semiotic schemata. In this context, the heroes are 'pantextual' image/text creators like William Blake, an 'iconoclastic maker of icons', who juxtapose both graphic and typographic, words and images, within the same work (Mitchell 1994, p. 115).[60] Words and images should not be homogenized. They can accomplish different things. Their relationship can vary according to artefact and context; it may be as much about disjuncture, contrast and disagreement, as about similarity, analogy and resonance. The important thing, however, is to ask specifically what words and images are doing with, for and to each other, taking each element seriously on its own terms.

Often art pictures contain words or phonetic symbols. This is true of Japanese calligraphic art, but it also arises in modern art – Magritte's *Ceci n'est pas une pipe* is one obvious example. Cartoons also exemplify words and images dancing together mutually to create meaning and content. An interesting feature of pictures and other visual images is that they often create words around them as well as meanings within themselves – they become loquacious. Pictures are often surrounded by labels and catalogue entries that guide and sometimes hide the image from viewers. More than this, images spawn vast amounts of writing in art criticism, the history of art and so forth. Indeed, the less accessible an image is, the more writing it may create. Perhaps the more inferior the art work, the more words it generates.[61] This is particularly the case, perhaps, with non-representational and abstract art. Lack of obvious reference summons squadrons of words to rescue meaning from the world of shape and colour. This creates a semiotic storm of writing that allows viewers to access an alien visual realm.[62]

Words and images often belong integrally together. Attempts to keep them separate, or to subordinate one to the other, are probably less fruitful and sensible than trying generally to keep them together in a creative, dialectical relationship. A 'haptically' modified logocentrism might attempt to draw nearer to the realities of visual objects and create more intimate relations of friendship and fellowship with them rather than dismissing or subordinating them.

## Conclusion

In this chapter I have explored some aspects of attitudes towards visual images that may contribute to our not taking them seriously, mostly drawing on thinking that is oriented to art-like, representational and mimetic images. There is a considerable case to be made for the value of visual images. This value is easily denigrated in a logocentric, rationalist culture which has valued word over visual image, creating suspicion about images in general. This suspicion is amplified in the Christian theological tradition which generally allows only a very qualified role to some visual images, particularly within the context and practice of religion as such. Contemporary seers of images are also influenced by a range of factors that conspire to marginalize understanding and appreciation of the visual generally and visual images in particular. The contemporary context makes it difficult to take visual images and relationships with them seriously. The rift between words and images is an arbitrary and unhelpful one. However, practices of looking at, valuing and understanding visual images as the equal, and necessary, complement of words and concepts are still underdeveloped. It will take changes in all parts of our thought and practice, however, before visual images are appreciated fully for what they are, rather than being relegated to being mere decoration, illustration or distraction.

Having said that, art and other kinds of images pervade our lives and significantly condition our existence. Whether logocentric rationalists approve or not, people continue to enter into important relationships with visually available material images of all kinds, mostly in an unconscious and inarticulate way. In the next two chapters I will try to articulate some of the ways in which these relations with images can, or might, occur, and why some material images have power and significance for humans.

## Notes

1 Stafford (1996, p. 11) notes that there is a 'paradoxical ubiquity and degradation of images, everywhere transmitted, universally viewed, but as a category generally despised. Spectatorship . . . has become synonymous with empty gaping, not thought-provoking attention.'

2 Of course, there is a sense in which the whole world is an image to the eye, so an image is everything and nothing. I hope this restrictive differentiation, which is somewhat arbitrary, is an improvement on nothing.

3 James Elkins (1997, 1999, 2000, 2003) has almost single-handedly fought to develop a practical, critical notion of all things visual that includes all other kinds of visual objects and experiences from bank notes to natural land formations. He demonstrates how narrowly we have conceived visuality and the range of significant visual objects and experiences. Elkins' work demonstrates how much thinking and analysis is required to gain a full appreciation of all aspects of the visible world and

visual phenomena. It is a sign of the inadequate development of visual studies that we can only distinguish 'art' and 'non-art' images. There are many different kinds of non-art images, but we largely lack a typology for describing and discussing them, especially passive and invisible images (Cf. Elkins 1999, p. ix).

4 Elkins (1999, p. 54) writes: 'Art is a very loud word, blustery and often effectively empty.' Empty it may be, but it acts as a 'black hole' into which very nearly all human thinking about images has been sucked, to the detriment of much of our visual experience.

5 I follow Stephens (1998, ch. 5) here, interposing other ideas and material as appropriate.

6 There is a considerable debate about the relationship of images to space and time. It has been argued by some (see Jay 1994) that images minimize time in favour of de-historicized space as compared with information gathered by touch and hearing which depend upon linear development in time for their effective functioning.

7 See further, for example, Galison (2002), Jones and Galison (1998).

8 Oral culture, as opposed to literary culture, is also visual culture, and far more dependent upon pictures than texts.

9 Plato (1955, p. 382).

10 It is obvious that visual images are *superficial* and, in the case of paintings, only skin deep. They represent the appearances of things, the outside skin of what they depict.

11 Cf. Kemp (2001, pp. 26ff.). One of the founding myths of mimetic illusionistic painted images is the story of two painters, Zeuxis and Parrhasius, recorded by Pliny. 'Zeuxis produced a picture of grapes so dexterously that birds began to fly down to eat from the painted vine. Whereupon Parrhasius designed so lifelike a picture of a curtain that Zeuxis, proud of the verdict of the birds, requested that the curtain should now be drawn back and the picture displayed. When he realized his mistake . . . he yielded up the palm, saying that whereas he had managed to deceive only birds, Parrhasius had deceived an artist.' Quoted in Bryson (1983, p. 1).

12 Suspicions of deception, distraction and triviality hung around the development of early optical instruments such as microscopes which could be used to entertain and amaze as much as to educate and investigate (Wilson 1988, 1995). Scientists who used, and, indeed, still use, visual images to inform or amaze the public remain open to the suspicion of 'visual quackery' (Stafford 1993, p. 362). Cf. Galison (2002), Lynch and Woolgar (1990), Kemp (2000a, 2006), Jones and Galison (1998). Daguerre ran a profitable optical diorama show in Paris while also claiming to be a scientist (Crary 1999, p. 132). This kind of example is a parable of the ambivalence hanging around the seriousness of, and trust to be placed in, so-called 'scientific images'. Science has always depended for its popularity and public credibility upon being able to provide spectacular sights and images, such as air pumps (Shapin and Schaffer 1985) or the image of DNA (Kemp 2000b, 2003).

13 Hegel (1993, p. 96): 'Poetry is the universal art of the mind which has become free in its own nature, and which is not tied to find its realization in external sensuous matter, but expatiates exclusively in the inner space and inner time of ideas and images.'

14 For the mimetic power of images of the self see Gregory (1997, ch. 3) where he explores the magical powers of mirrors. Gregory explains that 'mirror' is closely related to *miraculum* or wonder in Latin: 'Mirrors *look* magical!' (Gregory 1997, p. 42). See also Taussig (1993, 1999). For more on mirrors see Melchior-Bonnet (2002).

15 'To describe the power of art in words constitutes, in the lines of T. S. Eliot, "a raid on the inarticulate, with shabby equipment"' (Zeki 1999, p. 9).

16 See, for example, Thomas (2001), Manguel (2002).

17 A number of recent critics have noted that even pictures situated in or close by texts to which they are taken to be integrally linked may have subtly or even very different knowledge and messages to communicate than their companion words. See, for example, Steinberg (1996). In relation to early Christian art, where one might assume that words strictly control meaning, Jensen (2000, pp. 3–4) believes that some images may have preceded texts and the texts then may be commentaries on the images: 'Images and words together constitute sacred symbols, and neither has inherent primacy over the other. Understanding this might require that we transcend modern culture's tendency to disengage symbols and words, and to value words as better or clearer communicative devices.'

18 Holly (1996, pp. 155ff.) arraigns the twentieth-century art interpreter, Erwin Panofsky (1955), as a kind of artistic Sherlock Holmes whose mission is to sweat pictures under iconographical and iconological analysis until they 'confess' their meanings and significance in words. She sees this as part of the 'phallocentric project of iconographic unlocking'.

19 See, for example, Gaut and McIver-Lopes (2001), Carroll (1999).

20 Burch Brown (2000).

21 See, for example, Edelman (1996), Idel (2001), Kuhnel (2001), Kunzl (2001), Wolfson (1994).

22 See Barasch (1992, ch. 1). Latour (2002, p. 23) observes that there is no way to observe the restrictive version of the second commandment. 'The only thing you can do to pretend that you observe it is to deny the work of your own hands, to repress the action ever present in the making . . . to erase the writing at the same time as you are writing it, to slap your hands at the same time they are manufacturing.'

23 Dyrness (2004). Barasch (1992, pp. 18ff.) notes that it is never made clear in the Bible why God forbids the making of images, either of natural things or of divinity itself.

24 Wolfson (1994). Cf., for example, Flannery-Dailey (2004) and Propp (1987).

25 While thinkers like Augustine believed that it would, in theory, be possible physically to see God, this was postponed indefinitely, particularly in this material world. See Miles (1983).

26 See further, for example, John of Damascus (1980), Besancon (2000), Barasch (1992), Ouspensky (1992).

27 I draw mainly on Pattison (1998, pp. 14ff.), supplementing this where necessary.

28 The argument might run that if an image is material and inanimate it cannot represent the living God so should not be worshipped or reverenced, whereas if it is material and animate then it represents gods other than the true God who cannot be captured in living form in images therefore it represents real but false gods or demons, in which case it should not be worshipped or reverenced either. See Barasch (1992), especially ch. 6.

29 See Dyrness (2004). Leonardo da Vinci, on the other hand, precisely admired the power of visual images and favoured illusions because of their 'ability to lure men into idolatry' (Mitchell 1994, p. 32). Leonardo was heir to a Christian tradition that God could be reached through the visual image rather than through words. Leonardo's altarpieces are a means of ascent towards the divine. See Farago (2003).

30 See further Wandel (1994).

31 Dyrness (2004, pp. 49ff.). Cf. Pattison (1998, p. 21).

32 Pattison (1998, pp. 22ff.).

33 Arguably, Gregory was, and remains, wrong. Mostly, religious images are not self-communicating to viewers, whether literate or non-literate. They need to be explained, and even then, they may be obscure. If you are familiar with the Bible, think about the number of biblical images that need to be explained to you when you look at the stained-glass windows in a church. They are as complex and uncommunicative as words, and people need to be inducted into them.

34 For example, Dyrness (2004), Harvey (1995, 1999), Morgan (1999), Gutjahr (2001), McDannell (1995, pp. 67ff.).

35 Barasch (1992, p. 205).

36 The third-century Christian theologian, Tertullian, with others, argued that the shaping of a person or humanoid image belongs to God alone. 'The artist, by forming a human image in stone or paint, or by impersonating a human being on stage, is competing with God, is attempting to usurp God's function. By so doing the artist becomes God's adversary. This ... brings the artist into close proximity with the devil, God's principal antagonist' (Barasch 1992, p. 118).

37 Brading (2001). Cf. Christian (1992), Orsi (1985).

38 For example, Dyrness (2001), Pattison (1998), Burch Brown (2000), de Gruchy (2001).

39 Elkins (2004).

40 Morgan (1996b, 1998, 1999). Cf. Harvey (1995, 1999).

41 For more on the elite ascetic aestheticism see, for example, Bourdieu (1984, ch. 1).

42 See Conran and Fraser (2004), Sweet (1998, 1999), Pavitt (2000), Starck (2003) to gain some idea of the range and penetration of design and designers into all parts of the contemporary world.

43 Galison (2002, p. 300) notes that, while images are integral to modern science, there is still anxiety about their capacity to convey truth rather than to deceive in a world where reason and logic are supposed to rule. There is an ongoing tension between the need to have images to convey and crystallize data and to dispose of them in a whirl of iconophobia and iconoclasm. The rejection of visual representation is related to childishness: 'when we ask what we are capable of knowing, we must put aside the childish playthings of the pictorial.'

44 Bourdieu (1984).

45 See, for example, Postman (1987).

46 See, for example, Elkins (1997), Williams (1999).

47 Plotinus: 'We are what we look upon and what we desire' (Miles 1985, p. 127).

48 Lynch (2005, p. 82) finds that the evidence that visual images damage people and affect behaviour is equivocal.

49 For example, Mitchell (1994).

50 Mitchell (1994, p. 163).

51 Mitchell (1994, pp. 152, 210). See also Elsner (2004). Bal (2003) argues that visual performances are best apprehended and appreciated through other visual performances: words provide thin translations of them.

52 Smith (1999).

53 Whiteley (1999, p. 119).

54 Hill (1999, p. 159). Commenting on similar postmodern scholarly attention to the embodied, emotional subject, Stoller (1997, p. xiv) notes: 'Two salient features

of the new embodied discourse, however, weaken its overall scholarly impact. First, even the most insightful writers consider the body as a text that can be read and analyzed. This analytical tack strips the body of its smells, tastes, texture and pains – its sensuousness. Second, recent writing on the body tends to be articulated in a curiously disembodied language.'

55 In the same vein, Gardiner (1999, p. 57) notes of the Jewish thinker Emanuel Levinas that he sees a strong correlation between vision and the 'reifying and domineering aspects of modernity, which was felt to denigrate the bodily, affective, and intersubjective qualities of human life.' It creates mastery, dominance and 'otherness'.

56 Brown (2004, p. 10) notes, 'words can be the occasion for idolatry no less than images. Spoken or written metaphor can be just a seductive and limiting as visual symbol . . . since so often listener or reader is unaware of what is occurring just beneath the surface.'

57 Berger (1972, p. 7).

58 See further, for example, Arnheim (1969, pp. 226ff.).

59 Nightingale (2005).

60 Holly (1996, p. 117) cites Leonardo as another pantextualist of this kind: 'Leonardo's words and images scroll together in a vortex of unfolding mobility . . . Words would unwrap in pictures, only to be metamorphosed back again at the other end of the line.'

61 Whiteley (1999).

62 Mitchell (1996, ch. 7) shows how the art critic Greenberg in a sense created and legitimated abstract art like that of Jackson Pollock by verbally theorizing around it. This neatly illustrates the dialectic relationship between image and word. The image needs to the word to gain popular understanding and access, while the word would not exist without the image.

# 5

# Relating to Visual Artefacts 1:
# Antecedent and Contextual Factors

People have always known, at least since Moses denounced the Golden Calf, that images were dangerous, that they can captivate the onlooker and steal the soul.

W. J. T. Mitchell, *Picture Theory*

The more power pictures have, the less we seem to know about how they operate.

Peter Weibel, 'An end to the end of art'

## Introduction

In the last chapter, I argued that there is much in Western culture that stops us from taking visual artefacts and images of all kinds seriously. I focused on art images and their like. However, the factors that may inhibit taking representational and mimetic images seriously include all other kinds of visible appearances of material artefacts within their penumbra. Visual images and objects can be cathected with considerable power, fear and anxiety. In the next two chapters, I will look at some of the factors that allow visual images to be perceived as powerful, or 'auratic', and the impact of these factors on human relationships with images.

As the epigraphs above suggest, visual images can have a powerful impact upon us and act as 'sticky eye traps'. Human lives and sight become entangled in webs of significant visual relationships, often with quite personal objects that are of no great aesthetic value or importance. However, mostly there is little conscious understanding of the nature of these relationships. We often do not know why something 'catches' the eye or become significant.

Many images and objects are specifically designed to meld into the background. This does not mean that they do not have conditioning effects upon us, or that we do not have some kind of relationship with them. However, it is almost impossible to begin to discuss the power of 'invisible' or semi-visible background images in everyday life. So here again I will focus on art-type images and speculate on the reasons why relatively prominent images have an impact in visual relationships. This might raise awareness about less obvious images.

I make this working assumption: it is useful to regard at least some pictures and prominent visible images as more like people than like inanimate objects.[1] This assumption is based on the insight that people have auratic relationships with objects:

> Experience of the aura rests on the transposition of a response common in human relationships to the relationship between the inanimate or natural object and man. The person we look at, or who feels he is looked at, looks at us in turn. To perceive the aura of an object we look at means to invest it with the ability to look at us in return. (Benjamin 1999, p. 184)

This perception challenges the taboo and absolute distinction in Western culture between animate beings like people and inanimate objects. I will discuss this further in a later chapter. However, I would like to suggest some pragmatic reasons for making this assumption here.

First, many people make important relationships with visible images. Sometimes these relationships are of supreme importance, so that the destruction of a visual image might affect a person more than a relative dying. For example, I felt physically sick when I contemplated the loss that would have accrued to me had Giotto's frescoes in Assisi been destroyed in the recent earthquake there.

There are many human faces and figures in the street, most not particularly memorable or important. Similarly, there are many images with which we have imperceptible or negligible relations. There are some human images and faces that are important to us, and there are some non-human visual images that enter a zone of intimacy with us. Each person is likely to find some images important; others may leave us entirely unaffected. The reasons for attachment or indifference to visual images are a complex mixture of conscious needs and liking, unconscious needs and fears, and different individual sensibilities.

Later I will discuss some of the ways in which visual artefacts are filled with intention, personhood, even, perhaps, a kind of secondary agency. Here, it is enough to suggest that humanly created visual artefacts have much human emotion, intentionality and agency put into them; this is easily sensed by human viewers.[2]

Sometimes, it takes more effort to retain a sense that visual artefacts are dead and wholly unpersonlike than to respond to them as personlike. This is particularly so with animated images, cartoons, films and TV programmes. Here, the image so closely indexes the human world that it is easy to mistake the imaginary for the real. Thus some TV actors are attacked in the streets because their fictional personae are taken to be real people. As with haptic touch, it may take an active effort of will and repression to maintain the sense that visual images and human beings are actually two completely different kinds of being that must be kept apart, and whose relationships are fundamentally distant. This repression may account for some of the anxiety that attends images in the shape of prohibitions against representation, idolatry, etc. I suggest this is because both images and persons transgress the species barrier that people, the creators of the images and artefacts, have erected to keep images in their place.

In my exploration of the nature of the relationships that can exist between visual objects and persons, I will first ground my discussion in some examples of how people can become entangled in significant relationships with visual objects. I identify some of the complex factors that might impinge upon relationships developing or failing to develop between people and visual things. These factors can be grouped into *antecedent factors* that predispose viewers (like knowledge of narratives, customs and practices), *contextual factors* that influence viewers while they are in the presence of visual images (such as position and display arrangements), and *inherent factors* that seem to flow from the nature of the visual object or image itself. This third group will be dealt with in the next chapter.

Having identified a pluralistic group of factors which make the visual relationship hard to predict or to analyse, I conclude the next chapter by returning to the personlike nature of some visual relationships, asking the question, Does it matter whether people engage in visual relationships, and what kinds of relationships they experience? I conclude that this does matter – and in practical terms. Indeed, close affective visual relationships with objects might sometimes be a matter of life and death.

## Experiences with visual objects

That people have significant relationships with visual objects cannot be doubted. In a study of strong, personal, emotional reactions to pictures, *Pictures and Tears,* James Elkins (2001) considers the ways in which people are jolted, assaulted and floored by pictures.

Contemporary Westerners live in an emotionally 'dry' environment; stoic intellectualism and postmodern irony mean that we fail to engage emotionally with pictures. It was not always so. People have been, and are, engaged, mostly unwittingly and unexpectedly, in turbulent emotional weather with them. They sometimes abduct or transport viewers into another world, so that they are either overwhelmed or drained by the experience.[3] Where the boundaries of the viewing self are breached, either by the fullness or the emptiness of a viewing experience, there is a flow of emotion that can evoke tears, or even prostrate viewers.

Elkins admits to staggering in front of the pictures in the Rothko Chapel in Texas, though he confesses that he has never been reduced to tears, or brought to the ground, by such an experience.[4] He is, however, not necessarily typical. 'Stendhal syndrome' is a set of temporary symptoms that afflict tourists to Italy, especially Florence. The symptoms of 'hysterical tourism' include crying, fainting, ranting, fevers and hallucinations.[5] People probably experience these symptoms in the presence of Renaissance masterpieces because they are predisposed to do so by romantic ideas which suggest that art works created by geniuses will evoke strong individual emotional responses. The syndrome, still going strong, dates from the second decade of the nineteenth century.

Fainting fits and ecstasies in cultural centres point to the emotional power potentially available in relationships between people and visual objects. They are not typical of general reactions to everyday visual artefacts.[6] To ground this chapter, therefore, I begin with some consideration of actual significant relationships with visual objects from the lives of ordinary people. As preparation for this, you might like to ask yourself the following questions:

- What sorts of relationships, if any, do I have with visual objects and the visual environment around me?
- Which visual objects do I value? Which would I miss? Why do I value them?
- Are there any visual objects that I feel required to attend to? Are there any I have a relationship with? Why this particular object?
- Are there any visual objects that arouse noticeable emotional responses in me, for example, pleasure, anger, puzzlement?
- What makes some visual objects sticky 'eye traps' for me?
- Have I ever been 'abducted' by a visual image or taken up into its world? How might I account for this experience?
- In thinking of any particular object why do I think I have a

relationship with it? What do I and the object respectively bring to the relationship?

- What sort of relationship do I think I am having, or not having, with visual objects and the visual environment when I am not attending to them?
- Do I have relationships with any visual objects that are more important to me than those with any people that I know? If I do, how do I explain this to myself?

One of the most interesting things that I have done in preparing this book is to talk to people about the visual images and artefacts that are important to them. It is quite common for people to volunteer that they have had important relationships with artefacts, sometimes of a deep, or even passionate, kind.

I have already volunteered my own passion for the frescoes of Giotto, but there are other works with which I feel my life is involved. The mosaic crucifix in the apse of the church of San Clemente in Rome, for example, Piero della Francesca's *The Baptism of Christ* in the London National Gallery, and John Piper's foliate head series of screen prints and etchings, spring readily to mind. I also have a relationship with a pastel portrait of an elderly lady that hangs on the wall of one of my friends' houses; it is warm and evocative, and I always look forward to seeing it.

On a less grandiose level, I own a small toby jug that belonged to my grandmother, and various other objects of no artistic importance provide context for my everyday life (see Plate 7). I do not reflect upon, or look at, these objects all the time, but I do think about them regularly, more than I do about some of my friends and relations.

One person to whom I spoke, a nun, told me that she had an ancient leather bag that was important to her. She spoke lovingly of how she polishes and maintains it. Another told me that when her mother was dying, she asked for a certain vase to be brought to her and she kept this beside her bed until she finally died. Significantly, her daughter is sorry that this object which had been around in her childhood is not hers now. A former airman recounted the experience of going into an art gallery and suddenly being grabbed by a particular picture of Russian peasants beholding an icon. He felt almost mystically transformed by his encounter with the work that almost sprang off the wall at him (he quickly and carefully informed me that religion and mysticism was not his thing).[7] Another man told me that he had the experience of an ordinary, mass-produced tablespoon becoming inexplicably fascinating and beautiful as he looked at it.

This is just a small, random collection of anecdotes about visible objects, great and small, personal and impersonal, owned and not owned, that have made an impact upon a very small group of people.[8] Other people have similar feelings and experiences about jewellery, kitchen utensils such as pepper mills, photographic images, and films. They seem to become part of that person's important life experience and identity, not just material flotsam and jetsam that float past ephemerally.[9]

Here is Alan Bennett sheepishly acknowledging a set of 'illicit' relations with everyday things in his diary:

> Note how personalized and peopled the material world is at a level almost beneath scrutiny. I'm thinking of the cutlery in the drawer or the crockery I every morning empty from the dishwasher. Some wooden spoons, for instance, I like, think of as friendly; others are impersonal or without character. Some bowls are favourites; others I have no feeling for at all. There is a friendly fork, a bad knife and a blue and white plate that is thicker than the others which I think of as taking the kick if I discriminate against it by using it less. Set down this seems close to insanity but it goes back to childhood when the entire household was populated with friends and not-friends and few objects were altogether inanimate, particularly knives and forks. (Bennett 2005, p. 284)

This kind of significant experience with visible images and objects is not uncommon, though it is mostly not publicly acknowledged. People feel somewhat embarrassed about being touched by, and relating to, material, inanimate things. These relationships are also quite intimate, personal and private, so nobody asks about them. They tend to be very difficult to articulate verbally.

Little academic research has been done on how people relate to individual objects, or on the character and meanings of these relationships. Even in the context of art and art museums, academics seem mostly uninterested in assessing what people bring to, and take away from, individual images.[10] Attention has mainly focused on the intentions and meanings of sponsors, creators and exhibitors, or the nature, iconography and meaning of images. But that such relationships exist cannot seriously be in doubt. For without some kind of relationship, or the possibility thereof, there would be no satisfaction or gratification in viewing visual objects.

Within the world of religion, relationships with visible objects are less concealed, though no less complex. Religious reality is mediated through images of one kind or another – statues of Hindu gods, of the Buddha, and of Christ and Mary abound.[11] Even in Protestantism, emblems, Bible illustrations and pictures of Jesus form an important point of connection with the divine.[12] Devotees see themselves as having a relationship with the divine, not with a piece of fashioned plaster or stone. However, it would seem that some images and particular representations have a greater religious significance and efficacy than others. A personal audience with Our Lady of Guadalupe, or the Madonna of 115th Street, may be deemed more efficacious than simply praying to any image of Mary.[13]

Outside the overtly religious world, visual images also develop important significances and relationships. Elkins (2004, p. 53) points to the iconic importance of pictures of Elvis Presley; he claims to have a friend who owns a picture of Elvis that weeps. People also have important relationships with public art. They touch, mutilate, destroy, and even place flowers beside public sculptures, indicating that passionate affective relationships are occurring (see Plate 4). It is not just representational or mimetic images that are so treated. Abstract sculptures can attract much feeling, positive and negative. And in ordinary everyday situations, it is not difficult to imagine how your work colleague would feel if you handled the photo of the family on her desk carelessly or with contempt.

Many people, at least some of the time, enter into important, emotionally significant relationships with a variety of visual objects, domestic and public, functional and decorative, great and small, famous and obscure. Sometimes, these relationships may have a direct, clearly understood, public significance. Mostly, their nature is not clearly articulated. Relationships are intersensorial, involving the whole embodied sensorium, including the emotions and non-symbolic senses of touch, smell and taste. They do not have to be verbally articulated to be of great significance.

In the remainder of this chapter, and in the next, I shall consider some of the factors that might render particular visual images significant to some people, some of the time. I will look at factors that have been advanced mainly in relation to art works. However, these factors might also come into play in relation to everyday, ordinary visible objects that do not attract the attention of theorists of vision and aesthetics. The threads of relationship and significance uniting viewers to visible objects are likely to be nearly as complex as those that constitute personal relationships between people.

## Factors contributing to the power and significance of relationships with images

Remarkably little is known about the factors that contribute to individuals and groups developing important relationships with visually available objects. It is clear from the kinds of examples adduced above (toby jugs, bags, vases) that it is not necessarily a matter of artistic merit. Some of the most powerful and influential religious images, for example, the statue of Our Lady of Rocamadour, are relatively small, crude and insignificant aesthetically. It is possible for people positively to love ugly or kitsch objects more than those that are ostensibly beautiful.[14] At the same time, some objects have a significance and power experienced by many viewers over the years, for example, Michelangelo's Sistine Chapel.

Before I speculate on some of the factors that may affect the kinds of relationships that people have with visual images, I want to emphasize again the relational nature of both sight and power.[15] It may sometimes seem that visual images have some kind of autonomous power to elicit particular responses and relations. But as in marriage, it takes at least two participants to make a relationship with power dynamics. Power and influence in relations between viewers and visual objects inhere in the relationship between them.

To examine some of the factors that may bear upon the nature of visual relationships, I will first look at the *antecedent factors* that condition the expectations of viewers before they encounter any visual object. Then I will examine *contextual factors* that might come into play when an object is being viewed. Finally, in the next chapter, I will look at some of the factors that are *inherent* in the image/object itself.

I should emphasize here not all of the factors identified may pertain in a particular visual relationship. Similarly, some of them may contradict, conflict, or be ambivalent. This necessary confusion cannot be resolved, only recognized and articulated.

## Antecedent factors in visual relationships

It is possible broadly to divide possible antecedent factors that people might bring to visual relationships with images into socio-cultural and individual/psychological categories. I will deal with the broadly socio-cultural factors first.

## Narratives

Perhaps the most important factor surrounding and conditioning the expectations of viewers of visual objects are stories told about objects. Significant objects that attract attention draw words and narratives to them and spawn stories.[16] These condition potential viewers to what they should want to see, what they will see, and to what the significance is of the seen object.

Thus objects are often seen through and with words, not just as visually discrete, uninterpreted phenomena. Words, for example, in art books and catalogues, establish the nature, place and importance of objects, orienting potential viewers. If objects fail to be, or to become, ennarrated, they may lose their social significance and value, and thus be completely ignored. So, for example, my toby jug is a small, poorly made object, of little aesthetic value. It has significance for me and my intimates because it is contextualized within a narrative about my family. I can give an historical account of where it has been and what it means to me that enhances its interest and significance. Similarly, an important social narrative can be advanced about history and significance of Giotto's fresco cycle in the Arena Chapel in Padua. This widely shared narrative concerns the development of Western civilization and culture which puts Giotto at the centre of visual development.[17] Thus people visit the Arena Chapel with reverence and awe, as instructed by their guidebooks.

Viewers, too, are shaped by narratives that tell them what it is to be a seer of certain kinds of objects. Thus Elkins discovered that his response to Bellini's *Ecstasy of St Francis* had been formed unwittingly and unconsciously by the individualized psychological narrative or intense emotional response articulated by Ruskin and other nineteenth-century critics to which he had somehow been exposed as a child.[18]

Narratives, verbal accounts and commentaries, construct, and condition in advance, the potential visual relationship which people might expect to have.

## Fame and reputation

One of the things that narratives do is to spread the fame and reputation of visual objects. These narratives may be supplemented with pictures, reproductions, and other images, that build up expectations of how wonderful the image is before ever a viewer encounters them.

1 The *Camera obscura*, which was used as a model for the relationship of mind to material reality by seventeenth-century philosophers, including Descartes. (Athanasius Kircher, *Ars Magna Lucis et Umbrae*, 1646.)

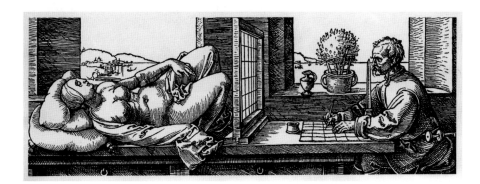

2 Perspectival, realistic representation became dominant in the West in the fourteenth and fifteenth centuries. This picture can be taken to symbolize many of the criticisms made of perspectival vision insofar as it is taken to be objectifying, distancing and dominating, as well as subordinating and reifying women within a kind of male gaze. (Detail from Albrecht Durer, *Draftsman drawing a nude*, woodcut, *c.* 1525.)

3 Anthony Gormley, *The Angel of the North*.

4 These photographs, taken in 2005, show how people touch and engage haptically with public visible objects. When the Bull in the Birmingham Bullring was damaged by vandals, some people left flowers and messages of sympathy for this inanimate object. (Laurence Broderick, *The Bronze Bull*.)

5 Perception is unified, embodied and intersensorial: the different senses should not artificially be separated from each other. This disconcerting image locates eyes in the hands. It is highly suggestive for haptic vision.
(Herbert Bayer, *The Lonely Metropolitan*, photomontage, 1932.)

6 Mary of Burgundy, *Book of Hours*. The Hours of Mary of Burgundy
(Ms1857 fol 14v), late 1470s, Vienna, Oesterreichische Nationalbibliothek.

7 The author's Toby jug: not all objects with which humans have important relationships are beautiful or culturally significant.

8  In pre-modern times it was not unusual for people to have lively, personlike relationships with inanimate objects, as St Francis did when he heard the crucifix in San Damiano speak to him with the voice of Christ.
(Giotto, *St Francis having a vision before the Crucifix in San Damiano*, from Basilica of St Francesco in Assisi.)

9 Jake Cress's 'animated furniture' demonstrates how easy it is for some inanimate objects to acquire the attribution of personlike features and even feelings. (Jake Cress, *Oops* and *Self-portrait*.)

Thus, years before seeing Leonardo's *Last Supper* on the wall of a monastery refectory in Milan, I had seen photographs, postcards, tapestries, small plaster models, imitations and parodies of the work. All of them, even the parodies, emphasize the huge social and cultural importance of this wall painting. (Not surprisingly, actually standing in the same room with it was a bit disappointing.)

## Setting and presentation

The importance of images is also indicated by their setting and presentation. Marcel Duchamp showed that the significance of a visual artefact could be entirely changed by placing a urinal upside down in an art gallery and designating it a modern sculpture, *The Fountain*.[19]

A dramatic natural setting might also give prominence, as in the case of *The Angel of the North* in Tyneside (see Plate 3). Sometimes a visual object might be given prominence by its setting in an important religious building or complex, or in a setting such as an art gallery or museum. Thus, the National Gallery in London, itself designed partly to imitate a religious space, using architecture first associated with Greek temples, is taken to be a kind of space that gives a sort of sacrality to its contents. People visiting it expect to see 'important' visual objects, and maybe to have some contemplative, quasi-spiritual experience.[20] People often talk in hushed, reverential tones in art galleries. Even within ordinary homes, the position of objects in prominent places can suggest a certain significance.[21] Some people use the mantelpiece, or the top of the television in their front rooms, as little shrines to family photographs. This draws the attention of the viewer to their importance, at least for the people who put them there.

## Uniqueness and rarity

The influential early twentieth-century cultural critic, Walter Benjamin, argued that mass production of images, such as the *Mona Lisa* or the *Last Supper*, was likely to deprive original visual objects of their mystique and auratic power (their power to create wonder) because they would be widely available, but cut off from their original ritual setting and function.[22] It seems that Benjamin was wrong. Far from depriving people of the need to see original images, mass reproduction seems to whet people's appetites to see the unique prototype, and to increase its auratic power.[23] Uniqueness and originality is a powerful force in draw-ing people to want to see the original that has such power to inspire mass reproduction in the first place.

## Nature and function

Many people have expectations based on their perception of an image's nature and function. They are often fairly clear as to what the nature of an image is, for example, whether it is designated as art, devotional object, or functional object.

With regard to function, in the case of religious images people may have heard how a particular image might heal or help in time of trou-ble. The image of St Jude, for example, might be thought to be particu-larly helpful in times of desperate need.[24] Outwith religion, too, images acquire a reputation for particular functions. Thus, some paintings are regarded as particularly sublime, impressive, and bound to move the viewer, for example, Michelangelo's Sistine Chapel. Other paintings, like Rothko's, might be deemed to be good for providing meditative or contemplative calm. Within the home, particular paintings or photo-graphs can be treasured because they provide good likeness or capture the spirit of the person; they might provide comfort or consolation. Thus, potential viewers may approach visual images with definite hopes and expectations of what an image might do for them, for example, healing, contemplative calm, vivid recollection. That these expectations may not be met does not abnegate this prospective readiness for par-ticular kinds of relationship and experience.

## 'Consecration' and sacralization[25]

From the written and spoken narratives that they have been exposed to, viewers often know before they see an image that it is special or signifi-cant. In religion, this specialness may have been created or enhanced by an act of ritual consecration, dedication or cultic recognition.[26] Some images, for example, tombs of saints, or reliquaries, are deemed to be filled with sacral power by virtue of their direct association with divine power; they require continuing recognition rather than formal conse-cration. Formal sacral power can continue to influence the way that images are perceived, even in a secular society among agnostic tourists. Many of the buildings and images they visit have been used for overt 'religious' reasons by believers.[27] Even religious pictures in galleries, isolated from their original contexts and meanings, can continue to have a religious as well as cultural resonance for viewers.[28]

Consecration and sacralization, the recognition of power and so on, do not only pertain to religious images. Commentators on the growth of tourism and leisure have noted the way in which particular objects and places come to have a de facto sacral status in that they are designated as particularly set apart by differentiation from other objects.[29] Thus, amidst the many landscapes of Britain, the Lake District and Scottish Highlands are differentiated as particularly moving and important. Effectively, secular pilgrimages are undertaken by visitors to see them, with some hope that some kind of profound, sublime experience might be available there.

A similar process occurs with individual visible objects. *The Angel of the North* is in danger of becoming a sacral object to which some kind of numinous power and identity is attributed, so that visitors are drawn to it (see Plate 3). And visitors to London would not want to miss seeing Nelson's Column in Trafalgar Square, or the Leonardo cartoon in the National Gallery next to it.

Association with a famous, inspired, artistic genius is a quick way to de facto consecration, leading viewers straight from the world of mere images to the anteroom of heaven whence inspiration comes.[30] While people may not anticipate worshipping these images, they still attribute more significance to objects like these, hallowed by narrative, past practice, custom and pilgrimage, than to other, equally impressive and beautiful, objects nearby. Often, people ignore significant objects under their noses because they are not formally designated by guides, guidebooks and other narratives as having the same kind of significance.[31]

## Visual images are bound up with other social functions and rites

So far, I have separated out some socio-cultural factors that might influence people's expectations of experiences and relationships with images. Analytic clarity is refuted in reality. All these factors mingle together in ways that are difficult to separate. So, for example, a person going to see the important Renaissance pictures and sculpture in Italy is likely to follow a well-defined pilgrimage trail to certain cities (Florence, Venice and Rome) in which particular loci and images have been identified in narratives and guidebooks. They will enter special buildings, religious and secular, and ritually view alongside other aesthetic pilgrims, gazing attentively and contemplatively at 'great' paintings by the geniuses of history. Their experience of viewing will be heavily structured by history and ritual.[32] Particular images are bound up in complex narratives and practices, many of them internalized by individuals unconsciously. Even within the domestic sphere, important, potentially relational images do not exist as isolated entities. They are situated within a matrix of personal and familial history, memory, narrative and ritual (consider the prominence of a photograph or a treasured object of a dead family member at a gathering of his or her survivors).[33] Viewing of images is conditioned by context and social norms that mostly pass unremarked. Without them, we would not know what to look at or understand the ostensible significance of what is to be seen.

I don't suppose I am alone in having been asked to look at an art, religious, or other image only to be disappointed with its lack of power or meaning for me. This may be attributable to inadequate socialization. When I look at the *Volto Santo* in the Cathedral at Lucca, for example, what I see is a rather crude, inert, non-life-like large wooden statue of Christ which is of no great aesthetic value. However, for many contemporary Luccesi this statue is alive; it is a miracle-working image that heals and helps. It requires reverence because of its capacity to bridge the gap between heaven and earth. Give me Tintoretto's *Last Supper* that hangs behind an altar a few feet away with its amazing perspective and dynamism. If I inhabited the narrative and ritual world that made and keeps the *Santo* sacred, however, I would almost certainly value it and relate more closely to it than to the mere work of art that is its near neighbour. Thus, aesthetically and religiously educated and socialized viewers can respond to images in completely different ways.

As well as the antecedent socio-cultural factors that condition potential responses and relationships with visual images, it is important to take into account the individual psychology of viewing and the temperament of individual viewers.

## Psychological factors

There seems to be little specific research into why different viewers are psychologically predisposed to relate to particular kinds of images beyond a general kind of assertion that people bring their experiences, attachments and preferences from the past to their present visual relationships.

Norman (2004), a cognitive psychologist of design, suggests that, in evolutionary terms, situations and objects that offer food, warmth or protection are likely to give rise to positive affect.[34] Within the visual realm, these conditions are likely to include bright, highly saturated hues, smiling faces, 'attractive' people, symmetrical objects, and rounded, smooth objects. Conditions that might be expected to produce automatic negative affect include bright lights, looming objects that are about to hit the observer, darkness, empty, flat terrain, crowded, dense terrain, crowds of people, misshapen human bodies, and snakes and spiders. These features might help to provide some kind of template for why we do or do not like certain kinds of visual experience and object.

Neurobiologists have recently begun to explore the relationship between visual neurology and art. They can clearly identify parts of the brain stimulated by particular kinds of images. They conclude that the brain is 'hard-wired' to be very sensitive to images of faces, moving creatures and landscapes – representations that are clearly important for human survival and flourishing.[35] Zeki (1999, pp. 9–10) argues that the function of art is to 'allow us to acquire knowledge not only about the particular object . . . but to generalize from that to many other objects and thus acquire knowledge about a wide variety of objects or faces'. Ramachandran (2003, p. 65) believes that it is a form of 'virtual reality simulation' that allows humans 'to practice scenarios in an internal simulation without incurring the energy cost or risks of a real rehearsal'.

However, non-psychologists regard the purpose of visual representation as being mainly to symbolize, rather than to gain knowledge.[36] Whatever the rights and wrongs of this argument, cognitive psychology presently has little insight into individual responses to visual images. Zeki (1999, pp. 217–18) concludes that we 'can say little about one of the major features of art, namely their power to disturb and arouse us emotionally'.[37]

We must therefore wait for neurology and cognitive psychology to make a substantive contribution to understanding of relationships with visible objects. Even when we know more about, for example, the relationship between personality type and image preferences, little will be known about the subjective importance and meaning of particular visual relationships.

*Psychodynamic factors*

Psychodynamic psychology is less coy about asserting the importance of individual character and psychology for visual relationship and experience. However, it is still general in its approach to visual objects.

For this kind of psychology, attachment to people and things is a major concern; the importance of relationships that can form with inanimate things through the mechanisms of transference and projection is recognized.[38] Most importantly, this kind of thinking roots relationships with objects of all kinds within the early, pre-linguistic, pre-symbolic multi-sensorial development of the infant and its experiences of desire, longing and attachment with its early caregivers. It is difficult to test empirically the veracity of psychodynamic insights into specific relations with visual objects. However, they are phenomenologically and experientially suggestive.[39]

Building on Lacan's work, Darian Leader believes that art works play upon a sense of absence, loss and void. Arguing that infants lose their unified relationship with the maternal object as they acquire language and become civilized, Leader suggests that 'loss creates desire, the yearning to re-find something we believe we once possessed. Art provides a special place within civilization to symbolize and elaborate this search' (Leader 2002, p. 75). However, the images created cannot fill the void they evoke. They act as 'a screen that separates us from the void and at the same time evokes it for us'. In this sense, the history of art can be regarded as the 'history of finding new ways to evoke what is missing in the world of images, the absence that makes us look' (Leader 2002, pp. 127, 146).

This kind of thinking is amplified in Bollas's consideration of aesthetic experience. Within the intimacy and unity of infant–mother dyad, the mother is a transformational object and environment which effects radical changes in the child's experience of the world. As the child grows, it moves away from the mother, the original transformational object, via transitional objects, so that it comes to relate to many other things. However, the original dyadic intimacy can be reignited so that 'a person feels uncannily embraced by an object' (Bollas 1987, p. 4). This experience of fusion re-enacts a pre-verbal ego memory and is often interpreted as an aesthetic moment.[40] Such moments evoke a psychosomatic sense of fusion that existentially recalls the original transformational object.[41]

Aesthetic moments with objects will often seem to promise transformation. These moments can be so important that the subject is likely to think of the object as being in some way sacred.[42] They can be filled with fear and hatred, and be negative as well as positive, for they evoke the feelings that were present at the beginning of emotional life. They are, however, 'profoundly moving because of the existential memory tapped' (Bollas 1987, p. 29). Bollas concludes,

Whether this moment occurs in a christian's conversion experience, a poet's reverie with his landscape, a listener's rapture in a symphony, or a reader's spell with his poem, such experiences crystallize time into a space where subject and object appear to achieve an intimate rendezvous . . . such moments . . . are fundamentally wordless occasions, notable for the subject's feeling and the fundamentally non-representational knowledge of being embraced by the aesthetic object . . . these occasions can sponsor a profound feeling of gratitude in the subject that can lead him into a lifelong quest for some other reacquaintance with the aesthetic object. (Bollas 1987, p. 31)

So powerful and unbidden are these momentary aesthetic experiences that they may be attributed as coming from the object which has 'chosen' the viewer (Bollas 1987, p. 32). Thus the object can be regarded as having unique importance, with inherent sacrality and power. In aesthetic experience of this kind, transformational objects may promise integration and hope, hence a quest to seek similar experiences with the same or different objects in future.

Most of this psychodynamic thought is general and directed towards high-point moments in experience. It does not deal with ordinary visual relationships with a wide variety of everyday objects which might evoke vague feelings of affection or dislike, rather than intense, specific feelings of love and hate. It is probably also the case that behavioural conditioning will partly determine individual responses to visual objects. So if a particular colour is linked to an unhappy experience it may put viewers off objects thus coloured. If a portrait of a face looks a bit like a favourite aunt, we may be predisposed to like it. However, all of this fails to provide a proper understanding of why particular individuals are likely to relate to specific objects as they do.

This, then, concludes my brief survey of some of the antecedent factors that might condition our responses and potential relationships with visual images before we actually get to see such images. Frustratingly, the extent to which each factor might be involved and the weight of its influence over any particular individual is very difficult to determine: 'Receptivities are as individual as snow crystals' (Steiner 1988, p. 191). There is still much to learn about the preconditions for relationships, positive and negative, with the visual aspect of objects.

## Specific contextual factors

Viewers encountering images of any kind, at any time, are profoundly affected by social and psychological factors which may condition their reactions and potential for engagement and relationship.

To start with the individual and psychology, clearly *the state of the person* (for example, their overall health, mood and state of receptiveness), plays an important part in what one notices and the extent to which one attends to it. If people are inwardly preoccupied or tired, they may not be able to engage much with images. On the other hand, they may be sensitive to particular kinds of images and objects that 'speak to their condition' in some way – even to the extent of seeing images that are not physically present.[43]

Similarly, the *personal expectations* with which an individual engages in a visual encounter can be significant. If I have high expectations, I may be visually engaged and delighted, but I may also be deeply disappointed, my disappointment being deepened by my idealistic expectations. Similarly, if I have low expectations of a particular visual object, say a kettle or a plug, I may miss out on having an engagement of some depth and value. Active seeing is highly selective, and past experience and expectations have an important effect upon present visual engagement.

The *place and time of viewing* can have an effect on the viewer's engagement with a visual object. I once stayed in the room in Florence where the stolen *Mona Lisa* was recovered in the early twentieth century. I doubt my experience of seeing the picture lying flat on the floor of a modest bedroom would be anything like seeing it displayed in the Louvre. Sister Wendy Becket reports that her encounters with significant pictures took place in solitude through the medium of looking at small postcards in her hermitage caravan. This distortion of size and medium of objects presumably affected what and how she was able to see.

*Time*, too, has an effect. One might feel entirely different about looking at Picasso's *Guernica* in Madrid the day after a terrorist attack than one did the day before. And the amount of time that one spends looking may affect the impact of a visual encounter. One of the reasons that films and other narratively structured artefacts like novels may move people more than static images is because people engage with them for longer, becoming more involved with them.[44] In the present era of saturation with visual objects we are perhaps less disposed to stand and stare. This may affect our relationships with them profoundly. *Historical and spatial context*, then, are likely to have a significant effect upon visual encounters.

*Social context*, too, must be taken into account. A solitary encounter with an image may be a very different experience from the one that occurs in the company of others. It is easy for humans to pick up ideas, expectations, moods and emotions from other people.[45] In a public space with people who are all looking at one work, I will probably want to see it, too. If people are paying only cursory attention to visual objects, I may well do likewise. I may decide rather consciously not to do what everyone else is doing as a sign of independence or rebellion – but even then my actions and attitudes are being partially shaped by others. And the absence of people might also influence experience.

## Conclusion

Having acknowledged some of the contextual personal and social factors that may influence viewers' encounters with visual objects, I will now outline some of the many factors perhaps inhering in the object and its setting that may also influence the kind of relationship that may or may not occur between visual objects and their viewers.

## Notes

1 Armstrong (2005) also discusses the importance of loving objects of beauty, of entering into appreciative relationships with them. Norman (2004), discussing objects both beautiful and ugly, points out that hatred is also a form of bonding with them, similar to, and perhaps representative of in some cases, the kind of relationship we might have with people.

2 Gell (1998).

3 Elkins (2001, pp. 71ff., 171ff.). Elkins (2001 pp. 71ff.) denotes this theory, derived from art theorist Bertrand Rouge, 'trance' or 'travelling' theory. He compares it to the spiritual journey of the shaman from the world of everyday reality to another realm with the picture serving as a bridge. For 'abduction' as a response to art works see Silverman (1996, pp. 93ff.). Silverman sees this kind of abduction in relation to pictures as a property of their auratic relationship with their viewers. Seduction and sexual metaphors are often used to explain the attractiveness of pictures and visual objects (cf. Norman 2004, pp. 111ff., Holly 1996).

4 Elkins (2001, pp. 74ff.) movingly discusses his teenage engagement with a picture, Giovanni Bellini's *The Ecstasy of St Francis*. He regrets the loss of his fascination with it which he attributes to his acquisition of art historical knowledge. Art historical knowledge is like cigarette smoking. It is very addictive, but it moves people from experience and engagement to more distant knowledge and understanding (Elkins 2001, p. 107). There is a loss. Most of Elkins' art historian contemporaries are unwilling to discuss their emotional reactions to pictures in public, seeing emotions as redundant and even embarrassing. He (2001, p. 54) points out that if pictures do not evoke emotional engagement and attachment, it is difficult to see what their point is or why it is worth spending time with them. Viewers want to be 'hit' or moved by pictures, not to have them hanging around for intellectual or decorative purposes.

5 Elkins (2001, pp. 43ff.).

6 de Bolla (2001, pp. 2–3) believes that aesthetic experience before art works is in the first instance affective experience evoked by the work. This can move from bodily experiences and mutism, being struck dumb, to rationcination and, eventually, to words.

7 Paul Tillich (1989, pp. 234–5) describes a similar experience – see below, pp. 146–7.

8 For more examples of significant relationships with visible/haptic objects see Norman (2004). Such objects can include tea-pots, cutting-knives, fruit-juicers and a variety of other everyday designed objects.

9 Sharp-eyed readers will have noticed that many of the objects I have mentioned are not just visible objects. Sight is not simply about the use of the eyes, but is rather a multisensorial, multidimensional experience that occurs over time. Haptic vision is not just an interesting idea, it is a phenomenological reality. People relate to the totality of things using the totality of themselves; they are not optically confined.

10 Zwijnenberg (2003, p. 112): 'To investigate the response of the beholder is in general not considered a part of the art historian's enterprise.'

11 See, for example, Pinney (2001), Orsi (1996), Christian (1992).

12 Morgan (1996b, 1998, 1999), Harvey (1995, 1999).

13 Brading (2001), Orsi (1985).

14 Norman (2004, p. 47): 'We like attractive things because of the way they make us feel. And in the realm of feelings, it is just as reasonable to become attached to and love things that are ugly as it is to dislike things that would be called attractive. Emotions reflect our personal experiences, associations and memories.'

15 See, for example, Levin (1988), Foucault (1979).

16 Mitchell (1994).

17 See Vasari (1991).

18 Elkins (2004, pp. 88–9).

19 Newhouse (2005, p. 8) writes: 'Placement has affected the perception of art ... since the first cave paintings. Where an artwork is seen – be it in a cave, a church, a palace, a museum, a commercial gallery, an outdoor space, or a private home – and where it is placed within that chosen space can confer a meaning that is religious, political, decorative, entertaining, moralizing, or educational.' Objects are often presented and considered in books and catalogues as if they had no context or relations to other objects or surrounding space. Light, elevation and isolation give importance to objects.

20 See Duncan (1995), Derlon (2002, p. 120).

21 Morgan (1998).

22 Benjamin (1999, pp. 211ff.).

23 MacCannell (1999, p. 48) argues, 'The work becomes "authentic" only after the first copy is produced. The reproductions *are* the aura, and the ritual ... *derives* from the relationship between the original object and its socially constructed importance.' (Emphasis original.)

24 Orsi (1996). Cf., for example, Hayum (1989), Orsi (1985), Brading (2001).

25 For more discussion of the importance and means used to consecrate objects see, for example, Freedberg (1989, ch. 5) and Gell (1998, ch. 7).

26 See Davis (1997, pp. 36–7).

27 See Horne (1984), Coleman and Elsner (1995), MacCannell (1999).

28 See, for example, Gaskell (2003), MacGregor (2000), Drury (1999).

29 Urry (2002, pp. 10ff.). MacCannell (1999) argues that tourism as a whole is a symbolic and ritual activity comparable to religion. It structures and creates a symbolic

world. Objects and sites are 'consecrated' as attractions within this religion and they are used as structuring nodes for the creation of the symbolic world.

30  Kris and Kurz (1979).

31  There is an iconographically rare and theologically extraordinary small, anonymous picture of Christ ascending the cross, climbing up a ladder in a determined way under his own volition, in the Accademia in Venice. I have never been able to track this picture down in a catalogue or seen a reproduction of it. Most people visiting the gallery completely ignore it because it is verbally and reproductively 'invisible'.

32  See MacCannell (1999, pp. 39ff.), Horne (1984).

33  See Csikszentmihalyi and Rochberg Halton (1981).

34  Norman (2004, pp. 29–30).

35  See, for example, Zeki (1999). Latto (1995) points out that most of the images that have been produced by humans (particularly Western humans) have been representations of other humans, animals or landscapes. Abstractionism is a strange and very modern aberration in this general context. Julius (2000, p. 72) adverts to the ironic experiment by two artists, Komar and Melamid, who asked Americans in 1993 what would be in their most wanted picture and least wanted picture. They most wanted a blue tinted landscape. They repeated this consultation in a number of countries. In all of them, people most wanted blue tinted landscapes and least wanted abstract art images. '"Can you believe it?" they exclaim, "Kenya and Iceland!" "And they both want blue landscapes."'

36  See Read (1951), Spivey (2005).

37  Ramachandran (2003, pp. 46–69) argues speculatively that there are ten universal neuroaesthetic laws of art.

38  Fonagy (2001).

39  It is in the sphere of design rather than high art that psychodynamic facts have been most consciously attended to in attempting to create relationships between visual objects and people. The Italian designer, Alberto Alessi, has been extensively influenced by the thought of Franco Fornari, who emphasizes the importance of emotions, and of D. W. Winnicott, who points up the need for toys and other objects of play that allow people to discover the happiness and security of childhood. '"In our deepest beings we respond to, and have an urgent need for childish objects," says Alessi. "Apparently uncomplicated, these kinds of objects give us pleasure and reassurance. Modernism temporarily purged us of these objects of enjoyment, but we are now ready for their return"' (Sweet 1998, p. 13).

40  Bollas (1987, p. 16).

41  'The aesthetic experience is an existential recollection of the time when communicating took place primarily through this illusion of deep rapport of subject and object. Being-with, as a form of dialogue, enabled the baby's adequate processing of his existence prior to his ability to process it through thought' (Bollas 1987, p. 32).

42  Bollas (1987, pp. 16–17).

43  Walker Bynum (2002).

44  Elkins (2001, p. 140).

45  Elkins (2001, p. 142): 'Noise, crowds, bright lights: it's a recipe for tear-lessness.'

# 6

# Relating to Visual Artefacts 2:
# Factors Inherent in Objects

If the poet . . . can inflame men with love . . . the painter has the power to do the same, and to an even greater degree, in that he can place in front of the lover the true likeness of that which is beloved, often making him kiss and speak to it . . . So much greater is the power of a painting over a man's mind that he may be enchanted and enraptured by a painting that does not represent any living woman.

Leonard da Vinci, *The Science of Art*

Monet makes me feel anxious. You may not agree that some of Monet's marks imply the tension I sense in them, but you cannot disagree that the marks themselves are tense . . . Emotions cannot be excluded from our responses to paint: these thoughts all happen too far from words to be something we can control. Substances occupy the body and the mind inextricably.

James Elkins, *What Painting Is*

## Introduction

For most of us, much of the time, relationships with objects, like relationships with people, may feel as though they are largely determined by the object itself. We do not think about the antecedent factors that bear upon us and prejudice our seeing – they are the 'water' we 'swim' in. Instead, we are likely to attribute our reactions to the qualities that inhere in objects, so 'they' make us feel uneasy, happy, sad, or whatever. We are probably not even conscious at all of the visual relationships that we have with many things around us. However, it is possible to suggest some factors that may come into play from objects themselves that may influence our relations with them, making them either sticky and easy to become entangled with, or repellent, and difficult to relate to.

## Physical attributes

Perhaps the place to begin is with an object's most obvious physical attributes – size, shape, line, colour, material of manufacture, texture, movement and dimensionality (two dimensions, as in a picture, or three, as in sculpture and architecture). These things are often immediately noticed about an object before it is more closely inspected. They fundamentally affect the way in which particular people may be able to relate to it.

*Size* is significant in helping people orient to an object. Large objects, in being overwhelming, may arouse feelings of awe such as those that used to be associated with the sublime.[1] However, tiny, intricate objects can be equally fascinating and demanding in their delicacy. Compare here, for example, the Antonello di Messina's tiny panel painting, *St Jerome in his Study*, in the London National Gallery, with Titian's gigantic *Assumption of the Virgin* in the Frari in Venice. Both images are immediately engaging, but they lie at opposite ends of the scale of grandiosity.

If an object is about the same size as a human being, capable of being carried or handled without extra effort, it may not particularly impress itself upon a viewer. However, both gigantic and miniature objects, in exaggerating normal parameters of size, may attract attention, causing reactions of attraction or repugnance.

Miniaturism invites very close attention. It fascinates because it metaphorically represents containment, hiddenness, subjectivity and inner space.[2] It is often associated with beauty. A very small object may fascinate because of the care and patience needed in looking at it and the skill required in its creation.[3]

Gigantic objects may equally impress and engage because of their signification of the super-human, the public, the natural and the open. They may hold the attention of the viewer because it is difficult to get a complete vision of what is there to be seen.

The *shape* of an object may also be significant for viewers. Humans may be predisposed to find certain shapes, such as symmetrical, or round and smooth objects, very pleasurable and attractive. Human-sized and human-shaped objects are also likely to be of interest. By contrast, jagged, angular, inconsistent and non-representational shapes may not be easy to relate to; many people find it very difficult to relate to abstract art. However, for some, the familiar and reassuring in terms of shape may be boring; they may be more drawn to more stimulating, irregular and non-symmetrical objects. Some people cannot bear square pictures, for example. Some of the reaction elicited by shapes is likely to be conditioned by culture. For example, in non-Western cultures, unconditioned by Western geometrical conventions, there might be an aversion to straight as opposed to curved lines in architecture and representation.[4]

*Colours* and *brightness* may also have an important effect on viewers. Generally, human beings seem predisposed to like primary colours that are quite bright and they enjoy the sense that things shine and have lustre.[5] It has been observed that 'blue is the West's favourite colour, far surpassing the others', and it has become increasingly popular since the thirteenth century.[6] However, here, too, culture plays a part. Rembrandt's very dark pictures in subdued tones, often lit from only one small light source, often seem just as attractive to people as the bright palette of the Impressionists like Monet. Education and taste come into the evaluation of whether the light and bright, or gloomy and dark hued, are highly esteemed. The social meaning and practice of colouration and hue changes considerably in different cultures and places.[7]

The *material* from which an object is made is important in conditioning responses. Precious materials like gold and jewels give an object extra interest because they are rare and unusual, as well as lustrous. Certain types of material like oil paint (widely used from the Renaissance onwards), and blue made from lapis lazuli (used before the Renaissance and the widespread use of oils), have also been used to signal the importance of particular objects and to attract viewers' attention and respect.[8] An oil painting surrounded with a gold frame is more likely to attract attention than a simple pencil drawing plainly framed in wood.

*Texture* also affects viewers' responses to objects. This is an under-researched area, but many people seem to have a predilection for touching significant objects that they 'like the look of'. Whether the object appears to be smooth or rough, lapidary or furry, wet or dry, cold or warm, metallic or skin-like, texture is likely to impact upon the viewer. Very smooth objects may be attractive, as may those that have a very rough, unfinished surface. Both of these features can be found in the sculptures of Michelangelo or Rodin, and they are part of what draws viewers into relationship with the object.

I have often been surprised by the actual textural *feel* of visual objects – smooth marble and bronze look cold, but they are often as warm as the surrounding air, while the velvety looking surface of a rusting public statue can be rough and chilly. Chased silver or gold looks rough but when touched feels perfectly flat. These sensual consonances and dissonances can become an important part of creating relationships between humans and visual artefacts. The *tactile availability* of an object is a very important aspect of its meaning and significance for humans.[9] It can make an object more interesting and attractive, but it might also prove repellent, limiting the affective relationship that might develop.

Living beings move and *movement* is an important sign of life. If objects are entirely inert and make or portray no movement, they are likely to be of less interest than objects that do. The attribution of life-like features to objects substantially increases the possibilities of relationship with them. In everyday life, objects with moving parts are picked up and fiddled with. In museums, if there are buttons that make things move, people quickly find and operate them. In art, a major Renaissance achievement was the rediscovery of the *contrapposto* gesture whereby one leg of a statue or figure was slightly bent behind the other. This created a slight corkscrew effect for the body portrayed so that it seemed to be alive and moving. In the case of moving screens on computers and films, this kind of relationship can become very intimate indeed as people identify with the artificially produced moving images.

*Dimensionality* is another aspect of objects that affects the kinds of relationships that they may enter into with humans. Humans experience depth as well as height and width. If objects are, or appear to be, three dimensional, this accords more closely with human perceptions of relevance and significance. Thus perspectival pictures or sculptures may be more interesting than those that are entirely flat surfaced. Perhaps this is why viewers have been slow to engage with and enjoy pictures like those of Mark Rothko and other abstract artists who emphasize the surface of paintings rather than attempting to portray the illusion of depth. People are happier to engage with modern computer screens providing the illusion of depth than with older word-processors that presented words on an apparently totally flat surface.

All the physical characteristics of objects that I have described here depend on human reaction to have any significance at all. In many ways, they are visceral factors; they have an immediate impact on the emotions which bears upon initial attraction and judgement about the object.[10] This instant, visceral, emotional response may later be modified in relationship with the object as people come to consider its context, use, functioning and its rationale.[11] The main thing to note here is that the characteristics blend together to provide a total visual effect; they are not found in isolation from each other. There is much scope for individual and societal variation in what might appear to be attractive or alluring. However, it seems likely that all of these factors available on first acquaintance with an object can, and do, pertain to the kinds of relationships which might then ensue.

## Contextual presentation

An important factor bearing upon the visual perception of an object is its contextual presentation, that is its setting and display.[12] Objects can be displayed in settings which enhance their apparent meaning and value such as grottos, churches or art galleries. In this context, they might be displayed on their own or mixed in with other artefacts. They may be positioned above or below the viewer, or at the same level. Some may be accessible and within arm's reach, while others may be distant and perhaps separated by some kind of barrier – ropes, water, glass, for example. They might be brightly illuminated by directed lighting sources, barely discernible amidst flickering candles, situated in shadows, or simply lit by ambient daylight. Some objects may be viewed from all angles and be totally available to sight, while others are hidden or partially veiled by clothes, flowers, coverings or decorations (veiling being a way of heightening anticipation and a sense of mystery).

Display and presentation give important messages to viewers and alter their responses. The quiet, dimly-lit, curtained room within which the Leonardo cartoon, *The Virgin Mary, the Christ, St Anne and St John the Baptist,* is displayed in the National Gallery in London, creates a sense of reverent gloom which silences viewers and perhaps leads them to have an anticipatory sense of awe and mystery at what they are going to see. This contrasts with the setting of Laurence Broderick's *The Bronze Bull* in the Birmingham Bullring which is visible in the open public square at all hours (see Plate 4). The bull evokes no sense of mystery whatsoever, though it does evoke a sense of physical power.

Often, setting and display may have more impact on the viewer than the object itself. St Francis' tomb in the basilica at Assisi is plain and visually rather uninteresting, situated in a low-light subterranean chapel – but the way towards it is lined with wonderful frescos that create a sense of anticipation. In this kind of context, image and setting blend together to create an emotional impact which influences the personal impact and relationship that a viewer might have with an object. Many finely made objects may be ignored or despised because they are not singled out for special presentation and display.

All of this highlights the importance of the relationships of objects with their settings and surrounding objects. Often, it is the juxtaposition and relationship of a number of objects with others in an overall pattern that together produces an impression on the viewer. Thus it is cumulative effect, not an individual object, that constitutes the grounds of attraction and potential relationship. I am thinking here of some of Antony Gormley's displays of multiple figures in particular visible contexts, but I might equally talk about the juxtaposition of ornaments and photographs on the top of a TV, or a mantelpiece, in a domestic setting. Objects modify the significance of other visible appearances in their vicinity.

## Technical factors

A range of factors that may draw people into relationship with images are those associated with its technical production and execution. These include aspects such as ingenuity, craftspersonship, technical competence and decorative features. For example, the impression of lustre and shininess produced without using gold in paintings, producing a sense of depth by the use of perspective, or the minute working of a surface to cover it with complex patterns, as in medieval Celtic hand-written books. To produce this kind of fascination, built upon technical competence and execution, the skill needed to produce a visual artefact must be beyond the competence of viewers, but not so far beyond that they cannot imagine being able to do it themselves.[13] Thus the complexity of the unique knotted patterns woven in fishermen's sweaters by their wives is a source of fascination and attachment. The same principle applies to all artistic thaumaturgy such as magic or acting upon the stage. People can see that it is not inhuman or miraculous. However, it displays a level of competence and ingenuity that is beyond them, so they can marvel at it. This fascination draws them into closer relationship with the object or performance.

Decoration is often taken to be rather an inferior feature of visual objects – optional flummery. However, decoration is 'intrinsically functional or else its presence would be inexplicable' (Gell 1998, p. 74). Complex patterns and details induce a sense of unfinished fascination with objects that ensures continuity of interest and relationship, making objects 'sticky' for the human gaze – as in the maze patterns in Celtic objects. They help to individualize and personalize objects, making similar things very different and distinct to their users and owners. By becoming involved in decorative patterns, people become attached to objects and more closely identified with them. However, intricate patterning sits ill with the minimalist temperament of modernity, which focuses upon line and shape rather than decoration; some patterning may be annoying rather than attractive to the contemporary gaze.

## Incompleteness, defacement and mutilation

Contrary, but equally powerful, factors that can engage the viewer are those of incompleteness, defacement and mutilation.

The complete image, perfect in every aspect and detail of representation, can make people stop and stare. They marvel at the detail and subtlety of a doll's house, for example, where everything looks real, and no feature has been omitted. However, incomplete images and objects have their own kind of charisma. Consider the unfinished statues of Michelangelo, or the suggestions of faces and other objects in many artists' drawings that somehow hook the viewer into a kind of speculative, imaginative relationship in which they try mentally to complete what is there. If the psychoanalysts are right in believing that visible art objects figure the void, then the presentation of nothingness, absence, or incompleteness acts as a lure.[14] A certain openness can be more attractive and evoke attentive desire more successfully than complete representation. Incompleteness, shadows, darkness and hiddenness in an object create a kind of space which the human viewer can imaginatively inhabit. In making viewers work hard in this way, images and objects create a space in the human mind and sensorium that engenders attachment. To pursue this thought haptically, space and hiddenness give viewers more to hold on to, and in working to grasp, they are grasped.

Defacement and mutilation, the diminishment, dismemberment, desecration and destruction of images can also create fascination and pulling power. In modern secularized society, people have little experience of the power of the sacred. However, the experience of defacement and desecration of images can unleash an enormous, uncanny power of shock and fascination:

> When the human body, a nation's flag, money, or a public statue is defaced, a strange surplus of negative energy is likely to be aroused within the defaced thing itself. It is now in a state of desecration, the closest many of us are going to get to the sacred in the modern world. (Taussig 1999, p. 1)

People who might not be interested in an image that is unmutilated can become fascinated by it when it is defaced. The Latin word *sacer*, from which 'sacred' derives, means both holy and accursed. The mutilation or desecration of some objects can seem to liberate some kind of concealed power or charisma from an object.[15] The mechanisms whereby this power becomes manifest are obscure. However, phenomenologically, this seems to be an accurate observation, at least sometimes.

> Defacement works on objects the way that jokes work on language, bringing out their inherent magic, nowhere more so than when those objects have become routinized and social, like money or the nation's flag . . . Defacement of such social things, however, brings a very angry God out of hiding . . . (Taussig 1999, p. 5)

This kind of desecration, whether of sacred or secular objects, may be one of the ways in which people become powerfully engaged by objects.

I find it difficult to look on the face of some Buddhist statues that have been mutilated and injured by the bullets of the iconoclastic Taleban in Afghanistan. Mysteriously, however, this kind of mutilation has made these images more emotionally sticky for me, more personlike, and more in need of my compassion. The defaced *Rokeby Venus* in the London National Gallery is in some ways a more moving work than it was before it was attacked with a knife by a suffragette.[16] Demonstrating the vulnerability of images, their human-like quality of being capable of being injured or destroyed rather than existing beyond life, death and history, can make them 'more real' (Taussig 1999, p. 54). Something can be added to a visual object by its diminishment.

## Content and representation

Hitherto I have not discussed the importance of actual content in discussing the relational potential of visible objects. It might be assumed that the most important, attractive aspects of visual objects, particularly art objects, are their subject matter and content.[17]

Humans are hard-wired to be very much aware of other human-like forms and faces and so our eyes are drawn to objects that depict these. Faces, in particular, are of enormous interest as they are a main site of communication, understanding and relationship from our infancy onwards.[18] We can, perhaps, each distinguish and remember up to one million faces; we are, then, instinctively drawn to depictions of faces, especially those that appear to be looking at us. Hence the famous quip about a painting being good if the eyes of the subject follow you around the room. Gaze and mutual gaze are an important part of interpersonal engagement. Thus many devotional and art images have as their focus the eyes of the figure represented; devotees and viewers become engaged in a kind of mutual gaze and communication which can feel very real indeed.[19]

Human and animal figures are important for human survival and flourishing, as are landscapes. So these subjects also have power to draw and retain attention in depictions and objects. Even if not directly depicted, humans may find living forms and personalities in things, so that 'there are penguins in our water jugs, and stout and self important persons in our kettles, graceful deer in our desks and oxen in our dining room tables' (de Botton 2006, p. 84). A form that much commends itself to humans is the dendric. Dendric forms are those that look like trees. They are ubiquitous throughout the world in lungs, blood vessels, road maps, family trees, organizational charts and elsewhere. They are to be found in religion and science, as well as in forests. It seems that humans have a particular affinity with dendric shapes, with their close affinity to the human shape (consider the 'trunk' of the human body) and to nature.[20]

The particular faces, figures and landscapes depicted and represented may also have significant resonances for viewers. Thus images of familiar or well-known figures like the Queen, the Virgin Mary, family members, or pets, may be a particular draw for some viewers. More abstract and less animate figures and representations, on the other hand, may act to deflect our gaze.

The elements of composition in a picture or sculpture help to gain and retain attention, too. As with the initial assessment of the object from a distance, style, colour, shape, texture, composition, symmetry, line, shade and light may all influence feelings about an image, helping to make it an eye-trap or repelling the gaze. Naturalistic and realist styles, for example, may be more assimilable and attractive than more symbolic or abstract ones. Here again, there is likely to be much variation of response between individuals and within different cultures.

A further important factor is the 'magic of mimesis'. Artistic mimesis, the copying and representation of objects in words or images, worried Plato who saw it as a powerful fraudulence that might deceive people. He was not the last thinker to note the power and fascination that mimetic representation engenders. Copying, then representing, or even representing by apparently copying something that does not have a 'real' material prototype (for example, a non-existent monster), seems to have within it a kind of magical power that is not entirely explicable.[21]

Mimesis allows humans to gain power over the thing portrayed, the Other. Something of the prototype, real or imagined, then inheres in the visual reproduction. It is attached to it in a quasi-material, tactile way which is perceived by the eye, 'an organ of tactility', on the plane where the object world and the visual copy merge (Taussig 1993, p. 35). Gaze grasps where touch falters. So there is a kind of tactile knowing of embodied knowledge whereby we get hold of an object visually by way of its reproduction. Mimetic reproduction is thus one of the factors that can endow objects with a living, animate quality to which human beings can personally relate.

All of this takes place on the edges of sensual seeing, imagination and the unconscious, enhancing the liminal and mysterious power of reproduction and reproductions:

> To ponder mimesis is to become sooner of later caught . . . in sticky webs of copy and contact, image and bodily involvement of the perceiver in the image, a complexity we too easily elide as nonmysterious with our facile use of terms such as identification, representation, expression, and so forth . . . (Taussig 1993, p. 21)

It is not appropriate to explore in depth the nature and effects of mimesis and representation here.[22] But it is important to note the continuing power and fascination of mimesis and its products, and the emotional impact that it has on viewers. Images that imitate or copy things can participate in enormous power. This is particularly so with images of religious or other important figures, taken to have some continuing connection with an invisible original.[23] Mimetic representations of individuals or phenomena can also excite extreme emotions of real attachment, liking and loathing. The subjects of photographs can feel that it is 'them' in the picture. If a picture or photo is criticized or mutilated, they can feel personally hurt (not so very far from the volt magic of sticking pins into wax images to injure people). It is not surprising that jilted lovers tear up the photographs of the erstwhile beloved. Nor is it accidental that the statues of dictators are erected to assert their real presence and destroyed with real passion when they are deposed. At a less personal level, Crick and Watson's double helix model of DNA, the *Mona Lisa* of scientific images, appears to place the powers of nature within our grasp in some sense (Kemp 2003).

Mimetic representation, then, 'catches' the eye and dynamizes relationships with visual objects. It is not surprising that artists and other technicians of the mimetic are regarded as having magical or thaumaturgic powers, albeit that these may now be levelled to some vague ideas of inspiration or imaginative ability.[24]

## Plenitude and emptiness

It may be that the images that have most power to evoke extreme human responses are those that contain either too much or too little.[25] Images characterized by plenitude, like the Sistine Chapel ceiling, are overwhelming. Empty or lonely images like those of the nineteenth-century painter Caspar Friedrich appear to be 'hungry'. They evoke a sense of void and painful absence. In either case, personal boundaries are ruptured; viewers are emotionally overcome and carried into the world of the picture. Elkins ascribes the power of Rothko's pictures to move people to their unique combination of both overwhelming and sucking out viewers with a mixture of presence and absence.

The play of overwhelming presence and absence may be thought to be based upon the idea of the absent and present divine. God is the unthought, unspoken known that underwrites the power of images. In this sense, art images are significant because they appeal to a fundamental sense of mystery. Within the secular world of art, this kind of thinking is deeply alien. However, perhaps the dry, ironic art of the modern Western world is tacitly nostalgic for the religious world that was perhaps the real source of image-making.[26] Images thus help to make divine grace known and present – but they also point to the deep mystery and unknowability of the ground of being. This may be why they evoke deep feelings of joy, awe and despair.

## Aesthetic factors

It is perhaps reasonable to assume that the main reason that we are likely to find objects attractive and to enter into relations with them is because they are basically beautiful and well crafted. People talk of the power of beauty to move and engage viewers, to fill them with longing and desire.

Beauty may be an important component in attracting and forging relationships between viewers and visual objects. However, many of the important visual relationships that people have with objects are not based on aesthetic superiority or appreciation. Most people probably do not value the pictures and other objects in their homes primarily for their aesthetic merits or beauty, but for their associations with memories or people.[27] Very few people actually consciously looked at visually available objects for their visual content or beauty. Indeed, people can love ugly objects as much as beautiful ones.[28] Often, people's most precious visible objects, like my toby jug, wholly lack aesthetic merit, but their relational significance remains undiminished.

Beauty is an elusive category. Plato and others believed it was a property that inhered in objects and could be clearly identified by viewers. Thus, the eighteenth-century artist Hogarth argued that a curve was the most beautiful shape imaginable because it had elements of continuity and change that would infallibly excite the admiration of viewers.[29] This view was disputed by those like Kant who argued that beauty was strictly subjectively perceived by the beholder, while simultaneously holding that judgements of beauty were universal and necessary.[30] A middle way suggests that there may be a degree of agreement about what is beautiful among viewers, allowing both objectivity and subjectivity to come into the discussion. However, in a pluralistic, multi-cultural, globalized world, the wide range of views and practices concerning what is deemed to be beautiful threatens even this middle view. In some cultures, for example, fat people are regarded as beautiful, while the opposite is true in contemporary Western society. While the symmetry, order and proportion associated with classical architecture is often thought desirable, this style is not beautiful in all settings, and it can be oppressive. Hence the revolt of the architect Gaudi and others in favour of naturalistic curves – deemed to be beautiful by some while condemned by others as hideous.

If there are as many different styles of beauty as there are styles of human happiness, then it is difficult to evaluate the content and effects of beauty for any one person or group of people.[31] Even where an object may widely be recognized to be beautiful, it can fail to engage viewers who may prefer to gaze upon their small plastic souvenir statues of the Eiffel Tower or reproductions of sentimental pictures of dogs.[32]

Beauty and aesthetics can contribute to some visual relationships, but they are not essential for strong relationships to occur. Indeed, it can be argued that beauty in the modern world has become a rather weak, non-specific category which denotes innocuous, domesticated and non-threatening pleasantness rather than implying huge impact upon the viewer.[33] When people cannot think of anything else to say about an object they vaguely like, they describe it as 'beautiful'.

## Familiarity/unfamiliarity

For some people, familiarity with an image, for example, a common devotional object such as a crucifix or an image like the *Mona Lisa*, deepens their relationship with it. However, for others, familiarity means that it simply becomes part of the background of their visual relational lives, even boring and tedious. Similarly, if an image is only glimpsed once or very occasionally, this may have an unforgettable, momentary impact on a viewer, but it can also mean that they fail to form a relationship with the object due to lack of familiarity. They might even be overwhelmed or frightened by its strangeness, so unable to assimilate or take it in.

Some Zen-influenced designers advocate only permitting indirect glimpses of beautiful views in order to increase fascination and appreciation.[34] This makes sense of one aspect of human viewing, the propensity to be intrigued by the unfamiliar and the wholly, or partially, withheld.[35] This tendency perhaps reaches its logical end in the fascination that people have for some images that have actually disappeared. Thus when the *Mona Lisa* was stolen from the Louvre in the early part of the last century, more people went to see the space where it had hung than had ever seen the picture itself. Similarly, when the mutilated statue *Phil and Liz naked down by the lake* was finally removed from its site in Canberra in 1995, people came to stare at the place where the (in)famous work had been.[36] It seems that visual images can actually attain more charisma and value by being partly or even completely unavailable to the sight.

That said, however, it also needs to be recognized that another, equally important, aspect of relationship with visual images is the need for familiarity and presence. Without the knowledge and familiarity of the picture built up over years and through a variety of media reproductions, the loss of the *Mona Lisa* might have inspired little interest. Many images are stolen and otherwise destroyed every day (think of the number of photographs in newspapers that are routinely pulped after only one cursory glance), but mostly this is ignored. It is only certain familiar images that can attract this kind of feeling of the importance of presence in absence.

Familiarity and novelty, availability and restriction, presence and absence all potentially affect relations with visual objects.

## Semiotic factors

Visual images, like words, can be understood as representational, language-like, symbolic media.[37] They are in large part a form of human communication of meaning.

Much of the satisfaction of viewing visual objects probably comes from a sense of assimilation of meaning, although it may not be possible to articulate this linguistically.[38] Thus visible objects that appear to communicate meaning of some kind, even if this is symbolic or otherwise coded, are likely to be of particular interest to viewers. Conversely, images that appear to communicate no pattern or meaning, or whose meaning is abstract and difficult to appreciate, are more likely to be ignored.

Some images, like medieval stained-glass windows, are created for the communication of meaning, even for the conveying of information. Others are less clear and more ambiguous. What is the meaning, for example, of Jackson Pollock's many abstract paintings?

A clear semiotic factor that affects potential relationships with objects is the use of written and spoken words in and around objects. Labels tell people what they are looking at in art galleries. Many objects also contain words within them, coming out of people's mouths, written on architectural features, or in other places. Hieronymous Bosch includes on one of his pictures, *The Seven Deadly Sins*, surrounding a staring eye-ball that represents the all-seeing and judgemental eye of God, the words, 'Beware, Beware, God is watching'. These words actually help to make explicit the main meaning of the image and to reduce the polysemic possibilities that might be present. In other examples, for instance, Blake's use of images alongside words, verbal and visual may live in tension, contradiction, or perpetual dialectic, enriching the fascination of a particular visual phenomenon.

An interesting example of the power of words to animate and increase the significance of objects is to be found in the stone created to celebrate the millennium in Carlisle. A granite stone was carved by a sculptor with an ancient curse, then placed in a prominent place in the city. In 2005, representations were made to have the stone removed because it was believed to be responsible for several floods, an outbreak of foot and mouth disease, and the failure of the city's football team! This example of belief in animating power of words in objects that then produce real effects demonstrates continuing human vulnerability to the influence of visual objects multiplied by the magic of words. Humans are suckers for the power of words – we even use the word 'spell' to describe our use of them, perpetuating the mystical properties of these marks on pages and things.[39] Words, within, and in interaction with, visual objects, have an exponential explanatory and amplificatory effect on the significance of the latter.

## Indexical factors

Images are full of human meanings, intentions, emotions and agency because they have been created intentionally by human beings. This is a key factor in making them personlike, so that it is possible to relate to objects in some ways like other human beings.

The endowment of objects with meaning, intention, agency and other personlike aspects that can then be recognized and responded to by human viewers is denoted 'indexicality' by anthropologists.[40] An object or phenomenon indexes a personal creator by embodying within itself some of the meanings, purposes and intentions of its originator. It becomes 'a congealed residue of performance and agency in object form, through which access to other persons can be attained, and via which their agency can be created' (Gell 1998, p. 68).

An artefact can become a kind of secondary agent, an extension of the person who originated it, reflecting some of the characteristics of that person's original acts and intentions. Indexical objects of this kind can include plays where actors re-enact and realize the intentions of authors so becoming an index of authorial meaning and intent, statues which represent and extend the lives and intentions of the people who commissioned them, or any other kind of artefact. Persons, too, can become indices of the divine if they are possessed by transcendent forces and behave according to their will and purpose. Thus a spirit-filled devotee who dances, or walks through coals of fire, embodying the divinity possessing them, becomes an index of that divinity.[41]

The more human meaning, intention and purpose an object is perceived to contain, the more personlike and complex it will appear, and the more likely people are to relate to it in a personal way. Thus portraits of human beings by human artists can be very powerful because they not only index the subjects who commissioned them, but also the artist who painted them.[42] Even the stick men children draw have some of this kind of indexical power of agency within them. Humans have often seen the created natural order as indexing the intentions, power and person of the divine, being predisposed to find patterns of meaning and purpose throughout the universe.[43] Pattern and apparent purpose indexes person. So a visible artefact easily evidences personal traces, albeit that the work itself is made of inanimate matter and its creator may be absent. People cheat death and extend their influence beyond it by creating indexical objects such as tombs, wills and institutions, that act as secondary agents, perpetuating their actions and intentions.

In the context of the indexicality of images, emotional expressiveness should also be mentioned. One reason that people endeavour to see particular images, and resonate with them, is that they appear to be charged with, and to communicate, emotional energy. This often evokes an affective reaction in the viewer. It is one of the most attractive and 'sticky' aspects of images, producing an effect of immediacy and communication whatever the actual content of an image or visual object. The viewer picks up the indexed emotional intentions and expressions of the object's creator. This is part of the satisfaction that comes from interacting with visual objects. Some objects have more complex emotions indexed within them than others. However, this aspect of the 'personality' of objects is in principle available in all artefacts as their viewers and handlers get to know them.[44] Indeed, without some kind of emotional content it may be difficult to form full and satisfying relationships with objects.

Created images and artefacts can be full of meaning, emotion and intention because they are created by human beings. They can be seen as indexing the person and agency of those who created them, attaining a kind of semi-autonomous secondary agency of their own.

Anthropologists argue that we find meaningful relationships with objects because other human beings have put meaning and significance there in the first place. However, this reductionist explanation would not necessarily be acceptable to viewers themselves. They might argue that the power of images comes from their actually being possessed or touched by a transcendent force. Thus, a statue or object really is connected to another non-human world or inhabited by a transcendent being, spirit, or god. This is the kind of argument that might be made for icons within Eastern Orthodox Christianity.[45] They are not regarded as human creations that simply index a general human perception of divine providence; they are directly connected to, and become a gateway to, the heavenly, non-human world. If an image really does embody a divine spirit, or index the person and will of a transcendent reality, or god, viewers will feel compelled into personal response and relationship with it; this might be characterized by awe and fear, as much as by love and intimacy.[46]

This concludes my survey of just some of the varied factors that might inhere in and around visual objects when they are viewed. These range from physical and stylistic factors to indexicality and the animation of images by some kind of living spirit. Different factors may come into play with different images seen by different viewers at particular times and places. In principle, all of them may bear upon the kinds of experiences and relationships that viewers may have with visual objects, as do the antecedent and contextual factors considered earlier.

## Seeing as a relational activity

Complex relations come into play among the factors in each group I identified, and between each group. For example, I might on the whole not relate easily to very large objects, but I might very much resonate to human figures and faces. So I might be prepared to enter into a relationship with a gargantuan human figure in a way that I would not be if the huge object were simply abstract in shape and pattern. This complexity is compounded by the nature, expectations and situation of the viewer.

In any particular perceptual context, it is difficult to isolate the key factors that create or militate against significant relationship with a particular visual image. Very few of us, for example, can really explain precisely why a particular object had such a profound impact upon us when we saw it in a particular context at a specific time, or why it left us feeling indifferent when next we saw it.

The intersensorial interplay of factors impinging upon the creation of relations with visual objects is perhaps one of the things that makes them personlike. Critics like Holly (1996) write of the play between viewer and object, a dance-like movement of continually evolving perspective and interpretation that allows relationships to evolve. Like the people we meet, visual objects change their meanings and significances constantly. This instability and change may itself help images to become lively eye-traps that seduce viewers into inarticulate, but important, relationships. Arguably, if this kind of dynamic play does not occur, the object dies or becomes invisible to the sight of the viewer. Only if it continues to engender living and changing responses does the image abduct or hail the viewer, enter their world, and have some transformative effect. Like Keats' Grecian urn, the object may not move or behave entirely like an animate object, but it can still contain and engender movement, changing in relation to persons who come within its range and intersect with its personlike indexicality and other features. Dynamism could thus be a main part of the stickiness of objects that excites human emotions and entangles people with them. So just as we look at visual objects, there is a sense in which they look back at us – they keep an eye on us and we can sense their presence. All of which reinforces the case for thinking of at least some visual objects as more like people than inanimate things.

144

David Carrier argues that in the case of art works deliberately intended to attract and engage the viewer, there are at least four possible basic relationships. First, the spectator can simply stand before the work and behold it in an objective, non-involved way as a kind of Cartesian viewer. Second, a more mutual relationship can occur in which the spectator sees the work and allows him- or herself to be looked at by the work. Beyond this, third, the spectator can become absorbed into the work. Finally, the work elides the spectator's presence so there is no recognition of the spectator or their separate gaze.[47] In all three of the later possible relationships, a more personal, mutual, dynamic, socio-political perspective on relating to visual objects than that of one-way detached gaze is posited. This better reflects the active, involved nature of relating to visual objects which has been the subject of this chapter.

Some visual images survive for many centuries. Like the humans who created them, visual images can be both curiously strong and resistant, surviving to create many new relationships while at the same time being vulnerable to change and decay – a painting can be shredded with a knife in a few moments.[48] An image might last for millennia, or only a couple of days. Whatever their transience, fortitude or longevity, some artefacts have a well-developed, if ill-understood, capacity to create important relations with people. This capacity needs to be both acknowledged and much better analysed.

This speculative discussion about factors that may affect relationships with visual artefacts has leant heavily upon insights and examples from art-like objects. Discussions about art objects or well-known devotional objects may collude with the marginalization of the important everyday relationships people have with the visual objects of all kinds. These are of primary and continuing importance. Indeed, it can be argued that in many ways our lives depend upon appropriate affective relationships with common, everyday visual artefacts. If these are not made, then our lives may be substantially impoverished. They may even be at risk.

A dramatic example of the life-threatening and life-enhancing potential of visual relationships in everyday life is provided by motorcycle crash-helmets. The first crash-helmets were developed in the 1940s by doctors and scientists. However, the helmets were widely rejected by riders, being thought unattractive and cumbersome. It was only when industrial designers became involved in reconceiving and remodelling helmets that they began to be acceptable to riders, especially the young men who were most likely to have accidents. Now helmets are very carefully designed not only to protect people's heads, but also to look good, to attract their attention and affective assent. Good design that promotes visual affectivity and attachment to objects has, in this instance, helped to save thousands of young lives.

This awareness of the importance of creating potential visual affectivity with objects is increasingly important to producers, advertisers and designers (Norman 2004). If things look ugly or unattractive, people will not buy or use them. Norman asserts that 'attractive things work better':

> Shape and form matter. The physical feel and texture of the materials matter. Heft matters. Visceral design is all about immediate emotional impact. It has to feel good, look good. Sensuality and sexuality play roles . . . otherwise highly rated products may be turned down if they do not appeal to the aesthetic sense of the potential buyer. (Norman 2004, p. 69)

It is not just first impression that creates an affective relationship with an object, nor is it the case that simple, brightly coloured objects are the only ones that are intriguing and attractive for viewers. People build up a relationship through presence and usage and may become increasingly fond of an object's visual appearance, or indeed indifferent to it. However, the importance of appearance and establishing a strong initial visual relationship cannot be underestimated.

## Conclusion

People can, and do, enter into significant, emotionally charged relationships with visual objects. I have focused here on relationships with visual objects that are designed to attract attention to themselves, such as art works, and have attempted to draw out some of the factors that might impinge upon the emergence of such relationships. I have identified a large number of factors, antecedent, contextual, and inherent, that might bear upon whether or not people enter into significant relationships with visible things. These factors are complex, multisensorial, dynamic, and hard to distinguish analytically; they inhere in viewers, in objects, and in the relational space between them.

Even with awareness of some of the factors identified above, it is very difficult to predict how different elements will react together for any individual so that they might have some kind of significant relationship with a visible image or artefact.

For example, the theologian, Paul Tillich, had the experience of being physically shaken by Sandro Botticelli's *The Madonna with Singing*

*Angels* when he saw it in Berlin after several years of ministering in the trenches of World War One. This moment affected Tillich's whole life, giving him 'the keys for the interpretation of human existence', as well as 'vital joy and spiritual truth' (Tillich 1989, pp. 234–5). Tillich did not regard this artistic and aesthetic experience as equivalent to being grasped by the power of the divine presence. However, he argued that 'there is an analogy between revelation and what I felt'. It went beyond encounters with everyday reality to open up depths 'experienced in no other way'.

What was it that produced this reaction? Was it the culturally engendered expectations about seeing Renaissance masterpieces transmitted through narrative that he had internalized? Perhaps seeing the image in the setting of a culturally sacralized place such as an art gallery triggered his response, or, maybe, the charisma of being in the presence of a cultural artefact deemed to be uplifting.

The picture was a religious one, created and consecrated to aid devotion. Was that what gave it its power? Or was it the genius of its painter? Maybe it was the bright colours, the sweet faces of the people in it with their direct and enticing gaze, or the symmetry and attractiveness of the figures in the picture, that helped Tillich engage with it. Or perhaps the picture evoked a sense of presence, or absence, that was overwhelming for him after his traumatic experience in the trenches.

It is likely that Tillich's mood affected him, and his account of the incident suggests that he was on his own. Perhaps the physical attributes of the picture – its being round, bright, deeply coloured, smoothly textured, and embodying movement in its subjects – was what enabled this object to grab him. Maybe it was the magic of mimesis that reached across to Tillich as he encountered some of the power that came from Botticelli's capacity to make life-like things in the material world. It may be that it was the fact that he was familiar with it from seeing it reproduced in the magazines he had studied in the trenches by lamplight that allowed him to be touched. But equally, it may have been seeing a familiar object in an unfamiliar setting that breached his personal boundaries. Tillich himself thought he was moved aesthetically by beauty analogous with divine revelation, although he admitted that it was not the most beautiful picture in the gallery at the time. But, who knows, perhaps the power of the picture came from divine power and revelation itself?

We simply do not know exactly why Tillich was abducted and shaken by this particular artefact. Nor did Tillich, or he might well have tried to replicate the experience. Similarly, I cannot predict for myself what kind of visible artefact might draw me in to attending to it, when this might happen, or the circumstances in which this might occur. However, that this kind of relationship can occur, and that some of the complex factors we have considered here are likely to be involved, seems a reasonable supposition.

This concludes my exploration of some of the factors that might impinge upon relationships with visual objects. A wide variety of factors contribute to the potential relationship between viewers and visible artefacts. It might be tempting to think that images have a kind of autonomous power which compels a certain kind of relationship with viewers. However, the factors which impact on relationships between humans and visual artefacts are complex; they inhere in viewers, in objects, and in the space between them. The sticky webs of attachment that bind viewers to visual objects are complex, multisensorial, and hard to categorize analytically. They are largely beyond conscious awareness, pre-symbolic, and difficult to articulate.

Nonetheless, the quest to understand the meaning and importance of visual relationships and the factors that impinge upon them is an important one. It is essential to pursue it better to understand ourselves and the artefacts that surround us so that we can live responsibly and responsively in the material world. This will affect our economic, personal and social lives, as well as our competence to engage with, and fully enjoy, relationships with visual objects.

## Notes

1 For the sublime, past and present, see, for example, Burke (1990), Ashfield and de Bolla (1996), Beckley (2001).

2 Stewart (1993).

3 See Burke (1990) for beauty. Elkins (2001, p. 60) records one of his correspondents finding Rembrandt paintings oppressive – their smallness seemed to exclude this particular viewer.

4 Gregory (1998, pp. 150–51). Wartofsky (Jay 1994, p. 5) argues that 'human vision is itself an artefact, produced by other artefacts, namely pictures'. Kemp (2006, pp. 13–84) explores the dominance of the perspectival box in structuring Western vision. Cf. Kemp (1990).

5 Norman (2004, p. 67).

6 Pastoureau (2001, p. 179). Cf. Pleij (2004, p. 17), Julius (2000, p. 72).

7 See Gage (1995, 2000), Pleij (2004).

8 See Berger (1972).

9 Johnson (2002).

10 Norman (2004, pp. 5, 7).

11 Norman (2004, p. 5) distinguishes three different aspects of design. The visceral

aspect is concerned with appearances and immediate, automatic emotional and sensory response. The behavioural aspect has to do with the pleasure and effectiveness of use of an object. The reflective aspect has to do with rationalization and intellectualization of the object and is involved in the cognitive, interpretive level of people rather than in their immediate emotionally powered judgement. The behavioural and reflective levels are sensitive to experience, training and education. In practice, the three levels inevitably get mixed together.

12 Newhouse (2005).

13 Gell (1998, pp. 73ff.).

14 See, for example, Lacan (1981), Leader (2002).

15 Taussig (1999, p. 52).

16 Freedberg (1989, pp. 409, 425).

17 Lopes (2005).

18 See, for example, Kemp (2004), Bruce and Young (1998), Cole (1998), McNeill (1998), Wright (1991), Ayers (2003).

19 *Darshan* is a Hindu term meaning gaining 'blessing through the eyes' from the gods. 'Darshan is a gift or an offering made by the superior to the inferior, and it consists of the "gift of appearance" imagined as a material transfer of some blessing . . . To place oneself before the idol of the god, therefore, is to lay oneself open to the divine gaze and to internalize the divine image . . . Darshan is thus very much a two-way affair. The gaze directed by the god towards the worshipper confers his blessing; conversely, the worshipper reaches out and touches god . . . Devotee and god mirror each other in gazing at each other. What the devotee sees is the idol looking at him or her, performing an act of looking mirroring his or her own' (Gell 1998, pp. 116–18). Eye contact and mutual looking is often the basic mechanism for religious intersubjectivity (Morgan 2005a, pp. 48ff.). What is more surprising, perhaps, is that in Judaism and Protestantism people appear to be able to relate to God without any kind of physically embodied and mediated divine gaze (but cf. Harvey (1995, 1999), Julius (2000) and Bland (2000)).

20 See, for example, Kwint (2005), Rival (1998), Ingold (2000, pp. 134ff.), Thomas (1984, pp. 198–223).

21 Kemp (2001b, pp. 26–7). 'The wonder of mimesis lies in the copy drawing on the character and power of the original, to the point whereby the representation may even assume that character and that power' (Taussig 1993, p. xiii).

22 For more on the embodied nature of mimesis see, for example, Benjamin (1999, p. 211). Marks (2000, p. 138) notes: 'Tactile epistemology involves a relationship to the world of mimesis, as opposed to symbolic representation . . . Mimesis is thus a form of representation based on a particular, material contact at a particular moment, such as that between a child at play and an airplane, a moth and the bark of a tree . . . Mimesis, in which one calls up the presence of the other materially, is an indexical, rather than iconic, relation of similarity.'

23 See Pinney (2001).

24 Leonardo thought that the magical power of visual art to produce objects that appeared to be alive was one of the most attractive aspects of his work (Kemp 2001, pp. 26ff.). This power usurps the power of God who alone can create living beings, above all humanity, in the divine image.

25 Elkins (2001, pp. 174ff.).

26 Elkins (2001, p. 201).

27 Csikszentmihalyi and Rochberg Halton (1981, p. 178).

28 Norman (2004, p. 47).

29 Armstrong (2005, pp. 3ff.).

30 Kant (1997, pp. 18ff) and Armstrong (2005, p. 51).

31 Armstrong (2005, p. 146).

32 Norman (2004, p. 47).

33 Elkins (2001, pp. 35–6). Cf. Burke (1990).

34 Norman (2004, pp. 109ff.).

35 Veiling and partial lighting also set up dynamics of seeing and not seeing that intrigue viewers. See, for example, Tanizaki (2001) for the value of shadows and Levin (1999) for the importance of partial seeing as part of the fascination of images. Concealment is part of revelation and relationship in the gaze between object and viewer. See further, for example, Morgan (2005b), Meyer and Pels (2003).

36 See Leader (2002), Taussig (1999).

37 Hall (1997).

38 Sturken and Cartwright (2001, chs. 1 and 2).

39 Abram (1997, p. 133).

40 Gell (1998, ch. 5).

41 Gell (1998, p. 67). Cf. Pinney (2001), Stoller (1997).

42 Elkins brilliantly explores artistic indexicality in oil painting, pointing out that to encounter a picture is to encounter the embodied moods and actions of an artist beyond the content and subject of the picture. 'Meaning does not depend on what paintings are about: it is there at a lower level, in every inch of a canvas. Substances occupy the mind by invading it with thoughts of the artist's body at work' (Elkins 2000b, p. 96).

43 See Guthrie (1993) and Daston (1998, 2002). 'Even if the iconoclasts succeeded in destroying all representations made by human beings, the world would still be full of images: *natura pingit* – nature paints' (Daston 2002, p. 136).

44 Norman (2004, pp. 56ff.) discusses the 'personality of products' in a rather different and more limited sense than I am using here. He suggests product personality structure must be designed so that it is consistent and looks and behaves as it should. In particular, it needs to fit in with its brand. Brands, he suggests, are 'all about emotions. And emotions are all about judgment. Brands are signifiers or our emotional responses, which is why they are so important in the world of commerce' (Norman 2004, p. 60). Emotional relations with products are based on trust in brands.

45 Ouspensky (1992 vol. 1, pp. 7ff.).

46 Cf. Otto (1950).

47 Holly (1996, pp. 69ff.). The fourth mode of viewing or exchanging gaze is very similar to Marks's 'haptic visuality'. See Marks (2000, pp. 162ff.).

48 Bennett (2005, p. 189) notes, 'Paintings more often than not have quite violent and eventful lives; they are loved, after all, and so naturally they get interfered with and touched up and, their admirers being fickle, when they get to seem a little old-fashioned they are dressed up a bit to suit the taste of the time. They limp into the present coated with centuries of make-up but still trying to keep body and soul together.'

# 7

# The Matter of Visual Objects

We have forgotten how to initiate intimacy with objects.

James Elkins, *Pictures and Tears*

If you think that interacting with things is not important, just try to remember the last time that you were not engaged in some sort of 'material interaction'.

Tim Dant, *Materiality and Society*

## Introduction

One reason we find it difficult to look visual artefacts 'in the eye' is that we live in a culture where objects or things are regarded as of little value. Western culture is often described as materialistic, implying human over-involvement with material things. Often, however, this relationship is actually denied. The world is divided. On one side of the divide stand well-differentiated orders of biological, animate, intentional, living and responsive creatures such as animals and human beings. These have some social and moral significance, are admitted into the realm of communication, and are often held to deserve respect and consideration. On the other side are inanimate, non-organic, non-living, non-intentional objects. These exist only for the benefit and use of the animate, living order. Being non-communicative and inanimate, they are accorded little respect.

Figure 2 (see p. 152) illustrates the way that the world is divided up and attended to by Western humans. Curiously, inanimate non-sentient artefacts that owe their being directly to human action are placed beneath attention to non-sentient natural things for which humans have no direct responsibility.

Non-haptic, distancing ways of seeing in both religious and secular worlds have reinforced the devaluation of the material dimension of objects. Thus becoming consciously and willingly involved in important relationships with this aspect of objects is regarded as basically unnecessary, even taboo. The material is subordinate and incidental for

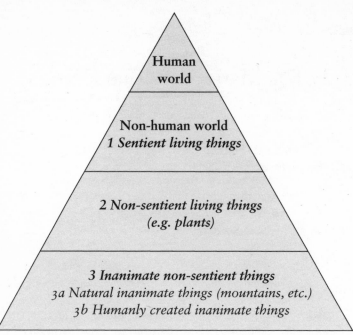

Figure 2: *The difference between the human and non-human world.*

intellectual and spiritual perception of 'higher' mental and metaphysical realities.

Within the world of high art and aesthetics, the material dimension of visual objects tends to be neglected; it is just a vehicle for representational ends. Focusing on the symbolic, signifying dimensions of visual objects diminishes attention to their materiality.[1] This also happens in Christianity where visual objects are mostly looked past, or through, to see the divine beyond.[2] Even the sacramental tradition, which emphasizes the importance of the material creation for the mediation of divinity, enables the materiality of objects to be dissolved to access spiritual realities.[3] A man who looks on glass on it may stay his eye, and consider its material reality, nature and importance. Or, as George Herbert suggests, the glass can be passed through and transcended so that the heavens can be seen.[4] Mostly, looking through objects has commended itself to Christians.

While the whole created order, in the form of 'creation' or 'nature', has attracted some consideration with the rise of the ecological movement, the realm of things is not regarded as part of the animate, human world.[5] In particular, artefacts, the work of human hands, are accorded limited status. They are treated as if they have no respectworthy ends or value other than those arbitrarily conferred upon them by human usage or neglect. Largely excluded from the moral community and from moral concern, they are consigned to the non-differentiated vocabulary of 'stuff', or 'things'. If pictures or other objects move from the realm of silent and abstract meaning to active relationships with human beings, this is discomforting or embarrassing; things are meant to have a subordinate significance – though they often exceed this.[6]

Objects, particularly artefactual objects, the work of human hands, can be seen as companions in our human world. They are more person-like than might be assumed. They may, therefore, deserve more consideration than contemporary Westerners often give them. Like persons, artefacts have a corporeal reality. Here, I want to delve further into the material dimension of relations with visible objects to open up ways of taking them more seriously and entering into appropriate relationships with them more fully.

Relationships with inanimate visible artefacts are real, important, common and ubiquitous, if unnoticed and often unacknowledged. Objects of all kinds play an important part in forming identity, self and culture. Humans are humans in large part because of their symbolic and non-symbolic relationships with the artefactual world. These may be denied and repressed, but not eliminated. A more positive approach would be to overcome unthinking taboos and embarrassments to foster fuller and more honest, appreciative attitudes to relationships with things under the aegis of haptic sight. Haptic sight as a model for perception implies taking the material nature of objects absolutely seriously.

The prevailing indifference to material objects and the divide that is perpetuated between the animate and inanimate worlds should be questioned. Having outlined something of the history of the rise of the absolutely divided worlds of animate and inanimate creatures, I will consider what sustains this distinction today. In the next chapter, I will then question whether or not this distinction is actually sustainable.

## Alienation from material objects

Western moderns may not particularly want to think carefully about, or seriously relate to, material objects. However, it was not ever thus. In the medieval world, material artefacts often displayed qualities and characteristics of persons and became involved in relations with humans. St Francis engaged with a painted crucifix in San Damiano (see Plate 8):

> As with eyes full of tears he gazed upon the Lord's Cross, he heard with his bodily ears a Voice proceeding from that Cross, saying thrice, 'Francis, go and repair My House, which, as thou seest, is falling utterly into ruin.' (St Francis of Assisi 1963, p. 311)

This episode seems curious, perhaps bizarre, to us now. In the contemporary West, objects, even devotional objects, are not supposed to speak or show signs of life. The crucifix that spoke to Francis looks reassuringly like a figure painted on wood; it has never moved or spoken in my presence, however closely I have attended to it. It is beautiful in its simplicity. But it seems as dead as a Dodo. Its importance lies in its historical significance in a culture in which objects became animated and seemed to share some of the characteristics of people, including powers of speech, movement and communication.

Francis was not alone in experiencing the personlike power of material images. Eleventh-century icons were regarded by some devotees as 'living beings' who seemed 'to speak graciously with their mouths to all who look on them' (Belting 1994, pp. 261–2). Like the relics of saints in the West, icons were regarded as having a continuing and living relationship with their prototypes, so they were capable of movement and action.[7]

So embodied and personlike did images become that they moved. Stories of images bleeding or weeping were commonplace. One image of Christ was reputed to have been made to bleed by being pierced with a lance, while the *Volto Santo* in Lucca is reputed to have slipped off and thrown a silver shoe as a gift to a poor troubadour.[8] An image of the crucified Christ once hit a recalcitrant nun, while an image of the Virgin Mary transported the Casa Santa and itself, from Nazareth to Loreto.[9] Images were sometimes treated as if the saint or holy person they represented were in them, 'working miracles through their image' (Belting 1994, p. 308). The Virgin, particularly, was reputed to act miraculously through her image, and the cult of St Francis, a 'second Christ' who bore the stigmata, was spread by icons before which miracles occurred.[10] As images became more life-like and had more emotional expressions, people frequently felt that they spoke to, and with, them. Effectively, the distinction between inert object and living being was often suspended:[11]

[I]n later mediaeval Italy, pictures could make people cry – not just once, but for years. They could hurt people and make them bleed. Pictures were capable of healing, blessing, and even transfiguring the people who saw them. Viewers were wounded, and even paralyzed: they were, in effect, assaulted by paintings. (Elkins 2001, p. 169)[12]

Personlike relationships between individuals and visual devotional objects continue. Christian (1992) documents the phenomenon of moving, weeping and sweating crucifixes in Catholic rural Spain just after World War One, while Orsi (1996) highlights the importance of the visual image of St Jude for his effectiveness in relationships with his contemporary Catholic devotees in North America. Morgan (1998, p. 156), in a completely different context, documents a picture of the *Head of Christ* by the Protestant artist, Walter Sallman, secreting oil in 1993 among other, similar miraculous phenomena witnessed by North American Protestants. I have already alluded to a picture of Elvis Presley in the American mid-West that weeps.[13] In early 2007, a new sculpture of Jesus cleansing the Temple in the Liverpool Academy of Art, by atheist sculptor Brian Burgess, was reported to be giving out sparks from its eyes. The result was crowds of people coming to venerate and pray before the work, with many reporting seeing the sparks themselves.

To Western moderns, this kind of material, personlike relationship with images seems the stuff of myth, legend, or metaphor.[14] It comes from a superstitious, animistic age, or from the credulous, ill-educated parts of the world. The people who experience such phenomena have a tenuous grasp of reality. Or they have a poorly differentiated and individuated personality, so they projectively animate images and fail to distinguish the material from the mental. Or they are full of wishful hopes. Or perhaps they are so devotionally transported that they attain some kind of quasi-personal relationship with sacred images. Or they are carried along by group norms and narratives that make such things plausible. Or maybe they are just trapped in world-views and language systems that force them to attribute agency and life to images because they have no other way of talking about meaningful, important religious experiences.[15]

For modern psychological rationalists, the era of dynamic, personlike relations with objects is over, especially outwith the world of devotion. The material world is wholly differentiated from the human world, and the boundary between things and sentient beings is absolute. The boundary is marked by a pejorative, pathologizing vocabulary of words like 'fetishism', 'animism' and 'primitivism'. This creates a realm of wordless abomination into which sensible people will not wander.

Despite living in a materialist culture, driven by the creation and consumption of material objects, moderns are dissuaded from considering their relationships with visual objects by a taboo against thinking of them as in any way personlike.

I contend that this taboo should be challenged. *Visible objects need to be treated as more like persons than things if we are to develop a proper respect and appreciation for them.*

To explore this hypothesis, I will structure my discussion with these questions in mind:

1 How, why, and when, did artefactual images 'die'? How did they come to be relegated to the realm of 'things', deprived of any personlike qualities?
2 Why do we continue to assert the absolute difference between inanimate artefacts and living beings?
3 Are we quite sure that humanly created visual objects do not have personlike aspects to them?
4 Are we really modern? Do we, in fact, continue to have covert personlike relationships with artefacts and objects?

I am interested in considering all visible objects. As ever, however, I will be heavily dependent on work done on the nature and fate of art and religious objects.

Against prevailing Western views of the human, which see persons as atomized, integrated, autonomous psychological selves inhabiting an animate world distinct from the inanimate, and whose existence ends with biological death, I suggest that personhood is diffuse and porous. In a more ecological view of the person and perception, humans diffuse themselves into objects and things in various ways, perpetuating aspects of their existence beyond actual presence and biological death.[16] Thus Monet's emotions and intentions can be sensed from the material marks he left on canvas in his pictures.[17] At the same time, artefacts and objects, the expressions of human diffusion and intentionality, help to shape the human ecology and persons in both symbolic and non-symbolic ways. Thus chairs make symbolic statements about status and social order, but also non-symbolically determine posture and help to shape the body.[18] They establish our social position – and give us varicose veins! The material and immaterial, the personal and the artefactual, mutually interpenetrate each other. Relations between diffuse persons and objects are complex and necessarily obscure. However, if this general approach is correct, personlike relations between objects are not just possible, they are inevitable.

## The 'death' of 'living' material images

Not all images are regarded as totally inanimate in the contemporary industrialized Western world. Within the Christian religious world, Catholic and Protestant, some images are regarded as very much alive and active. Particularly in Catholicism, there remains a flourishing tradition of active, miracle-working images which still attract devotion and pilgrimage. However, within the secular societies, particularly those shaped by a predominantly Protestant tradition, the only sorts of artefactual images and objects that are supposed to be animated are those that have been made to move by direct, deliberate human agency. Thus computer screens, televisions and films are wonderfully animated, but this is not because they are in themselves personlike, but because they have been made to act by human agents who create them using rational technology. Thus there is no secret, mystery or autonomy to their operation, amazing though it may seem to viewers.

A huge distance has been travelled since Byzantine worshippers regarded themselves as the objects of the vision of God mediated through the eyes and presence of images in churches, to the present day, when images are regarded as inanimate objects for the aesthetic consumption of sovereign viewers.[19]

One radical account of this process is offered by Freedberg (1989). Over the centuries our basic responses or desire and longing aroused by pictures have become repressed. Images are, and always have been powerful, appealing to human longings and desires. They produce a sense of life which provokes basic emotional reactions:

> People are sexually aroused by pictures and sculptures; they break pictures and sculptures; they mutilate them, kiss them, cry before them, and go on journeys to them; they are calmed by them, stirred by them, and incited to revolt. They give thanks by means of them, expect to be elevated by them, and are moved to the highest levels of empathy and fear . . . They do so in societies we call primitive and in modern societies . . . (Freedberg 1989, p. 1)

However, this sense of the living, personlike artefact is threatening, difficult and ungovernable. So in modern, rational society images are relegated to the realm of art.[20] Images which continue to disturb people and engage them, such a pornography and advertising, are not regarded as art. Art denotes the category of neutered images that are not troublesome.[21] Categorizing images thus brings about their neutralization and death.[22]

With the rise of art, instead of being interested in the function of images as religious and mediating forces, people became more interested in their form and content as objects in themselves. Devotional pictures, removed from their original settings and pinned, like so many dead butterflies, to the walls of secular art galleries, are no longer able to speak or create deep affective devotional relationships with viewers.[23] Religious art objects, re-assigned to the category of the aesthetic, have lost their fetishistic power. Museums, then, are like cemeteries, giving value to things that are outside life and safely dead. They are 'prestigious places for locking things up' (Clifford 1998, pp. 231, 226).[24]

I have concentrated here on religious images moving from active quasi-personal characteristics and relationships within a devotional setting to being dead objects of aesthetic appreciation because more is written about these objects than any others. They have often also been more significant in more people's lives than other objects. Before the Reformation, most of what is now called art took the form of religious imagery. The progress of these images into art is clear, while many images created since the Reformation have never been anything but art.[25]

Thus far, I have highlighted the lively nature of some kinds of material images, and hence the historically relative condition in which moderns now find themselves. While viewers may be encouraged to experience a sense of enlightenment, spiritual nourishment, or personal restoration within the secular rituals of visiting art galleries under the guiding ethos of aestheticism, they are not generally supposed to be engaged in quasi-personal relationships with objects. They are encouraged to be recollected in contemplative tranquility, not to throw themselves at the feet of images.[26] In secular, aesthetic culture, images and visible artefacts are not allowed to do things, or to manifest personlike attributes and qualities.

The movement of material images from living religious, personlike significance and relationship, to dead artefact and object over the last six centuries has been accompanied by the rejection of seeing the world as animated or potentially animated. While religious images have been turned into lifeless art objects, many more recent and 'lesser' artefacts have never been candidates for animated or personlike status. They have simply come into being as 'things' with little significance beyond that. An important and absolute dualism has come to exist between artefacts and persons. This is reflected in life, as well as in language.[27]

## Why is the world of 'things' a dead, non-personlike world?

What was it that led to the dissolution of a world-view in which humans and things might have personlike relationships? The short answer to this is that in some way the notion of a chain of being, in which all of creation, human and non-human, is integrally connected in symbolic and communicative relationships, was destroyed.

Probably the most important factor in the systematic de-animation of the material world was the rise of the secularized scientific world-view from the sixteenth century onwards. However, it is first worth pointing to a few antecedent factors.[28]

Platonic philosophy, with its hierarchical, but integrated, view of the world ranging from the ideal at the top through to inanimate material-ity at the bottom gives some importance to matter within a great chain of being.[29] However, the place of matter is a very subordinate one, far from the higher realms of reason and ideas. This basic philosophical world-view does much to set the scene for the denigration of matter and its relegation to insignificance.

Religious anti-idolatrous teaching is another important precursor to the devaluing of the artefactual world and its separation from that of living, animate and human beings. In various places in the Old Testa-ment, most notably in Isaiah 44.9ff., there are passages that caution people against making objects that then become idols that are wor-shipped. Any object that could become effectual or animated might become an alternative site of devotion.

This kind of teaching has always been available within the Christian tradition. It was extensively expounded by the Reformers, particularly Calvin. Calvin was determined to turn people away from the use of images so they would discern God's invisible image in the theatre of the world and in the faces of other human beings.[30] This anti-idolatrous tradition continues to be influential. Protestants pride themselves on their worship of the living God and their stand against giving more than instrumental significance to the work of human hands.[31] Further-more, material goods, diligently made, and acquired in collaboration with the divine plan and will, should not to be allowed to divert ascetic Protestants from the pursuit of the heavenly blessings.[32] The material world is thus regarded with some suspicion, while it is exploited in the name of human stewardship of the divine purpose.

The Christian tradition is not entirely anti-material or dismissive of the importance of material creation. By contrast with contemporary Platonic philosophy, Alexandrian theologians in the early centuries of the church insisted that since the physical world was God's creation it was part of divine good purpose.[33] It must be 'read' as a kind of symbolic text which could be interpreted in both physical and spiritual senses. This valuing of the physical world (not initially based on the doctrinal implications of incarnation, as it tends to be in the modern world), meant that the world was treated as a kind of sign by theologians like Basil and Augustine. This tradition of understanding the world as a legible symbol lasted until the seventeenth century.[34]

The physical, visible world, though important, was subordinated to, and a way towards, the inner and spiritual. One passed through and beyond it to the greater non-corporeal truths to be found within by contemplation.[35] Nonetheless, in the eleventh, twelfth and thirteenth centuries, thinkers like Aquinas, Hildegaard of Bingen and Hugh of St Victor emphasized the importance of experiential knowledge of the world.[36] Everything, visible and invisible, spiritual and material, mortal and immortal was linked together. The whole of creation was a manifestation of the divine purpose; living things and inanimate objects were as revelatory of meaning and intelligibility as the written texts and words that were eventually to silence them.

The thirteenth-century Oxford 'proto-scientist', Robert Grosseteste, was able to maintain that even a speck of dust could be seen as imaging and mirroring the Creator, while human beings summed up the fullness of creation as microcosm to macrocosm.[37] Indeed, Grosseteste's experiments in optics and understanding light were not so much daring premonitions of scientific enquiry into the workings of the world for its own sake, as part of an integrated theological programme of attempting to read the text of material creation better to understand the mind and purpose of its Creator.[38] In this sense, the divine was immanent in every part of reality. The boundary between the material and the spiritual, the animate and the inanimate, was potentially transparent and porous. It was in this context that Francis could be addressed by the divine through a material object.

The book of nature, symbolically revealing the divine when read by rightly disposed human beings using reason, was closed, and the great chain of being shattered, by the Reformation. With Luther's emphasis on the central importance of the biblical text as God's self-communication, 'Meaning and intelligibility were ascribed to words and texts, but denied to living things and inanimate objects' (Harrison 1998, p. 120). Nature and the visible world were divested of symbolic importance, and the book of nature was read in a new way by seventeenth-century experimental scientists like Hooke, Newton and Wren.[39]

Within this new intellectual regime, the natural world became essentially an object of exploration in its own right. It was still thought to be the work of God, but the cultures of belief and of exploration gradually began to separate, with objective and objectivizing scientific methods dominating the latter. Although science and belief never completely separated, the study of objects and nature for their own sake, independent of theological or symbolic meaning, has become dominant.[40]

A key marker in this process was the thought of René Descartes.[41] He theorized the mind and the self as autonomous, and independent from the external material world.[42] This dualistic philosophical perspective underwrote, and reflected, the kinds of world-views and scientific experimentation that increasingly treated the natural world and the world of objects as inanimate and autonomous, the sphere of objective scientific investigation, rather than symbolic or sacramental revelation. Most importantly, relations with this world lay outside the realm of morality.[43]

Within two centuries of the Reformation, experimental science with its objectification of the natural world was dominant among the educated classes in Northern Europe. The heavens filled with mystic meaning were now no more than skies full of physical objects. Simultaneously, the Reformers' anti-idolatrous protest against the dominance of material objects such as statues and pictures in religion removed such objects from the religious sphere.[44] The proper study of theology was humanity. Knowledge and love of God were not to be encountered externally in matter and space in a material sacramental system, but in time, and in human minds and souls illuminated by the word of sacred Scripture.[45] Rather than looking outwards into the material world to find mediating sources of grace and knowledge of God, psychologized believers literally shut their eyes in prayer and meditation to find the divine within the individual person.[46] Individualistic Protestant piety fostered the emergence of the autonomous psychological self, interested in humanity, and with a mission to act as God's vice-regent or steward in the world, but independent of nature and the world of objects except insofar as these could be used to foster human flourishing.[47]

An emergent feature of the post-Reformation world, with its fostering of objective scientific experimentation, was the discovery of rational patterns and universal laws of nature. This formal rationality increased its influence in all parts of life and society.[48] Both bureaucratic organization and the rise of capitalism conspired with science to emphasize the importance of human agency and planning in the world. Explanation replaced mystery. Rationality contributed to the growth of demystified secular society in which animism, gods, mystery and irrationality became redundant in a world focused on human thought and intentions. Thus the world has formally become increasingly disenchanted, explained, and objectified, with little space for mystery and divinity, least of all in relation to artefacts and objects.[49] By the time nineteenth-century anthropologists studied non-Western societies, they were able to use words like 'primitive', 'animism' and 'fetishism' to describe the apparently irrational behaviour of humans who did not appear to realize that the human and material worlds were now firmly separated.[50]

From the sixteenth century onwards, human society, the world of culture and politics, became completely separate from nature, with analytic science regarded as the paradigm rational activity.[51] People would not weep before statues or be assaulted by them in the rationalist, humanistic aniconic world of the Enlightenment – at least among the Protestant intelligentsia. By the time of Kant and Hegel, the appreciation of objects was fundamentally distant, objective and intellectual. The rise of the category of art and its formal institutions, like galleries and museums, accompanied by the theorization of response in rational philosophical aesthetics, testifies to the separation of animate humans from inanimate objects.[52] Devotional objects and 'primitive' fetishes could now be placed in museums for intellectual stimulation and curiosity, a trend which has only recently begun to be reversed.[53]

Eventually, within this dualistic split between worlds, the divine was mostly written out of the material world. The latter came to be seen as an independent reality existing on its own without the need or possibility of divine plan or intervention.[54] Nature and the material realm were finally silenced, except insofar as human scientists chose to interpret and speak metaphorically on their behalf.

A further development that bears upon the evolution of the present dualistic perspective, where the world of objects is completely separated from that of living beings, is represented by the rise of consumer capitalism. The free exploitation of the deanimated and desacralized material world for financial profit, has been closely associated with Protestantism.[55] Protestantism is perhaps also partly responsible for the stimulation of the appetite for unlimited hedonistic consumption of inessential goods.

In most human societies need is self-limiting, and there is a restricted desire for acquisition. The rise of 'autonomous imaginative hedonism', fuelling the rise of the desire for unlimited consumption beyond basic need in Western Europe from the eighteenth century, therefore needs explanation (Campbell 1987, p. 77). This could only occur in a society in which individuals felt that they needed to fulfil emotional desires and gain hedonistic stimulation to be happy. The definition and refinement of the autonomous imaginative self, who seeks satisfaction through emotional stimulation via the acquisition of objects and experience, arose in large part because of the influence of Protestant pietism. This focused individuals upon their inner psychological states and gave them a primary vocabulary of personal emotion as part of their response to the divine.[56]

The autonomous, imaginative, emotional, hedonistic self lives in a world of day-dreaming and fantasizing about the stimulation that might be gained from the purchase of new experiences or objects. The need for constant emotional stimulation and gratification can never be permanently satisfied by particular goods and objects. Renewed stimulus is always required. Thus material objects acquired to provide emotional gratification are not seen and treated as things having value in themselves. Rather, they often become symbols and signs of something else, such as social status.[57] In consumerist market capitalism, actual things are seen past and through; they are not primarily valued for their material capacities and qualities. They are not produced or acquired to meet real physical needs, but rather to address the individuals' sentimental and symbolic needs for meaning, belonging and emotional stimulation. They increasingly become characterized by instantaneity, ephemerality and disposability.[58]

Consumerist materialism thus paradoxically helps to spiritualize, disembody and dematerialize the importance of objects while simultaneously seeming obsessed with exploiting material resources and increasing consumption. Materialist spirituality and consumptive practice is largely unconcerned with the reality of particular material things. To continue to flourish, it must deny any value or personlike respect to the material world. According such value and respect would be acknowledging a limit on market activity, ostensibly undertaken for the benefit of the animate, living beings.

The stage is set then for thinkers like Marx and Engels who see the material world in terms of the evolution and purposes of human beings. The materialists, despite their name, contributed to the downgrading and suspicion of the natural world and the world of objects with their theories of reification, alienation, fetishism and the like. Basically, they argued that human energy and agency became objectified within the products of labour and manufacture which stand over against humanity as 'thieves' of human essence, relationality and identity.[59] For Marx, objects are unnaturally animated; they exercise the power of humans and their pursuit by humans is then analogous to the power and influence of religion.[60] Furthermore, the world of human creation and objects under capitalism is radically ruptured and fallen; it represents a realm of captivity in which people are owned and controlled by the works of their own hands. Thus materialist-influenced humanist thinkers easily harbour contempt or suspicion for the material world and the world of objects; it has no significance except insofar as it might one day be restored to enabling human flourishing. Paradoxically, then, 'the materialists are not interested in the material' (Molotch 2003, p. 6).

Materialist thinkers provide one strand of critique leading contemporaries to nurture suspicions about the value of the inanimate material world, especially the world of mass-produced artefacts. Their devaluation of objects is matched by that of romantics, Christians, and others of good conscience, who, in blaming materialism and consumption for many of the ills of the world, often seem to arraign the artefactual world itself for existing.

Inhabitants of Western capitalist society often wistfully laud pre-industrial societies, where people own fewer things and enjoy richer human relationships, as if the relationship with objects under capitalism inevitably contributes to a devaluation of human flourishing.[61] For many religious and morally concerned Westerners, then, goods are automatically bads, or at least deeply suspect.[62] They are liable to lead the human race and individuals astray, as did the idols of old. Rather in the same way that women have been blamed by men for luring them into acts of rape and violence, humans blame objects for tempting them into consumerist extravagance and indulgence.

Thus artefacts themselves may be treated effectively as polluting dirt, matter out of place, in a society that continues to create them exponentially. They may be demonized and treated as if they were automatically addictive and destructive, like cigarettes. Concomitantly, far from being loved, cared for, enjoyed and appreciated, they must be controlled and limited to minimize their harmful effects. For very positive reasons, paradoxically, a kind of unthinking anti-materialism, powered by humanistic and ecological concern, prevents us from looking more closely at objects and taking them seriously. The demonization of artefacts contributes to an anti-materialist spiritualization of the world.

Critics of the curiously anti-material fantasy world of market capitalism have thus helped to denigrate the world of material artefacts. They were deemed to be mystified and misleading representations of alienated human potential and capacity that should not be accorded the power and significance that they had.[63]

Regarding artefacts and objects as inappropriate, exploitative and destructive in themselves is a widely shared attitude in the West. Ecologists and others point to the dangers of material exploitation and hyperacquisition. However, they risk cathecting the material world and artefacts with an aura of evil. This is reminiscent of concerns in the early Jewish and Christian traditions that all objects, especially those made by human hands, have the potential to become living, exploitative idols that lead the world and humanity astray. This enduring tradition preserves the importance of humanity and the priority of its relationship to a living divinity in whose image humanity is made, fostering radical humanism.[64] Unfortunately, however, the material world of objects, especially artefacts, is regarded as inferior, and possibly evil.

Why is the world of 'things' regarded as a dead, inanimate and totally non-personlike world by Western moderns in developed societies? A combination of forces over the last few centuries has led to the gradual yet absolute functional separation of the animate world of persons (and to a certain extent, living creatures) and that of material objects. Basic Renaissance humanism that made 'man the measure of all things' was supplemented by growing objectification and rationalization of the world that led to a fundamental disenchantment of the material realm and a clear separation of reasoning, living humans from the material world of 'things'.

Capitalism, bureaucracy, and objectifying scientific thinking, as well as more ancient theological thinking about the dangers of idolatry and the lowly place accorded to the material world in philosophy, combined to produce a ratio-instrumental attitude to the inanimate creation, especially the realm of artefacts conceived and made by human agency. This allows contemporary 'rational' humans, whether religious or not, to use the material environment and its contents as they please.

Paradoxically, the disenchanted, materialist world-view that supports the mass production and consumption of artefacts, does not actually value these objects for themselves. They have limited emotional and symbolic importance, but they are thought to have no interests or rights of their own. Many people would regard it as insulting if they were accused of loving their material possessions. Love as a quality is generally restricted to relationships between sentient, animate beings, possibly including some higher animals. Thus the realm of things is maintained in an inferior position, mostly outwith moral consideration, and relations with it are undifferentiated and general. Insofar as artefacts may be 'idolatrous' by virtue of their fetishistic intimacy, dynamism and power, they are condemned and disparaged.

## Conclusion

There is a taboo that prevents people from entering into living, person-like relations with objects and artefacts. This may represent a fear that they may not be as passive and inanimate as humans like to think. Much of the contemporary way of life in the West depends on the understanding that the inanimate, non-sentient world is 'other' than human, so it does not deserve much consideration or respect. The world may not be fully disenchanted, religion and belief may not be completely moribund, and the planet may be regarded as a living ecosystem by ecologists and nature mystics. However, the realm of artefacts (pictures, sculptures, cars, buildings, etc.), is passive and dead. It is unnecessary to think about its nature and welfare so long as it supports human life, desire, need and flourishing:

> One of the features of later modernity is that myriads of material objects are created and used as tools; if we ever stop to think about them, we regard them as 'mere' objects that do not in anyway [*sic*] compete with humans for status as beings. Objects are there for us to use and dispose of in whatever way we wish; we may treat them well or badly without any concern for their rights or feelings because they have none. Just as people in other civilizations treated slaves or animals . . . we treat objects as possessions, chattels over which we have complete dominion. (Dant 2005, p. 62)

If this is a generally accurate caricature of contemporary attitudes to the realm of objects, in the next chapter I will try to subvert its supposed veracity by looking at the nature of objects and their power. Many artefacts and things have more personlike qualities and powers than we might care to admit. Indeed, the nature and identity of the human, animate world is inextricably bound up with the world of things at all levels of individual and social existence. Objects generally, and visible objects particularly, therefore, deserve more attention and respect.

I go on to suggest that, in practice, contemporary humans do engage in personlike relations with things. The divide between the human and the 'thing' world is not absolute. Instead of being denied, much as human dependence on money is denied, the connections between humans and visible objects need to be better understood and nurtured.

Only thus can proper friendly relations be enjoyed to the full, rather than being used within the spirit of ratio-instrumental exploitation. It may even be that humans and objects could begin to experience the kinds of relationships in which objects might again begin to speak, either literally or metaphorically. But this can only happen if humans have a willingness to attend and listen across the divide.[65]

# Notes

1 See, for example, Panofsky (1955), Gombrich (1977).

2 See, for example, Brown (2004), Inge (2003), de Gruchy (2001), Dyrness (2001).

3 McFague (1997).

4 'The Elixir', in Herbert (1961, pp. 175–6).

5 McFague (1997) argues strongly for a theological revaluation of relationships with the material world, via haptic-like sight, but nowhere does she consider relations with artefacts and humanly created inanimate objects.

6 Compare the lavish attention given to a selective range of objects, for example, famous pictures and sculptures. This is often criticized by those who think we should spend the money and attention on living human beings.

7 'The image, with the bodily appearance of a sculpture, was an agent of religious experience as it represented the reality of the presence of the holy in the world on terms similar to those of the relic. Image and relic explained each other' (Belting 1994, p. 302). For the animation of images by relics see further Gell (1998, pp. 141ff.).

8 Belting (1994, p. 305).

9 Freedberg (1989, pp. 309–10).

10 Davidson (1998).

11 Freedberg (1989, p. 311). Cf. Belting (1994, pp. 308–10, 362, 410).

12 Elkins (2001, pp. 167–8) cites the example of St Catherine of Siena who was paralysed while looking at Giotto's *Navicella* in Rome in 1380 and received the stigmata while looking at a crucifixion. Many lives of the saints report dynamic relationships with statues and religious artefacts. See, for example, St Teresa of Avila (1957).

13 Elkins (2004, p. 53).

14 Walker Bynum (2002).

15 McDannell (1995) believes that in patriarchal society and religion, non-abstract material relationships with objects are seen to be the province of the emotional, the weak, the simple, and the regressed. They are often associated with women and the domestic rather than the public and intellectual spheres.

16 Gell (1998). Cf. Ingold (2000).

17 Elkins (2000b, pp. 97–8).

18 Cranz (2000).

19 Bryson (1983, p. 98) comments on Byzantine looking practices: 'So far from being a spatial or temporal point, the viewer of the ecclesiastical image is an embodied presence in motion through a circular temporality of text and a choreographic . . . space of vision . . . The body does not see itself; the gaze under which it moves is not yet the introjected gaze of the Other, but of God.'

20 Freedberg (1989, p. 374) notes: 'all images work as religious images, including beautiful and artistic ones. All visual representation must be held in check – as the ancients knew . . . because of its strong ability to involve the beholder and to transcend natural law. It is dead but it can come alive; it is mute but has a presence that can move and speak; and it has such a hold on the imagination that it informs dreams and

produces fantasies that are adulterous . . . it is an irrationality that a rational society must keep in check.'

21 'The power of images is much greater than is generally admitted . . . we repress the evidence of responses clearly revealed by past behaviour because we are too embarrassed by it, and . . . because we fear the strength of the effects of images on ourselves . . . Much of our sophisticated talk about art is simply an evasion' (Freedberg 1989, p. 429). For Freedberg (1998, pp. 42ff.), what anthropologists used to call primitivism is that which is not repressed. It has little place in the cool world of art.

22 With the advent of modernity, images were relegated to being part of the natural world rather than being regarded as potentially active manifestations of sacred persons. See Belting (1994, p. 471).

23 Elkins (2001, p. 121). Though Gaskell (2003) shows that pictures can move from sacred to secular and back again in some circumstances.

24 It was Adorno who first linked museums with mausoleums. A museum is like a family sepulchre for works of art (Tamen 2001, p. 65).

25 Staniszewski (1995, ch. 2) suggests that the distinctive category of art arises along with the transformation of people into individual citizen subjects in the eighteenth century within liberal democracy and capitalism, and that, linked to the right to own and exchange, it functions as an emblem of modern subjecthood (which is individualized, atomized and psychologized).

26 Duncan (1995, p. 14) notes that art galleries arose at the same time as Kant was developing his non-religious aesthetics: 'The eighteenth century's design of art and aesthetic experience as major topics for critical and philosophical inquiry is itself part of a broad and general tendency to furnish the secular with new value. In this sense, the invention of aesthetics can be understood as a transference of spiritual values from the sacred realm into secular time and space . . . In philosophy, the liminal became specified as the aesthetic experience, a moment of moral and rational disengagement that leads to or produces some kind of revelation or transformation. Meanwhile the appearance of art galleries and museums gave the aesthetic cult its own ritual precinct.'

27 Appadurai (1986, pp. 12–13) observes that 'anthropology is excessively dualistic: "us and them"; "materialist and religious"; "objectification of persons" versus "personification of things"; "market exchange" versus "reciprocity"; and so forth.' Anthropology merely reflects wider Western social assumptions in making these dualistic distinctions (Ingold 2000).

28 Abram (1997) argues for another antecedent factor bringing about a fundamental gap between humans and the material world that precedes any of those mentioned here in relation to modernity. This is the rise of non-referential abstract language, eventually written, evolved in Hebrew and Greek civilizations. When language becomes detached from place and material objects, and is self-reflexive and self-referential, Abram argues, material objects and specific places become less important. Australian aboriginal language and poetry, by contrast, has never become detached from material reality and context in this way.

29 Lovejoy (1936).
30 Dyrness (2004, ch. 3).
31 See, for example, Ellul (1987), Dyrness (2001).
32 Weber (1976).
33 Harrison (1998, p. 15).
34 Harrison (1998, p. 15).
35 Harrison (1998, ch. 1).
36 Harrison (1998, ch. 2).

37 Harrison (1998, p. 47).

38 Crombie (1953). The poetic highpoint of this tradition which mingles optics, philosophy and theology is Dante's *Paradise* (Dante 1986). For more on the theological significance of light and optics in the medieval world see, for example, Hills (1987), Lindberg (1976), von Simson (1988), Park (1997).

39 For background to this see, for example, Funkenstein (1986) and Shapin and Schaffer (1985). Shapin and Schaffer argue that the (artificial) disjunction between science and culture reflects a basic conflict between Boyle and Hobbes who created separate realms for each. See further Latour (1993) for the implications of this dualism.

40 See further, for example, Brooke and Cantor (2000), Chapman (2001).

41 Descartes takes over some key attitudes to nature from Christianity: 'that it exists primarily as a resource rather than as something to be contemplated with enjoyment, that man has the right to use it as he will, that it is not sacred, that man's relations with it are not governed by moral principles' (Passmore 1974, p. 20).

42 Rorty (1980, ch. 2).

43 Passmore (1974, p. 20).

44 See Dyrness (2004), Koerner (2004a).

45 See Morgan (1998, p. 182). 'In the seventeenth century . . . "supernatural", the substantive, began to connote a realm of being . . . "outside" the world we know. With "nature" now deemed single, homogenous and self-contained, we labelled "supernatural" that other world inhabited (some said) by ghosts and poltergeists, by demons, angels and suchlike extraterrestrials – and by God.' Thus, 'By the end of the seventeenth century, "believing in God" . . . had become a matter of supposing that there is, outside the world we know, a large and powerful entity called "God".' Mysticism then becomes 'a matter of unusual experiences . . . of a God to whom the rest of us have, at best, precarious and inferential access through the thick filters of the world' (Lash 1996, pp. 168, 169, 171).

46 See Dyrness (2001). 'Spiritual struggle in its form as Protestant ethic denies the outside a reality in itself; denies the value of being present in the world' (Sennett 1992, pp. 65–6).

47 See Dyrness (2004).

48 Ritzer (1999, pp. 62ff.).

49 For more on disenchantment by rationalization, a Weberian concept, see Gerth and Wright Mills (1948), Brown (2004), Ritzer (1999), Bennett (2001).

50 Harvey (2005).

51 Latour (1993).

52 See Staniszewski (1995, ch. 2), Duncan (1995). Romanticism in aesthetic theory can be seen partly as an attempt to re-enchant the world (Morgan 1996a).

53 Edwards, Gosden and Phillips (2006).

54 Latour (1993, p. 33) notes that God is 'crossed out' and made totally transcendent so the divine has no influence in either science or society but can be appealed to as a transcendent court of appeal when there are conflicts between the laws of nature and the laws of society. Even religious people can live their lives without direct divine intervention or interference in this kind of environment.

55 Weber (1976).

56 Campbell (1987). Sennett (1992, p. 45) observes that the 'Puritan eye could only see within itself.'

57 Appadurai (1986, p. 38) notes that luxury goods are not necessities but incarnated signs.

58 Harvey (1989, p. 286).

59 Miller (1987, ch. 3). Insofar as commodities represent congealed relations of distorted, unjust class relations in capitalist society they reflect the ills and woes of wider social forces and forms. They are, as it were, symptoms of illness which must be cured before objects can be valued properly. Bennett (2001, pp. 113ff.) argues that Marx's account of fetishism is not capacious enough to account for our fascination with commercial goods.

60 Bennett (2001, p. 117).

61 Miller (1987, pp. 204ff.) argues against both left-wing materialist critics of fetishism and romantic critics of complex industrialized consumerist societies that there can be no culture without objects, that not all objects are bad or non-productive, and that goods are not just saleable commodities – they can have multiple uses and meanings. They share in the contradictions of society, having the potential for good and ill and they can be a means of reappropriation, sublation and self-realization in social relations.

62 See Molotch (2003, pp. 5, 227) for goods being regarded as bads.

63 Mitchell (1986, ch. 6) discusses Marx's ideas of fetishism of commodities and suggests that these could just as easily be conceived as a critique of idolatry. For more on fetishism, see, for example, Mulvey (1996, pp. 1ff.), Dant (1999), Marks (2000). For Marx, fetishism is the over-valuation of objects. Dant (1999, ch. 3) fundamentally criticizes both Marx and Freud for taking a realist, essentialist view of overvalued, fetish objects. He sees the fetish object as being the product of social meanings and human discourse that ascribe certain qualities to objects. If an object is overvalued and ascribed qualities of desire and fascination, this is not an intrinsic quality of the object, although these qualities become part of it in a particular discursive framework. The fetish is therefore 'real' because it partakes in the world of meanings, not because of anything inherent in itself.

64 See Kaufman (2004).

65 Mitchell (1996).

# 8

# Communicating with Visual Artefacts

Objects are for us, often without our recognizing it, the companions of our actions, our emotions and our thoughts. They not only accompany us from the cradle to the grave. They precede us in the one and survive us in the other. Tomorrow they will speak our language. But are they not already speaking to us, and sometimes much better than with words?

S. Tisseron, *Comment L'Ésprit Vient aux Objets*

We are human only in contact, and conviviality, with what is not human.

David Abram, *The Spell of the Sensuous*

## Introduction

If an absolute divide exists between the human/animate world and the inanimate world of things, objects cannot be regarded as personlike except by some kind of romantic wishful thinking or poetic trope. In this chapter, however, I consider whether all objects can, in fact, be confined to a separate realm. Recently, a number of thinkers have begun to question the absolute gap between human and inanimate realms. Here, I will look at the fluid nature of personhood and question whether it is a quality that can be attributed only to humans. I will then go on to consider some of the thinking that explains how personlike qualities might be found incarnated in material artefacts. I will suggest that a case can be made for seeing at least some artefacts as having personlike qualities.

## Confounding categories/personal confusion

In an anthropocentric world-view, material objects are generally deemed ineligible for designation as persons. Persons must be living members of the species *Homo sapiens*; there is the implication that as an individual you should breathe, eat, excrete, die, think rationally, have intentions, purposes and agency, and use language, to cite but some of the common characteristics attributed to persons (Snyder 2004, p. 196). (Religious thinkers might include the possession of a god-reflecting soul or animate divine indwelling of the body as a part of the eligibility for personhood.[1])

This helpful clarity about the nature and qualities of personhood soon begins to disintegrate. Some humans are not treated as persons. Slaves, still to be found today, are humans who are reduced to voiceless objects and chattels of others. Human foetuses, babies and small children are sometimes treated as persons with rights, sometimes not. It is within my lifetime that babies have been acknowledged to have the capacity to feel pain. Individuals with serious learning difficulties and other mental incompetences, as well as the demented and those in comas, may also drop out of the category of personhood. Meanwhile, some kinds of animals, notably primates, are now regarded as having personlike qualities and rights. They are thought to suffer in ways analogous to humans, and to possess qualities like the ability to communicate and relate to others.[2]

This demonstrates the precarious, often contingent, attribution of personhood.[3] The 'friends of interpretable objects' such as buildings, wildernesses, or rainforests, can attribute rights, and even speech, to these inanimate things. In the past, soulless material objects had intentions or actions attributed to them.[4] So statues, haystacks and other things were regarded as agents that could be tried and punished like humans: 'as late as 1892, a Russian bell was brought back from the Siberian exile to which it was sentenced in 1591' (Tamen 2001, p. 79).[5]

The 'fable of personification' allows objects to acquire the mask of personhood and become legally liable (Tamen 2001, p. 85). This is not mysterious. The recognition and honouring of personhood in humans or other parts of creation comes from humans. The attribution and possession of personhood is, therefore, contingent. Both humans and non-humans can, if humans wish, be honoured with personlike status and attributes. Equally, they can be deprived of it.[6]

The Western restriction of personhood attribution to human individuals, while material things are regarded as impersonal, is not universal:

> we take it more or less for granted that things – physical objects and rights to them – represent the natural universe of commodities. At the opposite pole we place people, who represent the natural universe of individuation and singularization. This conceptual polarity . . . is recent, and, culturally speaking, exceptional. (Kopytoff 1986, p. 64)

Some animals and objects are treated as though they have more importance and voice than some humans. The *Mona Lisa* is allotted more interest, respect and resource than most African children. The latter die in their thousands, while the *Mona Lisa* has money and attention lavished upon her/it.[7]

The convenient, functional fiction that objects and humans, by definition and ontological position, share little in common, cannot necessarily be sustained. Nor should it be. Humanly created objects and artefacts are often full of intention, meaning, emotion and purpose. In many ways, they act as distributed persons or secondary agents. They are not exactly the same as human persons; they are not organic, do not suffer pain, and do not die, in the same way as humans. However, they do have some qualities of personhood.

In this context, it makes sense to define personhood non-biologically and non-essentially, thus:

> Persons are those with whom other persons interact with varying degrees of reciprocity. Persons may be spoken with. Objects, by contrast, are usually spoken about. Persons are volitional, relational, cultural and social beings. They demonstrate intentionality and agency with varying degrees of autonomy and freedom. (Harvey 2005, p. xvii)[8]

As a hospital chaplain, I sometimes saw the dead bodies of people I had ministered to while they were alive. One thing that intrigued me was that people's hair and fingernails continued to grow after they had lost consciousness and been pronounced dead. Similarly, I could see people gradually becoming more corpse-like as they neared death. Death is, in some ways, a gradual process. Just as people gradually become persons out of foetuses at the beginning of life, they gradually cease to be living embodied persons at the end. But even when people have ceased to be present and to exist biologically, they continue to have influence, leaving 'bits' of themselves behind in the things they have created or caused to happen, in their wills, and in the images and memories that others have of them.[9]

Developing the insight that persons and biologically living humans are not necessarily identical, anthropologist Alfred Gell expounds a theory of extended and distributed personhood which can manifest itself in objects. Humans emit aspects of themselves in what might be called *eidolata*, 'skins' or bits that come from them, but then have some kind of independent existence apart from them. So their personhood becomes 'distributed in the milieu, beyond the body boundary' (Gell 1998, p. 104).[10] Thus in volt magic, toenails, hair, possessions, and other things that have been intimately involved with a particular individual, can represent that person and be regarded as a continuing embodied part of them (so destroying or damaging these *eidolata* can be seen as wounding the person from whom they came).

Objects such as tombs, buildings, portraits and wills also extend the real existence of personal presence and agency in time. I researched this book at Jesus College, Oxford. There, I became acquainted with college benefactors like the splendidly named knights, Sir Eubule Thelwall, and Sir Leoline Jenkins, who died over three hundred years ago. Not only did the estates and wishes of these luminaries continue to influence the running of the college in the twenty-first century, we ate under the gaze of their portraits. Before long, I began to feel that I almost knew these people. If they were not actually present, it was as if they were just away for a while, perhaps in another room.

The distribution and extension of the personal agency and characteristics into other people and things is called 'indexicality'. St Paul's Cathedral in London indexes its architect, Christopher Wren. It embodies his ideas and intentions. A book indexes both its author and the people who print and bind it.[11] A dance indexes its choreographer, and a symphony performance indexes both its composer, and the conductor and players who perform it. In the same way, a picture can index both the person who commissioned it and the artist who painted it.

The point that I am making here is that personhood is not hermetically confined within living human bodies. Personhood extends 'beyond the confines of biological life via indexes distributed in the milieu' (Gell 1998, p. 223). Personal interests and effects can transcend and survive physical bodily existence. Personhood is, therefore, often distributed beyond the living body, as well as being focused within it. Existence in a living human body is not an essential condition for the continuation of personhood and agency. A person's continuing agency can be experienced by others through distributed objects and institutions closely associated with them. Persons, then, are 'the sum total of the indexes which testify, in life and subsequently, to the biographical existence of this or that individual' (Gell 1998, p. 222).

Building on the insight that the agency and presence of human agents can be extended and distributed through objects, Gell develops a theory of art applicable to all objects everywhere, not just to the high art of Western culture. Objects that are taken to be art are those that appear to index their creators; thus perceivers discover in them some sense of human purpose and intentionality. This enables viewers to have meaningful relationships with them.[12]

The person who creates an object, the primary agent, does so with purpose and intention. This is then embodied in the created object. Personal intention is realized in material form. In this marriage between intention and materiality, secondary social agency is born.

The created artefact may not be biologically alive, or genetically human. However, its embodiment of human intention gives it some of the qualities of its creator. As a secondary agent, it can resist, or have effects upon, other agents. The object abducts agency from, as well as being an index of, its creator. It puts humans who encounter it in contact with the intentional being who brought it into existence. They find a 'congealed' residue of performance and agency within it, 'through which access to other persons can be attained, and via which their agency can be created' (Gell 1998, p. 68). They may have to behave towards it as they would towards a person. Indeed, if agency is sufficiently ingenious and indecipherable, a 'technology of enchantment' occurs, so the object is treated exactly like a person (Gell 1998, pp. 70–71). Thus the relationships that humans have with images of the gods are not symbolic, they are personal, because they represent a direct encounter between agents and persons.[13] Effectively, this makes us all everyday idolaters, entering into meaningful personlike relationships with objects throughout our lives.

As an *eidolon* or index of a creative intentional mind, the object can be internalized within a perceiver. Perceivers can take in the 'skins' of other persons found in objects so they become part of them. Thus material created objects, expressions of distributed personal agency and intention, help create the human persons who ingest them.[14]

Gell claims that art and other objects that materially embody human will and intention are 'the equivalent of persons, or more precisely, social agents'. They must, therefore, be 'considered as persons' (Gell 1998, pp. 7, 9).[15] This conclusion is arrived at by extending the notion of personhood beyond the biological human being, making intention and will central to personhood and agency, and by dissolving the absolute boundary between living humans and inanimate substance in the case of intentionally created objects.

In this section I have suggested that some common notions of personhood which confine it solely and automatically within biologically living human beings are misleading. Aspects of personhood understood as intention, purpose and agency can be attributed, distributed and recognized in created material objects that index their creators. It is, therefore, inevitable that humans will have personlike relations with objects, especially those that express the minds and wills of their creators particularly clearly. The world of humanly created objects is full of personhood. However, it is also true to say that the world of persons is full of objects and objecthood that shape humans. I will now look more closely at the way that objects and people relate in creating and shaping human individuals, cultures and societies.

## Artefact–human relationships in society

Human life and society are inextricably bound up with, and shaped by, interactions between humans and things. Our lives our bound up with 'stuff', with material objects that shape us and realize our intentions and goals, as well as being shaped by us.[16]

Given the mutually constructive nature of the worlds of humans and things, little research has been conducted into how these worlds are constituted and interact at societal and individual levels. It is only recently that scholars have begun to look in detail at this. This reflects the taboo against breaking the barriers between the human and inanimate worlds. In particular, scholars have been uninterested in what things which are not sold do for individuals and groups.[17] They have also largely neglected to study the ways in which commodities (things that are produced and offered for sale) become personalized and intermingle with human agents after they have been sold.

Even in the articulate zone of human–artefact relationships covered by art history, studies of these relationships have tended to be rather generalized, focusing on their symbolic and meaning-creating dimensions.[18] Very few studies have concentrated on the non-symbolic relationships of particular objects with people in which the latter are recognized to have some quasi-autonomous social agency of their own.[19] The study of material civilization and 'the ordinary and everyday interactions of people with objects' has been strangely neglected in what purports to be a materialist culture (Dant 2005, p. 33).[20]

Hereinafter, I shall take it as axiomatic that artefacts and things simultaneously participate in both matter and meaning, they are cultural and practical, symbolic and useful. They are not just background stage settings to human action, personality, identity, culture and society (Gosden and Marshall 1999, p. 169). They are, in fact, integral to, and actively constitutive of, human action and meanings. While many things are certainly 'humble' and self-effacing, they have concrete form and existence. They help to shape the human and non-human worlds physically, psychologically, culturally and socially.[21]

A good example of the double role of objects as participating in both meaning and symbol, and materiality and usefulness, is the car.[22] The choice and possession of a car can be a symbolic thing, reflecting status, fashion and attitudes to social norms and customs. Thus a Morris Minor owner may be differently perceived than a Ferrari owner. Symbolically, your car 'says' a lot about you. However, it does not just contribute to personal meaning and identity. Non-symbolically, a car is of practical use. It facilitates and extends what an individual can actually do, who they can relate to, where they can go. It may fundamentally change one's relationship with family, friends and the environment. Thus one not only conceives of oneself and others differently, one relates differently to the external environment. Both materially and symbolically, then, the car helps to constitute the person and actions of its owner or driver.[23]

A number of studies have been undertaken on the symbolic and meaning involvement of objects.[24] The most relevant and detailed study here is the ethnographic study of domestic things and possessions undertaken by Csikszentmihalyi and Rochberg Halton (1981) in the USA. This suggests that things that people assemble around them within the home are vitally constitutive of the identity and meanings of the self. The things that people cherish (mostly furniture, not art, and mostly for reasons of stored memories that establish continuity, rather than for aesthetic reasons) connect them to wider meanings and life purposes. If identity is constituted around meanings and goals, then domestic objects form a supportive microcosm of symbolic meanings that reminds us of this. Thus a person who possesses a gun, even if they do not use it, is constituted symbolically by this possession as a gun-owner, and this becomes part of their fundamental identity. They conceive of themselves differently from, say, bicycle owners, as agents or persons.

This kind of useful study of meaning and symbolism, unfortunately, ignores the materiality of objects themselves, and the everyday interactions that people have with them. For greater insight into the non-symbolic dimension of human relations with things, I turn to social scientist Tim Dant. Drawing upon the thought of Heidegger, Merleau-Ponty and others, he suggests that 'human agency is invested in material objects through emotion, through meaning, through perception, and through interconnection' (2005, p. 61). Artefacts do not have a life of their own, but because they are closely bound up with their human creators and users, they come to have some independent and autonomous agency (or even personality) of their own.

From Gell, Dant adopts the notion that objects acquire a real secondary agency and intentionality that indexes their creators, but is separate from them. From the French psychoanalyst, Tisseron, he adopts the idea that objects, by virtue of their entanglement in human relationships in their creation and use, become deeply involved in emotions and persons. As they are used, these emotional and personal features become apparent. The American psychologist, Gibson (1986), advances the idea that objects offer certain 'affordances'; they are perceived to have their own invariant qualities and intentions embodied within them. So, for example, a path affords a means of getting from A to B. This notion of affordance inheres in the object, though it may be differently perceived by perceivers in different contexts.[25] This means that objects have their own character and 'personality' which is unalterable – a pen cannot be a light bulb, or realize the intentions and affordances of a car.[26] Finally, Dant draws on the work of the French social scientist, Bruno Latour and his associates and their Actor-Network Theory (ANT). This suggests that artefacts with their own inbuilt intentions, affordances and secondary agency become involved in patterns of interaction with other agents, human and non-human, to resist and assist, to hinder and to play. Particular objects cannot be made to do absolutely anything – a picture hook cannot take you to the moon. Thus human action and agency is limited and facilitated in turns by interaction with objects.[27] ANT holds that, effectively, agency is often shared between humans and objects. Thus a soldier is a combination of human and weapon. If either component is missing, the fighting unit does not exist.[28]

Dant argues that when people relate to artefacts they are relating to 'the human agency that has been "congealed" within it' (Dant 2005, p. 146). Objects and artefacts have their own personality and agency that interacts with humans and affects what they can do and be. Humans therefore develop embodied skills and practices that are shaped by their non-reflective, non-symbolic use of objects. So, for example, 'the knives and forks that in western culture are part of our eating many meals shape our interaction with the food we are bringing to our bodies and so affect our behaviour' (Dant 2005, p. 137). Techniques of the body incorporate material objects. Thus, for example, tennis rackets and bicycle wheels are integral to the development of skills of tennis playing and cycle riding. Objects within the social network therefore 'call out' particular human responses, providing both limits and opportunities for human action and helping to shape human identity.[29]

Dant empirically explores the embodied, non-symbolic, relationship between humans and objects in a study of garage mechanics at work. Here, tools and components come into contact with humans who have to change and adapt their own behaviour to accommodate their instruments and materials. This is not a symbolic, articulate or reflective process, but one that is built upon everyday use. A reciprocal interaction between objects and persons engaged in a network of relationships informed by the living intentionality and will of the active humans and the congealed intentionality and agency of the objects occurs. This is a relationship between social agents within a particular cultural context. We learn patterns of material relationship appropriate to our culture just as we learn language. In experiencing embodied relationships with cultural objects, humans experience the other, and the other's intentions and emotions, within the secondary agency of the material object.[30]

Artefacts impinge upon humans symbolically and materially. Material usage shapes human life, cultures and persons, as much as the symbolic dimension of the relationship.

Let me share a personal example. I have a round-shouldered stoop. This is the product of a lifetime spent sitting down at desks and poring over books and computers. I am also lop-sided because, for years, I used a heavy briefcase that hung off the end of my right arm, eventually weakening my back. In both these instances, I have been shaped by the material agency and intentionality embodied in a range of different artefacts such as chairs, desks, computers, books, and bags with handles rather than shoulder straps.

This is not a symbolic shaping of my mind and body by artefacts; it is material. And this material shaping probably affects the way that I look at the world and the way people react to me because I now tend to look downwards rather than up. My personality is probably conditioned by the reactions that people have to me physically. These will be partly based on my appearance. Thus the materiality of objects and the intentions and agency contained within them actively helps to shape me physically, psychologically and socially. I am shaped by the secondary agency embodied in the objects that I use. And in this sense, artefacts enable the intentions of absent humans fundamentally to affect me.

Artefacts, then, are one of the main ways in which cultures and persons live on and perpetuate themselves. This is mostly done tacitly and non-verbally, so it is little analysed. But it is no less effective for that. Tim Dant puts it well: 'As we use material objects to shape our lives and realize our intentions and goals, so they shape us, guiding us in the ways of our society.'[31]

If artefacts are full of meaning, emotion and intention, if they have qualities of secondary agency, resistance and facilitation that affect humans, then it is likely that humans will have personlike relations with them. These relations might include qualities such as respect for the form, purposes and intentions of some objects, not merely casual usage.

Some artefacts, art objects for example, have more complex human emotion, intentionality, meaning and ingenuity invested in their creation and consumption than others such as plugs and screws. It is therefore likely that these will receive more respect and consideration. However, this line of thought suggests that all artefacts are worthy of more human interest than they normally receive. Dant (2005, p. 62) summarizes the position:

> [A] myriad of material objects are created and used as tools; if we ever stop to think about them, we regard them as 'mere' objects that do not in anyway [sic] compete with humans for status as beings. Objects are there for us to use and dispose of in whatever way we wish; we may treat them well or badly without any concern for their rights or feelings because they have none. Just as people in other civilizations treated slaves or animals . . . so we treat objects as possessions . . . over which we have complete dominion. But when we are not thinking about it 'rationally', we do sometimes ascribe human characteristics to objects, just as we do to animals.

It is, then, realistic and normal to respond to perceived personlike features such as agency and intentionality in a personlike way. This means that it is not entirely fanciful or metaphorical to describe artefacts as having lives, personalities, and even biographies. As social actors, they intersect with humans to create meaning and patterns of functioning. In this process, they change.[32] The notion of the life and life history of objects and artefacts has been extensively explored by anthropologists committed to the metaphor of biography for studying objects.[33]

Objects, particularly those that come to be intimately associated with people as non-alienable personal possessions, can be regarded as having their own cultural biographies. Once they have come into someone's possession, they may acquire all sorts of meanings and functions, eventually acquiring a history by association with people and events that adds to and changes their significance. Physically, too, objects may be changed by their usage – showing signs of wear, for example, as in the patina or rust that may accumulate on metal artefacts.[34] As they move through history and different contexts, they can gain multiple biographies, technical, social, economic, which witness to their 'lives'.[35] Thus an axe-head produced for ritual purposes in one society may then acquire a cultural or aesthetic biography when it arrives in a Western museum. There is the danger that stories that give objects meaning in one context may be forgotten, but objects themselves continue to bear the signs of having lived with other agents. Even when an object is repositioned in a new context, where new meanings may emerge, these renewals are never fully complete: they 'bring with them fragments of old lives, threads of earlier meanings' (Gosden and Marshall 1999, p. 178).

This kind of approach has been applied to the lives of Indian images of gods. For Hindus, properly consecrated images of gods are alive and active because they are animated by the divinities they represent. Rituals around the enlivened image such as bathing, feeding, putting to bed ensure that the liveliness of the image is assured. Such images may be displaced or removed – there are many images of them in Western museums. But they may continue to have direct personal relations with their beholders, 'animated as much by their own histories and by their varied interactions with different communities of response as by the deities they represent and support' (Davis 1997, p. 13).[36]

Even images that are locked away by aesthetes in museums continue to have lives and interactions with humans, outlasting eras and cultures to have several very different biographies. At one time the traffic from temples to museums was one way; images entering the aesthetic, art-historical purview never returned to devotional use. Now, however, there are some examples of religious and ritual objects regaining or forging new religious biographies in new circumstances. Thus the most important icon in Russia, the thousand-year-old 'Virgin of Vladimir', kept in the secular state Tretyakov Gallery in Moscow since the Russian revolution, is now once again allowed to be used in the Orthodox liturgy on special occasions.[37] It has moved from the sacred realm, to the secular, and now partly back again, acquiring new uses and audiences upon its travels. For religious viewers, this icon presences the divine; they venerate it even within its secular museum context. Thus, silenced images can once again begin to speak and interact.

Animated discussion often surrounds the use of devotional artefacts for aesthetic purposes. So even if images do not themselves speak and act, they provoke talk and action around them, a fact that enriches their biographies. They continue to be treated as 'characters' within human discourse.

A somewhat different approach is taken in Hoskins' account of 'biographical objects'. Based on research in Eastern Indonesia, Hoskins (1998, pp. 12–13) argues that in a non-psychological society, where people might best be characterized as 'dividuals' rather than 'individuals', not conceiving of themselves as atomized, independent psychological agents, some objects effectively become a part of, surrogate for, or extension of the self.[38] These biographical objects are things within the domestic sphere with which people have lifelong relationships: 'they share our lives with us, and if they gradually deteriorate and fade with the years, we recognize our own aging in the mirror of these personal possessions' (Hoskins 1998, p. 8). Identities and biographies tend to be formed around them. They are personally meaningful, centred on the person, and often created in whole or in part by him or her. They have an identity which is localized, particular and individual, as compared to mechanically reproduced commodities where relationships are globalized and generalized.

Western society is full of psychological, bounded, acquisitive, individualized, masterful selves. It mostly does not recognize the creation of biographical objects bound up with fundamental personal identity. Even here, however, some objects acquire a biographical dimension, sharing in the lives and histories of their owners and acquiring a patina as a gloss of age and use.[39] I have a couple of ancient pens that have accompanied me through my academic life. Originally, they indexed the designers and the artisans of the Parker pen company. Now their nibs and shells have been battered, bent, and changed by me so they fit my hand, even as my hand has been modified by them. Their capacity for material and symbolic relationship has thus been changed, even as their significance to their owner has grown.

Even in contemporary consumer society, the division between persons and artefacts is not absolute. A study of mail-order catalogues found that the way to commend products to people was to portray objects in terms of personal identities and relationships, whether those of the producers or the potential users.[40] Mass-produced commodities appeal to their market only if potential buyers can begin to personalize them. To move from the category of alien commodity to personal possession, an object must be encased with the symbolism of humanity and relationship. A symbolic association of a saleable object with a web of people who have in a sense become part of the object is necessary if it is to be attractive to others.

In this section, I have selectively reviewed some of the thinking emerging in the literature of social science about the significance and plausibility of important, personlike relations between humans and objects. This suggests that a good case can be made for regarding artefacts as in some ways personlike. The qualities and attributes of personhood are not exclusively confined to the species *Homo sapiens*. In the light of this exploration, the surprise is not that humans have close personlike relationships with objects, but that that we so often fail to recognize the personlike attributes of objects and their importance for our lives.

While it is often unnecessary to recognize the personlike qualities and nature of either humans or objects, it is possible in principle to recognize the congealed intentionality, purpose and meaning bound up in artefacts. To do this more actively might be life-enriching and life-enhancing for humans, and perhaps for objects, too. But to suggest that artefacts and objects need to have their 'lives' enhanced is to suggest that they are potentially of equivalent importance to humans, that they are candidates for humanization.

I now want to look at this issue more critically, posing the issue sharply by asking, Can objects really speak? Or is this kind of attribution to objects just a misleading academic trope or metaphor which will turn us all into misguided idolaters, worshippers of the works of our own hands? This kind of attribution highlights the importance of taking the autonomous communicative and other personlike qualities of artefacts seriously.

## Can things 'speak' anymore?

St Francis was addressed by a painted crucifix. The kind of world-view and circumstances that allowed Francis and others to experience animated relations with artefacts has largely disappeared in the West. However, it is likely that within the realm of contemporary visual religion, people continue to have experiences of talking and acting images.

While in the devotional world images may carry on their business as usual with some people, generally this world of intimate, personlike and animated relationship with artefacts is disdained as some kind of animism. However, it is possible, without requiring the reappearance of angels, gods and heavenly powers, to create a plausible theory of artefactual agency and embodiment of intention that goes some way towards supporting the notion that humans and non-human objects can enjoy personlike relationships.

We lack a good phenomenology of such relationships because they are regarded as in some ways taboo. Existing beyond, and perhaps deeper than, words, we do not have a nuanced vocabulary for describing and deepening them either. If dumb animals are a problem in terms of linguistics, dumb artefacts presently defeat Western descriptive and expressive powers. Indeed, language reflects and reinforces the profound dualism that exists between the universe of people and the universe of objects.[41] Even to try and speak of objects in personlike ways feels strange. What cannot plausibly be articulated in words in a logocentric world may not be believed, experienced or acted upon. Those who try to extend words across the gaps between non-linguistic objects and the world of language using persons may be deemed daft. Snyder (2004, p. 196) puts the point well:

> Granting a voice to inanimate things can strike us as torturing, perhaps even violating language. Some philosophers . . . locate the distinction between things and persons in what they take to be the unique human capacity to use language. Beings are human . . . if, and only if they have the capacity to talk (and not merely to make sounds . . .).

Words, then, are part of the problem in taking artefacts and objects seriously. They continually reinforce the boundaries between human and non-human worlds, to the detriment of the latter. However, without them there is little possibility that humans can even begin to take the artefactual world more seriously. Words, language and objects belong inextricably together perhaps. But at the very moment that we start to use words to describe and explore this world, they begin to sound blunt, inappropriate, crazy. How can objects speak, have interests, needs, and so on? The vocabulary itself seems misplaced, even though it reflects important concerns and instincts about a world too often ignored.

Discourse generally has often felt like this as new areas and topics of concern have arisen into human consciousness. Women, disabled people, gays, and others confined to the edges of society and language as 'objects', have played with, and distorted, language awkwardly and shockingly to articulate an identity for themselves. Gradually the language they use becomes part of the common word pool and no longer feels strange.

Maybe objects and artefacts will never be human. Perhaps they will never originate their own words or articulate their intentions in language. But the baleful record of people in condemning humans and non-humans alike to mute objecthood suggests that we should perhaps be more open to considering whether personlike attributes and qualities might be discerned in things.

With these considerations in mind, I will briefly evaluate some recent attempts to discuss artefacts in terms of their speaking. Can objects actually speak in the same way that most humans do, or is this just a vivid, metaphorical way of suggesting that they convey meaning in the vicinity of humans? Most objects do not form the audible words usually associated with human speech. Even objects that do have 'speakers' and can make noises or utter words like radios, televisions and telephones do not convey their own autonomous meanings, purposes and words. So literally attributing speech to most objects is simply misplaced. However, a number of recent writers have attributed the power of speech and other similar personlike attributes directly, or indirectly, to objects.

Mitchell asks, 'What do pictures want?' He suggests that they want 'simply to be asked what they want, with the understanding that the answer may well be, nothing at all' (Mitchell 1996, p. 82). Mitchell sees pictures in particular as full of meanings and desires because of their personhood. They deserve respect and to be engaged in dialogue with their viewers. However, 'Pictures want equal rights with language, not to be turned into language' (Mitchell 1996, p. 82).

Mitchell here uses the notion of speech and linguistic communication metaphorically to suggest an attentive stance on the part of viewers to objects. Because pictures are full of meaning and emotion, and they are created to communicate these to viewers, they metaphorically 'speak' to and with viewers. But this is not a speech of words, nor should it be. Unlike St Francis, Mitchell does not expect to be hailed in intelligible words by pictures, but he does expect to have a communicative experience through and with them.

Tamen (2001) also notes the attribution of human-like qualities and attributes like intention, disposition and speech to objects. Among the kinds of non-human entities that seem to be able to be made to speak are wildernesses, forests, statues, paintings and companies. These are all non-human entities, many of them artefacts, to which people seem to be able to make claims such as, 'I know what that statue . . . means or needs' (Tamen 2001, p. 2). This implies that they enter into some kind of discussion or dialogue with the apparently non-responsive, non-reciprocating object in question. The 'speech' of non-human objects emanates from human language users. Groups or societies of human beings become 'friends of interpretable objects'. In interpreting them, they make them 'speak'.[42]

This kind of personification of parts of the inanimate world can be traced to systems of representation in the legal world where inanimate objects such as bells and statues can attract liability and responsibility of injuries caused. Thus all manner of things can be made to 'speak', but only if the right human societies are to hand. Societies of friends of interpretable objects include those that can make churches and museum objects speak, and who can discern the interests and intentions of statues and corporate bodies.[43]

With a basic notion of legal representation and interpretation, it is reasonable that things (as well as people) can in some sense speak. But this is clearly metaphorical and to do with the conferring of a certain kind of status within the human world.

The most vigorous proponent of the direct speech of objects is Lorraine Daston, editor of *Things that Talk* (2004). Introducing a collection of essays that look at various (primarily visual) objects such as glass flowers, soap bubbles, photographs, columns, islands and Rorschach cards, Daston asserts that these things

> talk; they do not merely repeat. They are not instruments for recording and playing back the human voice . . . Cartesian anthropocentrism, which asserts the monopoly on language for human beings, is a form of narcissism that condemns things merely to echo what people say . . . Yet the things treated in these pages manifest something of the plenitude, spontantaneity, and fitness of utterance Descartes ascribed to language. (Daston 2004, pp. 11–12)

Some things do not just speak by 'interpretation, projection and puppetry' (Daston 2004, p. 15). Underlying any overt semiotic meaning that may be conveyed by objects is an innate capacity in some circumstances to speak; they 'communicate by what they are as well as by how they mean' (Daston 2004, p. 20). Thus it is important to think with things, not words. If objects are regarded as speechless, it may be because there are too many words around them. Daston's book, then, attempts to 'make things eloquent without resorting to ventriloquism or projection'. Humans 'need things not only to talk about but to talk with' (Daston 2004, pp. 9, 12). The things discussed in the book are loquacious because they are unique or unstable objects that cannot be fitted into clear categories. Thus they seem to be animated in some way. It is only when objects become normalized, categorized, well formed and familiar that they appear to die or stop talking.

Ultimately, for Daston, the capacity of objects for speech is a matter of human activity and interpretation. Objects cause talk within interpretative communities, certainly. It is not clear that they can really speak for themselves, even if they actively engender talk around them. While Daston tries to get beyond metaphoric talk in trying to take the material agency and communicative power of objects seriously, she remains firmly stuck in the metaphorical. None of the objects discussed in the book really speak for themselves (how could they, without breath and tongues?) though, like many objects, they evoke some brilliant linguistic performances from their human interpreters.

So back to the original question, Can objects speak? Yes, in the sense that they evoke talk and interpretation in human communities. Yes, too, in the sense that some artefacts and objects are full of meaning, emotion and communication because these have been placed within them by their human creators – and not just at the overtly semiotic level. Objects can extend the community of meaning and interpretation and act as lifelike agents when they are in the vicinity of sense-making, language-speaking humans.

However, they do not speak, if speaking is understood to be the independent, intentional, coherent expression of audible words and concepts. The loquacity of objects must then be regarded as a metaphor for the fact that some artefacts communicate important and multiple meanings and significances to their human fellows.

Using the concept of speech in relation to objects heightens the importance of the meanings and significance that inhere in objects. This can spring out upon humans, prompting them into words and the attribution of lively agency to objects. However, to attribute direct humanlike speech to objects pushes language to the limit where it fails. It is to impose a human linguistic category upon the non-human, non-symbolic material world. This is a kind of colonization, albeit well intentioned.

If we are to take objects seriously, and on their own terms, we may need entirely to change our categories and terms for dealing with, and thinking about, them. Perhaps it is important not to force categories usually applied to persons on to objects in the hope that they will live up to human hopes and expectations of them and behave and communicate in human personlike ways. It might be more appropriate to think about the nature of the communications and relationships which could be possible between humans and artefacts. In the long term, different words, attributions and categories may be needed for describing and relating to objects on their own terms. We do not expect animals to speak or to join the realm of language. This does not stop us relating to them closely, or appreciating and respecting them. Why should we expect more of, or attribute more to, artefacts than we do to other parts of the non-human natural order? We have a lot to learn about how we perceive, take in and appreciate the meanings and emotions incarnated in objects, as well as about respecting their embodied intentions, purposes and ends.

Do objects enter into and significantly participate in the human world of meaning, emotion and intention, acting as agents and creating and modifying attitudes and language? Emphatically yes. Do they speak in the way that humans generally think of as audible speech acts? Emphatically and perhaps disappointingly, no, they do not.

## Are we as modern as we think we are? Everyday 'animism'

Objects may not speak in the ways humans do. However, they do participate in material and symbolic social relationships with people and other objects, and they do have personlike qualities. I want now to identify the possibility and reality of personlike relationships with objects in everyday life.

Perhaps modern Western people living in an ostensibly disenchanted world are not as removed from important relationships with dumb objects as they might assume:

> We have never stopped building our collectives with raw materials made of poor humans and humble nonhumans. How could we be capable of disenchanting the world, when every day our laboratories and our factories populate the world with hundreds of hybrids stranger than those of the day before? . . . How could we be rationalists, when we still don't see beyond the tip of our own noses? How could we be materialists, when every matter we invent possesses new properties that no single matter allows us to unify? . . . How could we be chilled by the cold breath of the sciences, when the sciences are hot and fragile, human and controversial, full of thinking reeds [*sic*] and of subjects who are themselves inhabited by things? (Latour 1993, p. 115)

Thus social scientist Bruno Latour questions the thesis that the modern Western world is a 'disenchanted' one in which reason and explanation have replaced mystery, and humans and things have been segregated into separate realms. The human and artefactual, the cultural and scientific worlds, cannot be neatly divided; they pollute, co-inhabit and co-construct each other.[44] The modern world is, in practice, a partnership between human and inanimate agents. However, the latter are denied representation, voice or consideration in the human affairs that largely determine the future of all entities on the face of the earth.[45]

Like Latour, I think it likely that Westerners are not as 'modern' and species-centred as they sometimes think. In practice, we are everyday animists. Reading, for example, can be seen as a form of animism as readers encounter text as animate, living mystery. We fix our eyes on black marks on a page, and instantly we begin to hear voices, spoken words. We start to see strange places and witness other people's lives.[46] Some people describe books as 'friends' and value their libraries more than their families. This is entirely understandable, because books strongly index their authors. A bit of me is trapped in the pages of this book and you are relating to it as you read! This is normal, indeed, unexceptional.

We are, then, friends and acquaintances of objects with which we have relationships. If the obfuscating rhetoric of idolatry, primitivism, fetishism, anthropomorphism and animism were removed from these kinds of relationships, we might have better, more considerate, more satisfactory relationships with artefacts that respect their inbuilt agency, intentions and contributions.

So what is the evidence that we make relationships with visual artefacts and attribute to them personal characteristics? An easy place to start here is in the art gallery with pictures. Here, 'even if we do not commit full-blown idolatry, we do verge on it all the time' (Gell 1998, p. 62). Paintings are full of human intention, meaning and emotion. Often, they have humans as their subjects. It can be difficult not to personify them, treating them as animated beings, quasi-agents, or mock persons.[47] They have a particular significance

> midway between the objective and the subjective, things that purportedly incarnate selves (both individual and collective) as objects, the word made flesh . . . Hence the difficulty of placing these kinds of things squarely on one side or another of the subjective/objective or art/nature divide might have been anticipated, though it is perhaps more surprising to find them athwart the person/thing divide as well. (Daston 2004, p. 22)

Mitchell squirms at this magical, premodern, subjectivizing attitude towards pictures whereby they are constituted as animated beings, even as he advocates that it should be accepted and understood. Recognizing that 'the idea of personhood of pictures is just as alive in the modern world as it was in traditional societies', he points to the example of ostensibly cold-blooded art historians who know that images are materially constituted and not alive but 'regularly talk and act as if pictures had will, consciousness, agency, and desire' (Mitchell 1996, pp. 72, 73). Mitchell sees pictures as being in a subaltern, stigmatized position to the humans who look at them, rather like slaves and women.[48]

I have noted several other examples of people relating to art-type objects in personlike ways, for example, hitting or mutilating them to 'punish' the prototypes they represent, stroking them, caring for them, and nurturing them. Some pictures acquire so much personhood and agency that they are better cared for than human infants.

It is not just in the realm of high art that people have personlike relations with visible artefacts. In everyday life people have 'animistic' relationships with the objects around them insofar as they appear to be social agents.[49] Children's dolls and toy animals often become real parts of human families, entering into social relations for a while and having character, desire, need and will attributed to them by their owners. A lost toy can be as important to a child as a lost sibling. And 'what is (Michelangelo's) *David* if it is not a big doll for grown-ups?' (Gell 1998, p. 18).

Perhaps the most common and intense personlike relationships with artefacts are those that take place between musicians and their instruments. Old string instruments, in particular, are frequently named by their owners. They have 'voices' and are cared for and maintained like vulnerable children, some travelling in their own seats on airplanes and trains. Many have to be with their owners at all times, and they act as extensions or even parts of their players. They are held close to the body, touching intimate places such as the lips or the breasts. Their users are devastated if they are lost or damaged.

Sometimes, instruments are regarded as gendered, and treated as quasi-partners, spouses, or family members; the performer and the instrument are regarded (and present themselves) as an 'item'. The comedian/cellist Rebecca Carrington, for example, talks about her two-hundred-year-old cello as a partner. 'He' is called Joe after his maker, Joseph Hill. This instrument indexes a person who died centuries ago, but part of whose being continues to interact with a contemporary young woman. This kind of intimate, personlike relationship to an instrument is seen as unexceptional, even admirable and necessary, when it could easily be condemned as anthropomorphic animism, or even idolatry.

Frequently, advanced machines that appear to have an amount of agency and personhood of their own become engaged in complex personlike relationships. Cars and motorcycles, for example, are often perceived to have a kind of personality and given a name, particularly if they engage their users in lengthy, complex joint activities such as long journeys and extensive, complex repairs. If they let their users down, the latter may hold the former personally and morally culpable – remember John Cleese in *Fawlty Towers* beating his failing car with a branch. If a car is damaged, the owner may feel that an injury has been done to them, just as they may feel personally violated if their possessions have been destroyed or damaged. Objects within social relationships thus become a conduit for agency and feelings.[50]

For better or worse, then, we appear frequently to enter into relations and even audible, if often one-sided, conversations with the artefacts that share our worlds. We do not mistake objects for humans so much as detecting agency, intentionality and other human-like characteristics and traces in them; these prompt us to interact with them in personlike ways.[51] Indeed, designers expend much effort deliberately trying to give objects personality so they will fit better into the human world. Incorporating emotional response into artefacts allows them better to enter into helpful relations with humans.[52] Thus it is likely that we will have ever more personlike relations with objects and the gap between human and artefactual worlds will be steadily diminished.[53]

Contemporary religion also contains instances of 'everyday animism'. I have already mentioned the relationships that some devotees have with statues of deities and other objects that represent divinity. Within Catholicism and Orthodoxy, this kind of mediated relationship with the divine is neither unusual nor proscribed. What, however, of those ostensibly aniconic religious traditions such as Judaism, Islam and Protestant Christianity where people are supposed to transcend objects in order to worship the invisible, living God who cannot be trapped within the material?

It is actually difficult to find a religious tradition that makes no use of visual objects to mediate and realize divine presence.[54] Within Judaism, for example, the written text of the Torah has often been regarded as far more than simply 'another text' which can be treated in any way its owner or handler wishes. For some Jews, the Torah has been treated as containing divine presence and essence. Many of the anthropomorphic, iconic aspects of God in the Hebrew Scriptures, such as the brightness that flows from the face of the divine, may have been transferred to the material text of the Torah. It is itself an index of the divine, in some ways still attached to divinity; the text and its divine author remain in some way one. Thus it can be used, for example, in kabbalistic mystical practices, as a way to access the direct presence of an embodied, but invisible, God.[55] The Torah scroll is often venerated and treated with the respect normally reserved only for animate beings.

While Islam does not have a doctrine of divine indwelling in the text of the Qur'an, Muslims similarly accord the actual text of this book great physical respect – witness the international outrage that ensued when it was alleged that copies of the Qur'an had been defaced by the US authorities in the Guantanamo Bay prison camp. In Protestantism the Bible, too, is treated with reverence as a physical object that mediates the divine word and in some ways seems to embody this word.[56] Thus, some Christians, including me, would be very upset to see the Bible mutilated, torn, or used carelessly in any way.

Although Protestantism theoretically has a very 'low' view of the printed text of the Bible it seems to gain iconic and personlike status, so damaging the book is perhaps to damage the God it indexes – and certainly to damage the community of people who take the text to be sacred and physically identify with it.[57] Thus many Protestants continue to behave towards the Bible as if it not only conveys the message of God, but also embodies divine presence. In some parts of Protestantism, such as Anglicanism, the Bible and other objects are kissed and treated in reverential, personlike ways, as statues or other objects might be in more iconic religions like Buddhism. Even in aniconic religion, then, it is difficult to escape having personlike, haptic visual relations with objects, even if 'rationally' or theologically they are nothing more than 'things'.[58]

Not all relations with material objects are personlike or haptic. And they do not necessarily have the depth that might be developed with (some) other human beings. We only have personlike relationships with some objects, not all – and the relations we may have with artefacts may change over time and space, as do our relations with human beings.[59] However, insofar as we do have such relationships, it might be helpful to rescue them from the opprobrium of 'idolatry' and 'fetishism' and the shadow of a materialist spirituality that devalues material artefacts. If we cannot avoid important personlike relations with artefacts, it might be more constructive to familiarize ourselves with, and get better at them, even if this swims against the tide of disenchantment and unbridled rational utility. Overt, articulate, rather than covert, relationships might be better all round.

We need to ask ourselves whether it is better to live in a world rich in an ever-increasing flow of material objects that are ignored, used, discarded, silenced and speechless, or to live in a world of more conscious human-artefactual relations, where the personal and social is recognized in the work of human hands, and the work of objects in constructing humanity is given due weight and acknowledgement.

## On not seeing through photographic images

One way of earthing some of the issues raised in this chapter, and also of returning directly to the visual, and to the nature of intimate, haptic sight, is to consider the material nature of photographs.

Photographs are ubiquitous in modern life. It is estimated that Americans take around 550 snaps per second; this adds up to millions of photographs per year.[60] They are easily reproduced in newspapers, books, etc., reaching wide audiences rapidly. Like other artefacts, photographs exist as both symbolic and non-symbolic objects. They are images to be deciphered in a semiotic way, but also tactile material objects. Both elements are important in considering their place in human life and relationships.

It is not difficult to recognize the symbolic significance of photographs. So, for example, many people would acknowledge that the photographs with which they surround themselves help to locate them within a meaningful world of family, friends, memories, etc. Csikszentmihalyi and Rochberg Halton (1981) in their survey of attitudes to domestic objects found that photographs were the objects most frequently kept and displayed for visual consumption, being used mainly to preserve memories of significant events and people.[61]

The materiality of photographs and their existence as material objects that have indexicality and a non-symbolic role as social agents is, however, often ignored. Viewers mostly suppress their consciousness of the photograph as a material object to see what it depicts.[62] This is a good example of looking through visual artefacts to see something within and beyond, rather than actually paying attention to the material nature of the object itself. Without material form and substance, the photograph would not exist or have the impact that it does. Furthermore, the material form, substance and presentation are bound up with the creation of symbolic meaning, identity and purpose. Photographs have meanings both as images and objects. Yet the latter aspect is often taken to be secondary to the subject depicted in the photograph. Photographs as objects are ubiquitous and influential, but they are also humble and oft ignored.

Engaging with the contemporary 'material turn' which moves away from language and semiotics to consider material objects on their own terms, some scholars have recently asserted the importance of the material reality of photographic objects:

> Photographs ... have 'volume, opacity, tactility, and a physical presence in the world' ... and are thus enmeshed with subjective, embodied and sensuous interactions. These characteristics cannot be reduced to an abstract status as a commodity, nor to a set of meanings or ideologies that take the image as their pretext. Instead, they occupy spaces, move into different spaces, following lines of passage and usage that project them through the world. (Edwards and Hart 2004, p. 1)

The materiality of a photograph is comprised of the substance from which it is made – paper and chemicals – and from presentational forms surrounding the former such as frames, albums, mounts. Both these forms of materiality carry physical traces of usage and time. Looking at a photograph, viewers, often without awareness, see its substance, its presentational form, and the marks of time and use inscribed on it. These elements contribute to the photograph's social biography as it has moved through processes of production, exchange, usage and meaning creation and interpretation.[63] Such biographical details contribute to the relationship that photographs have with their producers, owners and viewers, contributing a subliminal, material presence.

For example, the paper and chemicals from which a photograph is made (the quality of paper used, the use of platinum) may express a particular kind of intentionality such as the desire for permanence. The presentational form in a frame or album conditions the way in which the photograph is seen and understood; it reflects personal and cultural norms, values and functions. So placing photographs in an elaborate, leather-bound album resembling a family Bible may indicate a sacralized valuing of them which may then suggest more than casual glancing to viewers.

Materiality also impinges in the ways photographs are used and marked by usage. Well-thumbed photographs, or those that are stained, creased or faded, may bear witness to a long history of usage in social relations and exchanges. It is sometimes possible to deduce things about the nature of these relationships from careful inspection.[64]

Photographs are often used in exchange and gifts, becoming further materially involved in important human relationships. A portrait photograph of an important person given to someone else can indicate friendship or patronage. The material giving and receiving here may be more important than the actual image itself. Photographs can also be used as physical votive offerings or objects of intercession. Thus, 'layers of photographs accrue around religious images and shrines . . . Family photographs, wedding photographs, even foetal scans become votive offerings, objects mediating between peoples and their god' (Edwards and Hart 2004, p. 13). Here again, the aesthetic or other merits of the content of the image may be mostly secondary to the material reality and placing of the photograph that contains it.

Finally, photographs can become materially entangled in many ways with their possessors and viewers, literally sharing their bodily space and existence, modifying, expressing and extending their identity. Photographs are not just looked at. They are materially engaged in many different ways, for example, by being worn or touched.[65] Indeed, some photographs may not be seen at all because they are concealed in a locket, or within clothing. Nonetheless, people still engage in important and intimate material relationships with them, though these are haptic and touching, rather than optical. Consider all those photographs contained in wallets and purses, mostly unseen, but often kept closely about the person as an important part of the everyday personal world.

Some Tibetan Buddhist monks, forbidden to display images publicly, wear a photo-icon of the Dalai Lama under the robes: 'Positioned close to the heart, it can be literally embraced' (Harris 2004, p. 139). In an essay on the use of a locket containing both a photograph and some hair, Batchen (2004) shows how some photographs are designed to be worn and felt, to move along with their wearers' bodies. This is photography that is 'literally put in motion: twisting, turning, bouncing, sharing the folds, volumes and movements of the wearer and his or her apparel' (Batchen 2004, p. 36).

While academics often ignore the material, physical nature of photographic objects, this is not true of ordinary viewers. They often move beyond merely looking at photographs to touching, kissing and caressing them. Photographs are not just treated as optical images, but as textured, optical-tactile objects.[66] Edwards (1999, p. 228) notes of people looking at photographs that, 'the describing of content is accompanied by . . . an almost insuperable desire to touch, even stroke, the image. Again the viewer is brought into bodily contact with the trace of the remembered.' Indeed, some photographs can come to be treated as relics 'traced off the living; that which was there, like "pignora" of the saints. Like relics . . . ordinary remains (family snapshots) become treasured, linking object to traces of the past, the dead, a fetishized focus of devotion' (Edwards 1999, p. 226).

Photographs are particularly prone to being identified with their prototypes or referents. They are easily treated as intimate indexes and active expressions of their originals, for they appear to be traced from their subjects, to have had direct tactile contact with them.[67] They may indeed appear to be emanations generated by the referent itself, rather like a skin or *eidolon* that has slipped away from its original and become attached to the photographic paper:[68]

> As a footprint is to a foot, so is a photograph to its referent . . . the photograph is 'something directly stencilled off the real itself'. Indexicality, then, is a major source of photography's privileged status within modern culture. For . . . the camera does more than just see the world; it is also touched by it. (Batchen 2004, p. 40)

It is this almost substantial, emanationist idea of image or *eidolon* becoming embodied in the physical reality of the photograph that informs Barthes' (1997) famous essay on photography, *Camera Lucida*. The photograph provides a certificate of presence of that which has been, not just a resemblance. The indexicality of the photograph 'allows it to transcend mere resemblance and conjure a "subject", a presence that lingers' (Batchen 2004, p. 40). This 'allows an imagined exchange of touches between subject, photograph, and viewer'. There is a sense, then, in which the photograph brings the dead to life. The there-then becomes the here-now in an imagined exchange of touches between viewer, photograph and subject.[69]

Understood in this way, it is not surprising that Barthes and others have been jolted, seized and caressed by photographs. Nor should we be amazed that people want to touch and fondle photographs, as well as to burn them in anger with the persons and subjects they index. Perhaps it is this sense of haptic connection that gives photographs of massacres and atrocities their power. Even at the level of passionless everyday existence, we can look at images of ourselves in photographs and sometimes feel sad or pleased at the way we once looked. This ongoing sense of responsibility for the image caught in the object suggests that we still feel a kind of physical connection, however casual and remote, to the person indexed in the photograph.[70] Perhaps we are not so very far away from the Tibetan Buddhists who treat photographs as bodies that 'can be born, become ill, and die' (Harris 2004, p. 139).

## Conclusion

The purpose of looking in some depth at photographs here has been to earth the earlier discussion about the personlike nature of material visual objects. The case of photographs may be an extreme one – photographs, in their creation and subject matter, often closely and directly index human being with which viewers are likely to closely identify. However, they help to illustrate my general case that humans can and do engage in personlike, haptic visual relations with at least some objects. This relationship is based on the integrated symbolic and material realities of the object. Many people engage in everyday animism and personlike relations with photographic images, regularly, unselfconsciously, and without shame. Perhaps, then, we are not as clearly segregated from the material world as we might like to think. While photographs do not literally speak to us, they may 'address', affect, and relate to us in such a way that, if they are not in fact persons, in many ways they might just as well be. Looking more carefully at and with, instead of through, material artefacts like photographs, we might be able to have deeper, more satisfying relations with them.

# Notes

1 In practice, Westerners identify the essence of selfhood/personhood with the conscious mind enclosed by the physical container of the body. It is the mind as the locus of ideas, plans, memories and feelings that is valued over and above the biological organism located within the ecology of relations with all manner of beings, human and non-human. Humans emphasize their distance from the material ecology rather than their belonging within it. See Ingold (2000, pp. 95ff.).

2 For example, Midgley (1983).

3 For historical and anthropological perspectives on the evolution and arbitrariness of Western concepts of the biologically bounded, genetically human, psychological individual as person see Carrithers, Collins and Lukes (1985). Christianity has played an important part in creating this concept of the person (Taylor 1989).

4 'As most statues were probably heavy enough to kill people, and enough like people to be paradigms of intention-bearing soulless objects, they were frequently used as examples of the class of guilty soulless objects' (Tamen 2001, p. 80).

5 Animals like rats and weevils, corpses, and other things like haystacks have also been arraigned in legal proceedings. See Kadri (2006, ch. 5).

6 Gell (1998, p. 124) suggests that animacy is a quality dependent on the attribution of subjectivity and intentionality rather than biological life. He notes that 'there is a sense in which human beings themselves are "stocks and stones" – only rather twitchy ones – and when human beings are asleep, insensible, or . . . dead, the resemblance becomes much closer.' Social agency does not require biological life.

7 I write on the eve of the G8 Summit in 2005, themed as an event to 'make poverty history', and only days after the *Mona Lisa* was expensively rehoused in the Louvre at a cost of several million pounds.

8 For the Cree people, 'personhood is not the manifest form of humanity; rather the human is one of many outward forms of personhood' (Ingold 2000, p. 50).

9 It is perhaps worth reminding modern psychological individualists that as recently as the nineteenth century in Britain it was believed, following orthodox Christian doctrine, that an integral relationship continued to exist between corpses and souls that had passed on. Hence the fear of destruction of bodily remains by cremation or dissection, and the brave gesture of Jeremy Bentham in having himself embalmed at death. See Richardson (1989).

10 A familiar example of the distributed person can be found in everyday life. Most people have images of people whom they have met, but no longer see, firmly in their mind's eyes. You probably have a clear mental image of your parents, even if they are dead. More disconcertingly, you may have adopted some of their physical mannerisms and attitudes. And if you have children, for instance, you may well have heard a voice coming out of you that is your mother's or your father's, as you rebuke them or pass on some 'wisdom'. In this sense, people give off bits of themselves, *eidolata* or skins, visible and invisible, that pass into other people's lives and characters. Thus aspects of their person survive their absence or death.

11 I have long thought that inside every academic thesis, however obscure, is a person trying to get out. I now realize that in some ways theses and books actually contain diffused parts of their authors who are indexed in them. Perhaps that is why writing is sometimes such a difficult and depleting business which can leave the writer empty and exhausted.

12 It is because the natural order appears to have indexical purpose and intention that humans have posited a humanlike creator agent, or God, according to some theorists. Cf. Guthrie (1993), Daston (1998).

13 Gell (1998, p. 135).

14 Gell (1998, p. 223).

15 Gell (1998, p. 123): 'All that may be necessary for stocks and stones to become "social agents" . . . is that there should be actual human persons/agents "in the neighbourhood" of these inert objects, not that they should be biologically human persons themselves.'

16 See Dant (2005, p. x). 'We spend most of our waking time more or less alone, not interacting with anyone. But we are always living with the things that have been produced within our society, things which have a cultural resonance that makes the flow of our lives seem familiar . . . material things accompany the activities of our body and provide the environment for everything we do . . . these material things are human made, shaped or placed in accordance with the conventions of our culture . . . much of what society gives to people that is useful, is stuff' (Dant 2005, p. ix).

17 See Miller (1987), Dant (1999, 2005).

18 See, for example, Csikszentmihalyi and Rochberg Halton (1981).

19 Dant (2005, ch. 2), Edwards and Hart (2004, ch. 1).

20 Curiously, it is probably anthropologists and ethnographers working for commercial organizations who are undertaking most research into relations with objects for product design and marketing purposes. Their findings are often commercially confidential.

21 Edwards and Hart (2004, p. 4), Miller (1987, ch. 6).

22 Dant (2005, p. 146).

23 Clothes have a similarly complex set of material and symbolic functions. On the one hand, they keep people warm and protect them from the elements. At the same time, they are signifiers of the identity and social position of the wearer within a particular cultural context. Cf. Dant (1999, ch. 5). Schaffer (2004) considers how soap acted as both symbol and mundane useful substance in the nineteenth century.

24 For example, Bourdieu (1984).

25 Gibson (1986, p. 139): 'the affordance, being invariant, is always there to be perceived. An affordance is not bestowed upon an object by a need of an observer and his act of perceiving it. The object offers what it does because it is what it is.'

26 Norman (2004, ch. 2) discusses how 'personality' is deliberately designed into products by designers.

27 You can test out this theory of intentionality and secondary agency yourself by picking up any humanly created artefact. Even the most obscure objects often quickly reveal their possible uses and the intentions of their creators. They will also resist arbitrary usage for just any purpose. The reason that my computer will not do everything I want it to is because it embodies the purposes and intentions of other primary agents, persons who have created it with certain clear purposes in mind. These, and the material substance and form of the machine constrain, resist and shape my own reactions and possibilities.

28 See further, Dant (2005, ch. 4), Latour (2005).

29 Dant (1999, p. 122, 2005, p. 5).

30 See Dant (2005, pp. 135, 104). Artefacts mould physique and physical identity, too. Medieval archers not only had a distinctive purpose and identity in the military, they also had thicker arm bones than their contemporaries from firing their bows.

31 Dant (2005, p. x).

32 See Thomas (1991). Gosden and Marshall (1999, p. 169) note, 'as people and objects gather time, movement and change, they are constantly transformed, and these transformations of person and object are tied up with each other.' Norman (2004, p. 221) notes: 'Objects themselves change . . . Things are chipped and broken. But much as we may complain about marks, dents, and stains, they also make the objects personal – ours. Each item is special. Each mark, each burn, each dent, and each repair all contain a story, and it is stories that make things special.'

33 Gosden and Marshall (1999), Kopytoff (1986).

34 Dant (2005, p. 25).

35 Kopytoff (1986).

36 Cf. Nooter Roberts and Roberts (1997).

37 See further Gaskell (2003).

38 Strathern (1998, pp. 13ff.).

39 Hoskins (1998, p. 193).

40 Carrier (1990).

41 Kopytoff (1986, p. 84): 'Whatever the complex reasons, the conceptual distinction between the universe of people and the universe of objects has become axiomatic in the West in the mid-twentieth century.' Ingold (2000) underlines this mind-centred dualism whereby humans try to write themselves out of the material world.

42 'The sole business of various societies of friends of interpretable objects consists in attributing intentions and language to various bits and pieces of the world, making what non-members call "all kinds of unexpected things" speak' (Tamen 2001, p. 137).

43 Tamen (2001, p. 4).

44 Ingold (2000) similarly questions the separation of humans and culture from the realm of biology and things. All are bound together, though this is denied in modernist mentalist dualism.

45 Hence Latour's call (1993, pp. 142f.) for a 'Parliament of Things' where the interests, needs and contributions of non-animate objects are recognized.

46 See Abram (1997, pp. 131–2, 245). Relations with Scripture, *living* word, often retain this relationship explicitly. See further, for example, Wolfson (1994), Idel (2001).

47 Mitchell (1996, p. 81).

48 Mitchell (1996, p. 81). Some artists deliberately set out to make their pictures into agents. Koerner (2004b, p. 37) situates Hieronymous Bosch at the conjunction of reification and fetishism in art and suggests, 'Bosch never tires of announcing that the things he makes are potentially active agents that engage with viewers as if they were the persons and their viewers were mere things. His Seven Deadly Sins in the Prado gives evil and its ends the shape of a giant round eye that "sees" the picture's beholder . . . we become the passive object of this picture's gaze . . . In the Seven Deadly Sins, inside the dark pupil of its centre, we glimpse the agent of our surveillance: rising from his tomb, Christ looks out at us from the all-seeing picture. Not only does the object see; it also talks. "Beware, beware, God sees," warns text on the iris's inner edge.'

49 See Thomas (1984, pp. 212–22) for the power of human emotional, and other, engagements with trees in England. Trees are not artefacts, but they are inanimate. This has not prevented them from being heavily invested with human attributes, similar to those invested in pets.

50 Cf. Gell (1998, pp. 18–19).

51 Guthrie (1993) points out that humans are predisposed to see animated and anthropomorphic personlike forces in the world.

52 Norman (2004, ch. 6).

53 See Graham (2002).

54 Morgan (2005, pp. 9ff.).

55 Idel (2001, p. 197).

56 Morgan (2005, p. 10): 'English-speaking Protestants . . . have long displayed their Bibles in ornate bindings, enthroned in parlours. And the use of the red-letter . . . Bible, which marks the spoken words of Jesus in red type, is a noteworthy instance of the way some Protestants experience the iconicity of the biblical text.'

57 David Morgan (personal communication) argues that the Bible is 'the textual residue of divinely uttered words'.

58 On the day I wrote this paragraph, 28 June 2005, the Bishop of Southwark talked on the radio about an oak pectoral cross that he possesses. He asserted that he thought it was special because it was carved from the timber of a ship that had been present at the battle of Trafalgar. It appears, then, that even bishops cannot escape from a kind of everyday animism whereby things that have been present to events or people somehow become filled with personlike presence and meaning, if only in a minor kind of way.

59 Dant (1998, p. 38): 'humans interact with objects sometimes as if they are human, sometimes because through them we can interact with other humans and sometimes because they reflect back something of who we think we are.'

60 Batchen (2004, p. 42).

61 Edwards (1999, p. 222) observes, 'photographs express a desire for memory and the act of keeping a photograph is, like other souvenirs, an act of faith in the future. They are made to hold the fleeting, to still time, to create memory . . . In their relationship with their referent, their reality effect and their irreducible pastness, photographs impose themselves upon memory.'

62 Edwards and Hart (2004, p. 2).

63 Edwards and Hart (2004, p. 5).

64 Hanganu (2004) deduces from the pin holes in some photographs of Romanian religious images that they are likely to have been used devotionally.

65 Edwards and Hart (2004, p. 13).

66 See Edwards and Hart (2004, p. 9).

67 The inventors of photography like Fox Talbot thought that reality itself directly transferred itself onto the photograph (literally, a drawing by light). Talbot called his book of early photographs *The Pencil of Nature*, implying just such a direct view of emanation of the image onto the medium (see further Schaaf (2000), Wilder (2003)). The US courts originally regarded the sun as the author of photographs and therefore as the witness to the events recorded. Only later did photographs come to be regarded as documents authored by a photographer (Snyder 2004). At this point photographs ceased to 'speak' for themselves.

68 Gell (1999, p. 104) notes that in making a representational image 'the image of the prototype is bound to, or fixed and imprisoned within the index'. Thus 'I am the cause of the form that my representation takes, I am responsible for it . . . I can blame the photographer for taking the picture, but I cannot blame him for the way the picture came out.'

69 Batchen (2004, pp. 40–41). See also Barthes (1977, pp. 44–5).

70 Gell (1998, p. 104).

# 9

# Deepening Personlike Relationships with Visual Artefacts

Viewed comprehensively, human beings are makers and users of things. Some things need to be inanimate; others must be animate. Some images we want simply to show us where the toilet is, others we want to talk to us, reveal the nature of God, or heal our ills, or make our wives pregnant or husbands fertile. We both animate and dis-animate, even in the same breath, and we alternately turn the inanimate into the animate and back again. We personify endlessly and ignore people, animals and things shamelessly.

David Morgan

Prior to all our verbal reflections, at the level of our spontaneous, sensorial engagement with the world around us, we are *all* animists.

David Abram, *The Spell of the Sensuous*

## Introduction

Consideration of visuality in the modern world cannot be confined to the restricted realm of high-art images, with its emphasis on symbolic meaning and semiotic communication. It must also take in the visual aspect of all objects. Haptic sight as a governing model, or scopic regime, for multi-sensual perception implies taking the relational aspect of all perceptual experience seriously. Thus attention must be directed not only at art works but also at other, more humble objects with a visual aspect. In principle, any perceptually available artefact is one that can be related to by humans. Not all objects, any more than all people, are related to in the same ways. But, in principle, all kinds of relationships, some of which may be deeply appreciative and important, can be entered into with material artefacts.

Many moderns perhaps devalue artefacts by seeing through and past them. In this chapter I want to discuss attitudes and ways in which we might increase our visual perception and responsiveness in relation to visually available objects of all kinds. Thus I change from broad analysis and description towards prescription, from comprehension to concrete response and responsibility. What, then, might be done about seeing things differently, and in regard to our relationships and responsibilities to visual artefacts?

I want to argue that we need to appreciate visual objects of all kinds to a much greater extent than hitherto. Indeed, I suggest that we need to love them! That implies attending to them, respecting their ends and intentions, trying to see them for what they are, and not just for what they might do for humans, attempting to understand them, and manifesting many of the other attitudes and behaviours that we are accustomed to find in human personal loving relationships. We need to wonder with and at them, as we do at some of our fellow human beings. Like their human creators, they are full of craft, meaning, intention, emotion and communication. Like humans, they are 'little worlds made cunningly' (Donne 1990, p. 83), however commonplace, mundane, numerous, or humble they may be. They may even be revelatory to us, deepening our perceptions and relationships with the material world. At least some of them, some of the time, deserve much more attention and respect than they normally receive in the world of 'normal blindness' (Levin 1988, p. 58). Humans close their eyes to so much.[1] It is important both to realize the limits of our vision and then to expand it to include a wider and different range of objects than those privileged by their designation as art, by their cost, or by their rarity. Artistic or unusual artefacts should be included – but why stop looking with keen, intersensory, embodied attention when we turn away from this restricted range of unique or rare objects?

## Objections to 'loving' and treating visual artefacts as personlike

Humans can, and do, enter into personlike relations with some objects. My argument is that we need to recognize and take responsibility for these, understanding them better. However, both secular and religious contemporaries share considerable reservations about conferring personlike significance on the works of human hands. In this section, I consider some of the barriers and objections that might be advanced against deepening personlike relationships with artefacts.

## We are not animists or primitives

The first objection to loving artefacts, or respecting them as having personlike features, is that this might seem to imply that we are animists, or primitives. Animism is the attribution of some kind of life or animation to inanimate things. Western observers first used it as a term to describe the behaviour of 'primitive' non-Western peoples who appeared to attribute personlike properties to objects of worship like statues or fetishes which were believed to be inhabited by spirits.[2] To recognize personlike attributes in artefacts, and to treat them in some respects as personlike, might, therefore, be seen as a return to primitive, animistic ways.

This objection can be met in several ways. First, there must now be doubts about whether the vocabulary of progressive versus primitive is any longer appropriate in a world where the diversity and value of different cultures is increasingly recognized. Second, the whole notion and value of 'progress' is problematic when the dangers and costs of technological progress are considered, especially in the face of impending ecological disaster.[3] Awareness is dawning that animist, fetishist, 'primitive' societies often have more balanced, less harmful, richer relationships with their ecologies.[4] Third, animists were never mindless idolaters who took matter to be divine. They were perfectly able to distinguish between gods and their representations, but nonetheless able to accept and respect the mediating role of the material in shaping their lives.[5]

Fourth, and more important, is the argument that we have never really been modern (Latour 1993). While it has been convenient to think of people in non-Western, less industrially developed cultures as completely different, primitive and animist, there is all sorts of animism in late capitalist society. The objection that we should not have personlike relations with objects falls in the face of the phenomenological reality that we do have such relationships. Indeed, the language of animism is unhelpful because it stops us treating these relationships seriously. Animism sounds vaguely shameful and infantile – we should have grown out of it. However, it can be redefined in a more positive way:

> Animists are people who recognize that the world is full of persons, only some of whom are human, and that life is always lived in relationship with others. Animism is lived out in various ways that are all about learning to act respectfully (carefully and constructively) towards and among other persons. Persons are beings, rather than objects, who are animated and social towards

others . . . animism is . . . concerned with learning how to be a good person in respectful relationships with other persons. (Harvey 2005, p. xi)

If animism is thus positively and constructively understood, we need to grow into it rather than out of it: 'The new animism names worldviews and lifeways in which people seek to know how they might respectfully and properly engage with other persons' (Harvey 2005, p. xiv).

Moving beyond disparaging understandings of animism, primitivism and fetishism allows better understanding of what humans actually do with objects in everyday life. This will break down barriers between objects and people. It will also challenge prejudices against peoples and cultures which do not fit into Western modes of identity and interaction with the world.

The suggestion that we should regard some objects as having person-like qualities is not based upon requiring belief that the world is alive and inspired from outside. It is based on the phenomenological observation of Western people who do, in fact, treat some objects as having person-like qualities. It is also grounded in the argument that artefacts have personlike qualities and interact in personal ways because they have been created by human persons who have filled them with intention, emotion, agency and communication. Humans do not need to become closet supernaturalists to give significance and value to artefacts.

## We are not romantics or re-enchanters of the world

Some social scientists argue that while the world has become explained and disenchanted by the rationalism inherent in science, technology, bureaucracy and capitalism, people cannot bear living without mystery, depth, spirit, magic and, perhaps, some kind of divinity, beyond the facts of existence and calculability.[6] However 'officially' rational the world is, people find ways of re-enchanting it so it becomes habitable and meaningful.

This kind of thinking implies that those who acknowledge some element of reality and wonder in relating in a personlike way to natural or artefactual objects are retreating into a kind of fantasy world. Thus, the Romantic movement, which invested such importance in human relations with nature, using concepts like the sublime to suggest a more than instrumental, rational relationship with nature, seems to point towards a covert resacralization of the world without conventional theism.[7]

The idea of relating to non-human things in a personlike way can appear to be nostalgia, romanticism, or wilful non-realism. Because we do not want to think of the non-human universe as empty of sentient and mysterious beings, we attempt magically to reintroduce these in the form of relating in a personlike way to everyday artefacts. This is a flight from reality back into social and individual infancy where it was possible to regard the world as magically charged and full of wonder. In the face of this, it could be argued that, if we are to take responsibility for the world, we need to engage with it without enchantment, mystery and magic.

Using notions like disenchantment, re-enchantment and romanticism can imply that, if there is no god, then humans must substitute magic to fill any gaps in reality and make the world hospitable. Westerners usually take magic to be antithetical to reason and explanation, a childish substitute for reason. The dualistic and implicitly progressivist vocabulary that is used here is unhelpful. It would, perhaps, be useful to jettison concepts like enchantment and disenchantment in thinking about human–artefact relations.

One response to this kind of point is that perhaps the world really does continue to be enchanted and to have mysterious, invisible, spiritual dimensions. Perhaps humans 'enchant', or are enchanted by, the world because they are responding from what they are to what it is. If it is, in fact, mysterious, magical, spirit-filled, then humans cannot help responding to this.[8]

However, it is not necessary to believe in God, magic, or the need for re-enchantment, to acknowledge that, like some persons, artefacts can inspire wonder, delight, enchantment and awe, just as some scientific discoveries do. Furthermore, this kind of response to some artefacts is valuable; it properly recognizes their capacity for relationship and personal meaning construction. It also attaches people to objects and the world in which they have to live.[9] Without some kind of deep engagement with the material world and the amazing objects it contains, humans may not be able to engage fully with the reality before them. Even philosophy and science, the servants of rationality, are not inimical to wonder and awe.[10] Tim Ingold (2006, p. 9) argues for the desirability of re-animating the Western tradition of thought to recover 'the sense of astonishment banished from official science'.

In the present context, the critics of re-enchantment, nostalgia, theism and romanticism are aiming at the wrong target. It is not necessarily wrong to criticize these things. But this should not be taken as an argument that humans should not make personlike relationships with objects that are full of hidden, but not necessarily mystical, personhood.

If humans can have deep, incomprehensible and wonderful relations with people, they should be allowed to enjoy something of the same experience with artefacts without accusations that this is 'just magical thinking'. Indeed, it is perhaps unrealistic, magical thinking to ignore the existence of deep, significant relations with objects, especially if this obstructs dealing justly and ethically with the material world.

## We are not materialists or servants of objects

Although Western society is commonly (and mostly pejoratively) described as 'materialist', there is wide resistance to the notion that humans are essentially materialists, or slaves of the objects that they acquire and use. In this context, materialism might be taken to imply that goods and commodities have substantial influence over the ends and means whereby we live our lives. The idea that humans are substantially influenced and driven by our attachments to mere things seems ignoble and vulgar. Most people, perhaps, like to think of themselves as using things for higher ends. We are not enthralled to them like the proverbial misers of old.

Here again, a series of assumptions and ideas get unhelpfully compounded. What is being objected to is not so much that humans are material beings, or that they make and have relations with material artefacts, but the suspicion that to acknowledge such relationships is to admit to a kind of idolatry, a misuse of objects that overvalues them. This overvaluing (designated fetishism by Marx) means that somehow we are enslaved or enthralled to artefacts; they control and possess us rather than our possessing and controlling them. The objection is not, then, to objects themselves. It is to the power that they may be given in the lives of animate human beings.

The answer to this objection is not to assert that humans should not be materialistic and unconcerned with material things. It is not the fault of objects themselves if humans become obsessed by them. Rather, artefacts, and human relations with them, need to be opened for critical examination.

A spiritualizing materialist ideology that pretends that objects, and relations with them, are somehow shameful, even as it encourages increasing consumption and obsolescence, is not helpful here. That which is shameful, for example, enthrallment to objects, must be hidden and treated as an abomination that stands outside the human community, the realm of words and articulate consideration.[11] From thence, it haunts human consciousness without direct evaluation. This is much what happens in the case of money. Because people cannot admit to loving money, they fail to love and assess it appropriately. It then becomes a haunting presence, rather than an appropriately used commodity.

If we were to be real materialists, overt connoisseurs and lovers of material artefacts, we might be able to see objects in perspective and relate to them more fully instead of regarding them as a kind of naughty temptation to be denied. In particular, it is important to distinguish advocating overt and articulate relationships with objects from any implication that we should idolize, worship or overvalue objects. The latter may be more likely to occur when the former is ignored.


## We are humanists

One particular moral objection to personlike relations with objects is that the focus of human beings should be other human beings.[12] If artefacts and objects are allowed to captivate us, then we might love them rather than other humans. So they should be eschewed and related to only according to necessity. Both religious and secular ascetics would argue that artefacts should be kept strictly under control. Relations with them should be minimal and functional in the interests of social and ecological justice and flourishing.

Here again, arguments about not blaming artefacts for the abuses that humans indulge in with them apply. Again, it is important to avoid a spiritualizing materialism that fails to be take artefacts seriously. And a further set of considerations about the place of artefacts in people's lives must be emphasized. Artefacts are intimately involved in people's lives and the human community, helping to form identity and to shape the totality of existence. It seems, then, unrealistic to minimize human interdependence with artefacts, to exclude their importance for us, and our responsibility towards them. This denigrates artefacts and distorts the reality and potential richness of human life shared appropriately with them.

A study of domestic objects found that people who denied meanings to objects also lacked close networks of human relationship: 'Those who were most vocal about prizing friendship over material concerns seemed to be the most lonely and isolated.' While it may be pathological to be over-attached to possessions so that their loss destroys the self, 'to deny meanings to objects is not necessarily a sign of being in close contact with people' (Csikszentmihalyi and Rochberg Halton 1981, p. 164). Attachment to, and relationship with, objects is not necessarily a sign of anti-humanism.[13] It may be a signifier of the ability to attach to things in general, including humans. This capacity is indispensable to human society and flourishing.

## *There are too many artefacts for us to love them properly*

This is a more concrete and practical objection than the others. The world is full of artefacts; there are probably many more artefacts than people in existence. The current Argos catalogue alone contains more than 16,000 of them, each available for purchase today. Even on a blasted moor, walkers are accompanied by watches, compasses, shoes, clothes, maps, etc., each one an intricately made object. There are so many objects of all shapes, sizes, and functions, that it is impossible to discriminate between them and relate to them properly. Humans do not have the will, energy or capacity to do so.

There is some substance in this objection. Clearly, we cannot attend to all artefacts equally. Often, we might not even get as far as recognizing their existence or consciously identifying their nature and significance. Objects are often humble and retiring.

However, the recognition that we cannot give equal attention to each and every artefact is not an argument for ignoring relationships with all objects. Much the same point could be made in regard to relationships with humans. In practice, we cannot relate to all people with equal seriousness and attention, a fact recognized by moral philosophers. St Augustine (1997, p. 21) noted in the fourth century that: 'you cannot do good to all people equally, so you should take particular thought for those who . . . happen to be particularly close to you in terms of place, time, or any other circumstance.'

We ignore quite a lot of people, quite a lot of the time, using them as background objects in much the same way that we treat many artefacts. This is not morally heinous, but it does not justify always treating all people as background objects. It is perfectly reasonable that our attention to artefacts should be selective. But this does not provide grounds for avoiding some attentive relationships with some significant artefacts at least some of the time. It is an impoverishment if we wilfully fail to discern and explore our relationships with the intimate objects that help to shape our identity and life.

## Conclusion

Many of the objections and anxieties outlined above with reference to recognizing and fostering personlike relationships with artefacts have some legitimacy. However, on close inspection, they can mostly be seen to be somewhat misconceived. Contemporary human beings, as a matter of fact and observation, enter into personlike relationships with objects and/or attribute personlike qualities to them in practice. Some of those who enter into such relations may indeed be animists, re-enchanters, premoderns, wilful non-realists, romantics, theists. However, there is no need to adopt any of these positions or assumptions to see artefacts as personlike.

That is not to say that artefacts cannot evoke a sense of mystery and enchantment in relationship with humans – just as some other humans do. And humans can become enthralled in overvaluing objects. However, a progressive and denigratory vocabulary of animism, primitivism, fetishism, enchantment, materialism, idolatry, etc., damns the recognition of personlike qualities and relationships by association. Maintaining the phenomenological reality of personlike relationships with objects along the lines of relations with other humans substantially weakens many of the apparent objections and anxieties in this area. It should then be possible to perceive and engage in these relationships more clearly and appreciatively.

Having cleared this ground, I will look now at some positive reasons for loving and caring for artefacts in personlike relationships.

## Why humans should love and care about artefacts

Arguably, we cannot attain or recognize our full humanity unless we appreciate the significance of relationships with objects that humans have made and which help to form humanity. In this context, it is not misplaced to transfer the language that we apply to personal relationships to relations with the natural world.[14] This permits movement into richer, less exploitative relationships with things, deepening understanding both of things themselves, and of ourselves. The perceptual paradigm for doing this is that of reciprocal haptic, mutual, attentive gaze.

Code (1991, pp. 164–5) establishes an epistemological principle of mutual reciprocity between things and people thus:

[A]fter Heisenberg's formulation of the 'uncertainty principle', it is no longer possible to assert unequivocally that objects of study are inert in and untouched by the observational processes even of physics. Once that point is acknowledged, it is no longer so easy to draw rigid lines separating responsive from unresponsive objects. Moving to a framework of 'second person' knowledge ... calls ... for a recognition that rocks and cells, and scientists, are located in many relationships to one another, all of which are open to analysis and critique.

Moving from relations of domination and exploitation to greater mutual recognition and respect on the model of personal relationships opens possibilities of insight and understanding. So, arguably, people should try to structure their relations with things in the nuanced way that they do with their human intimates as a paradigm for relating to the world.[15] The use of the paradigm of personal relations provides a general basis for considering mutual relations between persons and objects.

Theologian Sallie McFague (1997) argues that humans should love and respect all aspects of creation in 'subject–subjects' relationships, rather than in the mode of dualistic subject–object relations. Human life is constituted of all manner of relations, including those with the physical, material universe.[16] Thus the notion of personlike relationship should be paradigmatic of our approach to the world and things. The subject–object paradigm implicit in ocularcentrism privileges the isolated controlling observer and objectifies both people and things, to the detriment of good relationships and the flourishing of the planet. In this context, it is better 'to elevate trees and mushrooms, the sun and the moon, ticks and tigers, to subjects' than to reduce everything and everyone to objects: 'If we see them as subjects ... we are more likely to treat all others, whether human or nonhuman, in a manner that respects their integrity and differences' (McFague 1997, p. 47).

This ecological, subject–subjects model of relating to the world recognizes that agency, activity and influence are not confined to humans, alone regarded as alive, active and influential in a passive, unchanging world of things. It acknowledges that the world 'is composed of living, changing, growing, mutually related, interdependent entities, of which human beings are one' (McFague 1997, p. 96). In this context, everything is on a continuum of subjectivity. All entities are, to some extent, subjects, and never merely objects: 'the knower and the known are more alike than they are different' (McFague 1997, p. 97). It returns humans to a world in which ecological relationships assume a primary importance. While these relationships have never actually been lost, they have been repressed and submerged in the dominant Western model of dualistic subject–object relations. The latter have emphasized disembodied mind and intellect over embodied material relating.[17]

Subject–subjects relations might best be nurtured by a practice of loving, haptic, attentive gaze which allows intimacy between fellow subjects without the annihilation of difference.[18] This is very different from the gaze of the Cartesian 'arrogant eye' that is detached, manipulative, exploitative and controlling.

A number of feminist philosophers and theologians implicitly allow for subject–subjects relations with all of material reality, animate or inanimate.[19] However, unaccountably, they omit to include artefacts as an important class of subjects with which to relate appreciatively. So my next task is to advance some reasons for taking personlike, subject–subjects relations with artefacts specifically seriously.

## Artefacts represent one of the highest forms of human creation and self-realization

Ever since *Homo sapiens* started to manipulate the natural environment, and created tools to do this, humanly formed artefacts have represented some of the highest forms of creation and self-realization. Because the world is full of artefacts encountered every day, it can easily be forgotten just how important those things are, and what they represent in terms of human endeavour, thought and craft.[20]

The human intellect and body, interacting with matter, shapes and produces artefacts that vastly extend the scope of human survival and flourishing, from the flint axe-head to the personal computer. From washers to sculptures, artefacts are full of human purpose, craft, emotion and communication. Often they are amazingly complex and ingenious achievements, both practically and aesthetically, solving complex problems and providing whole new ranges of possibilities.

However, their very proliferation and familiarity prevents the recognition that many things around us are 'fearfully and wonderfully made'. Artefacts affect not only what humans can do, but also how we conceive ourselves and our culture. That we treat most of them so casually belies their significance for us.

## *Artefacts are useful*

Artefacts have a huge variety of uses – functional, aesthetic, symbolic, identity-shaping, etc. Indeed to identify something an artefact is to recognize that it has been deliberately created for some purpose. Steve Woolgar, a sociologist of science, collects artefacts that have no discernible purpose, meaning, or use. After a lifetime of searching, he has only found one such artefact. The uses and meanings of objects change over time as they move into different contexts – books can become doorstops, horse brasses can become decorations. However, the use and value of objects is often assumed rather than understood and evaluated. Perhaps this is mostly how it should be. Many objects, like grilles, screws and switches are performing optimally when they humbly perform their roles so that they do not attract attention.

Artefacts are the servants of human intentions and purposes, so it is appropriate to understand better how they are used. In a real sense, humans enter into moral relations with objects which are mutually constitutive or destructive. Our relationships with them can destroy them, enhance them, or abuse them. We should therefore consider the relations that we have with objects in the context of the ways that we use them, rather than thoughtlessly deploying them without regard to their own inherent intentions and uses. I don't suppose I am the only person to have broken a chisel by applying it inappropriately to the wrong material. This represents a failure to relate properly to an artefact.

## *Artefacts are admirable and delightful*

Artefacts are not just quiescent, passive servants of human intentions, they can be quite dazzling, fascinating and delightful. It is not just nature that enchants:

> Man-made complexities also can provoke wonder, surprise, and disorientation. Take, for example, the exciting and unnerving power that personal computers can wield over their owners, as when one finds it difficult to pull oneself away from the screen after playing around on the Internet too long. (Bennett 2001, p. 171)

Most people will have had experiences of artefacts that amaze, at least initially – gadgets in cars, stereo headphones, animated film effects, particular buildings or pictures. They enhance our lives and imaginations and open up new possibilities.

Often, however, the wonders of artefacts are dismissed or denied. Maybe this is because they are associated with the 'evils' of technology, consumerism, or mass production.[21] This does scant justice to the ingenuity of the artefacts' creators, or to the value of the objects themselves. It is easy to stop recognizing and appreciating artefactual wonders. This represents a loss to perceivers and a diminishment of the value that could characterize relationships between artefacts and humans.

We need to rediscover the everyday wonder of artefacts. I still find airplanes miraculously beautiful as I see them flying high in the sky. I wish I could retain the same kind of appreciation for the many other objects that have become commonplace, silent and invisible in my life.

## Humans should be responsible for what they have created, obtained and use

Artefacts can be seen as being a bit like children. They would not exist without the prevenient actions of human beings. Moreover, they can be seen as embodiments of human action and intention, and they index their creators. They embody meanings, purposes and emotions, and they can have lasting effects upon other humans and objects – over centuries, even, in the case of some buildings, jewels and pictures.

As with children, humans have some general responsibility for their creations and their effects. Dead historical creators cannot take responsibility for the uses and effects of the artefacts they bring into being. However, it seems reasonable that we should be mindful of the artefacts that we create as well as the ways in which we possess and use them. This is partly a responsibility towards the rest of the human race, but also towards the things themselves.

If, for example, I discard an old but usable computer in a rubbish tip, there is a sense in which I bring its life prematurely to an end. This is irresponsible when a machine might have a substantial life beyond its original user. I would not dream of consigning my children to the rubbish tip. Perhaps we should treat the artefacts around us more like children than like disposable 'stuff'. Thus we would honour the effort, resource and ingenuity that went into the creation of an artefact and its inherent powers, as well as partly justifying our part in devouring the common creation to possess and use such an object.

# Seeing Things

## *Artefacts form part of, and help to shape, the moral community*

Artefacts help to shape human identity and community.[22] They help us to understand ourselves, and they create the context of possibilities and constraints within which humans live. They do things to, and for, people, as well as for other objects. Cars not only help symbolically to indicate social status and identity, but also non-symbolically allow people to travel long distances in particular ways, changing their fundamental views of themselves and their capacities. It can even be argued that 'human vision is itself an artefact, produced by other artefacts, namely pictures' (Jay 1994, p. 5). Perspectival pictures, for example, shape Western viewers' understanding of what is real, what can be seen, and how it can be seen.[23] Thus, scientific images are most likely to be meaningful when they follow the conventions of perspectival art and landscape painting.[24]

It can thus be argued that artefacts are, in some sense, participating members of the moral community. They are subjects and agents within a community of subjects, not just objects. Artefacts are not mortal, organic, primary agents with free will and independent intentions, features often associated with the capacity for ethically responsible action and participation in the moral community. Nor can they assume symmetrical reciprocal responsibilities towards humans. However, insofar as they act as subjects and agents to facilitate and constrain, and can themselves be acted upon, they have moral significance within the wider ethical community.

Arguably, the personlike features that have been embodied in objects, and the effects they have upon sentient persons, entitle them to some kind of moral consideration from human beings. Asymmetrical relations do not imply that entities that cannot reciprocate in kind have no status. Thus children and animals are accorded respect and rights, even though they cannot assume reciprocal responsibilities. The language of rights is also increasingly used in relation to wildernesses, oceans and other parts of nature. However, rights-based morality and ethics as normative for all relationships is questionable. It may be more appropriate in approaching non-human entities to adopt an approach based on solidarity and care.[25] This extends the boundaries of moral vision, response and responsibility beyond a narrowly understood set of intra-human relationships.[26]

In practice, some artefacts are accorded honorary person status within the moral community. Famous pictures and sculptures often have their well-being and survival privileged over the needs of mortals. In wartime, for example, pictures and stained-glass windows may be evacuated from cities before the citizens. This is appropriate, because they are important participants in cultural identity and memory. I suggest that this kind of status might in principle be accorded to all artefacts. Not every artefact is as important to the human moral community as every human being. Nor does every artefact deserve exactly the same respect and treatment as a sentient creature (artefacts are not conscious of their own pain if they are mutilated or disfigured, for example). However, they should receive some real consideration from humans. Their needs and interests should be appropriately respected; this might constrain the freedom of humans to do with them what they will.

Some artefacts deserve a great deal of attention and respect because of their continuing importance in the network of relations between people and the world. Notions of where the moral community begins and ends therefore need some revision within the paradigm of subject–subjects relationships. If we fail to allow artefacts proper place and respect, then we might fail to take responsibility not just for the realm of artefacts, but also the human realm which intersects with, and is shaped coterminously, with it.

## Objectification does not serve artefacts or humans well

The modern Western habit of treating artefacts as objects, not as subjects capable of entering into personlike relationships, has probably not served artefacts, the world, or humans well. It has been expedient in terms of economic expansion and consumption to regard humanity as the only part of the world that is morally significant. A 'lifeless' creation is open to unbridled manipulation by human will and interests, leading to mass production and consumption which has been valuable to humans in the short term. However, it has had a downside to it.

Living in a world characterized by the insatiable illusions of hyper-consumption, artefacts are easily purchased, little treasured, then thoughtlessly disposed of. Instead of allowing attention to become fixed upon the nature, purposes and functions of objects, they are seen past and through. This is not respectful of artefacts themselves, or of their potential. It leads inexorably to the exhaustion and pollution of the earth's resources. It is not good for humans insofar as they fail to engage properly with the material environment in which they are immersed.

As meaning and symbol-making creatures, humans could have a different attitude that would be much more limited and specific. They could have a respectful and appreciative attitude to the artefacts they possess and use, investing fewer objects with greater meaning.[27] Instead of this, they live in a consumptionist psychosis in which their needs can never be satisfied. The exploitative inattention to artefacts threatens the long-term survival of the planet and of the human race itself. It leads to a process of accelerated entropy whereby the realm of artefacts moves, with the human community, ever more rapidly towards the production of crud.

## Humans need to become more attached to the world

It is part of human growth and development that we need to be attached to persons and other objects.[28] If we fail to invest in the people and things around us, normal development is disrupted, and we skate across the top of our lives and experience without properly valuing it. We may even be incapable of trusting ourselves and develop so-called narcissistic disorders as individuals, or as societies.[29] Symptomatically, we may then move on from one thing to the next without really engaging with the people and things around us. This is highly consonant with market consumerism whereby we satisfy our deep inner longings and desires for meaning and belonging by acquiring more things that will not satisfy our bodily or symbolic needs.[30] Advertisers play upon this pathology, encouraging the fantasy that the object which is about to be acquired is the very one that will solve our needs for esteem, belonging, affection, etc.

In this context, then, we need to become more attached to the reality of the artefacts we presently possess, rather than perpetually seeking the transformational object that lies just out of reach on the horizon. Discovering the experience of enchantment with artefacts in everyday life is one way in which we can better be attached to the world, and so be happier and perhaps more responsive and responsible agents in the world.

Against the Weberian disenchantment thesis, it can be argued that the human experience of enchantment has never disappeared; it has transmuted as society has changed. Enchantment can be understood as a moment of pure presence in which a state of wonder produces a temporary suspension of time and movement. It involves

a surprising encounter, a meeting with something that you did not expect and are not fully prepared to engage. Contained within this . . . are (1) a pleasurable feeling of being charmed by the novel and as yet unprocessed encounter and (2) a more . . . uncanny feeling of being disrupted or torn out of one's default sensory-psychic-intellectual disposition. The overall effect of enchantment is a mood of fullness, plenitude, or liveliness, a sense of having had one's nerves or circulation or concentration powers tuned up or recharged . . . a fleeting return to childlike excitement about life. (Bennett 2001, p. 5)

This experience, which can be cultivated and developed, though never completely controlled or predicted, firmly attaches people to life and anchors them in valuing the experience of living.[31] It can overflow into a sense of ethical generosity and loving response to people and things that can powerfully motivate moral behaviour. Thus it can overcome cynicism and detachment. (This active, embodied, appreciative attachment is very close to some of the key elements of haptic vision.) Energizing enchantment and attachment is to be found in many places, including social movements, humans, animals and human-electronic interfaces.[32] Cultivating minor experiences of enchantment in everyday life can help to develop a sense of joyful attachment with all parts of the world, including the artefactual world and the wonders it contains.

The concept of 'enchantment' may not be the most helpful one to use here. I would prefer to talk of joyful attachment through grasping the wonders of the people and things in the environment around us. Cultivating a sense of wonder and attachment in relation to artefacts is exactly the right approach if they are to be seen and valued for what they are on their own terms. It might moderate Western attitudes of unthinking acquisition, consumption and disposal, engaging humans more deeply in personlike relations with all parts of the subject–subjects world.

## If humans loved artefacts more, we would need fewer of them

In the hyperconsumptive world inhabited by Westerners, people seek more artefacts to address their desire for emotional stimulation. Because artefacts are not valued for their own sake, or appreciated in their material complexity and reality, this quest is symbolic, disembodied, and basically antimaterialist. Western society has an unlimited capacity for the purchase, consumption and discarding of artefacts, perhaps because we cannot invest enough affection, attention and attachment in the artefacts already surrounding us.

If humans cultivated more intimate, friendly and loving relationships with artefacts, along the lines of relationships with people, then we would be less inclined easily to purchase, consume and discard them. Loving attention is not something that can be afforded to every thing or person of one's acquaintance. Humans therefore invest their attachment and affection in a finite number of other humans. They try to get to know them well and become interested in all aspects of their lives.

It is precisely this approach I want to suggest in relation to artefacts. If we paid attention to objects, spent time trying to understand them, admire them, etc., we might find that we did not want to have a lot of superficial relationships with a wide range of artefacts. If we chose our artefacts with care and tried harder to nurture relationships with them, this might limit our desires and consumption, for we would find greater meaning and value in that which we already have. This would be likely to be good for artefacts themselves, for consumption-driven humans, and for the earth which cannot afford the epidemic disposability of objects that presently prevails.[33]

This approach implies a considerable change in the way that artefacts are produced and designed. Modernist sensibility dictates that objects shall be initially seductive, auratic and highly desirable, but that this enchantment should quickly fade, so that acquisitive individuals will want to move on to buy more artefacts. If long-term, entangled relations with artefacts are deemed to be desirable then 'emotional design' will need to change to allow people to become more involved with objects. This may require changes in the features that permit people to get involved with objects over the long term. Perhaps, then, lines will become less clean and decoration will become intricate so that objects are more engaging and intriguing.[34]

In this part of the chapter, I have set out a range of miscellaneous considerations that suggest that there is real benefit and value in loving and respecting objects in personlike ways. This approach is rooted in the notion that the subject–subjects relation is a more appropriate paradigm for humans in relating to the material world than the dualistic subject–object model that has dominated in the ocularcentric West hitherto. To become more aware of, and responsive towards, artefacts is, I have hypothesized, likely to be of substantial benefit to artefacts themselves, to humans, and to the earth as a whole. However, before concluding this chapter on a very positive note, it is important to pose a difficult question, which is this: Do all artefacts deserve our loving gaze and attention?

## Do all artefacts deserve loving gaze and attention?

It is perhaps easy to fall into a romantic haze about appreciating and loving objects more, and seeing them more haptically. But do all artefacts deserve human respect and attention? What about swords, arrows, guns, bombs, fighter planes and weapons of mass-destruction, which function perfectly, and may be visually delightful and fascinating, but whose purpose is essentially destructive? Do they deserve the respectful friendship of humans? I don't have time to deal with this important question in detail, but I would like to make a few sketchy points in response to it.

First, let it be remembered that artefacts exist because humans have created them. They index the intentions, emotions and material interventions of their creators. So they are our responsibility, whether we like them and their embodied purposes or not.

Second, and equally uncomfortably, these artefacts enter into important material and symbolic relations with human individuals and communities which fundamentally shape them. What is a soldier but the combination of a human and a gun?[35] It will not do for us to avert our eyes from this kind of relationship, unless we want it to remain unexamined and unchallenged. We should attempt to look all artefacts in the eye, even if this is difficult for us.

Third, we must be careful of blaming objects themselves for the intentions of the creators that they index. Maybe there is a point at which it is appropriate to admire fundamentally destructive things like pikes, knives and swords, particularly if they are ornately decorated and unlikely to be used for their original aggressive purposes.

Finally, acknowledging the possibility of appreciative, personlike relationships with artefacts does not imply admiration for everything that an object is or does. Love and attention do not necessarily indicate approval. People can love their children while deploring their characters and actions. We can have regard and respect both for people and artefacts that we don't like.

My conclusion here is that, in general, we should err on the side of trying to pay loving subject–subject attention to all artefacts, even those we despise, fear or loathe. Such attention might help us to control or channel our feelings and relationships more effectively. This might be more appropriate than ignoring artefacts that then haunt our lives and worlds unconsciously. It probably behoves us in this context to exercise a certain amount of 'ethical patience' before moving to quick judgements about things, based on insufficient understandings and appreciations of what they are or might do.[36]

And in this connection, it is worth remembering that relationships with some apparently non-destructive, beautiful artefacts, for example, paintings like the *Mona Lisa*, can themselves have ambivalent, even negative, effects upon people and the world. They can become consumers of affection, money and attention that might be more appropriately expended elsewhere. On the day that the summit to end world poverty in Scotland began in 2005, the Louvre announced that they had just finished spending several million euros on re-housing the *Mona Lisa*. The iconoclastic reformers of the sixteenth century would certainly have had something to say about the potential effects of this on human life and well-being.[37] As with so many other areas of life and morality, then, the issues involved are complex and ambiguous.

## Conclusion

If we can recover a sense of wonder at the marvel of particular artefacts to which we have become loving friends, using the paradigm of multisensorial, haptic vision rather than distancing ocular perspectivalism, human lives are likely to be richer, differently meaningful, and less based upon acquisition and consumption. Cultivating a sense of intimate, joyful attachment to, and appreciation of, specific artefacts which we befriend will broaden our understanding of ourselves and the world, while reducing the need to acquire yet more things that are seen past and through.

The challenge is to expand the boundaries of human community and concern, dissolving traditional boundaries between subjects and objects, things and people, to create appropriate friendship and fellowship with artefacts. We need to develop a sense of answerability in relation to artefacts of all kinds, not just high-art objects. This should be characterized by what Steiner (1989, p. 8) calls 'responding responsibility'. A recognition of mutually shaping reciprocity in relationships of immediacy and personal engagement should allow humans to become more effective respondents, answerers in action, with material objects.[38] This will not only preserve and enhance the status of the objects themselves, but may also make us more human.[39]

Bachelard observes that 'whenever we live close to familiar, everyday things, we begin once again to live slowly, thanks to their fellowship, and so yield to dreams which have a past, yet in which there is always something fresh and new' (McAllester Jones 1991, p. 157). Taking the example of an oil lamp, a 'kindly object' that 'keeps faith' with humans, Bachelard points out that 'Every evening at the appointed time, the lamp does its "good deed" for us' (McAllester Jones 1991, p. 159). It is a 'creating creature' that is effectively the 'germ of another world'. Adopting the same respectful attitude to other humble and kindly artefacts that share our lives might help humans to have more interesting, richer lives. It will certainly allow artefacts to have a fuller place in the world beyond mere utility.

How then might theoretical appreciation and commitment to friendship and fellowship with artefacts be turned into an actual attitude or behaviour of embodied, loving attention that will change the way we perceive and interact with objects? It is to this that I now turn.

## Notes

1 Levin (1999, p. 186) asks, 'To what do we shut our eyes?'

2 Harvey (2005, p. xiii) notes, 'The term clearly began as an expression of a nest of insulting approaches to indigenous peoples and to the earliest putatively religious humans. It was, and sometimes remains, a colonialist slur.'

3 See Beck (1992).

4 See Abram (1997).

5 Gell (1998). Terms like 'idolatry', 'animism' and 'fetishism' are never self-chosen designations; they are always pejorative, negative accusations from those who consider themselves superior. 'The image warriors always make the same mistake: they naively believe in naïve belief' (Latour 2002, p. 33).

6 Bennett (2001, pp. 56ff.). Cf. Ritzer (1999).

7 Morgan (1996a).

8 Morgan observes: 'Weber's argument for the disenchantment of modern, rationalist, bureaucratic, capitalist society ignores far too much in modern life. Protestantism and modern science certainly do urge us to instrumentalize nature, but Protestantism enchants the Bible as God's Word. And science is dumb about anything it can't measure. It has no authority to say anything about it, and it must remain quiet about anything that does not fall within the empirical range of its callipers. This leaves a lot of room for enchantment' (Morgan, personal communication).

9 Bennett (2001).

10 Midgley (2001, pp. 180ff.). In the *Theaetetus*, (155d), Plato asserts that 'wonder is the feeling of the philosopher, and philosophy begins in wonder'.

11 Pattison (2000).

12 Scarry (2000) notes that one of the reasons that consideration of beauty has been downgraded within the humanities over the last two decades is the spurious idea that attending to beauty distracts attention from matters of suffering and justice. She argues, on the contrary, that attention to beauty actually decentres the self and presses viewers to wider care and lateral attention to people and the world, producing caring and creative acts, an overflowing of moral concern. Scarry sees beautiful objects as

# Seeing Things

basically innocent victims in a misplaced attack here, though, of course, there are dangers in aesthetic enthrallment to some kinds of artefacts. I think she might perhaps suggest that if they enthral and do not produce a broadening of ethical concern for justice, then perhaps they are not really beautiful. Scarry also warns against seeing sight and gaze as inherently damaging to the things beheld. Actually, in the mutually life-giving relationship between objects and humans, it may be humans who risk being changed by objects – the experience of Dante and others when they beheld beauty.

13 In this connection, it is interesting to note that the first group of official 'friends' of inanimate artefacts to be founded was the Friends of Canterbury Cathedral in 1927. This organization was founded by the great Christian humanist, Bishop George Bell, who later became famous for his opposition to the destruction of thousands of people in the saturation bombing of Dresden in World War Two.

14 Code (1991, p. 163). Cf. McFague (1997), Abram (1997).

15 Code (1991, p. 165).

16 McFague (1997, p. 37).

17 Ingold (2000).

18 McFague (1997, p. 97).

19 For example, Code (1991), McFague (1987, 1993, 1997), Ruether (1992).

20 Lash (1996, p. 94) notes: 'First . . . there are very many different kinds of things. Secondly . . . there are many different ways that we know the kinds of things there are. Thirdly . . . competent description of kinds of things and ways of knowing demands attentiveness to the history of how things and descriptions came to be the way they are.'

21 Molotch (2003, pp. 5–6).

22 Dant (2005).

23 See, for example, Gombrich (1977), Berger (1972), Kemp (2006).

24 Kemp (2000b), Jones and Galison (1998).

25 McFague (1997, p. 40).

26 'A care ethic . . . is based on the model of subjects in relationship, although the subjects are not necessarily all human ones and the burden of ethical responsibility can fall unevenly. The language of care – interest, concern, respect, nurture, paying attention, empathy, relationality – seems more appropriate for human interaction with the natural world . . . than does the rights language' (McFague 1997, p. 40). Compare McFague (1997, pp. 155ff.) on solidarity. An emphasis on care for things that matter and significant everyday relationships, as opposed to law and rights, is typical of some feminist approaches to ethics. See further, for example, Noddings (1986).

27 Csikszentmihalyi and Rochberg Halton (1981).

28 Fonagy (2001).

29 See Lasch (1991).

30 Campbell (1987) and Berger (1972).

31 Bennett (2001, pp. 159–60). Steiner (1989, p. 179) writes of unbidden encounters with (art) objects: 'That which comes to *call* on us – that idiom . . . connotes both spontaneous visitation and summons – will very often do so unbidden.' Steiner calls this experience of penetration an 'unelected affinity' or alchemical 'sympathy' which is based upon some kind of presymbolic recognition.

32 Bennett (2001, p. 84).

33 I am arguing here for the development of real friendship or fellowship with artefacts, along the lines suggested by Bachelard. Bachelard believed that this friendship actually makes humans more human. In times when complex artefacts were much rarer than they are now, it is not difficult to believe that people treasured and

222

used them more, drawing into much closer relations of use, friendship and fellowship with them.

34 Gell (1998).
35 Dant (2005).
36 Dyson (2001, p. 118).
37 Wandel (1994).
38 Steiner (1989, pp. 8ff.).
39 McAllester Jones (1991, p. 155).

# 10

# Loving Artefacts –
# Approaches and Practicalities

Relation is reciprocity. My You acts on me as I act on it. Our students teach us, our works form us . . . How we are educated by children, by animals! Inscrutably involved, we live in the currents of universal reciprocity.

Martin Buber, *I and Thou*

Our eyes are far too good for us. They show us so much that we can't take it all in, so we shut out most of the world, and try to look at things as briskly and efficiently as possible. What happens if we stop and take the time to look more carefully? Then the world unfolds like a flower, full of colours and shapes that we had never suspected.

James Elkins, *How to Use Your Eyes*

## Introduction

Earlier on in the book, haptic vision, a rather diverse, incoherent alternative scopic regime to ocularcentric perspectivalism, was described and discussed, mainly phenomenologically, using the work of anthropologists and visual theorists.[1] Now I want to reintroduce haptic vision as a normative approach for engaging in relations with artefacts, drawing on the work of philosophers and theologians. Vision, like conscience, is 'a capacity to be developed and a task to be achieved' (Levin 1988, p. 14). The development of haptic, appreciative, embodied, multisensory, non-objectivizing perception as a response to the material world, as expressed in the practical cultivation of the loving eye, is the subject here. This provides an undergirding approach for dealing with non-human artefacts in personlike ways. Beyond the general advocacy of attentive haptic vision as a scopic regime, I will tentatively explore some ways in which loving, attentive gaze might be cultivated in everyday encounters with artefacts. This with a view to creating deeper relations of fellowship and friendship with the inanimate objects that share the human world.

## Cultivating the loving eye

In the last chapter, I argued for treating all objects on a subject–subjects basis. This loving, appreciative approach might be translated into practice by developing the loving eye.[2] Arguably, Western society has cultivated the 'arrogant' or 'nihilistic' eye.[3] This has been conceived as distant, controlling, disconnected, individualistic and unrelational. Sight is isolated from other bodily senses in the scopic regime of Cartesian perspectivalism, and regarded as dominating them. The corrective to this is to develop a loving, connected, haptic 'eye' that is based on a more relational, holistic, embodied model of perception whereby all the senses are used together in an integrated sensorium.

The basic paradigm of perception should be one based on touch.[4] 'Touch reminds us that reality is made up of others; touch is a lesson in "objectivity"' (McFague 1997, p. 94). It relates perceivers immediately to the physical environment. It is two-way and mutual – one cannot touch without being touched – and it reveals the world as both resistant and responsive.[5] Haptic, 'touching', vision is thus 'a relational, embodied, responsive paying attention to the others in their particularity and difference' (McFague 1997, p. 94). The loving, haptic eye respects others for what they are. It embodies the dynamics of mutual intimacy and distance characteristic of human gaze within primary loving relationships.[6] Thus it acknowledges and appreciates without owning, taking over, or controlling. It is tactful and courteous, aspiring to intimacy while appropriately recognizing otherness and difference.[7] In this context, viewers must learn to perceive things as they are, and to curb their fantasies and imaginative projections.[8]

It is difficult for humans to look carefully at things in themselves because vision is cathected with personal wishes, illusions and fantasies that colour the world.[9] The autonomous, psychological self is itself a 'dazzling object' (Murdoch 1985, p. 35). Thus, it is important to cultivate the richness of intersensorial perception; the appreciation of difference 'depends on perception, not imagination' (McFague 1997, p. 114). To attain perceptual courtesy and tact, we must become apprentices to the other, allowing artefacts to become our teachers and guides. Thus we properly befriend them.[10]

In attending to humans, generally the more one comes to appreciate their differentness and separateness 'the harder it becomes to treat a person as a thing' (Murdoch 1985, p. 6). In the present context, the more the separateness and otherness of artefacts is realized in disciplined, intimate perception, the harder it becomes to treat them as undifferentiated 'stuff' or 'things'. Thus attentive, just and loving haptic gaze should enable viewers to 'grow by looking' (Murdoch 1985, pp. 31, 34) as they broaden their sympathies with objects of all kinds, as well as with the humans who created them.[11]


## Looking artefacts in the eye

There is much rhetoric and exhortation to look more carefully and more lovingly at things, particularly art works, in the world. Iris Murdoch, for example, argues that great art manifests a kind of objective beauty which draws viewers to itself, taking them away from self and selfish concerns so they see things as they truly are in their multiplicity and otherness. Truth, goodness and beauty are integrally linked. Thus the process of developing attentive gaze is a moral quest; it adds value to the world surrounding the moral agent. Many theorists of this kind believe that we need to develop a more contemplative, receptive sense of sight, the better to appreciate and value the world.

There are two problems with this kind of laudable exhortation. First, it is mostly the 'beautiful' that is the object of the theorists' interest. However, I am concerned with artefacts that are not necessarily conventionally 'beautiful'. In principle, they, too, deserve some personlike attention, along with the more restricted range of objects that constitute high art. Any object gazed upon lovingly might become wonderful and beautiful as its meanings and reality unfold.[12]

Second, the philosophers tend to leave their exhortations to more contemplative, loosely haptic, viewing at a high level of generality. The assumption seems to be that beautiful objects will somehow mystically compel and draw the eye. Beauty, whether physical, spiritual, moral, or personal, is simply 'waiting for our love' (Armstrong 2005, p. 162). It is just a matter of surrendering to artefacts to engage in personally transformative experience that will add value and interest to objects.

I want now to make the challenge of relating to ordinary artefacts via the paradigm of haptic, visual perception more concrete. We cannot guarantee to have meaningful personlike relations with all objects (and, indeed, we should not aspire to this, any more than we can, or need to, have personlike relations with every human being on earth).[13] However, we can do some things to enhance our subject–subjects perception of visually available artefacts.

I feel diffident and inadequate in trying to suggest ways in which haptic, more appreciative perceptual relationships with artefacts might be developed. I am not a sensitive, articulate, or well-trained seer, as an artist might be. Second, I am not very good at relating to artefacts myself – I often misuse and break them. Third, the kind of haptic, relational seeing that I am advocating as complementary to distant, optical seeing has not really been effectively described or outlined by anyone. Perhaps this is because it is pre-verbal, embodied and non-symbolic so that it pushes on the limits of words. It is experienced rather than articulated, analysed and taught.

## Widening the purview of vision

Almost all the familiar or useful things around us put on a 'cap of invisibility'.[14] Humans see only as much as is necessary for their purposes; this is very little, just enough, to identify objects and persons, which then effectively disappear. Only very distinctive objects specifically designed to be looked at, such as art masterpieces, are really attended to. And even these can become part of the wallpaper over time. Our vision, then, is selective.

If we are going to develop attentive, loving gaze with artefacts, the cap of invisibility – or perhaps more accurately, the opaque glasses of assumption – must be removed, so we can look things in the eye. Here, then, are some preliminary moves that we might make in trying to include artefacts more deliberately in perceptual relationships.

One way in which we might become more responsive to visual artefacts is simply to use our eyes better. Vision is a dynamic, partial process. What we think we see is often a rather incomplete, holey, 'best guess' at what is visually available to our eyes.[15] Thus we often fail to see what is before us. We need, then, both to become better seers of particular objects, and to widen the purview of our gaze to consider more visually available material artefacts.

In this twofold quest, Elkins (2000a) is one of the few guides available. Elkins wants people to use their eyes more concertedly and with more patience. His recipe is profoundly simple – and very difficult:

> It's about stopping and taking the time simply to look, and keep looking, until the details of the world slowly reveal themselves . . . Even a postage stamp suddenly begins to speak about its time and place, and the thoughts of the person who designed it. (Elkins 2000a, pp. vii–viii)

Elkins commends prolonged, attentive seeing in everyday life. In considering all manner of easily available, everyday sights, from culverts and sunsets, to fingerprints and Chinese scripts, he argues people should attend to things that are commonplace and ordinary: 'Once you start seeing them, the world . . . will gather before your eyes and become thick with meaning' (Elkins 2000a, p. ix).

This suggests a way of concretizing the notion of loving attention through haptic vision, and entering into personlike relationships with objects that deepen our experience of living. If, then, we want to enter into more subject–subjects type relationships with artefacts and other visual phenomena we might undertake a two-stage process.

First, it would be useful if we simply *noticed* the variety and kinds of visual artefacts around us instead of assuming their existence and looking past them. It might be helpful initially to develop some categories for thinking about visual artefacts. For example, there might be some artefacts that are basically intended to be passive and unnoticed. Others might be intended to do something and be very obvious, for example, door handles, cars. It might also be useful to begin to notice what sorts of relationships we have with various kinds of objects. Are they, for example, careful, appreciative, casual, vital, loving, indifferent, or something else? Which artefacts do we look forward to encountering? Which do we try to avoid? Are there artefacts to which we give a lot of care and attention? Do some of them need special care because of their material structure? Just noticing how we deal with artefacts, visually, haptically and aurally, in this way might begin to raise awareness of relationships with them and help in thinking about how we might relate to them differently or more adequately.

Second, it might then be appropriate to begin *to look at and think about some particular artefacts more specifically*. Maybe we might take one familiar artefact and try to perceive it carefully for an extended period of time (say, at least five minutes), defamiliarizing it, and allowing it to teach us something of the nature, purposes and intentions that are ignored when we simply use it occasionally and casually. For example, a few minutes spent looking carefully at a spoon might prove revelatory.

It might be appropriate to adapt the advice Elkins (2000b, pp. 210ff.) gives to those who want to deepen their appreciation and relationships with paintings. First, be on your own so you can concentrate and be calm. Second, focus on particular objects and not try to see everything in equal depth at the same time. Third, minimize distractions, for example, the sight and sound of other people. Fourth, take your time and move around; you may need to look at the object many times before it 'decides to speak'. Fifth, pay full attention and concentrate on what you see. This allows self-forgetting absorption. Sixth, be faithful – go back to look at the artefact again in future.

On the desk in front of me I have some wooden pipes with a beautiful grain, several books with beautiful covers and attractive print fonts, a small, intricately designed box of matches, several files, and a few pens of which I am fond. Perhaps I should take the trouble to give each of these objects a prolonged viewing, rather than just using them or look-ing past them. They have all been carefully designed by someone and bear the imprint of much human ingenuity and indexicality. It might help if I picked them up, too, and thought about the texture and feel of these things to fully appreciate their otherness.

Maybe my life, perceptive powers, and capacity to enter into appre-ciative, personlike relations with them would be substantially deepened by offering them some sustained attention. It might be further enhanced if I were also to touch and feel them, noticing the texture of each one. It is the work of a moment to pull my keys out of my pocket and turn them over in my hands, looking at them and beginning to notice the tiny marks and indentations that these ingenious and useful objects were created with, and which they have acquired during their life with me. And it would perhaps also make some sense if I were to try to see how the various artefacts to which I have access actually work and were made. If I get bored with objects readily to hand, I could look more carefully at the books that surround me and the pictures I have put on the wall. The latter, like the photographs of my family and friends, tend to get ignored because they have become a routine part of my everyday working life. I might even try to appreciate and gaze more lovingly at, instead of through, the ingenious little laptop computer which I am using to write this.

One of the advantages of everyday artefacts is that they are readily available and can easily be touched and seen from different perspec-tives. Unlike art in galleries, we can become intimately acquainted with the artefacts that surround us, they can be engaged at leisure. There is no sign or interdict saying 'Do not touch' or 'Move on so someone else can have a look'.

We need to look more carefully and concertedly. We also need to widen the range of objects that we take to be significant. Traditionally, recognized works of art, antiques and other socially designated objects of note have been the focus of sustained gaze and attention. But fascination can be found in gazing upon objects and artefacts that are traditionally ignored or just used, for example, x-rays, scripts, coins, engineering drawings, banknotes, maps. This list might be extended to other domestic objects such as cutlery, light fittings, furniture, cooking utensils, lawnmowers, tools, bicycles, musical instruments, and much more.

All of these objects are carefully designed and produced by humans. Freighted with purpose and intention, they have a particular feel, weight, appearance and usage. We often have quite intimate but unreflective relationships with such artefacts, having regard mainly to their utility rather than their 'character', appearance and being. A more contemplative, multisensory, appreciative approach to everyday objects could increase our respect for the artefacts themselves, for those who created them, and for the world around us. What we need to do is to stop and look and sense more carefully, to open our eyes and other senses to relate to individual objects rather than seeing past them as clones of a particular class of things that are just a backdrop to life.

## Understanding relationships with artefacts

To enter into more personlike, haptic, relationships with material artefacts it would be helpful if we more consciously audited the kinds of relationships that we have with them, so their significance or potential significance in our lives might be better appreciated.

First, then, *how do we relate to particular artefacts sensually?* Which of our senses are engaged when we encounter them? Are they tactile, visible, audible and smelly, or only some of these things? Some objects, such as sculptures high up on buildings, we might simply look at from afar. Others, like dolls and forks for example, we might also touch, hear, or even put in our mouths.[16] I am myself an inveterate sniffer, as well as reader, of books! No particular sensory approach to an object is necessarily better or more adequate than any other, but we often fail to observe and reflect upon our perceptual relations and the stimulus that emerges in relations with artefacts at even the most basic level. We are thus limited in our capacity to identify and magnify the kind of perceptual encounter that we have with them.

For example, we may not notice that we are frustrated by not being able to touch a particularly interesting looking object. The acknowledgement of this would bring to consciousness valuable data both about the artefact itself and about our actual or fantasized possible relationship with it.[17] We would thus be taking the object more seriously in its material reality.

Second, *what are our relationships, rights, responsibilities and feelings about artefacts?* For most people, perhaps, there are two main classes of artefacts, based on ownership. There are those that belong to us, with which we can do as we like without impediment, and those that belong to someone else. The second type of object is not available for us to use without some kind of permission or sanction pertaining.

Beyond ownership, there are issues of responsibilities and rights in relation to artefacts, both individually and corporately. Do I have any responsibility for public sculptures, for example? If someone tries to mutilate them should I stop them? Do I myself have a right to mutilate or modify an object that does not belong to me if I find it offensive or think that my intervention will improve it? If an object that I have a relationship with, for example, a friend's picture, is damaged or in danger of neglect, do I have a responsibility to ensure that it is cared for? If I value an artefact much more than its owners or users seem to, should I have more access to it, or even take it without their permission to look after it 'better' (as the British did with the Elgin Marbles from the Parthenon)?

It might also be useful occasionally to consider what sort of relations we have with objects in our immediate sphere of influence and significance. Do we just possess them without any further consideration? Do we use them? Do we look at them or have some other kind of sensual relationship with them? Are the relations we have with them simply symbolic – I keep that picture because it was given to me by my mother – or do we engage directly with the object itself in some way, for example, perhaps by speaking to it, or worshipping through it? What, if any, are my responsibilities for this particular artefact's well-being and care? Would it matter if it was not there?

With some artefacts, we have straightforward instrumental relationships. They are used by us to do things with. Thus reading glasses help me to see what I have written on the page and I don't have any particular relationship with them beyond this. However, other artefacts may have a more symbolic, reflexive role in human lives. For example, as a writer I use a range of fountain pens to scribble notes. The pens are directly useful to me, but they also help to define me – they are part of my identity as a writer, and they remind me of who I am (in part) and what I do.

A third kind of relationship is that of extension of the self. A bike, for example, extends the self so that I can become a certain kind of person – the kind of person who is mobile and able to do things that are not available to the pedestrian. Other artefacts extend the self by distributing it. Thus a book, or a picture, can make an author's, or artist's, meanings and intentions known well beyond the original locus and time of production.

Artefacts that are both symbolic and extending can become an important part of the human self, so that their loss or damage can be genuinely traumatic for people. I care about the well-being of my pens and my bike. If they get lost or damaged, I feel diminished and guilty.

A fourth sort of relationship is that of mediation. Artefacts can be important in mediating relations with other people or things. Photographs, for example, may be exchanged as tokens of love and affection between people, and the rings exchanged at a wedding, arguably, actually create the marriage. Similarly, tools used in making things mediate between human intentions and the matter upon which they work. In this context, specific artefacts may be vital for relationships to exist or flourish.

This is a rough, ready and incomplete typology of relationships with artefacts, indicative rather than comprehensive. In practice, artefacts may function in all these ways – and more – simultaneously. Those that possess all these relational qualities are likely to be few, very precious, and intimate to people. They become 'biographical objects', practically and personally indispensable parts of people's lives with which humans have vital long-term relationships.[18] We perhaps need to become more aware of the actual and potential relationships that we are having with artefacts, and of the functions that they perform for us.

The typology I have outlined of some ways of relating to artefacts does not take into account important factors that may affect the usage, symbolism and significance surrounding them that arise in different places and circumstances. Some things (like bicycles) actually do something, others (like wallpaper) are just passively there. Some artefacts are readily visible, others are hidden or difficult to see. Some (like oil portraits of relatives) are valued because of their costliness and uniqueness, others (like family snapshots) because of their replicability, cheapness and ubiquity. Some artefacts (like knives) may be used all the time, others (like cut-glass decanters) may only appear on special occasions. The factors that make an artefact important and engage it in symbolic or non-symbolic relations of personlike significance with particular human beings are, then, very complex.

Within the context of exploring subject–subjects relations with things in general and personlike relationships with objects, we need to ask more evaluative questions. What kind of relationship am I having with the visual artefacts around me? Are there objects that I ignore? Does this matter? To what extent is the relationship I have with a particular artefact mutual and respectful? Do I overvalue or undervalue this artefact? Do I feel that it has power over me so that I am obsessed with it and give it too much attention? How might my relationships with artefacts be more appreciative? Is the level of relationship that I have with any particular object appropriate and good for me and for it? What is my emotional and personal investment in this artefact? Does relating to it leave me indifferent or frustrated, or does it give me pleasure? Would it be possible for me to improve my relationship with visually available artefacts?

These are exactly the kinds of questions that can arise in relating to human beings. They are appropriate here, because, as I have suggested, there are various ways in which we can and do actually fall into person-like relations with objects, as well as with other members of our own species.

Looking in haptic terms requires us to read visual things for their meaning, but also to acknowledge our material experience of being with them.[19] Relating to a painting is not just a matter of deciphering its symbolism or meaning. It is also an encounter with a piece of cloth with muddy marks made upon it that reflect the material possibilities of paint and human muscle movements.[20]

I have to say that looking closely at the cloth and mud rather than trying to look through them to find aesthetic or symbolic meaning has begun to give me much pleasure. I feel more in contact with the picture and its painter than I did when I just asked myself questions like, Is it beautiful? What about it is beautiful? What aspects of this picture do I like? These abstract, symbolic ways of looking maintain a distance from artefacts that makes them less rewarding to be with.

I can now slow down my viewing of pictures and other objects by paying close attention to the material shape and surface of them. These not only witness to the indexicality of their originators, but also often to the biography of the object through which it has become the unique thing that it is.

## Conclusion: cultivating joyous attachment

We need to increase both the range and the depth of our attachment to artefacts. To do this, we need to cultivate a loving, attentive gaze, the kind of haptic perception that pays close attention to particular objects in their own right. Doing this will enrich our own lives. We may also become more aware of the interests, purposes and needs of artefacts so they are given more appropriate appreciation and respect.

I am not enthusiastic about the notion of re-enchanting the world. This seems to imply that people are not able to cope with the realities and responsibilities of contemporary existence, and that a sense of magic and mystery can be manufactured at will to make life seem deeper and less bleak in the secularized Western world. If, however, enchantment means recognizing that humans have an abiding capacity for wonder and awe, and that there is a need for human attachment, both to other humans and to the world of objects, which is ignited by a sense of belonging and relationship (understandings summed up in the notion of 'joyful attachment'), the experience that lies behind the concept is fundamental. The concept of enchantment is linguistically related, within the Indo-European group of languages, both to singing (chanting) and to smiling.[21] A sign of increased sensitivity and engagement in relations with artefacts that are perceived to have a capacity for creating wonder around them revealed in mutual, loving gaze might be that we actually smile and sing more. In their own right, even mass-produced objects can be quite wonderful, enchanting and delightful. Perhaps there is a certain prejudice against acknowledging the delights of ordinary visible artefacts because they are associated with the evils of technology, consumerism, or mass production. But this failure to engage with, and smile at, the real delights that everyday visible artefacts provide represents a diminishment in relationships between artefacts and humans. Childish wonder and pleasure at the artefacts we encounter in the world is not necessarily something we should seek to avoid. It adds value to everyday life, as well as to the objects we possess and use. I agree with Jane Bennett (2001, p. 171) when she protests, 'Why must nature be the exclusive form of enchantment? Can't – don't – numerous human artefacts also fascinate and inspire?'[22]

We can easily find ourselves smiling at, and with, artefacts, as well as people. There is no reason why taking personlike relationships with artefacts more seriously should engulf us only in philosophical gloom and a greater sense of responsibility. Joyful attachment, based on haptic, appreciative vision as a paradigm, might expand pleasure in the world, not just exacerbate the ascetic guilt that turns goods into bads, or requires that ordinary viewers become scholars of complex understandings of the visual world like art historians or psychologists. Good, attentive looking, appropriate perceiving, does not have to be heavy or difficult to be worthwhile. If wealth is a matter of appreciating what is good rather than acquiring goods, the capacity to enter more fully into personlike relations with artefacts can only make us richer – and with a good deal less damage to the environment and to artefacts themselves in the long run.[23] This is a way of drawing nearer to reality rather than an attempt at flight from unfriendly facts:

> To dignify and engage with the subjective experience of the senses is not to deny reality, nor is it a return to fetishism or romanticism. Rather it is a better way to appreciate human imagination and experience. (Edwards, Gosden and Phillips 2006, p. 25)

## Notes

1 A scopic regime is 'an integrated complex of visual theories and practices' (Jay 1988, p. 4). I would argue that 'integration' may not be a feature of haptic sight. Its theories and practices hang loosely together in antithesis to Cartesian perspectivalism, itself perhaps less integrated than one might think.

2 Levin (1988, p. 99) characterizes *theoria* as 'attentive looking', a capacity to be appreciative, open and responsive to the realities within visual experience. Steiner (1988, p. 69), drawing on the Greek roots of the concept, characterizes it as properly comprised of both perception and appropriate conduct.

3 See McFague (1997, p. 33), Levin (1988). 'The eye of the body respects and admires the physical, the concrete, and the diverse, rather than searching for the abstract, the general, and the same, as does the eye of the mind' (McFague 1997, p. 94).

4 Murdoch, Code and McFague seem unaware of the work done in the 1950s on touch and relationship by John Macmurray, though McFague has been influenced tacitly by Macmurray through Bonifazi (1967). In referring to the embodied 'tactual', over against the visual, as the bedrock for personhood and relationships to others, Macmurray anticipates much of what is commended by Murdoch *et al*. He comes to the importance of the haptic without apparent knowledge of Heidegger and Merleau-Ponty. Macmurray (1991, p. 111) writes: 'Tactual perception is our only means of having a direct and immediate awareness of the Other as existent.' Thanks to Adam Hood for pointing me to Macmurray's contribution.

5 McFague (1997, p. 93).

6 For example, Ayers (2003), Wright (1991) and Stern (1985). 'Objectivist discussions of vision rarely mention one of its aspects that develops in infancy, is crucial to infant development, and figures prominently in personal relationships. That aspect is direct eye contact between people: a symmetrical act of mutual recognition in which neither need be passive and neither in control' (Code 1991, p. 144).

7 Steiner (1989, pp. 148ff.) discusses the importance of tact in engaging with art works. Tact, in this context is comprised of 'ways in which we allow ourselves to touch or not to touch, to be touched or not to be touched by the presence of the other.' Steiner argues for a 'courtesy of perception' comprising 'tact of heart'.

8 McFague (1997, p. 114).

9 Murdoch (1985, p. 64) writes of the illusory, fantasy dimension of ordinary seeing: 'Almost all art is a form of fantasy-consolation and few artists achieve the vision of the real.'

10 See McFague (1997, pp. 115, 116). Murdoch (1985, p. 66) writes: 'It is in the capacity to love, that is to see, that the liberation of the soul from fantasy consists. The freedom which is a proper human goal is the freedom from fantasy . . .' Moore (1996, p. 128) warns, however, that idealism and imagination focuses our attention away from the ordinary world and the minor experiences of wonder and difference that can be experienced there. See also Bennett (2001, p. 176).

11 Murdoch (1985, p. 34) uses 'the word "attention" . . . to express the idea of a just and loving gaze directed upon an individual reality.'

12 'Love is knowledge of the individual' (Murdoch 1985, p. 28). This could in principle include all kinds of individuals, including artefacts, flowers, trees, and much more.

13 Augustine (1997, p. 21) notes, 'you cannot do good to all people equally, so you should take particular thought for those who . . . happen to be particularly close to you in terms of place, time, or any other circumstances.'

14 Fry (1937, p. 29).

15 See Elkins (1997), Gregory (1998).

16 The architect, Pallasmaa (2005, p. 59), recounts how, on entering a particular building, he 'felt compelled to kneel and touch the delicately shining white marble threshold of the front door with his tongue'.

17 See Johnson (2002).

18 See Hoskins (1998).

19 Elkins (1999).

20 See Elkins (2000b).

21 Bennett (2001, pp. 5ff.).

22 Bennett (2001, p. 171).

23 Armstrong (2005, p. 161).

# I I

# Touching God: Christians and Relationships with Visible Artefacts

Is not this the carpenter's son? Is not his mother called Mary? And are not his brothers James and Joseph and Simon and Judas?

Matthew 13.55 (RSV)

The more ethically and morally superior the religion, the more it presents an abstract deity who need not be approached through the material.

Colleen McDannell, *Material Christianity*

## Introduction

Little space has been devoted in this book to religion or the divine. I have based the case for broader, more appreciative, comprehensive approaches to relationships with artefacts on arguments and experience available to most Western people without the need to resacralize the universe.

However, I work in the tradition of Western Protestant Christian theology. In this last chapter I want to consider how Christianity might contribute to the task of thinking about contemporary relations with visual objects.[1] There are obstacles and prejudices that contemporary Christians might need to overcome sympathetically to engage with this approach. However, there are also strands of Christian thought that are consonant with taking the world of everyday visual artefacts seriously. Christian thought may even support a deeper, more sustained basis for relating responsively and responsibly to the world of visual objects than secular thinking, especially in its incarnationally based concern for creation and the wider terrestrial ecology. Hitherto, this potential has mostly not been developed, except in relation to high art.

As far as I can see, there is absolutely no reason why Christian believers and thinkers should not accept the value of developing personlike relationships with artefacts of all kinds, from 'high' art to 'low' design and technology. These relationships need not supplant relationships with people, nor fixate people upon objects rather than upon the divine. Indeed, developing them might help to get artefacts better into perspective so they are less likely to become enthralling idols. A more attentive attitude to relations with artefacts might be seen as part of the responsibility of Christians in their role as co-creators made in the image of the divine and as stewards and friends of the whole of creation. They are, after all, the works of human hands.

Unfortunately, there is very little evidence to suggest that Christians, especially theologically minded Protestant Christians, give much attention to this aspect of life in thought or practice. Some Christians do find a place for material artefacts as vital aids to devotion and religious practice.[2] Others have an interest in the aesthetic qualities of works of high art and architecture as a means of gaining access to beauty and truth – important aspects of the divine – and insights into the human condition.[3] But there focused attention upon artefacts seems to end.

Christians and Christianity are not positively against visual artefacts or relationships with them. Rather, there appears to be a gap in their purview which makes this area of little interest beyond the area of high art and symbolism. While there is growing interest in the natural world, ecology, the future of the planet, and issues that relate to caring for the natural world, the realm of humanly made artefacts, especially everyday objects, does not capture the Christian imagination. This despite the fact that Christianity is a self-confessed materialist religion that theologically rejects any notion of separation between the divine and the whole of creation, which is of supreme importance to its Creator.

Paul Tillich wrote in 1963:

> The religious significance of the inorganic [artefactual] is immense, but it is rarely considered by theology. In most theological discussions the general term 'nature' [art] covers all particular dimensions of the 'natural' [artefactual] . . . A 'theology of the inorganic [artefactual]' is lacking. (Tillich 1978, p. 18)

He might very well have concluded the same today.[4] My insertions within this quotation suggest that Tillich's general point about the neglect of things inorganic was, and remains, equally apposite in thinking about the artefactual. Simone Weil (1959, p. 116) puts the matter plangently: 'How can Christianity call itself catholic if the universe itself is left out?'

## Inhibitors: what stops Christians from taking relationships with artefacts seriously?

Christianity is not concertedly and articulately against thinking about or relating more closely to artefacts. However, mostly it has not really considered such relationships. There is just a space where thought about artefacts might be.[5] It is not, then, possible to create a concerted critique of Christian thought. All I can do is to point to some of the largely implicit ideas and trends that might have led to Christianity's ignoring this area.

### Cultural conformity

Like most Westerners, Christians tend to think of the artefactual realm as existing for human use and disposal at will. Protestant Christianity might be arraigned as a major force in evacuating the material, spatial world of theological significance, and thus spiritualizing and etherealizing religion in the West. Conforming to contemporary cultural norms, it has not much advocated taking the artefactual world seriously. If there are inhibitors as to the uses to which artefacts might be put, these are not couched in terms of the well-being and intentions of artefacts or the character of the relationships within which they find themselves. There may be interest in a few artefacts that are specially designated for symbolic, relational purposes, for example, works of art, particularly works with religious themes, symbols, or meanings.[6] But, for the most part, Christians are no more interested stewards or friends of the artefactual order than their secular contemporaries.

The issue of creating positive responsive and responsible relationships with visible artefacts is not distinctive to Christianity. Christians share the 'normal blindness' of their non-religious Western peers. There are some factors inhibiting positive relations with artefacts, however, that emerge directly from the Christian tradition.

### Asceticism

One factor which probably does bear upon the Christian indifference to artefacts, and fuller relationships with them, is the long tradition of asceticism and denial of personal material property. Jesus commands his followers to dispose of possessions to feed the poor and follow him (cf. Mark 10.21), with the implication that possessions and money get in the way of discipleship. He warns of storing up treasures upon earth, and of the dangers of trying to serve God and Mammon. Several of his parables, particularly in the Gospel of Luke, seem to imply that earthly riches are a barrier to the Kingdom of Heaven. The parable of Dives and Lazarus (Luke 16.19–31) illustrates the dangers of becoming indifferent to the needs of the poor, while that of the rich fool (Luke 12.16–21) demonstrates how people should trust in divine providence and judgement rather than in personal wealth. In the Lucan Beatitudes, the wealthy are cursed (Luke 6.24f.). The Son of Man travels light, with no family, home or place to lay his head. He expects his followers similarly to share what they have with their new-found brothers and sisters. Thus they will be rewarded in heaven. This tradition continues through the New Testament and beyond. Thus, monks were expected to live frugally, a tradition which coalesced in a routine vow of poverty. St Francis, the *alter Christus* of the medieval period, took Lady Poverty as his mistress, giving away and rejecting all wealth and comfort.

While Francis was wandering the hills of Umbria, however, others were amassing wealth and jewels in honour of God and the Church, though ostensibly this was corporate or divine rather than personal wealth, gathered in a devotional quest.[7] Nonetheless, the ascetic tradition has tended to create a normative feeling within Christianity that personal possessions are a hindrance to full discipleship such as that which monks and nuns can exercise. In the Reformed tradition, the acquisition of possessions for one's own pleasure and benefit was frowned upon in an environment underpinned by an ethos of 'inner worldly asceticism' (Weber 1976). Ascetic attitudes survive to the present day. They are found not only in monasticism and some forms of Protestantism, but also in movements such as liberation theology which emphasize God's commitment to the poor and the need for a radical discipleship that eschews personal acquisition and wealth.[8]

This brief consideration of the ascetic tradition indicates that personal property is problematic for Christians, especially if it prevents people from loving God and trusting divine call and providence and from responding to the needs of their neighbours. This general wariness of personal or overvalued possessions supports a general Christian indifference to artefacts, the kinds of things that often clutter up people's lives and engage their attention and affections over more important things. However, the Christian tradition mostly does not condemn objects themselves (as it condemns usury and the love of money).[9] It condemns their inappropriate and personal use and possession, especially if this threatens to lead people away from God. This distinction may be ignored such that it is objects and artefacts that are deemed to be evil, tempting and misleading, rather than the human desires and fantasies that implicate those things in ungodly attachments.

Against this undifferentiated miasma of condemnation and suspicion hanging around things, Ruskin's notion of wealth as the appreciation of good things rather than the accumulation of lots of things should be remembered.[10] This might imply that Christians should be ascetic in the sense that they do not allow things to come between them and God, God's will, and the needs of other people. However, within this, there is space for Christians to become more appreciative of a few things that they might either own or relate to. Joyful appreciation might then be valued over denied, furtive accumulation.

## *Idolatry*

St Paul summarizes the Jewish/Christian anti-idolatrous tradition in his condemnation of the 'enemies of God' who deserve to die:

> [S]ince the creation of the world, the invisible existence of God and his ever-lasting power have been clearly seen by the mind's understanding of created things. And so these people have no excuse . . . While they claimed to be wise, in fact they were so stupid that they exchanged the glory of the immortal God for an imitation, for the image of a mortal human being, or of birds, or animals, or crawling things . . . they have worshipped and served the creature instead of the Creator . . . (Rom. 1.20, 22, 25 NJB)

There is always the danger that people may fall prey to the mistake of overvaluing objects, attributing to them the power and worship due to God alone, and becoming enthralled to them.[11] Lash (1996, p. 51) asserts, 'all estimable things are "gods" and all of us are polytheists'. The question then,

> is not whether we shall worship, but in what direction our hearts might be set . . . We worship things as naturally as we breathe and speak . . . untutored, we set our hearts on things: on forces, elements, ideas; on people, dreams and institutions; on the world or on some item of its furnishing. We are spontaneously idolatrous . . . the great . . . 'religions' have served as schools in which we seek some education from idolatry. (Lash 1996, p. 50)

Spontaneous idolatry in relation to artefacts is explored by

Wolterstorff (1997) who criticizes the modern aesthetic contemplative tradition of taking art seriously for art's own sake. In aesthetic contemplation, art can become a form of religion, mysticism and salvation. Thus art objects become things of ultimate significance, persons almost. Artists become creative gods, and humans become their worshippers in a kind of cult (Wolterstorff 1997, p. 50). Wolterstorff (1997, p. 48) condemns contemplating objects for their own sake and thinking of them as having rights of their own.

The danger of spontaneous idolatry in relation to objects should be remembered. The essence of idolatry is that persons and things become confused (Koerner 2002, p. 166). However, this kind of critique of potential and actual idolatry need not be read as a condemnation of taking objects seriously, or entering into personlike relations with artefacts. Arguably, it is not possible to have religion that is independent of the mediation of visual images and artefacts.[12] Rowland (2005), considering idolatry in the New Testament, has argued that idols and potential idols are ubiquitous and unavoidable. Thus Christians must learn to live with them appropriately rather than pretending to live in an artefact- and idol-free zone.[13]

Proximate goods like relationships with humans and objects should not be allowed to usurp the place of God in human life, nor the end of worshipping the divine within and beyond the material world. However, artefacts and other parts of the created order might be deemed to have an important place in the divine creation and providence which should be appreciated, not despised. They can be seen as mediations of divine presence and a means of communicating with God rather than obstacles to religious life. Simone Weil (1959, p. 120) suggests that 'The beauty of the world is Christ's tender smile for us coming through matter'.[14]

It is perhaps a measure of humans' propensity to fall into overvaluing images that Christians tend to devalue all objects and artefacts. The anti-idolatrous, anti-iconic tradition, particularly in Protestant Christianity, can be interpreted as a blanket condemnation of artefacts in and of themselves rather than as a caution against placing things in the way of relationship with the living God. The prospect of idolatry dazzles and blinds humans to the importance of everyday objects. However, it might perhaps be better if we looked them more directly in the eye, and learned to live with and love them appropriately within a school of religion that teaches us how to value the material within the providence of God. And it should be noted that it is not just the visible and material that misleads human attention and devotion. Words, ideas and aspirations, the works of human immaterial imagination, can be just as dangerous as artefacts. An invisible God represented in words can be manipulated and managed more easily by theologians and ideologues, creating far more potential for destruction and error than mere material images (Brown 2004, p. 10). At least with artefacts and images, you can literally see what you are up against.

## Spiritualization and disembodiment

Christianity's central doctrine is that God becomes human and embodied in the man Jesus. This doctrine of the incarnation sets a fundamental value on flesh, physicality and embodiment. A number of studies, notably by feminist scholars, have emphasized the fundamental reality and importance of embodied existence and perception for Christianity from its earliest times.[15]

Unfortunately, post-Reformation Christianity for a long time emphasized the other-worldly and immaterial nature of God, faith and discipleship:

> In the seventeenth century, for the first time, 'supernatural', the substantive, began to connote a realm of being, a territory of existence, 'outside' the world we know. With 'nature' now deemed single, homogenous and self contained, we labelled 'supernatural' that other world inhabited (some said) by ghosts and poltergeists, by demons, angels and suchlike extraterrestrials – and by God. (Lash 1996, p. 168)

Religious, and particularly mystical, experiences then become not the whole of Christian embodied life lived in the totality of the material world to its fullest intensity, but 'unusual experiences, enjoyed by a handful of unusual individuals known as "mystics" . . . perpetuating the quite unchristian misapprehension that "experience of God" is, at best, something esoteric and, at worst, close cousin to the paranormal' (Lash 1996, p. 171).

This kind of spiritualizing, and erasure of God from the material, everyday world, has left many Christians seeking God inwardly in the psyche or in the world of words rather than in the realm of material objects.[16] To love and worship God then becomes a matter of cognition, seeking symbolic meaning, or personal feeling, rather than an engagement with the material world. This thin spiritualization of the divine, separated from the material, is a fundamental heresy: 'Humanity's failure to see the divine theophany in nature is of the same piece as its refusal to accept the divine theophany mediated through Jesus' (Wink 1986, p. 164).

There is now more interest in embodied Christian existence in the context of the material world, as witnessed by the growth of feminist theology and liturgical material that is profoundly conscious of relations with the whole of creation and its future.[17] However, there is still validity in Feuerbach's observation that 'Nature, the world, has no interest for Christians. The Christian thinks only of himself and salvation of his soul' (Bonifazi 1967, p. 75). Otherworldly and supernatural matters still preoccupy many Christians. Concern for 'nature' and the material world does not often extend into the realm of exploring relations with material objects and artefacts in the visible world generally. These things remain firmly dead and un-godlike; they do not share divine characteristics such as invisibility, spirit and reason.

Arguably, this kind of contempt for the material does not exist among many ordinary Christian believers, particularly women. McDannell (1995, p. 1) points out that many Christians have 'explored the meaning of the divine, the nature of death, the power of healing, and the experience of the body by interacting with a created world of images and shapes'. However, 'official', logocentric, doctrinally based Christianity has been more abstract and contemptuous of home-based, non-theological and non-verbal ways of apprehending the divine. Adopting a kind of aesthetic and intellectual elitism, it has tended to make religion art. That art reflects modernist, masculine values of nobility, strength, power, detachment, disinterestedness and abstraction, instead of emotion, involvement, localness and the stereotypical female qualities of sentimentality, superficiality and intimacy (McDannell 1995, p. 164). Even Catholicism has reformed itself to become more rationalistic, abstract, logocentric and theological, formally eschewing much of the materially based popular religious practice that was characteristic of it before Vatican II (Orsi 1996). Thus much domestically based, religious materialism is regarded as kitsch (Morgan 1998).

Perhaps, then, the debate about aesthetics and taste in Christianity has as much to do with the roles of men and women as anything else. Images and material objects are, however, important to both sexes:

> The antagonism of a few theologians to visual images and their injunctions to 'spiritual' – that is, verbal – worship of God reveals a fundamental disdain for the vast majority of human beings, women and men, whose perspective was based on the exigencies of physical existence, in other words for the educationally underprivileged who [have] not been trained to identify themselves with intellectual activity. (Miles 1985, p. 38)

'Official' Christianity often despises the material mediations of religion which are often closely associated with women, the home and the secular rather than the aesthetic, symbolic, discursive, intellectual, ecclesiastical and formally sacred. Unfortunately, religion requires emotional attachment as well as cognitive knowledge and assent, so it must be supported by mediations of sight, touch, smell and sound. If these are despised or absent, then religion itself may be weakened (McDannell 1995, p. 14).[18]

Recapturing a sense of the divine theophany in and through material things will demand changes of thought and practice that will constrain human action and choice. 'If nature is dead, then there are no restraints on exploiting it for profit' (Wink 1986, p. 155). If, however, artefacts and objects have that of God and humanity about them, they cannot be so readily used and exploited.

## Conservative suspicion of technology and commodification

The notion that the creation belongs to, and is ordered by, God into a pattern consonant with the divine will and good for its inhabitants, married with the doctrines of human sin and the fall of creation that uphold the fallibility of human action and the imperfect state of the world, means that Christians are often wary of human technology and innovation.[19] Sinful humans make interventions in the world that prove to be harmful and against the divine order, the argument seems to run, so one should be careful of human innovations and interventions that are supposedly progressive.[20] Thus, some churches have resisted inventions such as contraception, anaesthetics and blood transfusions, and shown grave suspicion of many other technologies such as genetic manipulation, the personification of machines, and the possibilities of developing post-humans whose bodies are substantially technologically enhanced and extended.[21]

The doctrine of sin and the fallibility of humans perhaps affects attitudes towards artefacts. Particularly in a world of mass production and commodification of objects, it may seem that artefacts in themselves are likely to be bad. The ways in which they are produced, exploiting the world's resources, are likely to be very bad. If technology is dubious or bad, then its artefactual products may be endowed with courtesy stigma.

There is a counterbalancing tradition in Christianity which characterizes humans as co-creators with God and active stewards, or 'gardeners', of creation (Wolterstorff 1997, pp. 76f.). Many of the objects and processes that have transformed the world have been produced under the aegis of this idea of humans' God-given creative potential and responsibility. It was Cistercian monks, for example, who first developed watermills. This more positive view of the creative power of humans often tends to be submerged beneath implicit, more conservative, anti-technological, anti-commodity attitudes. These lead to suspicion of the works of human hands regarded as sharing in corruption, unnaturalness and sin.[22]

The artefactual realm, while used and produced by Christians as much as any other group, does not figure positively in Christian thought and action. If an artefact is beautiful, it is lauded for its aesthetic, emotional and 'spiritual' value, particularly if it is unique and has been created by an inspired, creative individual designated an artist or craftsperson. Otherwise, at best, artefacts are just 'there'. They are cared for to the extent that they can be used, and otherwise ignored. They may be despised and treated as somehow not good, and certainly not of great concern to the divine except insofar as they can be used to prosecute the divine will. It is very difficult to find a positive view of specific, humanly created everyday visible artefacts within the literature of theology.

## Humans and nature – not artefacts

The Christian gospel of salvation pays little attention to artefacts. It seems to embrace two main categories. First, and most importantly, humans are the instruments and objects of God's purpose in the world. As active agents, repentant humans who hear the good news can become part of God's creative and re-creative processes, just as they were the agents of the fall of the world. Second, the creation as a whole is the object of God's love and care: 'creation had frustration imposed on it . . . with the intention that the whole creation itself might be freed from its slavery to corruption and brought into the same glorious freedom as the children of God' (Rom. 8.20, 21 NJB).

Between the whole of creation and the much narrower category of people, there is little differentiation of things, and their several destinies and purposes. Artefacts and all kinds of entities and objects theoretically enter into God's purposes, but there is little discussion of how they are to be used or appreciated either in the New Testament or subsequently, except in terms of ethics, justice and distribution of goods. Christian theology thinks in very general terms beyond the realm of the specifically human.[23] Thus, even in the twenty-first century, it talks broadly about such things as 'creation', or 'nature', which are taken to be of enormous value, even though they are too large really to comprehend. On the other hand, cars, pens, photographs and sculptures are mostly beneath detailed attention, despite being readily to hand and having considerable physical and symbolic influences on people, cultures and planet.

The focus on human beings within Christianity is understandable and appropriate. Humans as intentional agents certainly need salvation. The focus on the broad natural environment in which we live – lakes, rivers, hills, stars – is also to be welcomed, though it does suggest that Christians are biased towards some kind of rural, pastorally and organically related religion that cannot really speak to urban technological complexity dominated by machines and human creations. However, there is a hiatus in Christian thought and practice which allows little positive place for thinking about the importance of human creations and artefacts. This implies that humanly made 'things' are not that important in the divine scheme of things. However, because of their significant place within human society and relationships, this now seems an inadequate response.

## Bases for a positive theology of artefacts

A number of inhibiting factors contribute directly or indirectly to a lack of interest in artefacts within Christian thought and practice. These include a general disapproval of possessions, anxiety about the idolatrous potential of objects, disparagement and fear of the fruits of human technology, general spiritualization of religion so the material is excluded, the emphasis in Christianity upon human salvation, and a very generalized, non-specific concern for creation which largely ignores the works of human hands.

There are, however, a number of themes and traits within the Christian tradition, some of them central and well accepted, which provide a basis for creating more positive attitudes towards artefacts. Not many of them refer to artefacts as such, so it is a matter of turning them obliquely for their relevance to be perceived.

### Creation

The Bible begins with God creating the world and all this is in it, including the humans who will take forward God's creative and nurturing purpose. Genesis 1 constantly records that, as God creates another part of the world, 'God saw that it was good' (Gen. 1.10, 25, 31), or even 'very good'. This implies a fundamental stance of appreciation, God's enjoying things as they are, for what they are. The early part of Genesis also allocates to humans the job of mastering and dominating creation (Gen. 1.27) – a text which has sometimes contributed to the notion that humans can dispose of creation as they wish. But this has to be seen in the context of a positive view of nature and things.

> [The] three attitudes toward nature – appreciation, stewardship, and domina-
> tion – are graded, with appreciation ('it is good') being the primary one . . .
> Stewardship is also important in the text . . . But domination . . . the primary
> attitude of the West toward nature, takes up less than one verse of the thirty
> one verses in the chapter. (McFague 1997, p. 166)

The positive stance of appreciative perception of all that is made should be the one positively adopted by Christians. Christians should see the world as God sees it, and see God within it. This is a theme picked up by various Christians throughout history. Nicholas of Cusa, for example, regards God's sight as what makes and sustains things in being. It is concrete, haptic and sustaining: 'You . . . are my God who sees everything, and your seeing is your working. And thus you work all things' (Nicholas of Cusa 1997, p. 242).[24] Cusa thought that *theos* (God) and *theoria* (vision) were etymologically linked words, and so a fundamental property of God was God's creative sight.

For Cusa, and perhaps for us, the notion of God's loving, appreciative, sustaining, creative sight over everything that exists cannot exclude anything. It implies that artefacts, the works of human hands, also have their place within the divine providence. This taking of creation seriously might change attitudes to artefacts for, with and through them, we are partially able to see God, their ultimate originator and sustainer. If God's essence and sight penetrates all things, then humans who take the divine seriously should take seriously all parts and aspects of the material created order, not just natural phenomena such as trees, rivers and seas: 'You, Lord, see all things and each single thing at the same time. You are moved with all that are moved and stand with all that stand' (Nicholas of Cusa 1997, p. 252).

## Humans as made in the image of God and facilitators of the potential of creation

The doctrine of creation in Genesis already contains within it an understanding that humans are made in the image of God. However, they have lost the likeness of God. They need forgiveness of their sins and redemption to restore their likeness to the divine. This likeness, and the full vision of God, is restored in Christ, the incarnate Word of God. Despite the loss of the divine likeness, humans are still charged with stewardship over the creation. Furthermore, sharing the divine image, they share some of the same attributes of the divine, crucially, rationality. This allows humans a certain relationship or co-nature with the divine Word (Lossky 1983, pp. 58ff). Thus humans share in some of the divine work of creating and sustaining the world.

It is in the context of seeing humans as having some of the attributes and capacities of the divine that the making of, and caring for, artefacts should be seen. Just as humans share in some of the characteristics of the divine, artefacts might be entitled to some of the respect accorded to their creators insofar as they share in, index and express this. As creations of humans, themselves sharers in and stewards of creation, artefacts deserve some of the honour due to the creative force and purpose that lies behind them, albeit that some artefacts are not created for good purposes, and some are misused for evil purposes.

The Eastern Orthodox theological tradition emphasizes the progressive creation and ultimate perfection of the whole cosmos and the key role of humans within it. Building on the thinking of the Cappadocian Fathers, Maxim the Confessor, and others, it maintains that the whole of material creation, including soulless and lifeless matter, is the gift of God: 'If God created all things in order that they might share in his love, their purpose is to reach full participation in this love, that is, full communion with God' (Staniloae 2000, p. 17).

In this kind of theology, all matter contains *logoi*, divinely given reasons and potentials from its very beginnings (Staniloae 2000, p. 16). When matter is used, shaped, or formed, these *logoi* are changed and shaped by the *logoi* of the agents and things that they encounter. While material objects do not have reason, consciousness, or free will, they have their own destiny and potential. This is realized in partnership with sentient, rational human beings. If humans undertake their creative work with matter seriously, they can present God's gift back to God as an offering and contribute to the ultimate realization of the perfection which the deity wishes for all creation (Staniloae 2000, pp. 48ff.). Thus humans, matter, artefacts and the whole creation participate in the divine joy in creation.

From this perspective, any humanly created artefact is an expression of the totality of *logoi* that it has encountered and related with in the process of getting to where it presently is. Objects, then, are the sum total of the relationships they have experienced and contain divinely given potential which must be actualized. They are not finished things without past or future; they have biographies of their own which precede and succeed any particular encounter.

Material artefacts, as bearers of the interactions of multiple *logoi*, are personlike expressions of relations that can affect those who own, use and encounter them. They present the sum of the relations and interactions of *logoi* they come with. This may change the people or objects they come into contact with. In turn, an object may be changed within a new context or set of relationships, so it proceeds to the next bit of its history as a different kind of object from what it was before.

In this Orthodox view, humans cannot attain to perfection and the rediscovery of the likeness of God without taking the whole of material creation, and artefacts within that creation, absolutely seriously. There is no attaining heaven without the renewal and realization of the divinely given potential of the earth and everything it contains. Creation is a becoming, and both humans and other kinds of matter have a vital part in this becoming.[25]

## Biblical holism

From the perspective of individualized psychological agents, firmly enclosed within our own bodies, and living in a world that is divided between animate and inanimate, organic and non-organic creatures, it is difficult to appreciate the way that people regarded themselves and the objects they used in Old Testament times. It is likely that the biblical writers would have regarded the earth as alive; they would have made no fundamental distinction between the organic and the inorganic (Bonifazi 1967, pp. 182f.). The boundaries between the individual human being, other people and other things would have been more fluid, thus making it possible, for example, for people to travel in dreams and visions.[26]

Bonifazi (1967, p. 184) argues, 'nothing in itself is lifeless: all is therefore susceptible to the force and content of *nepesh* (life)'. Objects share the qualities of their possessors, so that to make a gift of something that belongs to you is to give something of yourself. The living earth is connected and its contents are irrevocably associated with humans in a covenant relationship. Both the creation and humanity share together in blessing and curse – they are effectively 'a psychic community' (Bonifazi 1967, p. 185). The crucial distinction, then, is not between people and things, but rather between that which exists because it is word enlivened by divine life (*dabhar*), and that which does not exist (*lo dabhar*).[27]

This all suggests another, biblical, ground for arguing that artefacts, like other things that exist, should be seen to have a position of respect in human life and activity.

## Incarnation

For Christians, the eventual outworking of the Jewish tradition of a God who is known materially and visibly, not just invisibly and supernaturally, and imaged as having a human body, was the incarnation; God embodied in human form in the man, Jesus. 'Incarnation' as a doctrinal phrase tends to be used as a loose theological justificatory and self-explanatory symbol for all kinds of Christian concern with the material creation. It is often used in an exhortatory, invocatory way to assert that God cares so much about the material world that the divine becomes part of it for its sake. However, the notion of incarnation supports a positive Christian attitude to flesh, embodiment, and the material order in creation, not least in representing the possibility of the material restoration of humanity in its relations with creation to the likeness of God. For Teilhard de Chardin, incarnation is the message that 'corporeality is the ultimate end of all God's ways' (quoted in Wink 1986, p. 170).

William Temple famously declared,

> Christianity . . . is the most avowedly materialist of all the great religions . . . By the very nature of its central doctrine, Christianity is committed to a belief in the ultimate significance of the historical process, and in the reality of matter and its place in the divine scheme. (Bonifazi 1967, p. 22)

Christianity is often anti-materialistic and spiritualizing in practice. However, the notion that divine incarnation dignifies all matter, and makes possible its perfection and blessing, provides a powerful basis for taking artefacts seriously. If artefacts are included within the purview of a God so concerned about the whole of creation that divinity becomes part of it, they can be regarded as part of the story of creation and redemption in which Christians participate. Universal salvation through Christ must involve the artefacts that humans shape and which shape them. The doctrine of incarnation points towards the intention and blessing of God upon the realization of this creative, salvific process. Maybe it is relevant here to recall that Jesus, the Word made flesh, was himself a carpenter – perhaps a man who made, lived with and understood the importance of artefacts, though none of the objects he may have made are ever alluded to or appear to have survived (cf. Mark 6.13).

## Redemption

Incarnation figures the value of matter and divine concern about the whole of material creation. The doctrine of redemption makes clear that all parts of creation, including, presumably, the artefacts that people make and interact with, are included in the ultimate realization of salvation in which God's will and Kingdom are realized on earth. 'We are well aware that the whole creation, until this time, has been groaning in labour pains' (Rom. 8.22 NJB). No New Testament writer actually discusses the place of artefacts and objects in the scheme of redemption. However, the intimate relationship of people with objects suggests that they cannot be excluded from the divine purpose. If artefacts and objects are to be part of the overall scheme of redemption, Christians should think carefully about how they interact with them in their everyday lives.

## Discerning beauty, goodness and truth

For many Christian theologians as well as philosophers, the material creation offers an arena in which God's nature and purposes can be discerned by means of reason and devotion.[28] If beauty, goodness and truth – key attributes of divinity – are to mean anything, they must be discernable within the material created order. Thus Simone Weil (1959, pp. 113ff.), for example, argues that God blesses humanity in the beauty of the material world and suggests that humans should offer a reciprocal care to that world. The implication is that artefacts, which embody some of the highest and most developed fruits of human purpose, intelligence and ingenuity married with the matter, should be seen as part of the human quest for recognizing divine beauty, goodness and truth. If artefacts are excluded as a means of discerning the nature and beauty of God, a major element of human intersection with reality is ignored.

## Horizontal 'sacramentalism'

An important way that the Christian tradition has found value in material things, including artefacts, is to see them in a sacramental light:

> The sacramental tradition assumes that God is present with us not only in the hearing of the Word and in the Eucharist but also in each and every being in creation . . . [It] should be acknowledged as contributing to a sense of the world as valuable – indeed, as holy – because it is a symbol of the divine and can help us reach God. (McFague 1997, p. 27)

Sacramentalism values the material world as an integral part of God's presence, care and self-revelation. However, this way of seeing can imply that material things are not of intrinsic value in themselves, but only insofar as they are 'seen through' to a 'higher' spiritual realm beyond this one. They are thus treated solely as a means to an end.[29]

Perhaps, then, the sacramental approach needs to be modified so that things are valued and appreciated for their own sake, not just as rungs on the ladder from the material world to some more spiritual, disembodied divine realm.[30] McFague advocates 'horizontal sacramentalism' in which things are both seen and valued for what they are, and seen in God. We need 'a way that allows us to love the natural world for its intrinsic worth, to love it, in all its differences and detail, in itself, for itself' (McFague 1997, p. 27).

St Francis exemplifies this approach. He both sees and values things for what they are with an intrinsic value of their own, brother sun, sister moon, but also sees them as signs that point towards the divine.[31] Perhaps it is not accidental that Francis and his followers created a revolution in piety that made visualization and visual objects such as Christmas cribs central to Christian discipleship.[32]

This stance of horizontal sacramentalism was also characteristic of people like William Blake and groups like the Shakers in the nineteenth century. The monk, Thomas Merton, himself a great proponent of the Benedictine tradition of handling 'the humblest material things with reverence and respect', writes: 'Neither the Shakers nor Blake would be disturbed by the thought that a work-a-day bench, cupboard, or table might . . . at the same time be furniture in and for heaven . . .'[33] For the Shakers, each material object had its own vocation; the work of the craftsperson was to ensure that things were made to be precisely what they were supposed to be. Artefacts were honestly and simply made for everyday use rather than for profit: 'The peculiar grace of a Shaker chair is due to the fact that it was made by someone capable of believing that an angel might come and sit on it.'[34]

The notion of seeing and dealing with material things as they are, for what they are, as well as for what they might stand for, and signify, is worthy of thought and emulation. If an attitude of 'horizontal sacra-mentalism' were extended to the whole created order, then artefacts, fearfully and wonderfully made by humans, might find a place both as objects of respect in their own right and as pointers towards the divine purpose and creativity. This would considerably enhance their value and importance.[35]

## Liberation and siding with the marginalized and voiceless

One of the main developments in Christian thought in the latter half of the twentieth century was that of liberation theology.[36] This theology holds that the Christian God is on the side of the marginalized and oppressed. Those who have been pushed to the edges are of most concern to a deity who comes among humanity as the incarnate Christ, one who serves the poor, abnegated and abused.

This divine concern for the oppressed can be extended to artefacts and material objects. It can be argued that nature and creation are made voiceless by human instrumental subject–object attitudes towards them. This is distorting and oppressive; it exposes creation to abuse and exploitation without appropriate responsibility and respect being shown to it by humans. Thus, nature as a whole should be regarded as part of the voiceless poor: 'Nature can be seen as the "new poor", not the poor that crowds out the human poor, but the "also" poor; and as such it demands our attention and care' (McFague 1997, p. 6). It needs to be respected and 'heard' if people are to have a more appropriate relationship with it. Christians, identifying with the God of the poor and oppressed, should commit themselves to oppressed nature.

Even within the created order broadly designated as 'nature', arte-facts are peculiarly neglected and despised, existing mostly beyond human language and attention. They are not even treated as a separate category deserving particular consideration for the relations that they have with humans and each other. Christians committed to the liberation and respect of creation might, therefore, be expected to have a special care for the realm of artefacts.[37]

## Loving all things

The Christian gospel bears witness to all-conquering and all-demanding love which flows out to all people and all things in imitation of, and thanksgiving for, God's love. For thinkers like Simone Weil (1959, pp. 116ff.), the material creation is one of the main places that humans might experience and reciprocate the love of God for humanity. Thus we need to love God by caring for material reality and recognizing divine beauty within it. Jesus' teaching and example suggests that love should have no bounds. If enemies are to be forgiven and accepted, how much more should 'innocent' parts of existence be respected, loved and cared for?[38]

The focused, but unbounded, selfless love exemplified in Jesus which respects, cares for, and delights in, the existence of others in their distinctiveness and connectedness should, in principle, include artefacts. Artefacts are among the highest fruits or human labour, and they are full of personlike qualities (unlike stars and planets). To love and be more respectful of artefacts might also be to learn how to love and care better for their creators and users. It would also constrain the unthinking use of objects, enhancing a sense of deep encounter with the world as subject rather than object.

## The world as God's body

Westerners have become accustomed to regarding God as a kind of separate and invisible being inhabiting a non-material realm of 'the supernatural' or 'heaven'. This thin, deistic view of an absent or hidden divinity has been challenged, particularly by feminist theologians.[39] They argue that models of God that allow for the material world to be seen as God's body are needed. God is the fundamental reality of this material realm. God has not disappeared or dispersed to become a *deus absconditus* (Luther's term), rather divinity is spread out in the whole of creation (McFague 1997, p. 146).[40] Because humans cannot stand outside this creation and see God as a separate 'object', it may seem that God is non-existent. The contrary is true. God is omni-existent, but 'ordinary blindness' makes us unable to discern this.

This kind of world- and material-affirming perspective on divinity provides a powerful incentive for taking artefacts, as well as other parts of the creation, seriously. If God is the ground, font and end of all being, and indwells it, then humans should take all aspects of it seriously, not treating any part of it as disposable crud, divisible from divinity and discipleship.

## The reality of Christian material mediations and images of God

While anti-iconism and iconoclasm has often been what Christians have preached, their practice has often included material representations and mediations of God. Even the most austere branches of Protestantism have material artefacts such as Bibles, pictures and church decorations that assist in establishing identity, aiding devotion, and accessing deity.[41] Christian and Jewish practice has always found a substantial place for imaging God and aspects of the divine in material artefacts.[42] This has not always been supported by articulated theologies. Indeed, sometimes, these theologies have despised or tried to minimize the evident need that many Christians feel to have some kind of visible mediation of the divine (Morgan 1998).

If Christian practice is taken as a significant datum in defining and developing tradition, there is a good case from historical and contemporary example for Christians taking relations with material objects and artefacts seriously. The alternative is to have an unhelpful theology of denial and repression which despises the needs and extensive experiences of ordinary Christians down the centuries. As one of David Morgan's respondents puts it, 'Pictures help me "see" who it is to whom I pray' (Morgan 1998, p. 157). Maybe visible artefacts in general, if taken more seriously, might help Christians better to see to whom it is that we pray.

## Transforming bodily sight

In 'The resurrection and the spiritual senses', Sarah Coakley argues that, to see the risen Christ, the women mentioned in the resurrection appearances in the Gospels had to have their sight transformed: 'the transformation of normal sense perception becomes the requisite of resurrection belief' (Coakley 2002, p. 152).

That discipleship in Christ might mean a transformation of the senses, as well as the mind, is an interesting and suggestive idea in the present context. If discipleship is not just about cognitive belief, and includes material and bodily transformation, as well as deepening of faith, perhaps part of being converted to Christ involves a commitment on the part of Christians to change their ways of seeing.[43]

Such a transformation of seeing and perception in the contemporary world might include a conversion to seeing visual artefacts differently and more relationally. If the world is God's body, and human grasp of the divine is to be material and embodied, as well as intellectual, humans need to see material artefacts in a different way in the quest to recognize the bodily reality of the risen Christ in the contemporary world. It is not enough to look for an invisible saviour in heaven. We need to change the focus and range of our vision to take artefacts seriously and see them in God, and in the Christ who completes creation.

## Conclusion: re-sighting Christianity

In this chapter, I have considered the silence and implicit aversion of Christianity to looking more closely at artefacts. There are traits within Christian tradition and practice that militate against taking relations with artefacts more seriously. These included anxieties about idolatry, technology, materialism and morality, as well as a preference for the verbal and aural (Miles 1985, p. 38). Close inspection of these traits does not reveal a coherent set of factors that preclude attention to artefacts. But they do raise awareness of certain real dangers that might arise if Christians, for example, become enthralled to objects or seek to amass large numbers of them.

There is a surprisingly impressive number of aspects of Christian tradition and practice that support a positive attitude to relationships with artefacts. These range from the basic goodness of creation and the God-given potential of matter, through doctrines of incarnation and redemption, to the responsibility of humans as being made in the image of God and the need to side with the inarticulate and oppressed, as well as to take the historic practice of Christians with visible artefacts seriously. Living in the resurrected Christ perhaps suggests a fundamental change in perceiving the world so the whole of divinely created and inspired creation, including artefacts, is seen with different eyes.

Again, these traits are disparate and various, and they mostly do not address the place of artefacts directly. However, they have a cumulative significance. While they do not amount to an imperative making artefacts central to Christianity, together they open a permissive, indicative space where material objects could enjoy a more important position. It seems strange, then, that artefacts, and other parts of 'inanimate', inorganic creation, have been neglected for so long.

There is a need to develop Christian theology and practice that values artefacts, and reflects on relationships with them more carefully and critically. It is desirable that Christians should move from theological assertion about things in general to pay specific perceptual attention to particular artefacts. We should attend more to artefacts in and for themselves, and become more aware of our relationships with them and their significance for us. This for the sake of the artefacts themselves – they have their own vulnerabilities – for the sake of the human race that is shaped with and by artefacts, for the sake of the planet which needs less mindless exploitation, and for the sake of God who made all that is and longs for the perfection and completion of creation in Christ. If we are really to see the glory of God through human beings, fully alive, then we need to have a different vision and perception of the artefacts that humans create and which partly constitute their identity.

Relationships with artefacts should not replace relationships with other humans.[44] This easily happens in Christianity; consider the way in which buildings, books and ideas become an excuse for failure to encounter and experience real, living humans – fetishism in action. St Irenaeus famously wrote, 'the glory of God is a living man [*sic*], while the life of man is the vision of God' (quoted in Lossky 1983, p. 40). I am commending a different, and fuller, way of embodied seeing and perceiving everything, not putting artefacts in the place of humans. Highlighting the importance of artefacts, and our relationships with them, should not denigrate humans, but should raise material reality to a position of more respect and interest within Western Christian thought and practice that reflects its actual place in shaping human life.

Westerners have unhelpfully over-emphasized the absolute difference between humans and artefacts. However, there are real differences between them. For example, as far as we can know, artefacts are not sentient and do not suffer pain. Sometimes, positive relationships with artefacts have been put ahead of alleviating human suffering; this cannot be lauded by Christians without thought and deliberation.

It is, however, important to be open to the development of more personlike relations with objects. This need not involve a quest for animism or re-enchantment. Rather, what is required is a recognition of the personlike creation and content of artefacts. This is both divine and human in origin. Humans are inveterate animists and anthropo-morphists, finding human-like traits, intentions and purposes every-where and deducing human-like agents who must be the authors of this.[45] This cannot be avoided, and it needs to be borne in mind when encountering events and objects. Artefacts need to be seen in God, not as divine in themselves.[46] When they are treated as gods, as complete ends in themselves, this must be a matter of concern.

What is needed is a kind of 'pastoral care' with, and for, artefacts. This should extend Christian vision, love and concern beyond the human, without losing sight of the human part of creation either. Learning to think about, relate to, and care for artefacts is an act of respect towards the God of creation and towards the humans who have collaborated in that creation and left parts of themselves within the material world. To respect and relate to artefacts is thus part of recognizing the reality of the communion of saints and persons through time. Much can be learned about humans, past and present, by relating fully to the arte-facts they have created and used symbolically and practically. If human lives and possibilities are shaped together and with artefacts of all sorts, caring for the creation demands that we understand and relate to them much more closely.

A move towards more personlike, caring, respectful relations with artefacts demands a fundamental change in relating to the world. Like all caring relationships, there will be cost and inconvenience; it will no longer be possible simply to treat things casually. This implicitly challenges the materialistic spirituality of consumption that devalues the importance of deep material perception. Humans are capable of changing the meanings and significance they give to things. We can do with much less if we love a few things more. However, this will involve basic changes in everyday thought and practice. Nothing less than a conversion, indeed.

There is here the hope of greater joy and appreciation in creation as a whole, a richer and deeper encounter with the world around us. Lash writes: 'in the school of Christianity, we learn to find God's presence animating all things' fresh, surprising liveliness – for from delight all beings come, "by joy they live and they return to joy"' (Lash 1996, p. 64). Ultimately, it is joy that Christians should seek and expect in the quest to take encounters and relationships with artefacts seri-ously – whether that comes from looking at religious masterpieces of the Renaissance in an art gallery, or from marvelling at the apposite simplicity of an everyday door hinge.

So, then, I wish you good looking!

# Notes

1 Like the 'West', Christianity is not monolithic and is composed of many perspectives, practices and traits between times and places. So this chapter is written at a high level of generalization. Its particular concern is with formal theology – this forms a tiny part of articulate Christian consciousness. It is heavily verbal, intellectual and elitist. This, I believe, may be part of the problem in seeing more widely and more deeply.

2 See, for example, Morgan (1998), Orsi (1985, 1996).

3 See, for example, Brown (2004), Burch Brown (2000), Drury (1999), Dyrness (2001).

4 Two notable exceptions to this generalization are, of course, the theological work and interest that has been expended on science, physics in particular, and on ecology. Vast though these fields are, inorganic, inanimate matter still generally receives little consideration beyond pious generalizations. In particular, the world of human creations is very under-assessed theologically except from a general ethical kind of perspective. See, however, Gorringe (2002), Brown (2004), Inge (2003).

5 Kaufman (2004, p. 41) arraigns anthropocentric Christian theology for its neglect of nature and ecology. It is curious that, within an anthropocentric theology, the works and products of human hands have been even more neglected than nature and ecology.

6 See, for example, Dyrness (2001), Drury (1999).

7 See Panofsky (1979, pp. 53ff.) and von Simson (1988). The arguments about the appropriateness of property and ownership within the Church in medieval times are well set out in Umberto Eco's novel, *The Name of the Rose* (1984).

8 See, for example, Pattison (1994).

9 See Ziesler (1973).

10 Armstrong (2005, p. 161).

11 Augustine (1997, pp. 9ff.) warns of the need to love God alone as an end and source of real pleasure. Material and corporeal things should only be used as a means towards that end: 'if we wish to return to the homeland where we can be happy we must use this world, not enjoy it . . .' Augustine is a vehement critic of idols of all kinds, and sees visible representations as 'superfluous human institutions' that threaten to foster 'selfish desires for temporal things' (Augustine 1997, pp. 52–4).

12 See, for example, Meyer (2006), McDannell (1995). Duffy (1992, 2001) provides an intriguing and poignant consideration of the importance of material religion in early modern England.

13 Those who claim to live free of artefacts and icons often have these things but simply live in a state of denial of them. The iconic nature of the Bible as a book in Protestantism is a case in point, and many Protestants have artefacts to which they are attached, for example, pulpits, banners, reading desks, photographs, scriptural illustrations, pictures and artefacts representing religious leaders like John Wesley. See further, for example, Harvey (1995, 1999), Morgan and Promey (2001), McDannell (1995). Even Calvin's early printed books had images and pictures around them

(Dyrness 2004, pp. 94ff.). 'Bible illustrations subvert the Protestant belief that the Word alone matters . . . when that Word arrives in the company of dozens . . . of interpretation-shaping illustrations' (Gutjahr 2001, p. 269).

14 McDannell (1995, p. 26) notes, 'Protestants, as well as Catholics, cherish religious images to the point that their devotions fuse the sign with the referent . . . many Protestants have intimate and powerful relationships with objects.'

15 See, for example, Walker Bynum (1995), Coakley (1997).

16 See, for example, Dyrness (2004). Sennett (1992) argues that the inward turn of Christianity began with Augustine's creation of a visual regime in which the outward, physical realm was separated from, and subordinated to, an inward, spiritual and contemplative journey. This represented a partial abandonment of the physical world that was sharpened by the interiority of the Reformation: 'The inner space of medieval Catholicism was physical, it was a space people could share. The inner space of Puritanism was the space of the most radical individualism and was impalpable. The Puritan eye could only see within itself.' Sennett goes on, 'Spiritual struggle in its form as Protestant ethic denies the outside a reality in itself; denies the value of being present in the world' (Sennett 1992, pp. 45, 65–6). This Christian pursuit of the hidden and inner led to the abandonment of the material, external environment, an abandonment only just being redressed by, for example, Gorringe (2002). Miles (1985, p. 3) observes that in Christianity, eyesight becomes feeling-toned insight.

17 See, for example, McFague (1993, 1997), Jantzen (1984) and Ruether (1992).

18 'Artefacts become particularly important in the lives of average Christians because objects can be exchanged, gifted, reinterpreted, and manipulated. People need objects to help establish and maintain relationships with supernatural characters, family, and friends . . . Religious meaning is not merely inherited or simply accessed through the intellect . . . We can no longer accept that "appearance" of religion is inconsequential to the "experience" of religion. The sensual elements of Christianity are not merely decorations that mask serious belief; it is through the visible world that the invisible world becomes known and felt' (McDannell 1995, p. 272). Morgan (1998) argues that popular, non-discursive material religion contributes directly to the business of living and meaning-making. Popular images have healing and comforting work to do that cannot be accomplished by the theologians' contemplative detachment and disinterest. See further, for example, Orsi (1985, 1996).

19 See, for example, Ellul (1964).

20 Drawing a fundamental line between things that are begotten and made, O'Donovan (1984, p. 65) writes of assisted procreation of humans: 'when we start making human beings we necessarily stop loving them; that which is made rather than begotten becomes something that we have at our disposal, not someone with whom we can engage in brotherly fellowship.' The phenomenological accuracy of this judgement is dubious, whether in relation to all children produced by artificial means, or in relation to all artefacts.

21 Christians have only just begun to consider technological developments that will reconfigure the human body, and so fundamental understandings of human nature. See Graham (2002).

22 The Scottish Churches Council in 1977 defined spirituality as an exploration into what is involved in becoming human which was itself conceived as 'an attempt to grow in sensitivity to self, to others, to the non-human creation, and to God who is within and beyond this totality' (McFague 1997, p. 10). Unfortunately, this positive declaration omits an affirmation of the human creation, the realm of artefacts, which escapes attention as a site of consideration.

23  Kaufman (2004, pp. 40f.).

24  Cusa mixes up the senses of the divinity to create a holistic creative perception of the world. So, for example, he writes (1997, p. 252): 'your gaze speaks, for your speaking is not other than your seeing, because they are not in reality different in you, who are absolute simplicity itself' (Nicholas of Cusa 1997, p. 252).

25  See Bonifazi (1967, pp. 144f.). This kind of thought is consonant with that of Pierre Teilhard de Chardin whose cosmic Christ contains and redeems all matter, summarizing and completing creation. See further Bonifazi (1967, pp. 190f.). Interestingly, de Chardin's thought in this direction emanated from seeing a picture of Christ and having a kind of mystical experience in which 'the whole universe vibrated without destroying the individuality of any single thing, while nervous lines of light threaded paths though all substance'. Quoted in Bonifazi (1967, p. 191).

26  See, for example, Flannery-Dailey (2004), Bonifazi (1967, p. 184).

27  Abram (1997, p. 248) approvingly notes that the Hebrew tradition, particularly through *kaballah*, preserves the inspirited nature of the whole of sensible creation.

28  See, for example, Burch Brown (2000), de Gruchy (2001).

29  Augustine (1997, pp. 9f.).

30  The classic contemplative tradition exemplified in thinkers like Augustine values the material as the beginning of the process of relating to God. However, the highest end of devotion and prayer is to ascend into the realm of the mind of God. It is not that materiality is left behind or totally alien here, but simply that it is seen as less important than the realm of mind and understanding. See Miles (1983) and Coakley (2002), for the movement from material earth to mind/heaven in the contemplation.

31  Seeing all things in God is also commended by Mechtild of Magdeburg: 'The day of my spiritual awakening was the day I saw and knew I saw all things in God and God in all things.' And again, 'The truly wise person kneels at the feet of all creatures' (Wink 1986, p. 166).

32  See further Derbes (1996) and MacGregor (2000, pp. 45ff.).

33  Andrews and Andrews (1966, p. viii). De Waal (1992, p. 106) writes of the Benedictine tradition: 'The garden tools or the pots and pans in the kitchen or pantry are to be treated with just as much care as the sacred vessels of the altar' so that the monastery becomes 'the house of God and the gate of heaven.'

34  Deming Andrews and Andrews (1966, p. ix).

35  Bonifazi (1967, p. 159) points out that while the sacrament of the Eucharist preserves a vital identification of Christ with matter, this has not spread to other parts of the material world.

36  See, for example, Rowland (1999).

37  Perhaps one should be cautious about characterizing visual artefacts as voiceless and so necessarily 'victims'. As we have seen elsewhere, turning visible objects into words is one way of ignoring their own visual reality. Perhaps invisibility is a better category for describing their marginalization – this is also a quality of poor and oppressed people who are looked through and past by others and thus confined to a realm of shame and non-participation (cf. Pattison 2000).

38  McFague (1997, p. 11) writes: 'The Christian practice of radical love knows no bounds: it does not stop at any border, even the human one.'

39  See, for example, McFague (1987, 1993), Ruether (1992), Jantzen (1984).

40  For more on *deus absconditus* see, for example, Dillenberger (1953), Ballentine (1983), Koerner (2004a).

41  See, for example, Dyrness (2004), Harvey (1995, 1999), Morgan (1998).

42 See further Mathews (1999), Edelman (1996), Assmann and Baumgarten (2001), McDannell (1995).

43 Miles (1983, pp. 141, 142) affirms the physical, bodily aspect of seeing in the work of St Augustine, 'father' of Western Christian theology. She writes: 'The continuity of physical and spiritual vision is frequently and strongly affirmed by Augustine.' The eye of the body and eye of the mind will both be present in the resurrection, and there will be physical sight of the immaterial: 'In the resurrection, the enjoyment of God will take the form of contemplation, the satisfaction of longing, the permanent embrace of the visual ray of the eye of the mind.' Like other feminists, Miles (1985, pp. 35ff.) argues that there is a need to acquire 'alternative lenses' of embodied seeing to appreciate images that 'are primarily addressed to comprehending physical existence, the great, lonely, yet universal preverbal experiences of birth, growth, maturation, pain, illness, ecstasy, weakness, age, sex, death'.

44 Both John of Damascus (1980, p. 76) and Calvin would agree that the primary locus for seeing the God on earth is in one's fellow human beings who share the image of God. '"God is to be admitted in his saints," wrote Calvin . . . In them God progressively restored the divine similitude, obscured and distorted by the effects of the Fall, to its original glory. Therefore, when believers gathered for worship, the meeting-house or chapel was resplendent with God's images' (Harvey 1999, p. 16).

45 See Guthrie (1993).

46 Cf. Augustine (1997, pp. 51–2).

# Bibliography

Abram, David, 1997, *The Spell of the Sensuous: Perception and Language in a More-than-Human World*, New York: Vintage Books.

Ackerman, Diane, 1990, *A Natural History of the Senses*, New York: Random House.

Alberti, Leon Battista, 1966, *On Painting*, New Haven CT: Yale University Press.

Alpers, Svetlana, 1983, *The Art of Describing: Dutch Art in the Seventeenth Century*, Chicago: University of Chicago Press.

Andrews, Edward Deming, and Faith Andrews, 1966, *Religion in Wood: A Book of Shaker Furniture*, Bloomington IN: University of Indiana Press.

Appadurai, Arjun, 1986, *The Social Life of Things: Commodities in Cultural Perspective*, Cambridge: Cambridge University Press.

Arendt, Hannah, 1978, *The Life of the Mind*, San Diego CA: Harcourt Inc.

Aristotle, 1986, *De Anima*, London: Penguin Books.

Armstrong, John, 2005, *The Secret Power of Beauty: Why Happiness is in the Eye of the Beholder*, London: Penguin Books.

Arnheim, Rudolf, 1969, *Visual Thinking*, Berkeley CA: University of California Press.

Ashfield, Andrew, and Peter de Bolla, eds, 1996, *The Sublime: A Reader in British Eighteenth-Century Theory*, Cambridge: Cambridge University Press.

Assmann, Jan, and Albert Baumgarten, eds, 2001, *Representation in Religion*, Leiden: Brill.

Atkinson, Janette, 1995, 'Through the Eyes of an Infant', in Gregory *et al.* 1995, 141–56.

Auge, Marc, 1999, *The War of Dreams: Studies in Ethno Fiction*, London: Pluto Press.

Augustine, St, 1997, *On Christian Teaching*, Oxford: Oxford University Press.

Ayers, Mary, 2003, *Mother–Infant Attachment and Psychoanalysis: The Eyes of Shame*, Hove: Brunner Routledge.

Bal, Mieke, 2003, 'Ecstatic Aesthetics: Metaphoring Bernini', in Farago and Zwijnenberg 2003, pp. 1–30.

Baldwin, Thomas, 2004, *Maurice Merleau-Ponty: Basic Writings*, London: Routledge.

Balentine, Samuel, 1983, *The Hidden God: The Hiding of the Face of God in the Old Testament*, Oxford: Oxford University Press.

Ball, Philip, 2002, *Bright Earth: Art and the Invention of Colour*, New York: Farrar, Straus and Giroux.

Banks, Marcus, and Howard Morphy, eds, 1997, *Rethinking Visual Anthropology*, New Haven CT: Yale University Press.

Barasch, Moshe, 1992, *Icon: Studies in the History of an Idea*, New York: New York University Press.

# Bibliography

Barasch, Moshe, 2001, *Blindness: The History of a Mental Image in Western Thought*, London: Routledge.

Barbalet, Jack, ed., 2002, *Emotions and Sociology*, Oxford: Blackwell.

Barry, Andrew, 1995, 'Reporting and Visualising', in Jenks 1995, pp. 42–57.

Barthes, Roland, 1977, *Image Music Text*, London: Fontana.

Barthes, Roland, 2000, *Camera Lucida: Reflections on Photography*, London: Vintage.

Bartsch, Shadi, 2000, 'The Philosopher as Narcissus: Vision, Sexuality, and Self-knowledge in Classical Antiquity', in Nelson 2000a, pp. 70–97.

Bataille, Georges, 1982, *Story of the Eye by Lord Auch*, London: Penguin Books.

Batchen, Geoffrey, 1997, *Burning with Desire*, Cambridge MA: MIT Press.

Batchen, Geoffrey, 2004, 'Ere the Substance Fade: Photography and Hair Jewellery', in Edwards and Hart 2004, pp. 32–46.

Baudrillard, Jean, 1994, *Simulacra and Simulation*, Ann Arbor MI: University of Michigan Press.

Baxandall, Michael, 1995, *Shadows and Enlightenment*, New Haven CT: Yale University Press.

Beck, Ulrich, 1992, *Risk Society*, London: Sage.

Beckley, Bill, ed., 2001, *Sticky Sublime*, New York: Allworth Press.

Begbie, Jeremy, ed., 2002, *Sounding the Depths: Theology through the Arts*, London: SCM Press.

Belting, Hans, 1994, *Likeness and Presence: A History of the Image before the Era of Art*, Chicago: Chicago University Press.

Belting, Hans, 2005, 'Image, Medium, Body: A New Approach to Iconology', *Critical Inquiry* 31: 302–19.

Benjamin, Walter, 1986, *Reflections*, New York: Schocken Books.

Benjamin, Walter, 1999, *Illuminations*, London: Pimlico.

Bennett, Alan, 2005, *Untold Stories*, London: Faber & Faber and Profile Books.

Bennett, Jane, 2001, *The Enchantment of Modern Life: Attachments, Crossings, and Ethics*, Princeton NJ: Princeton University Press.

Berger, John, 1972, *Ways of Seeing*, London: Penguin Books.

Bergson, Henri, 2004, *Matter and Memory*, Mineola NY: Dover Books.

Berryman, Edward, 2006, 'Taking Pictures of Jesus: Producing the Material Presence of a Divine Other', *Human Studies* 28: 431–52.

Besancon, Alain, 2000, *The Forbidden Image: An Intellectual History of Iconoclasm*, Chicago: Chicago University Press.

Bland, Kalman, 2000, *The Artless Jew: Medieval and Modern Affirmations and Denials of the Visual*, Princeton NJ: Princeton University Press.

Blumenberg, Hans, 1993, 'Light as a Metaphor for Truth', in Levin 1993, pp. 30–62.

Bollas, Christopher, 1987, *The Shadow of the Object: Psychoanalysis of the Unthought Known*, London: Free Association Books.

Bonifazi, Conrad, 1967, *A Theology of Things: A Study of Man in his Physical Environment*, Philadelphia PA: JB Lippincott Company.

Bourdieu, Pierre, 1984, *Distinction: A Social Critique of the Judgment of Taste*, Cambridge MA: Harvard University Press.

Bourdieu, Pierre, 1998, *Practical Reason*, Stanford CA: Stanford University Press.

Brading, D. A, 2001, *Mexican Phoenix: Our Lady of Guadalupe: Image and Tradition across Five Centuries*, Cambridge: Cambridge University Press.

Brooke, John Hedley, and Geoffrey Cantor, 2000, *Reconstructing Nature: The Engagement of Science and Religion*, New York: Oxford University Press.

Brown, David, 2004, *God and the Enchantment of Place: Reclaiming Human Experience*, Oxford: Oxford University Press.

Bruce, Vicki, and Andy Young, 1998, *In the Eye of the Beholder: The Science of Face Perception*, Oxford: Oxford University Press.

Bryson, Norman, 1983, *Vision and Painting: The Logic of the Gaze*, London: Macmillan.

Buber, Martin, 1970, *I and Thou*, Edinburgh: T & T Clark.

Buck-Morss, Susan, 1992, 'Aesthetics and Anaesthetics: Walter Benjamin's Artwork Essays Reconsidered', *October 62*: 3–41.

Bull, Malcolm, 1999, *Seeing Things Hidden: Apocalypse, Vision and Totality*, London: Verso.

Burch Brown, Frank, 2000, *Good Taste, Bad Taste, and Christian Taste*, Oxford: Oxford University Press.

Burke, Edmund, 1990, *A Philosophical Enquiry into the Origin of our Ideas of the Sublime and the Beautiful*, Oxford: Oxford University Press.

Burkitt, Ian, 2002, 'Complex Emotions: Relations, Feelings and Images in Emotional Experience', in Barbalet 2002, pp. 151–67.

Camille, Michael, 2000, 'Before the Gaze: The Internal Senses and Late Medieval Practices of Seeing', in Nelson 2000a, pp. 197–223.

Campbell, Colin, 1987, *The Romantic Ethic and the Spirit of Capitalism*, Oxford: Basil Blackwell.

Carrier, James, 1990, 'The Symbolism of Possession in Commodity Advertising', *Man* (NS) 25;4: 693–706.

Carrithers, Michael, Steven Collins and Steven Lukes, eds, 1985, *The Category of the Person: Anthropology, Philosophy, History*, Cambridge: Cambridge University Press.

Carroll, Noel, 1999, *Philosophy of Art*, London: Routledge.

Carruthers, Mary, 1998, *The Craft of Thought*, Cambridge: Cambridge University Press.

Chaplin, Elizabeth, 1994, *Sociology and Visual Representation*, London: Routledge.

Chapman, Allan, 2001, *Gods in the Sky*, London: Channel Four Books.

Christian, William, 1992, *Moving Crucifixes in Modern Spain*, Princeton NJ: Princeton University Press.

Claridge, Gordon, and Caroline Davis, 2003, *Personality and Psychological Disorders*, London: Arnold.

Classen, Constance, David Howes and Anthony Synnott, 1994, *Aroma: The Cultural History of Smell*, London: Routledge.

Clifford, James, 1998, *The Predicament of Culture: Twentieth-Century Ethnography, Literature and Art*, Cambridge MA: Harvard University Press.

Coakley, Sarah, 2002, *Powers and Submissions: Spirituality, Philosophy and Gender*, Oxford: Blackwell.

Coakley, Sarah, ed., 1997, *Religion and the Body*, Cambridge: Cambridge University Press.

Code, Lorraine, 1991, *What Can She Know? Feminist Theory and the Construction of Knowledge*, Ithaca NY: Cornell University Press.

Cole, Jonathan, 1998, *About Face*, Cambridge MA: MIT Press.

Coleman, Simon, and John Elsner, 1995, *Pilgrimage Past and Present*, London: British Museum Press.

Coleman, Simon, and John Elsner, eds, 2003, *Pilgrim Voices: Narrative and Authorship in Christian Pilgrimage*, New York: Berghahn Books.

# Bibliography

Collingwood, R. G., 1958, *The Principles of Art*, Oxford: Oxford University Press.

Colville, Ewan, 2006, 'Touching Scotland', Personal communication.

Connell, Janice, 1997, *The Visions of the Children: The Apparitions of the Blessed Mother at Medjugorje*, New York: St Martin's Press.

Conran, Terence, and Max Fraser, 2004, *Designers on Design*, London: Conran Octopus.

Cranz, Galen, 2000, *The Chair: Rethinking Culture, Body, and Design*, New York: WW Norton.

Crary, Jonathan, 1988, 'Modernizing Vision', in Foster 1988, pp. 29–43.

Crary, Jonathan, 1990, *Techniques of the Observer: On Vision and Modernity in the Nineteenth Century*, Cambridge MA: MIT Press.

Crary, Jonathan, 1999, *Suspensions of Perception: Attention, Spectacle, and Modern Culture*, Cambridge MA: MIT Press.

Crombie, A. C., 1953, *Robert Grosseteste and the Origins of Experimental Science 1100–1700*, Oxford: Oxford University Press.

Csikszentmihalyi, Mihaly, and Eugene Rochberg Halton, 1981, *The Meaning of Things: Domestic Symbols and the Self*, Cambridge: Cambridge University Press.

Dalrymple, William, 1998, *From the Holy Mountain*, London: Flamingo.

Dant, Tim, 1999, *Material Culture in the Social World*, Buckingham: Open University Press.

Dant, Tim, 2005, *Materiality and Society*, Maidenhead: Open University Press.

Dante, 1986, *Paradise*, Vol. 3 of *The Divine Comedy*, London: Penguin Books.

Danziger, Kurt, 1997, *Naming the Mind*, London: Sage.

Daston, Lorraine, 1998, 'Nature by Design', in Jones and Gallison 1998, 232–53.

Daston, Lorraine, 2002, 'Nature Paints', in Latour and Wiebel 2002, 136–8.

Daston, Lorraine, ed., 2004, *Things that Talk: Object Lessons from Art and Science*, New York: Zone Books.

Daston, Lorraine, and Peter Galison, 1992, 'The Image of Objectivity', *Representations* 40: 83–128.

Davidson, Arnold, 1998, 'Miracles of Bodily Transformation, or, How St Francis Received the Stigmata', in Jones and Galison 1998, 101–24.

Davies, Stephen, 1991, *Definitions of Art*, Ithaca NY: Cornell University Press.

Davis, Richard, 1997, *Lives of Indian Images*, Princeton NJ: Princeton University Press.

de Bolla, Peter, 2001, *Art Matters*, Cambridge MA: Harvard University Press.

Debord, Guy, 1995, *The Society of the Spectacle*, New York: Zone Books.

de Botton, Alain, 2006, *The Architecture of Happiness*, London: Hamish Hamilton.

de Gruchy, John, 2001, *Christianity, Art and Transformation*, Cambridge: Cambridge University Press.

Dennett, Daniel, 1993, *Consciousness Explained*, London: Penguin Books.

Derbes, Anne, 1996, *Picturing the Passion in Late Medieval Italy*, Cambridge: Cambridge University Press.

Derlon, Brigitte, 2002, 'From New Ireland to a Museum: Opposing Views of the Malanggan', in Latour and Wiebel 2002, pp. 139–42.

Derrida, Jacques, 1993, *Memoirs of the Blind: The Self-Portrait and Other Ruins*, Chicago: Chicago University Press.

de Waal, Esther, 1992, *A Seven Day Journey with Thomas Merton: Making a Private Retreat*, Guildford: Eagle.

Dillenberger, John, 1953, *God Hidden and Revealed*, Philadelphia: Muhlenberg Press.

Donne, John, 1949, *Complete Poetry and Selected Prose*, London: Nonesuch Press.

Donne, John, 1990, *John Donne: Selections from Divine Poems, Sermons, Devotions and Prayers*, New York: Paulist Press.

Drury, John, 1999, *Painting the Word: Christian Pictures and their Meanings*, New Haven CT: Yale University Press.

Duden, Barbara, 1993, *Disembodying Women*, Cambridge MA: Harvard University Press.

Duffy, Eamon, 1992, *The Stripping of the Altars: Traditional Religion in England 1400–1580*, New Haven CT: Yale University Press.

Duffy, Eamon, 2001, *The Voices of Morebath: Reformation and Rebellion in an English Village*, New Haven CT: Yale University Press.

Duffy, Eamon, 2006, *Marking the Hours: English People and their Prayers 1240–1570*, New Haven CT: Yale University Press.

Duncan, Carol, 1995, *Civilizing Rituals: Inside Public Art Museums*, London: Routledge.

Dyer, Richard, 2002, *The Matter of Images: Essays on Representation*, London: Routledge.

Dyrness, William, 2001, *Visual Faith: Art, Theology and Worship in Dialogue*, Grand Rapids MI: Baker Academic.

Dyrness, William, 2004, *Reformed Theology and Visual Culture: The Protestant Imagination from Calvin to Edwards*, Cambridge: Cambridge University Press.

Dyson, Michael, 2001, *Holler if You Hear Me: Searching for Tupac Shakur*, London: Plexus.

Eck, Diane, 1998, *Darshan: Seeing the Divine Image in India*, New York: Columbia University Press.

Eco, Umberto, 1984, *The Name of the Rose*, London: Picador.

Eco, Umberto, 2002, *Art and Beauty in the Middle Ages*, New Haven CT: Yale University Press.

Edelman, Diana, 1996, *The Triumph of the Elohim: From Yahwisms to Judaisms*, Grand Rapids MI: Eerdmans.

Edwards, Elizabeth, 1999, 'Photographs as Objects of Memory', in Kwint, Breward and Aynsley 1999, pp. 221–36.

Edwards, Elizabeth, Chris Gosden and Ruth Phillips, eds, 2006, *Sensible Objects: Colonialism, Museums and Material Culture*, Oxford: Berg.

Edwards, Elizabeth, and Janice Hart, eds, 2004, *Photographs Objects Histories: On the Materiality of the Images*, London: Routledge.

Ehrlmann, Veit, ed., 2004, *Hearing Cultures: Essays on Sound, Listening and Modernity*, Oxford: Berg.

Elkins, James, 1997, *The Object Stares Back: On the Nature of Seeing*, San Diego CA: Harcourt, Brace and Co.

Elkins, James, 1999, *The Domain of Images*, New York: Cornell University Press.

Elkins, James, 2000a, *How to Use your Eyes*, London: Routledge.

Elkins, James, 2000b, *What Painting Is*, London: Routledge.

Elkins, James, 2001, *Pictures and Tears*, London: Routledge.

Elkins, James, 2003, *Visual Studies: A Sceptical Introduction*, London: Routledge.

Elkins, James, 2004, *On the Strange Place of Religion in Contemporary Art*, London: Routledge.

Ellul, Jacques, 1964, *The Technological Society*, New York: Alfred Knopf, Inc.

Ellul, Jacques, 1985, *The Humiliation of the Word*, Grand Rapids MI: Eeerdmans.

Elsner, John, 2000, 'Between Mimesis and Divine Power: Visuality in the Greco-Roman World', in Nelson 2000a, pp. 45–69.

# Bibliography

Elsner, John, 2004, 'Seeing and Saying: A Psychoanalytic Account of Ekphrasis', *Helios* 31;1–2: 157–89.

Farago, Claire, 2003, 'Aesthetics before Art: Leonardo through the Looking Glass', in Farago and Zwijnenberg 2003, pp. 45–92.

Farago, Claire and Robert Zwijnenberg, eds, 2003, *Compelling Visuality: The Work of Art In and Out of History*, Minneapolis MN: University of Minnesota Press.

Finney, Paul, 1994, *The Invisible God: The Earliest Christians on Art*, Oxford: Oxford University Press.

Flannery-Dailey, Frances, 2004, *Dreamers, Scribes and Priests: Jewish Dreams in the Hellenistic and Roman Eras*, Leiden: Brill.

Fonagy, Peter, 2001, *Attachment Theory and Psychoanalysis*, New York: Other Press.

Foster, Hal, ed., 1988, *Vision and Visuality*, Seattle: Bay Press.

Foucault, Michel, 1979, *Discipline and Punish*, London: Penguin Books.

Francis of Assisi, St, 1963, *The Little Flowers of St Francis*, London: Dent.

Frank, Georgia, 2000, 'The Pilgrim's Gaze in the Age before Icons', in Nelson 2000a, pp. 98–115.

Freedberg, David, 1989, *The Power of Images: Studies in the History and Theory of Response*, Chicago: Chicago University Press.

Freeland, Cynthia, 2001, *Art Theory: A Very Short Introduction*, Oxford: Oxford University Press.

Freud, Sigmund, 1985a, *Art and Literature*, London: Penguin Books.

Freud, Sigmund, 1985b, *The Origins of Religion*, London: Penguin Books.

Freud, Sigmund, 1991, *The Interpretation of Dreams*, London: Penguin Books.

Frith, Chris, and Eve Johnstone, 2003, *Schizophrenia: A Very Short Introduction*, Oxford: Oxford University Press.

Fry, Roger, 1937, *Vision and Design*, Harmondsworth: Penguin Books.

Funkenstein, Amos, 1986, *Theology and the Scientific Imagination from the Middle Ages to the Seventeenth Century*, Princeton NJ: Princeton University Press.

Gadamer, Hans-Georg, 1989, *Truth and Method*, London: Sheed and Ward.

Gage, John, 1995, *Colour and Culture: Practice and Meaning from Antiquity to Abstraction*, London: Thames and Hudson.

Gage, John, 2000, *Colour and Meaning: Art, Science and Symbolism*, London: Thames and Hudson.

Galison, Peter, 2002, 'Images Scatter into Data, Data Gather into Images', in Latour and Weibel 2002, pp. 300–23.

Gardiner, Michael, 1999, 'Bakhtin and the Metaphorics of Perception', in Heywood and Sandywell 1999, pp. 57–73.

Gaskell, Ivan, 2003, 'Sacred to Profane and Back Again', in McClellan 2003, pp. 149–62.

Gaut, Berys, and Dominic McIver-Lopes, 2001, *The Routledge Companion to Aesthetics*, London: Routledge.

Gell, Alfred, 1998, *Art and Agency*, Oxford: Oxford University Press.

Gendlin, Eugene, 2003, *Focusing: How to Gain Access to Your Body's Knowledge*, London: Rider.

Gerth, H., and C. Wright Mills, 1948, *From Max Weber: Essays in Sociology*, London: Routledge and Kegan Paul.

Gibson, James, 1986, *The Ecological Approach to Visual Perception*, Hilldale NJ: Lawrence Erlbaum Associates.

Gombrich, Ernst, 1977, *Art and Illusion: A Study in the Psychology of Pictorial Representation*, London: Phaidon.

# Seeing Things

Gombrich, Ernst, 1995, *Shadows: The Depiction of Cast Shadows in Western Art*, London: National Gallery Publications.

Gorringe, Timothy, 2001, *The Education of Desire*, London: SCM Press.

Gorringe, Timothy, 2002, *A Theology of the Built Environment*, Cambridge: Cambridge University Press.

Gosden, Chris, and Yvonne Marshall, 1999, 'The Cultural Biography of Objects', *World Archaeology* 31;2: 169–78.

Graham, Elaine, 2002, *Representations of the Post/human: Monsters, Aliens and Others in Popular Culture*, Manchester: Manchester University Press.

Gravel, Peter, 1995, *The Malevolent Eye*, New York: Peter Lang.

Gregory, Richard, 1997, *Mirrors in Mind*, London: Penguin Books.

Gregory, Richard, 1998, *Eye and Brain: The Psychology of Seeing*, Oxford: Oxford University Press.

Gregory, Richard, ed., 2004, *The Oxford Companion to the Mind*, Oxford: Oxford University Press.

Gregory, Richard, John Harris, Priscilla Heard, and David Rose, 1995, *The Artful Eye*, Oxford: Oxford University Press.

Gruzinski, Serge, 2001, *Images at War: Mexico from Columbus to Blade Runner (1492–2019)*, Durham NC: Duke University Press.

Guthrie, Stewart, 1993, *Faces in the Clouds: A New Theory of Religion*, New York: Oxford University Press.

Gutjahr, Paul, 2001, 'American Protestant Bible Illustration from Copper Plates to Computers', in Morgan and Promey 2001, pp. 267–85.

Hahn, Cynthia, 2000, '*Visio Dei*: Changes in Medieval Visuality', in Nelson 2000a, pp. 169–96.

Hall, Stuart, ed., 1997, *Representation: Cultural Representations and Signifying Practices*, London: Sage.

Hanganu, Gabriel, 2004, 'Photo-cross: The Political and Social Lives of a Romanian Orthodox Photograph', in Edwards and Hart 2004, pp. 148–65.

Harris, Clare, 2004, 'The Photograph Reincarnate: The Dynamics of Tibetan Relations with Photography', in Edwards and Hart 2004, pp. 132–47.

Harris, Ruth, 1999, *Lourdes*, London: Viking Press.

Harrison, John, 2001, *Synaesthesia: The Strangest Thing*, Oxford: Oxford University Press.

Harrison, Peter, 1998, *The Bible, Protestantism and the Rise of Natural Science*, Cambridge: Cambridge University Press.

Harvey, David, 1989, *The Condition of Postmodernity*, Oxford: Blackwell.

Harvey, Graham, 2005, *Animism: Respecting the Living World*, London: Hurst and Company.

Harvey, John, 1995, *Visual Piety: The Visual Culture of Welsh Nonconformity*, Cardiff: University of Wales Press.

Harvey, John, 1999, *Image of the Invisible: The Visualization of Religion in the Welsh Nonconformist Tradition*, Cardiff: University of Wales Press.

Haynes, Deborah, 1997, *The Vocation of the Artist*, Cambridge: Cambridge University Press.

Hayum, Andree, 1989, *The Isenheim Altarpiece: God's Medicine and the Painter's Vision*, Princeton NJ: Princeton University Press.

Hebdige, Dick, 1995, 'Fabulous Confusion! Pop before Pop?', in Jenks 1995, pp. 96–122.

Hegel, Georg, 1993, *Introductory Lectures on Aesthetics*, London: Penguin Books.

Heller, Morton, ed., 2000, *Touch, Representation, and Blindness*, Oxford: Oxford University Press.

Herbert, George, 1961, *The Poems of George Herbert*, Oxford: Oxford University Press.

Heywood, Ian, and Barry Sandywell, eds, 1999, *Interpreting Visual Culture*, London: Routledge.

Hill, Diane, 1999, 'The "Real Realm": Value and Values in Recent Feminist Art', in Heywood and Sandywell 1999, pp. 143–61.

Hills, Paul, 1987, *The Light of Early Italian Painting*, New Haven CT: Yale University Press.

Holly, Michael Ann, 1996, *Past Looking: Historical Imagination and the Rhetoric of the Image*, Ithaca NY: Cornell University Press.

Holly, Michael Ann, 2003, 'Mourning and Method', in Farago and Zwijnenberg 2003, pp. 156–78.

Hooke, Robert, 2003, *Micrographia*, Mineola NY: Dover Publications.

Hopkins, David, 2004, *Dada and Surrealism: A Very Short Introduction*, Oxford: Oxford University Press.

Horne, Donald, 1984, *The Great Museum*, London: Pluto Press

Hoskins, Janet, 1998, *Biographical Objects: How Things Tell the Stories of People's Lives*, London: Routledge

Houlgate, Stephen, 1993, 'Vision, Reflection and Openness: The "Hegemony of Vision" from a Hegelian Point of View', in Levin 1993, pp. 87–123.

Howes, David, 2003, *Sensual Relations: Engaging the Senses in Culture and Social Theory*, Ann Arbor MI: University of Michigan Press.

Howes, David, ed., 2005, *Empire of the Senses*, Oxford: Berg.

Hull, John, 1991, *Touching the Rock: An Experience of Blindness*, London: Arrow Books.

Hull, John, 2001, *In the Beginning There was Darkness*, London: SCM Press.

Humphrey, Nicholas, 1993, *The Inner Eye*, London: Vintage.

Idel, Moshe, 2001, 'Torah: Between Presence and Representation of the Divine in Jewish Mysticism', in Assmann and Baumgarten 2001, pp. 197–236.

Ignatius of Loyola, St, 1996, *Personal Writings*, London: Penguin Books.

Inge, John, 2003, *A Christian Theology of Place*, Aldershot: Ashgate.

Ingold, Tim, 2000, *The Perception of the Environment: Essays in Livelihood, Dwelling and Skill*, Abingdon: Routledge.

Ingold, Tim, 2006, 'Rethinking the Animate, Re-animating Thought', *Ethnos* 71: 9–20.

Janaway, Christopher, 2001, 'Plato', in Gaut and McIver Lopes 2000, pp. 3–13.

Jantzen, Grace, 1984, *God's World, God's Body*, London: Darton, Longman and Todd.

Jantzen, Grace, 1995, *Gender, Power and Christian Mysticism*, Cambridge: Cambridge University Press.

Jay, Martin, 1988, 'Scopic Regimes of Modernity', in Foster 1988, pp. 3–23.

Jay, Martin, 1994, *Downcast Eyes: The Denigration of Vision in Twentieth-Century French Thought*, Berkeley CA: University of California Press.

Jenks, Chris, ed., 1995, *Visual Culture*, London: Routledge.

Jensen, Robin, 2000, *Understanding Early Christian Art*, London: Routledge.

John of Damascus, St, 1980, *On the Divine Images*, Crestwood NY: St Vladimir's Seminary Press.

Johnson, Geraldine, 2002, 'Touch, Tactility and the Reception of Sculpture in Early Modern Italy', in Smith and Wilde 2002, pp. 61–74.

Jonas, Hans, 1966, *The Phenomenon of Life: Toward a Philosophical Biology*, New York: Dell Publishing.

Jones, Caroline, and Peter Galison, eds, 1998, *Picturing Science Producing Art*, London: Routledge.

Jones, Lars, and Louisa Matthews, eds, *Coming About*, Cambridge MA: Harvard University Art Museum.

Judovitz, Dalia, 1993, 'Vision, Representation, and Technology in Descartes', in Levin 1993, pp. 63–86.

Julier, Guy, 2000, *The Culture of Design*, London: Sage.

Julius, Anthony, 2000, *Idolizing Pictures: Idolatry, Iconoclasm and Jewish Art*, London: Thames and Hudson.

Kadri, Sadkat, 2006, *The Trial: A History from Socrates to O. J. Simpson*, London: Harper Perennial.

Kant, Immanuel, 1987, *Critique of Judgment*, Indianapolis IN: Hackett.

Kaufman, Gordon, 2004, *In the Beginning ... Creativity*, Minneapolis: Fortress Press.

Kemp, Martin, 1990, *The Science of Art: Optical Themes in Western Art from Brunelleschi to Seurat*, New Haven CT: Yale University Press.

Kemp, Martin, 1990, 'Taking it on Trust: Form and Meaning in Naturalistic Representation', *Archives of Natural History* 17;2: 127–88.

Kemp, Martin, 2000a, *The Oxford History of Western Art*, Oxford: Oxford University Press.

Kemp, Martin, 2000b, *Visualizations: The Nature Book of Art and Science*, Oxford: Oxford University Press.

Kemp, Martin, 2001a, 'From Different Points of View: Correggio, Copernicus and the Mobile Observer', in Jones and Matthews 2001, pp. 207–12.

Kemp, Martin, ed., 2001b, *Leonardo on Painting*, New Haven CT: Yale University Press.

Kemp, Martin, 2003, 'The *Mona Lisa* of Modern Science', *Nature* 421: 416–19.

Kemp, Martin, 2006, *Seen/Unseen: Art, Science, and Intuition from Leonardo to the Hubble Telescope*, Oxford: Oxford University Press.

Kemp, Sandra, 2004, *Future Face: Image, Identity, Innovation*, London: Profile Books.

Kleege, Georgina, 1999, *Sight Unseen*, New Haven CT: Yale University Press.

Koerner, Josef, 2002, 'Icon as Iconoclash', in Latour and Weibel 2002, pp. 164–213.

Koerner, Joseph, 2004a, *The Reformation of the Image*, London: Reaktion Books.

Koerner, Joseph, 2004b, 'Bosch's Equipment', in Daston 2004, pp. 27–65.

Kopytoff, Igor, 1986, 'The Cultural Biography of Things: Commoditization as Process', in Appadurai 1986, pp. 64–91.

Kris, Ernst, and Otto Kurz, 1979, *Legend, Myth, and Magic in the Image of the Artist*, New Haven CT: Yale University Press.

Krauss, Rosalind, 1994, *The Optical Unconscious*, Cambridge MA: MIT Press.

Krell, David, ed., 1993, *Basic Writings: Martin Heidegger*, London: Routledge.

Kress, Gunther, and Theo van Leeuwen, 1996, *Reading Images: The Grammar of Visual Design*, London: Routledge.

Kuhnel, Bianca, 2001, 'Jewish Art and Iconoclasm: The Case of Sepphoris', in Assmann and Baumgarten 2001, pp. 161–80.

Kunzl, Hannelore, 2001, 'Jewish Artists and the Representation of God', in Assmann and Baumgarten 2001, pp. 149–60.

Kwint, Marius, 2005, 'Desiring Structures: Exhibiting the Dendritic Form', *Interdisciplinary Science Reviews* 3: 205–21.

# Bibliography

Kwint, Marius, Christopher Breward, and Jeremy Aynsley, eds, 1999, *Material Memories*, Oxford: Berg.

Lacan, Jacques, 1981, *The Four Fundamental Concepts of Psychoanalysis*, New York: WW Norton.

Lasch, Christopher, 1991, *The Culture of Narcissism: American Life in an Age of Diminishing Expectations*, New York: WW Norton.

Lash, Nicholas, 1996, *The Beginning and the End of 'Religion'*, Cambridge: Cambridge University Press.

Latour, Bruno, 1993, *We Have Never Been Modern*, Cambridge MA: Harvard University Press.

Latour, Bruno, 2002, 'What is iconoclash, or is there a world beyond the image wars?', in Latour and Weibel 2002, pp. 14–37.

Latour, Bruno, 2005, *Reassembling the Social: An Introduction to Actor-Network-Theory*, Oxford: Oxford University Press.

Latour, Bruno, and Peter Weibel, eds, 2002, *Iconoclash: Beyond the Image Wars in Science, Religion, and Art*, Cambridge MA: MIT Press.

Latto, Richard, 1995, The Brain of the Beholder', in Gregory *et al.*, 1995, pp. 66–94.

Leader, Darian, 2002, *Stealing the Mona Lisa: What Art Stops Us from Seeing*, London: Faber & Faber.

Levin, David, 1988, *The Opening of Vision: Nihilism and the Postmodern Situation*, London: Routledge.

Levin, David, ed., 1993, *Modernity and the Hegemony of Vision*, Berkeley CA: University of California Press.

Levin, David, 1999, 'My Philosophical Project and the Empty Jug', in Heywood and Sandywell 1999, pp. 185–97.

Levine, Lawrence, 1988, *Highbrow Lowbrow: The Emergence of Cultural Hierarchy in America*, Cambridge MA: Harvard University Press.

Lieb, Michael, 1991, *The Visionary Mode: Biblical Prophecy, Hermeneutics, and Cultural Change*, Ithaca NY: Cornell University Press.

Lieb, Michael, 1998, *Children of Ezekiel: Aliens, UFOs, the Crisis of Race, and the End of Time*, Durham NC: Duke University Press.

Lindberg, David, 1976, *Theories of Vision from Al-Kindi to Kepler*, Chicago: Chicago University Press.

Locke, John, 1997, *An Essay Concerning Human Understanding*, London: Penguin Books.

Lopes, Dominic, 2005, *Sight and Sensibility: Evaluating Pictures*, Oxford: Oxford University Press.

Lossky, Vladimir, 1983, *The Vision of God*, Crestwood NY: St Vladimir's Seminary Press.

Lovejoy, Arthur, 1936, *The Great Chain of Being*, Cambridge MA: Harvard University Press.

Lowden, John, 1997, *Early Christian and Byzantine Art*, London: Phaidon.

Lowe, Donald, 1982, *History of Bourgeois Perception*, Chicago: Chicago University Press.

Lynch, Gordon, 2005, *Understanding Theology and Popular Culture*, Oxford: Blackwell.

Lynch, Michael, and Steve Woolgar, eds, 1990, *Representation in Scientific Practice*, Cambridge MA: MIT Press.

MacCannell, Daniel, 1999, *The Tourist: A New Theory of the Leisure Class*, Berkeley CA: University of California Press.

MacGregor, Neil, 2000, *Seeing Salvation: Images of Christ in Art*, London: BBC.

Macmurray, John, 1991, *The Self as Agent*, Atlantic Highlands NJ: Humanities Press International.

Magee, Bryan, and Martin Milligan, 1998, *Sight Unseen*, London: Phoenix.

Manguel, Alberto, 2002, *Reading Pictures: What We Think about When We Look at Art*, New York: Random House Trade Paperbacks.

Maniura, Robert, 2003, 'Pilgrimage into Words and Images', in Coleman and Elsner 2003, pp. 40–60.

Marks, Laura, 2000, *The Skin of the Film*, Durham NC: Duke University Press.

Mathews, Thomas, 1999, *The Clash of Gods*, Princeton NJ: Princeton University Press.

Matthews, Eric, 2006, *Merleau-Ponty: A Guide for the Perplexed*, London: Continuum.

Maxwell, Meg, and Verena Tschudin, eds, 1990, *Seeing the Invisible: Modern Religious and Other Transcendent Experiences*, London: Arkana.

McAllester Jones, Mary, 1991, *Gaston Bachelard Subversive Humanist*, Madison: University of Wisconsin Press.

McClellan, Andrew, ed., 2003, *Art and Its Publics: Museum Studies at the Millennium*, Oxford: Blackwell.

McDannell, Colleen, 1995, *Material Christianity: Religion and Popular Culture in America*, New Haven CT: Yale University Press.

McFague, Sallie, 1987, *Models of God: Theology for an Ecological, Nuclear Age*, London: SCM Press.

McFague, Sallie, 1993, *The Body of God: An Ecological Theology*, London: SCM Press.

McFague, Sallie, 1997, *Super, Natural Christians*, London: SCM Press.

McNeill, Daniel, 1998, *The Face*, London: Penguin Books.

Melchior-Bonnet, Sabine, 2002, *The Mirror: A History*, London, Routledge.

Merleau-Ponty, Maurice, 1968, *The Visible and the Invisible*, Evanston ILL: Northwestern University Press.

Merleau-Ponty, Maurice, 2004, *Basic Writings*, London: Routledge.

Meyer, Birgit, 2006, 'Religious Revelation, Secrecy and the Limits of Visual Representation', unpublished paper.

Meyer, Birgit and Peter Pels, eds, 2003, *Magic and Modernity: Interfaces of Revelation and Concealment*, Stanford CA: Stanford University Press.

Midgley, Mary, 1983, *Animals and Why They Matter*, London: Penguin Books.

Midgley, Mary, 1989, *Wisdom, Information and Wonder: What is Knowledge For?* London: Routledge.

Midgley, Mary, 2001, *Science and Poetry*, London, Routledge.

Miles, Margaret, 1983, 'Vision: The Eye of the Body and the Eye of the Mind in St Augustine's *De Trinitate* and *Confessions*', *Journal of Religion* 63: 125–42.

Miles, Margaret, 1985, *Image as Insight*, Boston: Beacon Press.

Miles, Margaret, 1996, *Seeing and Believing: Religion and Values in the Movies*, Boston: Beacon Press.

Miller, Daniel, 1987, *Material Culture and Mass Consumption*, Oxford: Blackwell.

Miller, Daniel, ed., 1998, *Material Cultures: Why Some Things Matter*, Chicago: Chicago University Press.

Mirzoeff, Nicholas, 1999, *An Introduction to Visual Culture*, London: Routledge.

Mirzoeff, Nicholas, 2002, *The Visual Culture Reader*, London: Routledge.

Mitchell, W. J. T., 1986, *Iconology: Image, Text, Ideology*, Chicago: Chicago University Press.

# Bibliography

Mitchell, W. J. T., 1994, *Picture Theory*, Chicago: Chicago University Press.

Mitchell, W. J. T., 1996, 'What do Pictures *Really* Want?' *October* 77: 71–82.

Mitchell, W. J. T., 2002, 'Showing Seeing: A Critique of Visual Culture', in Mirzoeff 2002, pp. 86–101.

Molotch, Harvey, 2003, *Where Stuff Comes From: How Toasters, Toilets, Cars, Computers, and Many Other Things Come to Be as They Are*, New York: Routledge.

Monti, Anthony, 2003, *A Natural Theology of the Arts: Imprint of the Spirit*, Aldershot: Ashgate.

Moore, Thomas, 1996, *The Re-enchantment of Everyday Life*, New York: Harper Collins.

Moran, Joe, 2002, *Interdisciplinarity*, London: Routledge.

Morgan, David, 1996a, 'The Enchantment of Art: Abstraction and Empathy from German Romanticism to Expressionism', *Journal of the History of Ideas* 57;2: 317–41.

Morgan, David, ed., 1996b, *Icons of American Protestantism: The Art of Warner Sallman*, New Haven CT: Yale University Press.

Morgan, David, 1998, *Visual Piety: A History and Theory of Popular Religious Images*, Berkeley CA: University of California Press.

Morgan, David, 1999, *Protestants and Pictures: Religion, Visual Culture, and the Age of American Mass Production*, Oxford: Oxford University Press.

Morgan, David, 2005a, *The Sacred Gaze: Religious Visual Culture in Theory and Practice*, Berkeley CA: University of California Press.

Morgan, David, 2005b, 'The Visual Construction of the Sacred', unpublished paper.

Morgan, David, and Sally Promey, eds, 2001, *The Visual Culture of American Religions*, Berkeley CA: University of California Press.

Mulvey, Laura, 1996, *Fetishism and Curiosity*, London: British Film Institute.

Murdoch, Iris, 1985, *The Sovereignty of Good*, London: ARK.

Nelson, Robert, ed., 2000a, *Visuality Before and Beyond the Renaissance: Seeing as Others Saw*, Cambridge: Cambridge University Press.

Nelson, Robert, 2000b, 'To Say and to See: Ekphrasis and Vision in Byzantium', in Nelson 2000a, pp. 143–68.

Nettle, Daniel, 2001, *Strong Imagination: Madness, Creativity, and Human Nature*, Oxford: Oxford University Press.

Newhouse, Victoria, 2005, *Art and the Power of Placement*, New York: The Monacelli Press.

Nicholas of Cusa, 1997, *Selected Spiritual Writings*, New York: Paulist Press.

Nietzsche, Friedrich, 1969, *Thus Spoke Zarathustra*, London: Penguin Books.

Nightingale, Andrea, 2005, *Spectacles of Truth in Classical Greek Philosophy: Theoria in its Cultural Context*, Cambridge: Cambridge University Press.

Noddings, Nel, 1986, *Caring: A Feminine Approach to Ethics and Moral Education*, Los Angeles CA: University of California Press.

Nooter Roberts, Mary, 2006, 'Account of the Saint', Personal communication.

Nooter Roberts, Mary, and Allen Roberts, 1997, *A Sense of Wonder*, Pheonix AZ: Pheonix Art Museum.

Norman, Donald, 2004, *Emotional Design: Why We Love (or Hate) Everyday Things*, New York: Basic Books.

Oakes, Catherine, 1997, 'An Iconographical Study of the Virgin as Intercessor, Mediator and Purveyor of Meaning from the Twelfth to the Fifteenth Century', unpublished PhD thesis, University of Bristol.

O'Donovan, Oliver, 1984, *Begotten or Made?* Oxford: Oxford University Press.

O'Neill, John, 1995, 'Foucault's Optics: The (in) Vision of Mortality and Modernity', in Jenks 1995, pp. 190–201.

Orsi, Robert, 1985, *The Madonna of 115th Street: Faith and Community in Italian Harlem*, New Haven CT: Yale University Press.

Orsi, Robert, 1996, *Thank You, Saint Jude: Women's Devotion to the Patron Saint of Lost Causes*, New Haven CT: Yale University Press.

Otto, Rudolf, 1950, *The Idea of the Holy*, Oxford: Oxford University Press.

Ouspensky, Leonid, 1992, *Theology of the Icon*, two vols, Crestwood NY: St Vladimir's Seminary Press.

Pallasmaa, Juhani, 2005, *The Eyes of the Skin: Architecture and the Senses*, Chichester: John Wiley.

Panofsky, Erwin, 1955, *Meaning in the Visual Arts*, Garden City NY: Doubleday Anchor.

Panofsky, Erwin, ed., 1979, *Abbot Suger on the Abbey Church of St-Denis and its Art Treasures*, Princeton NJ: Princeton University Press.

Park, David, 1997, *The Fire Within the Eye: A Historical Essay on the Nature and Meaning of Light*, Princeton NJ: Princeton University Press.

Parker, Andrew, 2003, *In the Blink of an Eye*, Cambridge MA: Perseus Books.

Pashler, Howard, 1999, *The Psychology of Attention*, Cambridge MA: MIT Press.

Passmore, John, 1974, *Man's Responsibility for Nature: Ecological Problems and Western Traditions*, New York: Charles Scribner's Sons.

Pastoureau, Michel, 2001, *Blue: The History of a Colour*, Princeton: Princeton University Press.

Pattison, George, 1998, *Art, Modernity and Faith: Restoring the Image*, London: SCM Press.

Pattison, Stephen, 1994, *Pastoral Care and Liberation Theology*, Cambridge: Cambridge University Press.

Pattison, Stephen, 1997, *The Faith of the Managers: When Management Becomes Religion*, London: Cassell.

Pattison, Stephen, 2000, *Shame: Theory, Therapy, Theology*, Cambridge: Cambridge University Press.

Pattison, Stephen, and James Woodward, 'An Introduction to Pastoral and Practical Theology', in Woodward and Pattison 2000, pp. 1–19.

Paulson, William, 1987, *Enlightenment, Romanticism and the Blind in France*, Princeton NJ: Princeton University Press.

Pavitt, Jane, 2000, *Brand New*, London: Victoria and Albert Publications.

Pelikan, Jaroslav, 1997, *The Illustrated Jesus through the Centuries: His Place in the History of Culture*, New Haven CT: Yale University Press.

Pinney, Christopher, 2001, 'Piercing the Skin of the Idol', in Pinney and Thomas 2001, pp. 157–79.

Pinney, Christopher, and Nicholas Peterson, eds, 2003, *Photography's Other Histories*, Durham NC: Duke University Press.

Pinney, Christopher, and Nicholas Thomas, eds, 2001, *Beyond Aesthetics: Art and the Technologies of Enchantment*, Oxford: Berg.

Plato, 1955, *The Republic*, Harmondsworth: Penguin Books.

Plato, 1977, *Timaeus and Critias*, London: Penguin Books.

Pleij, Herman, 2004, *Colours Demonic and Divine: Shades of Meaning in the Middle Ages and After*, New York: Columbia University Press.

Poole, Deborah, 1997, *Vision, Race, and Modernity: A Visual Economy of the Andean*

*Image World*, Princeton NJ: Princeton University Press.

Postman, Neil, 1987, *Amusing Ourselves to Death*, London: Methuen.

Propp, William, 1987, 'The Skin of Moses' Face – Transfigured or Disfigured?' *Catholic Bible Quarterly* 49: 375–86.

Pylyshyn, Zenon, 2003, *Seeing and Visualizing: It's Not What You Think*, Cambridge MA: MIT Press.

Ramachandran, Vilayanur, 2003, *The Emerging Mind*, London: Profile Books.

Ramachandran, V. S., and Sandra Blakeslee, 1999, *Phantoms in the Brain*, London: Fourth Estate.

Read, Herbert, 1951, *Art and the Evolution of Man*, London: Freedom Press.

Ree, Jonathan, 1999, *I See a Voice: Language, Deafness and the Senses – a Philosophic History*, London: HarperCollins.

Richardson, Ruth, 1989, *Death, Dissection and the Destitute*, London: Penguin Books.

Ritzer, George, 1999, *Enchanting a Disenchanted World: Revolutionizing the Means of Consumption*, Thousand Oaks CA: Pine Forge Press.

Rival, Laura, ed., 1998, *The Social Life of Trees: Anthropological Perspectives on Tree Symbolism*, Oxford: Berg.

Rorty, Richard, 1980, *Philosophy and the Mirror of Nature*, Oxford: Blackwell.

Rose, Gillian, 2001, *Visual Methodologies*, London: Sage.

Rowland, Christopher, ed., 1999, *The Cambridge Companion to Liberation Theology*, Cambridge: Cambridge University Press.

Rowland, Christopher, 2005, 'Living with Idols: An Essay in Biblical Theology', unpublished paper.

Rubin, Miri, 1991, *Corpus Christi: The Eucharist in Late Medieval Culture*, Cambridge: Cambridge University Press.

Ruether, Rosemary Radford, 1992, *Gaia and God: An Ecofeminist Theology of Earth Healing*, London: SCM Press.

Sacks, Oliver, 1985, *The Man who Mistook His Wife for a Hat*, London: Picador.

Sacks, Oliver, 1991, *Seeing Voices*, London: Picador.

Sacks, Oliver, 1995, *An Anthropologist on Mars*, London: Picador.

Sacks, Oliver, 2005, 'The Mind's Eye: What the Blind See', in Howes 2000, pp. 25–42.

Sandywell, Barry, 1999, 'Specular Grammar: The Visual Rhetoric of Modernity', in Heywood and Sandywell 1999, pp. 30–56.

Scarry, Elaine, 2000, *On Beauty and Being Just*, London: Duckworth.

Schaaf, Larry, 2000, *The Photographic Art of William Henry Fox Talbot*, Princeton NJ: Princeton University Press.

Schaffer, Simon, 2004, 'A Science whose Business is Bursting: Soap Bubbles as Commodities in Classical Physics', in Daston 2004, 147–92.

Schama, Simon, 1999, *Rembrandt's Eyes*, London: Penguin Press.

Schivelbusch, Wolfgang, 1995, *Disenchanted Night: The Industrialisation of Light in the Nineteenth Century*, Berkeley CA: University of California Press.

Scholem, Gershom, 1995, *Major Trends in Jewish Mysticism*, New York: Schocken Books.

Scott, Robert, 2003, *The Gothic Enterprise: A Guide to Understanding the Medieval Cathedral*, Berkeley CA: University of California Press.

Sennett, Richard, 1992, *The Conscience of the Eye: The Design and Social Life of Cities*, New York: WW Norton.

Seremetakis, C. Nadia, ed., 1994, *The Senses Still: Perception and Memory as Material Culture in Modernity*, Chicago: Chicago University Press.

Shapin, Steven, and Simon Schaffer, 1985, *Leviathan and the Air Pump: Hobbes, Boyle and the Experimental Life*, Princeton NJ: Princeton University Press.

Silverman, Kaja, 1996, *The Threshold of the Visible World*, London: Routledge.

Smith, John, 1999, 'The Denigration of Vision and the Renewal of Painting', in Heywood and Sandywell 1999, pp. 162–82.

Snowden, Robert, Peter Thompson, and Thomas Troscianko, 2006, *Basic Vision: An Introduction to Visual Perception*, Oxford: Oxford University Press.

Snyder, Joel, 2004, '*Res ipsa loquitur*', in Daston 2004, pp. 195–221.

Spivey, Nigel, 2005, *How Art Made the World*, London: BBC Books.

Stafford, Barbara, 1993, *Body Criticism: Imaging the Unseen in Enlightenment Art and Medicine*, Cambridge MA: MIT Press.

Stafford, Barabara, 1996, *Good Looking: Essays on the Virtue of Images*, Cambridge MA: MIT Press.

Staniloae, Dumitru, 2000, *The Experience of God: Orthodox Dogmatic Theology: Volume II: The World: Creation and Deification*, Brookline MA: Holy Cross Orthodox Press.

Staniszewski, Mary Anne, 1995, *Believing is Seeing: Creating the Culture of Art*, London: Penguin Books.

Starck, Philippe, 2003, *Starck*, Cologne: Taschen.

Steadman, Philip, 2001, *Vermeer's Camera*, Oxford: Oxford University Press.

Steinberg, Leo, 1996, *The Sexuality of Christ in Renaissance Art and in Modern Oblivion*, Chicago: Chicago University Press.

Steiner, George, 1988, *Real Presences: Is There Anything in What We Say?* London: Faber & Faber.

Stephens, Mitchell, 1998, *The Rise of the Image the Fall of the Word*, New York: Oxford University Press.

Stern, Daniel, 1985, *The Interpersonal World of the Infant*, n.p.: Basic Books.

Stewart, Susan, 1993, *On Longing: Narratives of the Miniature, the Gigantic, the Souvenir, the Collection*, Durham NC: Duke University Press.

Stewart, Susan, 1999, 'Prologue: From the Museum of Touch', in Kwint *et al.* 1999, pp. 17–36.

Stewart, Susan, 2005, 'Remembering the Senses', in Howes 2005, pp. 59–69.

Stivers, Richard, 2001, *Technology as Magic: The Triumph of the Irrational*, London: Continuum.

Stoichita, Victor, 1995, *Visionary Experience in the Golden Age of Spanish Art*, London: Reaktion Books.

Stoller, Paul, 1997, *Sensuous Scholarship*, Philadelphia PA: Pennsylvania University Press.

Strathern, Marilyn, 1988, *The Gender of the Gift*, Berkeley CA: University of California Press.

Sturken, Marita, and Lisa Cartwright, 2001, *Practices of Looking: An Introduction to Visual Culture*, Oxford: Oxford University Press.

Summers, David, 2003, *Real Spaces: World Art History and the Rise of Western Modernism*, London: Phaidon.

Sweet, Fay, 1998, *Alessi: Art and Poetry*, London: Thames and Hudson.

Sweet, Fay, 1999, *Frog: Form Follows Emotion*, London: Thames and Hudson.

Tamen, Miguel, 2001, *Friends of Interpretable Objects*, Cambridge MA: Harvard University Press.

Tanizaki, Junichiro, 2001, *In Praise of Shadows*, London: Vintage.

Tanner, Jeremy, ed., 2003, *The Sociology of Art: A Reader*, London: Routledge.

# Bibliography

Taussig, Michael, 1993, *Mimesis and Alterity: A Particular History of the Senses*, London: Routledge.

Taussig, Michael, 1999, *Defacement: Public Secrecy and the Labour of the Negative*, Stanford: Stanford University Press.

Taves, Anne, 1999, *Fits, Trances and Visions: Experiencing Religion and Explaining Experience from Wesley to James*, Princeton NJ: Princeton University Press.

Taylor, Charles, 1989, *Sources of the Self*, Cambridge: Cambridge University Press.

Teresa of Avila, St, 1957, *The Life of St Teresa by Herself*, London: Penguin Books.

Thomas, Julia, ed., 2001, *Reading Images*, Basingstoke: Palgrave Macmillan.

Thomas, Keith, 1984, *Man and the Natural World: Changing Attitudes in England 1500–1800*, London: Penguin Books.

Thomas, Nicholas, 1991, *Entangled Objects: Exchange, Material Culture and Colonialism in the Pacific*, Cambridge MA: Harvard University Press.

Tillich, Paul, 1978, *Systematic Theology: Volume Three*, London: SCM Press.

Tillich, Paul, 1989, *On Art and Architecture*, New York: Crossroad.

Tomasello, Michael, 2000, *The Cultural Origins of Human Cognition*, Cambridge MA: Harvard University Press.

Trevarthen, Colwyn, 1995, 'Mother and Baby – Seeing Artfully Eye to Eye', in Gregory *et al.* 1995, pp. 157–200.

Turner, Denys, 1995, *The Darkness of God: Negativity in Christian Mysticism*, Cambridge: Cambridge University Press.

Urry, John, 2002, *The Tourist Gaze*, London: Sage.

Van Engen, John, 1988, *Devotio Moderna: Basic Writings*, New York: Paulist Press.

Vasari, Giorgio, 1991, *The Lives of the Artists*, Oxford: Oxford University Press.

Virilio, Paul, 1994, *The Vision Machine*, London: British Film Institute.

von Simson, Otto, 1988, *The Gothic Cathedral*, Princeton NJ: Princeton University Press.

Walker Bynum, Caroline, 1995, *The Resurrection of the Body*, New York: Columbia University Press.

Walker Bynum, Caroline, 2002, 'The Woman with the Pearl Necklace', *Common Knowledge* 8;2: 280–83.

Wandel, Lee, 1994, *Voracious Idols and Violent Hands: Iconoclasm in Reformation Zurich, Strasbourg, and Basel*, Cambridge: Cambridge University Press.

Watson, Lyall, 1999, *Jacobson's Organ and the Remarkable Nature of Smell*, London: Allen Lane.

Weber, Max, 1976, *The Protestant Ethic and the Spirit of Capitalism*, London: George Allen & Unwin.

Weibel, Peter, 2002, 'An End to the End of Art? On the Iconoclasm of Modern Art', in Latour and Weibel 2002, pp. 570–684.

Weil, Simone, 1959, *Waiting on God*, London: Fontana.

Weiskrantz, Lawrence, 1997, *Consciousness Lost and Found*, Oxford: Oxford University Press.

White, Patrick, 1996, *Riders in the Chariot*, London: Vintage.

Whiteley, Nigel, 1999, 'Readers of the Lost Art: Visuality and Particularity in Art Criticism', in Heywood and Sandywell 1999, pp. 99–122.

Wiebe, Phillip, 1997, *Visions of Jesus: Direct Encounters from the New Testament Today*, New York: Oxford University Press.

Wilder, Kelley, 2003, 'Ingenuity, Wonder and Profit: Language and the Invention of Photography', Unpublished DPhil thesis, University of Oxford.

Williams, Linda, 1999, *Hard Core: Power, Pleasure, and the 'Frenzy of the Visible'*,

Berkeley CA: University of California Press.

Wilson, Catherine, 1988, 'Visual Surface and Visual Symbol: The Microscope and the Occult in Early Modern Science', *Journal of the History of Ideas* 49: 85–108.

Wilson, Catherine, 1995, *The Invisible World: Early Modern Philosophy and the Invention of the Microscope*, Princeton NJ: Princeton University Press.

Wink, Walter, 1986, *Unmasking the Powers: The Invisible Forces that Determine Human Existence*, Philadelphia PA: Fortress Press.

Witham, Larry, 2005, *The Measure of God: Our Century-Long Struggle to Reconcile Science and Religion*. San Francisco CA: Harper Collins.

Wolfson, Elliot, 1994, *Through a Speculum that Shines: Vision and Imagination in Medieval Jewish Mysticism*, Princeton NJ: Princeton University Press.

Wolterstorff, Nicholas, 1997, *Art in Action: Toward a Christian Aesthetic*, Carlisle: Solway.

Woodward, James, and Stephen Pattison, eds, 2000, *The Blackwell Reader in Pastoral and Practical Theology*, Oxford: Blackwell.

Wright, Kenneth, 1991, *Vision and Separation: Between Mother and Baby*, London: Free Analysis Press.

Zajonc, Arthur, 1993, *Catch the Light: The Entwined Story of Light and Mind*, New York: Bantam Books.

Zaleski, Carol, 1987, *Otherworld Journeys: Accounts of Near-Death Experience in Medieval and Modern Times*, Oxford: Oxford University Press.

Zeki, Semir, 1999, *Inner Vision*, Oxford: Oxford University Press.

Zeman, Adam, 2004, *Consciousness: A User's Guide*. New Haven CT: Yale University Press.

Ziesler, J. A., 1973, *Christian Asceticism*, London: SPCK.

Zwijnenberg. Robert, 2003, 'Presence and Absence: On Leonardo da Vinci's *St John the Baptist*', in Farago and Zwijnenberg 2003, pp. 112–13.

# Acknowledgements

Lacan's notion of interlocking gaze, in Jacques Lacan, 1981, *The Four Fundamental Concepts of Psychoanalysis*, W.W. Norton, New York.

Albrecht Durer, *Draftsman drawing a picture of a nude*, woodcut, c.1525, Reproduced by permission: bpk / Kupferstchkabinett – Staatliche Museen zu Berlin.

Giotto, *St Francis having a vision before the Crucifix in San Damiano*, in the Basilica of St Francesco in Assisi. Reproduced by permission of the Bridgeman Art Gallery, London.

Athanasius Kircher, *Camera obscura*, 1646, Reproduced by permission of the Science Museum/Science & Society Picture Library, London.

Jake Cress, *Oops* and *Self-portrait*. Used by permission of Jake Cress.

Herbert Bayer, *The Lonely Metropolitan*. Used by permission of the Design and Artists Copyright Society, London.

Mary of Burgundy, *Book of Hours*. The Hours of Mary of Burgundy (Ms1857 fol 14v), reproduced by permission of Österreichische Nationalbibliothek, Wien.

# Index